Delivering Voice over Frame Relay and ATM

DANIEL MINOLI
EMMA MINOLI

WILEY COMPUTER PUBLISHING

John Wiley & Sons, Inc.
New York • Chichester • Weinheim • Brisbane • Singapore • Toronto

Publisher: Robert Ipsen
Editor: Marjorie Spencer
Managing Editor: Angela Murphy
Text Design & Composition: North Market Street Graphics, Lancaster, PA

Designations used by companies to distinguish their products are often claimed as trademarks. In all instances where John Wiley & Sons, Inc., is aware of a claim, the product names appear in initial capital or ALL CAPITAL LETTERS. Readers, however, should contact the appropriate companies for more complete information regarding trademarks and registration.

This book is printed on acid-free paper. ∞

Published by John Wiley & Sons, Inc.

Published simultaneously in Canada.

This publication is designed to provide accurate and authoritative information in regard to the subject matter covered. It is sold with the understanding that the publisher is not engaged in professional services. If professional advice or other expert assistance is required, the services of a competent professional person should be sought.

Library of Congress Cataloging-in-Publication Data:

Minoli, Daniel.
    Delivering voice over frame relay and ATM / Daniel Minoli, Emma Minoli.
        p.   cm.
    Includes bibliographical references and index.
    ISBN 0-471-25481-9 (cloth : alk. paper)
    1. Frame relay (Data transmission)   2. Asynchronous transfer mode.
3. Digital telephone systems.   4. Computer networks.   I. Minoli, Emma.   II. Title.
    TK5105.3.M56   1998
621.385—dc21   97-46553

Printed in the United States of America.
10 9 8 7 6 5 4 3

Contents

Chapter 5   Traditional Voice and Voice Signaling Systems   135

Chapter 6   Voice over Frame Relay   203

Chapter 7:   Voice over ATM Preliminaries   245

Chapter 8   VTOA Voice over ATM: Circuit Emulation Service   333

Chapter 9   VTOA Dynamic Bandwidth Utilization   365

Chapter 10   VTOA Interworking with Narrow-band/ISDN Services   379

Preface

This book follows the philosophy of the senior author: "All you need to know—no more, no less; no fuss, no mess . . ."

First there was the mainframe. Then there was the desktop. Then there was the enterprise network. Then came the intranet. This synthesis has evolved to the point where, as some say, "The computer is the network." But, in fact, we are now entering a quantum-change phase in the corporate landscape, whereby "the corporation is the network." A company's economic well-being, its ability to make money and achieve productivity breakthroughs, and its capacity to sustain stock market value all depend on having in place a multimedia, multipoint, multiservice, high-speed network.

Because of the flurry of activity in the enterprise networking industry in the 1990s—such as the rolling out of frame relay service, the deployment of upgraded desktop and backbone enterprise networks, the expanded use of the Internet, the introduction of intranets, and corporate deployment of ATM—the question naturally arises as to whether it makes economic sense to carry voice over data networks. Three variants are possible: (1) voice over frame relay, (2) voice over ATM, and (3) voice over IP (i.e., over routed enterprise networks and the Internet).

Integration has found reasonable effectiveness in the frame relay context for the support of small office/home office (SOHO) locations. However, since voice technology has been around for over a century and digital voice has been deployed since the early 1960s, the pertinent questions for corporate network planners are: (1) Are voice over packet networks a practical reality or just a technical possibility? (2) What technical alternatives are there? (3) How economical are voice over packet networks? (4) Is there customer premises equipment available to support voice over packet networks? (5) Can a standard PBX be supported? (6) What is the quality of voice? (7) Are there standards for voice over packet networks? (8) Besides enterprise networks, what other possibilities are there?

The Frame Relay Forum recently approved a specification to enable multivendor interoperability. The ATM Forum has similarly generated a series of specifications for the support of voice applications in a variety of settings. Proponents proclaimed 1997 as the "Year for Voice over Data," because a significant set of frame relay and ATM voice standards emerged that year. Since then, voice over packet networks (including the Internet) has continued to penetrate this arena. Planners are questioning which of these alternatives will ultimately win and/or are worth preparing for? From the current vantage point, besides traditional telephony, voice over frame relay seems to have the best chance to be used for commercial applications during the next few years. However, planners cannot afford to ignore the other evolving possibilities.

Based on years of research on voice over packet and voice (started in 1975 for the senior author), two texts have been generated by these authors and published by Wiley. This text covers voice over connection-oriented fast-packet transport technologies (frame relay and ATM); the other text covers voice over connectionless IP-based networks, including the Internet.

This book discusses the positioning of voice over ATM and voice over frame relay technology. ATM plays a role of its own merit in the frame relay discussions, since frame relay often is now delivered over ATM. This book provides a review of the technologies, digitization and integration methods, standards, and approaches in support of voice over data network.

After an introduction in Chapter 1, a basic review of the transport technologies is provided, as follows. Chapter 2 discusses frame relay and ATM technologies. An overview of voice digitization methods is provided in Chapter 3; it focuses on pulse code modulation (PCM) currently being used in ATM applications. Chapter 4 discusses adaptive differential PCM (ADPCM), currently being used, along with other methods, in frame relay. Chapter 5 discusses voice signaling mechanisms that have to be taken into account in voice over data networks. Voice over frame relay networks is discussed in Chapter 6. Chapter 7 starts the discussion on voice over ATM by covering a number of preliminaries. Chapter 8 covers in more detail circuit emulation service (AAL 1). Chapter 9 discusses dynamic bandwidth allocation when using circuit emulation service. Chapter 10 addresses the topic of network interworking of ISDN-based voice (e.g., originating on an ISDN-configured PBX) over ATM. Chapter 11 covers ATM voice telephony to the desktop via service interworking with ISDN. Finally, Chapter 12 provides a case study of voice over ATM using the newer AAL 2 mechanisms.

This book is aimed at technology and application developers, students, vendors, researchers, consultants, and corporate network planners.

Acknowledgments

The authors would like to thank Mr. Roy D. Rosner, ECI/Telematics, for contributing a major section to Chapter 2.

The authors would also like to thank Mr. Tony Ferrugia, Fore Systems, for providing early input and for contributions to Chapter 7.

Mr. Mike McLoughlin, General DataComm, is thanked for his insight on AAL 2 and the material supplied for Chapter 12.

The authors also thank Ms. Cecilia Fischus, Bellcore/SIA, for her help with Chapter 4.

Gabrielle Minoli is thanked for developing the index.

CHAPTER 1

Introduction and Motivation

1.1 Introduction

Voice communication remains and will continue to remain a critical requirement for corporate America, for world economies, and for residential users. Up to the early 1960s, commercial voice was strictly analog-based. For almost 40 years now, voice has been carried in ever greater shares in digital format. Yet, until recently, digital voice was not really carried in any meaningful way over *packet networks* (PNs), with the ensuing possibilities of statistical gains and lower costs. This is now poised to change. Because of the flurry of activity in the enterprise networking industry in the 1990s, such as rolling out of frame relay service, deployment of upgraded desktop and backbone enterprise networks, expanded use of the Internet, introduction of intranets, and corporate deployment of Asynchronous Transfer Mode (ATM) technology, the question naturally arises if it makes *economic* sense to "carry voice over packet networks."[1] Three variants are possible for packetized voice: (1) voice over frame relay, (2) voice over ATM, and (3) voice over the Internet Protocol (IP), that is, over routed enterprise networks, intranets, and the Internet.

Issues surrounding voice include economics, tariffs, traffic engineering, user-level quality, network's quality of service (QoS) and

1

queuing, network design, digitization and compression, and technical feasibility [1–56]. Driven by economics (the first item in our list), the interest in developing one integrated network to carry both packetized data and voice goes back to at least the mid-1970s (if not even earlier), when the Advanced Research Projects Agency (ARPA) sponsored studies to determine the technical possibility of doing so [1–12, 19–20]. Efforts in the Integrated Services Digital Network (ISDN) and ATM have also been aimed at voice support in general and multimedia in particular [57–70]. Efforts on the data side have included support of voice in local area networks (LANs), such as IEEE 802.9 and FDDI II [70], and enhancements to routers, IP (e.g., IPv6 and Resource Reservation Protocol, or RSVP), and network-layer handling of packets, such as multiprotocol label switching (MPLS), multiprotocols over ATM (MPOA), and tag switching/NetFlows.

Because of all this activity, technology has advanced to the point where quality voice can be delivered by packetized means, whether the voice is in traditional digital format or is compressed. Voice can now be delivered over connection-oriented data networks, specifically those based on frame relay and ATM, as well as over connectionless networks, specifically Internet Protocol (IP). This book focuses on ATM and frame relay, while a companion book, *Delivering Voice over IP Networks*, covers voice over IP [71]. The book aims at guiding network planners interested in applying this new technology to their environments.

In this book ATM and frame relay networks are simply called *packet networks*. As implied, many Fortune 500 companies now use PN services for corporate data, intranet, and electronic commerce applications. Hence, there is interest in addressing the question of services and media integration. Integration has found reasonable effectiveness in the frame relay context for the support of small office/home office (SOHO) locations. However, since voice technology has been around for over a century and digital voice has been deployed since the early 1960s, the pertinent questions for corporate network planners are: (1) Is voice over PN a practical reality or just a technical possibility? (2) What technical alternatives are there? (3) How economic is voice over PNs? (4) Is there customer premises equipment available to support voice over PNs? (5) Can a standard PBX be supported? (6) What is the quality of voice? (7) Are there standards for voice over PNs? (8) Besides enterprise networks, what other possibilities are there? (9) Are signaling and interworking with the traditional voice switches possible from the frame relay, ATM, and LAN/router switches, to support ubiquitous reach? These practical questions are examined in this book.

Is the following statement correct? "The bottom line at this juncture is that voice over PN is still in its infancy and is a technical novelty." Some carriers have demonstrated the feasibility of network-supported (on-net) ATM voice as well as IP/Internet-based voice; however, existing alternatives eliminate voice over ATM as the least-cost solution, except in specific situations. For frame relay, the economics are currently better, but frame relay does not now support important QoS metrics. It must be noted, however, that the applications, standards, maturity, and economics for voice over ATM, voice over frame relay, and voice over IP are all different. The hope of the developers is that voice over enterprise networks (IP/RSVP-based) will be possible. Routers are also being redesigned to support QoS-based policies—specifically, disciplined queue control (e.g., Cisco's Weighted Fair Queuing).

Equipment supporting voice—specifically, voice-enabled frame relay access devices (FRADs)—is now available from over a dozen vendors, and voice over frame relay technology is seeing commercial introduction. The Frame Relay Forum recently approved a specification to enable multivendor interoperability for on-net voice. The ATM Forum has similarly generated a series of specifications for the support of voice applications in a variety of settings. Proponents proclaimed 1997 the "Year for Voice over Data," perhaps because of the significant set of frame relay and ATM voice standards that emerged that year. Connectivity of frame-based voice to the public switched telephone network (PSTN), however, remains a future goal, at least at the practical service level.

In support of on-net and off-net connectivity, the ATM Forum recently approved four specifications for voice telephony over ATM (VTOA) using circuit emulation service (CES) as well as other ATM services. These specifications furnish the technical possibility for interconnection of private-network ATM voice with the PSTN; nonetheless, in general, PSTN connectivity of cell-based voice remains a future service. As already noted, when compared to voice over frame relay, the economics of voice over ATM are not yet as favorable, unless an organization already has an ATM-based enterprise network that uses ATM via edge multiplexers, and the organization is interested only in on-net voice for the time being. Off-net voice connectivity over an ATM network is just now being made available as individual case basis (ICB) applications by forward-looking carriers such as the Teleport Communications Group (TCG). As a spin, some carriers are looking also to use ATM totally internal to their network as a statistical multiplexing technology to derive higher Synchronous Optical Network (SONET)/Synchronous Digital Hierarchy (SDH) efficiencies. Such a *network interworking* arrangement would support voice in a fundamentally new way compared to today's synchronous networks. However, significant rollout of this radical architecture is not expected anytime soon.

Figure 1.1 depicts the various kinds of voice PNs discussed in this and the companion book. Planners are also asking which of the alternatives now emerging will ultimately win and/or are worth preparing for. From the current vantage point, besides traditional telephony, voice over frame relay seems to have the best chance to be used for commercial applications during the next few years; however, planners cannot afford to ignore the other evolving possibilities. Indeed, with the recent adoption of the Frame Relay Forum FRF.11 standard for voice over frame relay, it is likely that increased deployment of voice over Data Link Layer connection-oriented protocols will take place in enterprise networks, including wide area network (WAN) extensions. By contrast, some see voice over Network Layer connectionless protocols (specifically IP), and over the Internet, as being nearly free, and so would like to take advantage of this apparent bonanza without having to worry about owning their own WANs. Another advantage would be the ability to support off-net voice applications. However, the cost of the Internet, particularly for guaranteed grade of service, is going to continue to increase; thus, the economics will be changing in the next two to three years. Also, the ultimate benefits may be more the result of voice compression at the source than of the transport vehicle itself (namely, the Internet).

QoS plays a crucial role in support of voice over PNs. Table 1.1 depicts some of the key requirements for the support of voice, which any new alternative architecture is expected to accommodate; the table also shows requirements for IP-based solutions. QoS-enabled PNs are needed for voice applications. While ATM has

Figure 1.1
Voice over data networks: (a) Frame-relay-based voice interconnecting PBXs; (b) same as (a) but with public switched telephone network interconnection; (c) same as (a) but with frame relay provided via a core ATM network; also shows voice over ATM; (d) various voice over IP schemes, including (1) private-line connected routers, (2) IP over ATM (classical IP over ATM), (3) IP over MPOA/MPLS/tag switching/IP switching, (4) RSVP-based IP, (5) Internet delivery.

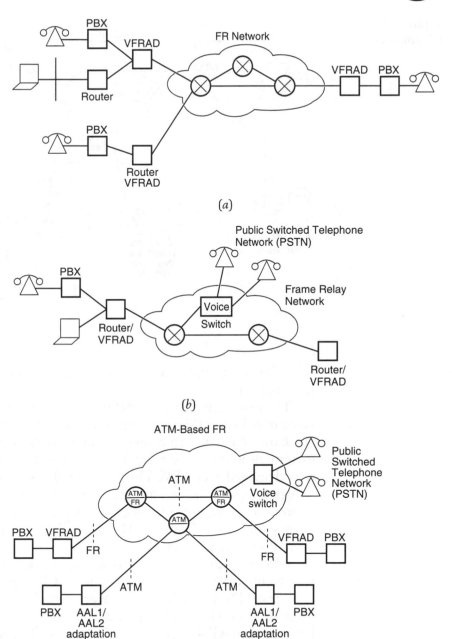

Figure 1.1
(Continued).

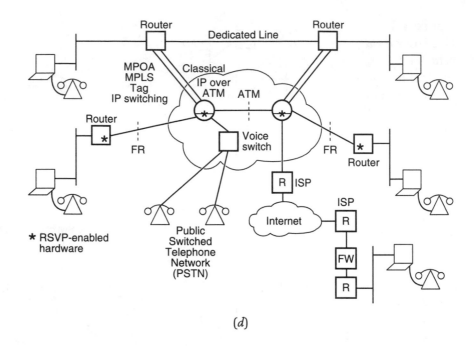

(*d*)

good QoS support, frame relay (not to mention IP) has more limited support.

The issues just discussed define the scope of the discourse of voice over PNs at this time. This book discusses the positioning of voice over ATM and voice over frame relay. ATM plays a role of its own merit in the frame relay discussions, since frame relay often is now delivered over ATM. The text provides a review of the technologies, digitization and integration methods, standards, and approaches in support of voice over fastpacket networks. As noted, a companion text, *Delivering Voice over IP Networks*, covers voice over IP and the Internet.

After an introduction in Chapter 1, a basic review of the transport technologies is provided, as follows. Chapter 2 discusses frame relay and ATM technologies. An overview of voice digitization methods is provided in Chapter 3; it focuses on PCM currently being used in ATM applications. Chapter 4 discusses ADPCM, currently being used, along with other methods, in frame relay. Chapter 5 discusses voice signaling mechanisms that have to be taken into account in voice over data networks. Voice over frame relay networks is discussed in Chapter 6. Chapter 7 starts the discussion

Table 1.1 Basic Voice-Feature Requirements for Voice over Data Applications

Feature	Description	Requirement in ATM	Requirement in IP net	Requirement in frame relay
Compression	Sub-PCM compression significantly reduces the amount of bandwidth used by a voice conversation, while maintaining high quality.	Nice to have.	Must have.	Must have.
Silence suppression	The ability to recover bandwidth during periods of silence in a conversation makes that bandwidth available for other users of the network.	Nice to have.	Must have.	Must have.
QoS	Assuring priority for voice transmission is critical. This keeps delay, delay variation, and loss to a tolerable minimum.	Must have. ATM has been developed with significant QoS/traffic management support.	Must have. Very little current support (type of service [TOS] not generally implemented in routers). There is a hope that the Resource Reservation Protocol (RSVP), which reserves resources across the network, will help. However, RSVP is only a protocol; intrinsic network bandwidth must be provided before a reservation can be made.	Must have. Frame relay does not explicitly support priority-based QoS. Recent development is attempting to address this limitation.
Signaling for voice traffic	Support of traditional PBXs and the associated signaling is critical.	Must have for real applications.	Must have for real applications.	Must have for real applications.
Echo control	Echo is annoying and disruptive. Control is key.	Must have for real applications.	Must have for real applications.	Must have for real applications.
Voice switching	Data network equipment can generally support on-net applications. Off-net is also critical. At the very least, the adjunct equipment must decide whether to route a call over the internal data network or route it to the PSTN.	Ability to route off-net is a must for real applications.	Ability to route off-net is a must for real applications.	Ability to route off-net is a must for real applications.

on voice over ATM by covering a number of preliminaries. Chapter 8 covers in more detail circuit emulation service (AAL 1). Chapter 9 discusses dynamic bandwidth allocation when using circuit emulation service. Chapter 10 addresses the topic of network interworking of ISDN-based voice (e.g., originating on an ISDN-configured PBX) over ATM. Chapter 11 covers ATM voice telephony to the desktop via service interworking with ISDN. Finally, Chapter 12 provides a case study of voice over ATM using the newer AAL 2 mechanisms.

Although not intended for scholarly research, this book does cover, as noted, many significant new technologies at the practical level. For original scholarly research, needed perhaps by developers, the reader is referred directly to IEEE technical magazines and IETF specifications. The coverage provided here should prove appropriate for corporate planners investigating whether there are any economic and productivity advantages to the introduction of these evolving technologies in their corporate enterprise networks.

Up to this point the reader may have noticed a relatively large number of acronyms (and more to follow), which are simply references to underlying technologies. Indeed, a large number of recent advancements come into play in delivery of voice over packet networks. The purpose of this book is to pull all of these technologies together, thereby providing a point of departure for readers and practitioners as they undertake an assessment of these new technologies with an eye to determine the productivity enhancements and/or cost savings that might ensue in a corporate setting.

ATM is mentioned extensively throughout this book because it is a technology in its own right at the LAN and even more so at the WAN level; it can be used to support frame relay services; it can be used to support classical IP applications; it can be used to support RSVP; it can be used to support newer Layer 3 services such as tag switching and IP switching; and it could be used intrinsic to the network (invisible to the end user, just to secure statistical gains). Hence, it will play an important role in coming years. However, its mention should not be construed as an endorsement of it as the technology of choice. The text aims at taking as clinical a stance of the various technologies, standalone or in combination, as possible. The use of ATM to support voice over IP is discussed in the companion text published by Wiley, *Delivering Voice over IP Networks*.

1.2 Evolving Packet Voice Applications and Directions

Because of the advances in the enterprise networking industry in the 1990s, such as the rollout of frame relay, the deployment of upgraded desktop and backbone enterprise networks, the expanded use of the Internet, the introduction of intranets, and corporate deployment of ATM, the question naturally arises if it makes sense from architectural and economic points of view to carry voice over data networks in general and ATM in particular. ATM has guaranteed QoS, which at the technology level would make it ideal for voice; however, other networks are being developed to support QoS—for example, RSVP and IPv6. Recently, there has been quite a lot of standardization activity for the support of voice over connection-oriented data networks (ATM in particular), but the question is: Will products and cost-effective services emerge in the next two to five years? The publication of standards is only a first step. It is worth noting, in this context, that several standards for voice over ATM have been around for over five years, since the 1992–93 ITU-T work in this area [65], but with limited commercial deployment.

ATM is a multimedia, multiservice, multipoint technology. Until the present, however, the practical focus of the industry has been on data applications. Major activities, such as the ATM Forum's specifications, LAN Emulation (LANE) and MPOA, have implicitly concentrated on data applications. ATM has in principle several intrinsic advantages over other networking technologies when it comes to voice:

1. ATM was designed from the start to be a multimedia, multiservice technology. The very format of the cell was arrived at by considering data, voice, and video payload requirements.

2. ATM supports extensive QoS and service classes capabilities. This allows time-sensitive traffic, such as voice, to be transported across the network in a reliable jitter-free manner. Service classes are supported, in part, by various ATM Adaptation Layers (AALs), discussed in Chapter 3.

3. Switches have been designed with effective traffic management capabilities—for example, call admission control, usage

parameter control, traffic shaping, cell tagging, cell discard, and per virtual channel (VC) queue management—to support the quality of service and service classes needed for the various applications, including voice.

4. Interworking with the PSTN should be relatively straightforward, since ISDN and ATM are similar, at least in terms of signaling.

The first three capabilities have already been put to good use in data applications. Somewhat complicating the discussion, however, is the fact that at this particular time, ATM to the desktop will not be popular at least until the turn of the century. This is because there are multiple competing technologies, some of which require only minimal infrastructure upgrade to be deployed. In particular, switched 100-Mbps Ethernet is well positioned to cover this space. When it comes to broadband WAN applications, however, ATM is the only available technology at this time. Hence, ATM is seeing deployment in this space, either as router-to-router technology or as campus switch–to–campus switch technology. The service is secured either via an organization-built WAN or via a carrier's public network. Where planners look to deploy voice over IP (rather than over ATM directly), it may still be the case that the backbone router network utilizes ATM.

The internetworking industry, particularly router vendors, are in the process of developing technology, standards, and equipment that will enable enterprise-network-based voice communication. Interestingly, this is a switch from the mid-1980s paradigm whereby planners deployed voice networks and then data could be carried for "free" (i.e., small incremental changes and charges); now planners deploy enterprise networks and overlay voice distribution over the data infrastructure, hopefully for small incremental changes and charges.

The next few years will see a tug-of-war between the compressed-voice methods and transport over connectionless networks and the traditional full-rate digitization methods and transport over connection-oriented networks. Indeed, during the early 1990s, significant advances in the design of digital signal processors (DSPs) occurred. A DSP is a microprocessor that is designed specifically to process digitized signals such as those found in voice and video applications. DSP development has allowed manufacturers to bring to market high-quality digitization algorithms that consume very little bandwidth. Voice compression algorithms make it possible to provide high-quality audio while making efficient use of bandwidth.

At this juncture, voice over ATM seems to have taken the approach of using traditional pulse code modulation (PCM). This tends to generate relatively high bit rates; however, given the throughput supported by ATM, these algorithms appear to be reasonable in the short term (until such time as carriers begin to use ATM ubiquitously inside the network—invisible to the end user— to gain statistical advantages; at such time the low-bit-rate-voice (LBRV) method will likely be employed). Given the fact that frame relay has much lower throughput capabilities, adaptive differential PCM (ADPCM) digitization and the vocoding methods similar, if not identical, to those recently standardized in the context of H.323 multimedia applications are more prevalent. When going all the way to IP-based solutions, where the guaranteed real-time throughput is even lower, the vocoding methods are a given. The most commonly used voice digitization/compression algorithms are as follows [72]:

- Pulse code modulation/adaptive differential pulse code modulation—ATM applications
- Code excited linear predication/algebraic code excited linear predication (CELP/ACELP)—frame relay and LAN/Internet-based multimedia
- Proprietary prestandards methods, such as adaptive transform coding/improved multiband excitation (ATC/IMBE)

The traditional PSTN algorithms, PCM and ADPCM, receive high (toll-quality) mean opinion scores (MOSs). Mean opinion scores of 4.4 for PCM and 4.1 for ADPCM are achieved by consuming 64-kbps bandwidth and 32-kbps bandwidth, respectively [72].

CELP/ACELP methods grew out of years of study at various research institutions. The three main elements of ACELP are: (1) Linear Predictive Coding (LPC) modeling of the vocal track, (2) sophisticated pitch extraction and coding, and (3) innovative excitation modeling and coding. Independent tests indicate that the perceived quality of voice is equal to or better than the industry-standard 32-kbps ADPCM (G.721). ACELP is rated with an MOS of approximately 4.2. The recent introduction of ACELP allows toll-quality voice transmissions over frame relay networks. A variation of the ACELP algorithm has recently been adopted by the International Telecommunications Union (ITU) for recommendation G.723.1 operating at 5.3 kbps [72].

Normally, complexity goes up and quality goes down as compression increases. The recent developments in very-low-bit-rate voice digitization (e.g., ACELP), however, demonstrate that voice can be compressed as low as 4.8 kbps and still achieve near toll quality. With low-cost toll-quality voice compression algorithms and management of voice and data transmission parameters, voice quality can be maintained in high-traffic networks. Until the present, voice over data networks has mostly been implemented in frame relay environments using a variety of compression schemes including prestandard versions of CELP/ACELP.

There are many integrated frame relay access devices on the market. Starting in the early 1990s, a number of FRAD manufacturers supported voice compression, echo cancellation, silence suppression, and dynamic bit-rate adaptation; fax and compressed data (4:1) were also supported. By the mid-1990s, many FRADs supported implementation of ITU-T's G.729 standard voice algorithm (ACELP) for compression rates below 16 kbps; however, interworking continued to be an issue. Also, many vendors used proprietary variations, and/or compressed voice to as low as 2.4 kbps. Some FRADs offered a choice of compression techniques. With the new FRF.11 specification, the issue of interworking should resolve itself in the 1998–99 time frame. Because of the fact that frame relay has limited QoS support, FRADs need to employ techniques such as predictive congestion management, jitter buffers, fragmentation, variable rates, prioritization, silence detection, and digital speech interpolation to retain acceptable voice quality levels.

Given the industry dynamics, it is difficult to predict which of the three technologies discussed here will emerge in first place in the next two to five years. Each of the alternatives has current (and developing) strengths as well as limitations. Hence, all three technologies should be tracked.

From a different point of departure but with the same end results, private branch exchange (PBX) vendors are beginning to redesign their equipment to be client/server-based. ATM-based switching technology, currently being introduced in data contexts, will gradually complement, then replace, traditional TDM/PCM switching architectures in PBXs, according to some, thereby changing the nature of the device and the room around it. This change will not occur instantly—Lucent and Nortel were reportedly planning to launch ATM-based PBX-type switching systems in 1998— but the kind of capabilities associated with the term *PBX* will clearly change. Lucent is already repositioning its Definity as an enterprise communication server that possesses, transports, switches, and stores multimedia signals. Other PBX vendors are likely to adopt a similar approach. These metamorphosed PBXs will have an open architecture, support multimedia communications, provide narrowband and broadband channels, and provide connectivity to both wireline and wireless terminals. All of the major PBX suppliers are preparing for desktop multimedia. Lucent and NEC have already announced ATM interface options, while Mitel and Intercom will reportedly use ATM/SONET to connect remote switching modules in the building. This will greatly impact the way telecommunications networks and infrastructure are conceived and designed, particularly given (1) the physically distributed nature of the new PBXs and (2) the fact that these devices will cease to be "different kinds of animals" and effectively will become LAN servers. But the question is: Will those servers be ATM- or IP-based?

These changes are part of a more encompassing Computer-Telephony Integration (CTI) initiative. CTI is rapidly becoming an important enabling technology, in the view of observers. With CTI, telephony functions will be melded into PCs for increased functionality and productivity. There is a clear desire to integrate at all three levels of the communication infrastructure in an organization: the support equipment, the wiring, and the applications (via CTI). Recently, Decisys (Sterling, Virginia) published what it sees as a migration strategy in the newly named field of *voiceLAN*. An outgrowth of CTI, the voiceLAN networking market has experienced a renewed level of interest in the recent past, as multimedia technologies have risen to the forefront of the applications hot list. The company sees the following migration track (although the actual migration steps may occur in different ways, the key thrust is toward a revamped PBX scenario and equipment room dynamics), which we describe for illustrative purposes.

Step 1: distributed PBX model. This step, beginning in the 1998–99 time frame at the technology level, will focus on breaking apart the existing PBX model and using the LAN as a simple transport vehicle for packetized voice between the telephone handset and the centralized PBX. Initially, ADPCM techniques supporting voice at 32 or 16 kbps will be used, but newer compression schemes will also be used. In general, there are four options for voice: ACELP, ADPCM, CELP, and PCM. ACELP and CELP are used for compression rates below 16 kbps. In 1995, ITU standardized the ACELP (ITU-T 729) voice algorithm for the coding of speech signals in wide area networks. ITU-T G.723.1 covering speech coding for multimedia communications at 5.3 and 6.3 kbps is based on multipulse maximum likelihood quantization (MP-MLQ). Some vendors use proprietary variations to compress voice to as low as 2.4 kbps.

Step 2: voice server and integrated voice/data PCs. This step is directed at integrating the telephone handset and the PC hardware. At the technology-supply level, this step could start in 1999 or 2000. Vendors will likely build both standalone handsets and new integrated handsets. As the deployment of voice-oriented devices matures in the LAN, vendors will begin to migrate from existing PBX-based hardware to open (standard PC server) platforms, reworking their features and functions into PC-based applications (this should begin to occur within the mass market in 2000, according to Decisys).

Step 3: As the technology behind voiceLAN matures, the desire and ability to build an integrated voice/data WAN connection will become important. WAN-enabled technologies, using voice over frame relay, ACELP, voice over ATM, and IP-based routing, may appear at the time.

Multimedia technologies such as H.323 may be a force of their own in this transition. The near-term synergy will be with IP networks.

Business voice requirements continue to be key for the overwhelming majority of businesses. There are several traditional and untraditional alternatives to the support of voice. On the traditional side, carriers such as AT&T, Sprint, MCI/Worldcom now have bulk-rate tariffs and/or pricing arrangements that provide voice services for less than $0.08 per minute. Voice over frame relay falls somewhere between the traditional and untraditional extremes; further toward the untraditional end is voice over ATM; voice over IP (for intranet/enterprise network applications) and voice over the Internet (for geographically dispersed applications) are fully in the untraditional camp. Bandwidth efficiency and quality are the principal trade-offs in this arena. Besides traditional telephony, voice over frame relay currently has the best chance to be used for commercial applications during the next couple of years.

Standards and products for voice over data networks are emerging because of a change in the economics of both public networks and private networks. Currently, a number of organizations have significant investments in private data facilities that have the capacity to carry additional on-net traffic with what is perceived to be little initial incremental expense; on the other hand, many corporate networks are already very congested (globally or at least in some segments) for data transmission, and so planners would be ill advised to add additional flows.

Figure 1.2 depicts some of the key voice over PN technologies available. The protocol stack approximately represents the kind of functionality that will be available in the interworking/adaptation device. Figure 1.2 shows:

- Voice over frame relay
- Voice over frame relay service—interworked to ATM
- Voice over ATM with ATM Adaptation Layer 1/constant bit rate (AAL 1/CBR), AAL 5/VBR (variable bit rate), or the newly introduced AAL 2/VBR
- Voice over IP carried in a frame relay network (e.g., LAN-originated and over a WAN)
- Voice over IP in a LAN
- Voice over IP over the Internet
- Voice over IP carried in an ATM network, using one of three available IP-carrying methods: classical IP over ATM (CIOA), LANE, or MPOA

As noted in Figure 1.2, there are two technical approaches for voice over ATM: one is via the constant-bit-rate service class and

Figure 1.2
Voice over data networks.

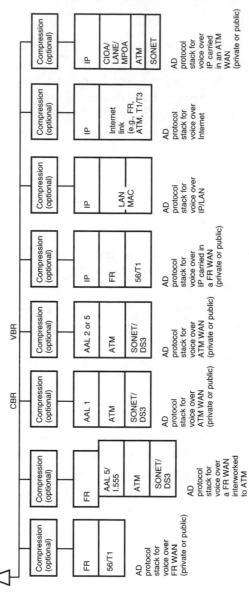

16

the use of AAL 1; the other is the variable-bit-rate service class and the use of AAL 5. The CBR approach is currently the most common of the two approaches and has been around for the longest. It is the method included in the recently approved VTOA specifications. One of the advantages is that it provides circuit emulation service, meaning that it gives a PBX the appearance that a T1 line is available, while in reality it is an ATM permanent virtual connection (PVC). The disadvantages of this approach are that (1) there is a need for higher bandwidth to recover a DS1 signal; (2) a mesh of end-to-end, point-to-point emulated circuits is required, generally without (carrier) network participation; and (3) there has been limited support of traditional voice telephony signaling. This in turn implies that voice is supportable only for on-net applications; that is, only the users at the various termination points of the organization's enterprise network are accessible, while other voice users are not accessible. At least in terms of the newly adopted ATM Forum VTOA specifications, this should begin to change.

On frame relay and/or IP networks, capabilities are needed to transform best effort communications into functionality that can support both streaming voice as well as bursty data traffic. QoS-enabled communication is the tool at hand (e.g., RSVP, tag switching, MPLS). ATM networks may or may not be utilized for best effort services, in the context of voice applications; for these applications, best effort services may be realized via IP-based methods. Originally ATM was designed to support CBR and VBR traffic types, with user-to-network traffic contracts. More recently, the computer industry has requested that best effort services such as available bit rate (ABR) and unspecified bit rate (UBR) be added (currently only a few switches/carriers support ABR).[2]

Beyond the publication of (fairly complex) specifications, there is a need for vendors to develop affordable and interoperable adaptation equipment. Today, if using ATM, the typical access device (edge multiplexer) for a medium-size branch location is actually an ATM-ready *router* that supports legacy ports on the user side and ATM on the network side. Many of these devices do not currently support CES. However, some edge multiplexers/routers now entering the market do support T1 interfaces on the user side, to connect PBXs utilizing circuit emulation. Frame relay access device support for voice over frame relay is probably going to be the near-term technology of choice for the majority of planners.

1.3 Packet Voice Is Leaving the Gate— Read On

A revolution in voice transmission and processing is coming. By the year 2005, it will be in full bloom. This book aims at beginning some of the discourse.

At this moment, voice over data networks suffers from a number of technical limitations, as follows:

1. *Voice over frame relay:* Until recently, no interoperability standards; specifications approved mid-1997; frame relay does not support quality of service; on-net only at the commercial level.

2. *Voice over ATM:* Still a technology novelty; expensive; quite a number of specifications approved late 1997; on-net only at the commercial level, except in special ICB situations.

3. *Voice over IP/Internet:* Few interoperability standards (e.g., H.323); IP does not support quality of service; IP-based networks usually overburdened, particularly at the router (and Internet router) level; enterprise networks not designed for isochronous traffic (like voice); on-net only (if deployed just over the enterprise network); could be off-net, if done across the Internet, but limited population currently equipped; little mainstream end-user equipment available at this juncture.

However, these restrictions will gradually be lifted in the next couple of years. In the rest of this book, the reader will find pertinent treatment of many of the factors and facets involved in this coming revolution. The reader may also wish to consult the companion text in this series, *Delivering Voice over IP Networks*, for the treatment of voice opportunities afforded by IP mechanisms.

References

1. D. Minoli. "General Geometric Arrival, Constant Server Queueing Problem with Applications to Packetized Voice." *ICC 1978 Conference Record* 3: 36.6.1–36.6.5.

2. D. Minoli with E. Lipper. "Mixed Classes of Traffic Obeying Different Queueing Rules with Reference to Integrated Packet Switched Networks." *1978 IEEE Canadian Conference on Communication and Power Record*, 1–4.

3. D. Minoli. "General Geometric Arrival, Discrete Server Queue." *NTC 1978 Conference Record*, 44.2.1–44.2.5.

4. D. Minoli. "Optimal Packet Length for Packet Voice Communication." *IEEE Transactions on Communication*, concise paper, COMM-27 (March 1979): 607–611.

5. D. Minoli. "Packetized Speech Network, Part 3: Delay Behavior and Performance Characteristics." *Australian Electronics Engineer* (August 1979): 59–68.

6. D. Minoli. "Packetized Speech Networks, Part 2: Queueing Model." *Australian Electronics Engineer* (July 1979): 68–76.

7. D. Minoli. "Packetized Speech Networks, Part 1: Overview." *Australian Electronics Engineer* (April 1979): 38–52.

8. D. Minoli. "Satellite On-Board Processing of Packetized Voice." *ICC 1979 Conference Record*, 58.4.1–58.4.5.

9. D. Minoli. "Issues in Packet Voice Communication." *Proceedings of IEE* 126(8): 729–740 (August 1979).

10. D. Minoli. "Some Design Parameters for PCM Based Packet Voice Communication." *1979 International Electrical/Electronics Conference Record*.

11. D. Minoli with K. Schneider. "Computing Average Loss Probability in a Circuit Switched Network." *IEEE Transactions on Communication*, COMM-28 (January 1980): 27–33.

12. D. Minoli with K. Schneider. "An Algorithm for Computing Average Loss Probability in a Circuit Switched Network." *Telecommunications Journal* 29-1 (June 1979): 28–37.

13. D. Minoli. "Digital Techniques in Sound Reproduction—Part 1." *Audio* (April 1980): 54–61.

14. D. Minoli with W. Nakamine. "Mersenne Numbers Rooted on 3 for Number Theoretic Transforms." *1980 IEEE International Conference on Acoustics, Speech and Signal Processing.*

15. D. Minoli. "Cost Effective Design of Local Access Networks Using Common Carriers Bulk Service Offering." *Electrical Communication* 55(2): 118–126 (1980).

16. D. Minoli. "Diseno Mas Economico de Redes de Acceso Locales Usando las Ofertas de Servicio Masivo de las Companias Explotadoras." *Communicaciones Electricas* 55(2): 118–126 (1980).

17. D. Minoli. "Gestaltung Kostengunstinger Anschlussnetze für das FAXPAK-Netz." *Elektrisches Nachrichtenwesen* 55(2): 118–126 (1980).

18. D. Minoli. "Optimisation de cout des reseaux d'acces locaux utilisant les options de tarif forfaitaires pour communications publiques." *Revue des telecommunicationes* 55(2): 118–126 (1980).

19. D. Minoli. "Digital Voice Communication over Digital Radio Links." *SIGCOMM Computer Communications Review* 9(4): 6–22 (October 1979).

20. D. Minoli. "Sizing Trunk Bundles Which Can Be Seized at Both Ends with Different Grade of Service." *IEEE Transactions on Communication* COMM-28(6): 794–801 (June 1980).

21. D. Minoli. "Getting the Most WATS for Every Communication Dollar." *Data Communications* (September 1980): 91–102.

22. D. Minoli. "Engineering Two-Ways Foreign Exchange Trunk Bundle Systems." *Computer Communication* 3(2): 69–76 (April 1980).

23. D. Minoli. "Digital Techniques in Sound Reproduction—Part 2." *Audio* (May 1980): 34–42.

24. D. Minoli. "Selection of Communications Facilities under a Multigraduated Tariff." *Computer Networks* 4(6): 295–301 (December 1980).

25. D. Minoli. "Optimal Allocation in a Multi-Resources Graduate Tariff Communication Environment." *Computer Communications* 3(4): 117–124 (August 1980).

26. D. Minoli. "Unmasking a Puzzling New Tariff: A Look at Some Hard Facts on WATS." *Telephony* 199(21): 24–27 (November 24, 1980).

27. D. Minoli. "A Case for Simpler Tariffs." *Telephony* 201(7): 22–24 (August 17, 1981).

28. D. Minoli. "Designing Large Scale Private Voice Networks." *Telephony* 201(12) 130ff (September 14, 1981).

29. D. Minoli. "Strategy in Multigraduated Tariffs under Random Usage." *Computer Communications* 4(6): 5–10 (December 1981).

30. D. Minoli. "A New Design Criterion for Store-and-Forward Networks." *Computer Networks* 7: 9–15 (1983).

31. D. Minoli. "Designing Practical Voice and Data Communications Networks—Part 1." *Computer World* (May 6, 1985): 67, 73.

32. D. Minoli. "All about Channel Banks: Technology Briefing." *DataPro Report* CA-80-010-902 (October 1987).

33. D. Minoli. "Evaluating Communications Alternatives—Part 1: Cost Analysis Methods." *DataPro Report* CA03-010-401 (June 1986).

34. D. Minoli. "Evaluating Communications Alternatives—Part 2: Pragmatic Network Design Issues." *DataPro Report* CA09-010-451 (June 1986).

35. D. Minoli. "Phone Changes Benefit Users." *Computer World* (May 12, 1986): 19, 23.

36. D. Minoli. "Integrated Voice/Data PBX." *Teleconnect* (May 1986): 75–78.

37. D. Minoli. "Engineering PBX Networks—Part 1: Design Modules." *DataPro Report* MT30-315-101 (September 1986).

38. D. Minoli. "Engineering PBX Networks—Part 2: Gathering Support Data." *DataPro Report* MT30-315-201 (September 1986).

39. D. Minoli. "ISDN Part 2." *Computer World* (January 20, 1986).

40. D. Minoli. "ISDN: Good News for the Communications Manager—Part 1." *Computer World* (January 13, 1986).

41. D. Minoli. "An Overview of ADPCM Transcoders." *DataPro Report* CA80-010-604 (November 1986).

42. D. Minoli. "Designing Voice Networks." *DataPro Report* 5401MVN (May 1995).

43. D. Minoli. "Traffic Engineering Basics." *DataPro Report* (June 1995).

44. D. Minoli. "Designing End-to-End Networks for New Multimedia Applications." *Proceedings, ICA*, Portland, OR, 1995.

45. D. Minoli. "Common Channel Signaling System Number 7." *DataPro Report* 8420 (March 1996).

46. D. Minoli. "Designing Voice Networks." *DataPro Report* 5401 (April 1996).

47. D. Minoli. "Queueing Fundamentals for Telecommunications." *DataPro Report* 5430 (January 1996).

48. D. Minoli. "Signaling Concepts." *DataPro Report* 2912 (February 1996).

49. D. Minoli. "Advanced Intelligent Networks." *DataPro Report* 3070 (March 1996).

50. D. Minoli. "Installing and Maintaining a Premises-Based Voice Wiring System." *DataPro Report* 5701 (March 1997).

51. D. Minoli. "Private T1 Networks for Business." *DataPro Report* (May 1996).

52. D. Minoli. "The Telephone Room Environment." *DataPro Report* 5720 (May 1996).

53. D. Minoli. "Traffic Engineering Basics." *DataPro Report* 5420 (July 1996).

54. D. Minoli. "Interstate Private Line Facilities." *DataPro Report* 3501 (August 1996).

55. D. Minoli. "T-Carrier Network Planning and Design." *DataPro Report* 5240 (September 1996).

56. D. Minoli. "AT&T Tariff 12." *DataPro Report* 3010 (November 1996).

57. D. Minoli. *Telecommunication Technologies Handbook*. Norwood, MA: Artech House, 1991.

58. D. Minoli. *Enterprise Networking: Fractional T1 to SONET, Frame Relay to BISDN*. Norwood, MA: Artech House, 1993.

59. D. Minoli and A. Schmidt. *MPOA: Building State-of-the-Art Intranets*. Greenwich, CT: Prentice-Hall/Manning, 1998.

60. D. Minoli and J. Amoss. *Broadband and ATM Switching Technology*. New York: McGraw-Hill, 1998.

61. D. Minoli and A. Schmidt. *Switched Network Services*. New York: Wiley, 1998.

62. D. Minoli and A. Alles. *LAN, LAN Emulation, and ATM*. Norwood, MA: Artech House, 1997.

63. D. Minoli. *Distance Learning: Broadband Applications*. Norwood, MA: Artech House, 1996.

64. D. Minoli. *Video Dialtone Technology: Digital Video over ADSL, HFC, FTTC, and ATM.* New York: McGraw-Hill, 1995.

65. D. Minoli and M. Vitella. *Cell Relay Service and ATM for Corporate Environments.* New York: McGraw-Hill, 1994.

66. D. Minoli and G. Dobrowski. *Signaling Principles for Frame Relay and Cell Relay Services.* Norwood, MA: Artech House, 1994.

67. D. Minoli. *Designing Broadband Networks.* Norwood, MA: Artech House, 1993.

68. D. Minoli and B. Keinath. *Distributed Multimedia through Broadband Communication Services.* Norwood, MA: Artech House, 1994.

69. D. Minoli and O. Eldib. *Telecommuting.* Norwood, MA: Artech House, 1995.

70. D. Minoli. *First, Second, and Next Generation LANs.* New York: McGraw-Hill, 1994.

71. D. Minoli and E. Minoli. *Delivering Voice over IP Networks.* New York: Wiley, 1998.

72. Act Networks Promotional Material, http://www.acti.com/vofr.htm.

Notes

[1] The term "voice over data networks" is also in vogue; we use the two interchangeably.

[2] These concepts are covered at length in Chapter 2.

CHAPTER 2

An Overview of Frame Relay and ATM Technologies

2.1 Introduction

This chapter provides an overview of frame relay and ATM technology and services. The chapter is intended as a synopsis only; the reader may consult any number of sources, if additional information is required.

2.2 Frame Relay

Motivations for frame relay services and technologies, as well as an introduction to that techology are provided in this section.

Frame Relay Drivers

Frame relay has become a major networking technology of the 1990s. Frame relay is a statistically supported, frame-based, connection-oriented data service that provides transparent transfer of information across a public or private network on a best effort basis. "Best effort" implies that there is no guarantee of delivery within a stipulated time window; the network can discard frames in congestion situations or when the user exceeds the traffic contract established with the carrier. The protocol provides a minimal set of functions to forward variable-sized data payloads through a network.

With the increased interest in full-featured, companywide connectivity for enterprise networks and intranets, access technology for SOHO support is playing an ever more important role in the total communication solution that corporate planners are seeking to deploy at this time. Specifically, there is interest in integrated multimedia access technology: Planners look for equipment that supports data, LAN, voice (compressed), videoconferencing, and fax applications over public or private frame relay networks, utilizing a single communication access facility. Remote branch offices are prime candidates for such entry-level, yet significantly important, connectivity equipment. Given the fact that there may be many remote locations, the cost effectiveness of the equipment and bandwidth efficiency are critical. At the same time, carriers, especially competitive local exchange carriers (CLECs), prefer to deliver only a single facility to a location and service all of the customer's needs in that manner. Frame relay is being positioned by the industry as that access technology, at least in the near term.

Many companies rely on public frame relay services from carriers such as AT&T, Sprint, TCG, and MCI/Worldcom. New pricing trends are also giving impetus to the voice-support question: In the recent past, frame relay services charges decreased, after several years of stability. Guaranteed bandwidth (committed information rate, or CIR) is generally charged in multiples of 8, 16, 32, or 64kbps. Some of the carriers are now also in the process of introducing switched services and frame relay–to-ATM interworking.

Frame relay has evolved from a solution for transmitting legacy and LAN data to handling more delay-sensitive protocols—for example, System Network Architecture (SNA)—to the current challenge of delivering voice and fax across WANs. In spite of all the hype about the World Wide Web, voice requirements continue to be key for the overwhelming majority of businesses. Besides traditional telephony, voice over frame relay currently has the best chance of all the voice over packet alternatives to be used for commercial applications during the next couple of years. Unfortunately, there is relatively little support for QoS in frame relay; however, given its relative ubiquity, there is a need to understand this technology. Initially, voice over frame relay makes sense over enterprise networks (even if implemented with public carrier frame relay services), rather than for generic off-net applications. Furthermore, it makes the most economic sense for calls between a company's domestic and international sites. However, as time goes by, there is the real possibility of central office (CO) interworking, allowing global access; the carrier in question, however, must deploy interworking equipment at the CO to achieve this.

Frame relay's key specifications for the service are ANSI's T1.617 and T1.618. The Frame Relay Forum (FRF) also developed a set of critical Implementation Agreements (IAs). This successful industry consortium continues in its efforts to promote use of frame relay products and services around the world, riding on the success of frame relay in North America and the growing markets in Europe and Asia. Key FRF specifications are FRF1.1, FRF.4, and FRF.8. Initially, these standards did not included intrinsic voice support; however, voice can be accommodated once a voice compression scheme is identified (so as to achieve greater packing density) and appropriate parameters for the frame relay service are established. Since 1997, a voice over frame relay standard has become available. Voice carriage over frame relay does not generally rely on pulse code modulation (PCM) techniques used to digitize voice since the early 1960s. PCM uses a constant stream of bits in a TDM channel; it requires 64 kbps, based on Nyquist's theorem and dynamic range/quantization considerations. Frame relay, on the other hand, is a form of statistical frame-based multiplexing with the associated possibility for frame-to-frame delay variation, frame loss, and jitter. In order to be able to support voice over a *shared* 64-kbps access/backbone frame relay link, the industry has moved, therefore, to compressed voice; at the same time, the issue of statistical jitter needs to be addressed. Video has used compression for many years; voice is now following suit.

Frame Relay Technology and Services

Frame relay service is a connection-oriented *fast-packet*[1] service supporting bursty traffic at medium speeds. The service has evolved as an improvement of packet switching service, supporting higher end-to-end throughput, lower delay, and less expensive user and network equipment. Frame relay accommodates applications such as wide area interconnection of LANs at the $n\times$56-kbps and 1.544-

Mbps rates. A frame relay interface (FRI) between the user and the network can support multiple sessions—specifically multiple virtual channels (VCs)—over a single physical access line, including, for example, VCs for data and voice. The term *relay* implies that the Layer 2 (Data Link Layer) data frame is not terminated and/or processed at the ends of each link in the network, but is relayed to the destination end point. Limiting Layer 2 functionality to the *core functions* (see Table 2.1) required to achieve this relaying implies that forwarding functions can be implemented in hardware, rather than in software, as was often done in packet switches, improving throughput/delay characteristics at the switch and at the interface. Frame relay implements only the core functions on a link-by-link basis; the other functions, particularly error recovery, are done on an end-to-end basis. Like X.25, frame relay specifies the interface between customer equipment and the network, whether public or private.

Frames with error are identified and discarded in the network, and user equipment is expected to recover higher-layer protocol data units (PDUs) using upper-layer protocols. Note that with fiber-based transmission facilities, bit error rate (BER) is improved, reducing the chance of transmission errors to a low probability. In a frame relay environment, the network can detect errors, but the correction is relegated to the end systems, using the Transmission Control Protocol (TCP), which, therefore, must be appropriately configured to support these tasks. Error conditions include lost, duplicated, misdelivered, discarded, and out-of-sequence frames.

Frame relay enables the transmission of variable-length data units over an assigned VC. VCs are identified by logical labels. Connection-oriented service involves a connection establishment phase, an information transfer phase, and a connection termination

Table 2.1   Data Link Layer Core Functions in Frame Relay

- Frame delimiting, alignment, and transparency
- Frame multiplexing/demultiplexing using the address field
- Inspection of the frame to ensure that it consists of an integer number of octets prior to zero bit insertion or following zero bit extraction
- Inspection of the frame to ensure that it is neither too long nor too short
- Detection of transmission errors

phase. A logical connection is set up between end systems prior to exchanging data. This is accomplished using the signaling mechanism or by administrative arrangement. Sequencing of data, flow control, and transparent error handling are some of the capabilities supported by a generic connection-oriented service. Frame relay service provides both a permanent virtual connection (PVC) service and a switched virtual connection (SVC) service. See Table 2.2. At the commercial level, nearly all implementations have been of the PVC kind. There is a possibility that SVC services could become available in the future. A PVC implementation establishes a fixed path through the network for each source-destination pair, which remains defined for a long period of time (weeks, months, or years). Since the setup is done once, it implies the allocation of some

Table 2.2   Virtual Circuits in Frame Relay

Permanent Virtual Circuits (PVCs)

A logical link or path between the originating and terminating routers. No resources are allocated to the link unless data is actually being sent. The link is set up by the administrator and remains in place for however long is needed (days, months, or years). The circuit is identified via the DLCI.

Switched Virtual Circuit (SVC)

A virtual circuit that is set up on a call-by-call basis. It is a future frame relay service, of particular importance to public frame relay networks. The circuit is identified via the DLCI.

Data Link Connection Identifier (DLCI)

A field in the frame indicating a particular logical link over which the frame should be transmitted. The field has local significance, since it can be changed by the switches as the frame traverses a single-node network (the input DLCI is mapped to an output DLCI). Multinode networks may pipeline cells to the network edges. In this case, VCIs are used and remapped. Access DLCIs are assigned by the network manager, while trunk VCIs are allocated dynamically. Toward the network, the switch associates each VCI with the physical address of the trunk over which the frame needs to be transmitted to reach its ultimate destination. Toward the user, VCIs are associated with the physical line supporting the DLCI identifying the user.

Virtual Circuit Identifier (VCI)

A label used by a cell switch to identify cells belonging to a given user. VCIs have local significance. These come into play in frame relay–to–ATM interworking cases.

resources regardless of the real-time traffic requirements or lack thereof. In SVC, resources are put in place only for the duration of the actual session (minutes or hours). SVC service signaling is based on a set of protocols common to all ISDN services. However, the implementations up to the late 1990s did not support the control plane, were not deployed in conjunction with ISDN, and have been based on PVCs. Frame relay can be obtained both as a private network technology or as a public network service.

Standards work for frame relay started in the mid-1980s; work accelerated in the late 1980s, after the publication of the first ITU-T frame relay standards. The basic frame relay protocol, described by the international standards committee, by the national standards committee, and even by the Frame Relay Forum, such as User-to-Network Interface (UNI) and Network-to-Network Interface (NNI) Implementation Agreements, has been augmented in recent years via additional agreements that detail techniques for structuring application data over the basic frame relay information field. These techniques enabled successful support for data applications such as LAN bridging, IP routing, SNA, and now voice. See Tables 2.3 and 2.4. Current key FRF specification activities are shown in Table 2.5.

Enterprise Networking Applications

Figure 2.1 depicts the integrated use of frame relay services in the context of an enterprise network. As noted, frame relay was originally developed to support the bursty traffic generated by LANs interconnected over WANs. In the early 1990s it was used as a cost-effective consolidation of distinct corporate networks, such as legacy SNA networks. Frame relay's low cost compared to meshes of dedicated lines, along with the first kind of traffic contracts available in the WAN market (ATM being the culmination in this respect) has made the service popular. For example, the user may be on a T1/DS1 line and contracts for 256 kbps of CIR with the carrier; but then the user could try to burst to higher levels and for a relatively long period of time. In general, users try to get away with the lowest possible CIR—even as low as 0—and then send more data. In that case, all of the relevant performance metrics, delay, jitter, and loss will be impacted.

The evolution in the private environment involves using customer-owned switches that provide FRIs to the routers and

Table 2.3 Basic Standards Apparatus for Frame Relay

UNI interface specification

Described in generalities in ITU-T Recommendation I.122 and first published in 1988, it is also described in FRF1.1. ANSI T1.606 provides a description of the frame relay service; the equivalent ITU-T recommendation is I.233.

Congestion management

The ANSI T1.606 Addendum describes congestion management; the equivalent ITU-T recommendation is I.370.

Frame format for data transfer

Based on a subset of ITU-T Q.921 (LAP-D), but extended with the flow control fields. The protocol is now known as Link Access Procedure F Core (LAP-F Core) and is defined in ANSI T1.618-1991; it is also defined in ITU-T's Q.922 Annex A adopted in 1992.[2]

Signaling

ITU-T Q.933 (an extension of ITU-T Q.931 used in ISDN) was developed to support SVC service. In the United States, T1.617-1991 describes access signaling, along with FRF.4.

PVC management functions

Included in T1.617 Annex D. The (Interim) Local Management Interface, or (I)LMI, makes it possible for the network to notify the end user of the addition, deletion, or presence of a PVC at a specified UNI (any such information received on a UNI applies to that particular UNI). Many of the features of the (I)LMI specifications contained in T1.617 were initially proposed by vendors and by the FRF.

(possibly) use cell relay/ATM technology between nodes. In the business and technological landscape of the 1990s it is prudent for the communication manager to look at networking solutions that will not have to be discarded after a couple of years to keep up with network growth or higher-speed networking needs or technologies. One answer to this problem is to *rely on a public carrier* and avoid setting up a private network, and secure the WAN switching hardware. The idea of a private frame relay network was more prevalent in the early 1990s when planners were using the point-to-point lines they had put in place in the mid to late 1980s to construct networks by simply adding switches. This approach, however, was soon discovered to be limited because it did not support companywide connectivity at the branch level. Some users may deploy hybrid frame relay networks: These users could utilize

Table 2.4   FRF Implementation Agreement

FRF.1.1	Date: January 19, 1996. User-to-Network (UNI) Implementation Agreement
FRF.2.1	Date: July 10, 1995. Frame Relay Network-to-Network (NNI) Implementation Agreement Version 2.1
FRF.3.1	Date: June 22, 1995. Multiprotocol Encapsulation (MEI) Implementation Agreement
FRF.4	Date: N/A. Switched Virtual Circuit (SVC) Implementation Agreement
FRF.5	Date: December 20, 1994. Frame Relay/ATM Network Interworking Implementation Agreement
FRF.6	Date: March 1994. Frame Relay Service Customer Network Management (MIB) Implementation Agreement
FRF.7	Date: October 21, 1994. Frame Relay PVC Multicast Service and Protocol Description
FRF.8	Date: April 14, 1995. Frame Relay / ATM PVC Service Interworking Implementation Agreement
FRF.9	Date: January 22, 1996. Data Compression over Frame Relay Implementation Agreement
FRF.10	Date: September 10, 1996. Frame Relay Network-to-Network SVC Implementation Agreement
FRF.11	Date: May 5, 1997. Voice over Frame Relay Implementation Agreement

their own frame relay backbone connecting major sites, and use a public frame relay network to connect secondary sites. In view of the growth in the population of LANs, carriers have realized the commercial opportunity to provide public PVC-based frame relay data services that support high-capacity access/throughput, coupled with the universal access, survivability, economies of scale, and efficiency available through resource sharing. SVC-based frame relay has some advantages, but it also has some limitations. As noted, the service may become available only later in the decade. Furthermore, a user needing to send data to some remote user on another LAN may not be willing to incur the call setup time each time a session is required. The way some people have gotten around the setup time issue in packet switched networks was to use long-duration SVCs: These are set up once and kept active for an appropriate amount of time, such as a day.

Although, initially, carrier frame relay networks were implemented as separate overlay networks, today many carriers' frame

Table 2.5 Key Recent Standardization Activities for Frame Relay

SNA Support

Work to bring frame relay into the mainstream of SNA business applications, through carrier services and advanced functionality in frame relay access devices (FRADs) and frame relay switches.

SVC Service

Work on FRF.10 (SVCs) at the Network-to-Network Interface (NNI). Ballot resolution is completed and has been forwarded to the board for ratification shortly.

Voice over Frame Relay (VOFR)

FRF.11 specifies procedures for the transport of packetized low-bit-rate voice over frame relay networks. This first-phase IA defines support for preconfigured connections allowing multivendor interoperability. The VOFR IA became available in mid-1997.

Frame Relay Fragmentation

This work will enable fragmentation and reassembly of frames at the FR UNI. Work in this area is under way and may be completed by press time.

Multilink Frame Relay at the UNI

This work will enable frame relay devices to use multiple physical links; in essence frame relay inverse muxing. This effort was expected to be completed by press time.

Work on Frame Relay–to-ATM (FR/ATM) SVC Service Interworking

This effort will define FR/ATM service interworking supporting SVCs, popular in ATM, and already defined for frame relay. This effort was expected to be completed by press time.

Frame Relay Network Service-Level Definitions

This effort will provide FR network performance definitions. This will enable service providers to deliver service levels that are uniform across diverse networks. It will provide users with a metric for use when determining if contracted service levels were rendered. Completion was expected by press time.

relay networks are integrated with ATM. This means that the switch supports frame relay User-to-Network Interface (UNI) to the user side, but internally it is an ATM switch connected to an ATM backbone. So, input frames are cellularized (typically on the input card), and the ATM quality of service and traffic/buffer management mechanisms are used to handle the derivative cells. On the output side, cells are either converted back to frames for immediate

Figure 2.1
Integration sought with frame relay.

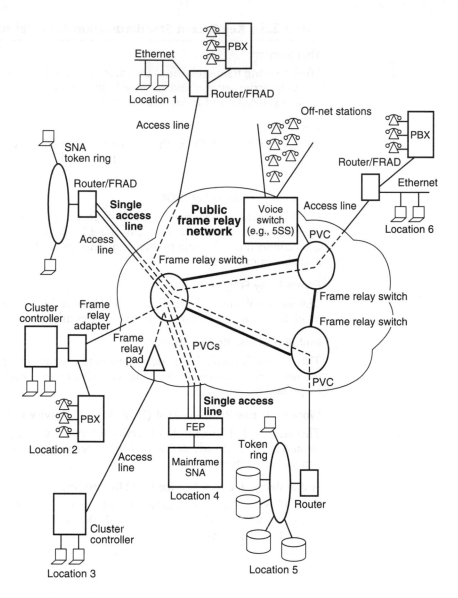

delivery or passed up to another switch for wide-area coverage. At the destination switch, cells are converted back to frames (having thereby achieved network interworking) or are delivered directly over an ATM link to the user. The user can in turn convert those cells back to frame relay (the advantage of this approach is that a high-speed link—e.g., 45 Mbps or 155 Mbps—can be used, rather than just a T1 link, as would be the case in a frame relay NNI). It should be noted that frame relay was not originally designed to support voice, while ATM has been developed from the beginning for this type of traffic mixing. In the frame over ATM case, QoS can be guaranteed to the cell stream but not necessarily to the frame stream. Clearly, better edge-to-edge behavior obtained via the ATM core network's QoS is a step in the right direction.

Additional Details on Frame Relay Technology and Services

The business trend is toward *interconnection of all company resources* into a seamless enterprisewide network. The paradigm now is that "the corporation is the network." However, such interconnection can become prohibitively expensive, unless it is done correctly. Corporations also see the emergence of *new LAN applications* in the 1990s, which must be supported by the enterprisewide network. In addition to voice, desktop videoconferencing via the newly approved ITU-T H.320 standards (H.323 in particular) may soon become a real requirement for enterprise networks. QoS support is therefore required. New high-bandwidth applications dictate the introduction of new high-capacity digital services and technologies in the corporate network. Frame relay is a step in that direction. High end-to-end throughput, low latency, cost-effective bandwidth-on-demand, and any-to-any connectivity are the order of the day. A major evolution in the way corporations connect their computers and the ubiquitous PC is already evident in progressive companies. Now, new equipment and new communication services allow corporations to redesign their networks and save money, while at the same time increase their capabilities and workforce productivity. The key to achieving these communication goals in a private network environment is frame relay over a cell relay platform, or a high-capacity public switched service such as frame relay over ATM.[3]

Frame relay is a multiplexed data networking capability supporting connectivity between user equipment (routers and private frame relay switches) and between frame relay switches, which was introduced in the late 1980s and early 1990s. The frame relay protocol supports only data transmission over a connection-oriented path; it enables the transmission of variable-length data units over an assigned virtual connection. Frame relay standards specify the user interface to a device or network supporting the service. In frame relay, this UNI is known as the FRI. The FRI is a standardized interface between customer equipment and a switch or a frame relay network. A two-layer protocol stack interface capability implemented at both endpoints of a link. A FRI supports access speeds of 56 kbps, $n\times64$ kbps, and 1.544 Mbps (2.048 Mbps in Europe). The service can be deployed (1) in a point-to-point link fashion between two routers, (2) using customer-owned frame relay switches (frame relay switches may employ cell relay on the trunk/NNI side[4]), and (3) utilizing a carrier-provided service.

Frame relay is a natural evolution of packet switching. Many of the principles still apply, although some of the error handling has changed, and the switches are much faster, being ASIC-based and operating at the 1- to 10-Gbps aggregate rate. Packet switching allows users to be easily added and interconnected, while following open international standards. But packet switching has traditionally been slow and the throughput has been limited.[5] These limitations became more accentuated with the new LAN applications that involve graphics, multimedia, desktop publishing, bulk file transfer, and other data-intensive requirements. This has led to the development of two solutions specifically aimed at LANs: frame relay and ATM. Frame relay supports bursty traffic at *medium speeds*. The introduction of switched Ethernet, 100-Mbps Ethernet, and gigabit Ethernet imply that, for major locations, frame relay is not enough. Organizations that have these kinds of desktop networks need to use ATM or ATM-based Transparent LAN Services (TLS) offered by a number of CLECs, notably TCG. Many progressive companies and early adopters are now introducing ATM on their campuses and WANs. The introduction of switched Ethernet, 100-Mbps Ethernet, and gigabit Ethernet is beginning to require interconnection between subnets at speeds ranging from 6 to 10 Mbps (achievable with inverse multiplexers and TLS), to as much as 45, 155, and 622 Mbps on ATM UNIs.

This section provides some additional details on frame relay services and technology.

Frame Relay Switches

A frame relay switch connects users, facilitating any-to-any connectivity. Connections are accomplished in real-time over the PVC (the PVC itself, however, must be previously established). The frame relay interface is only a definition of what the data stream into the frame relay network looks like. Equipment in the form of switches is needed in the network (private or public) to make the frame relay concept a reality. Like a packet or ATM switch, a frame relay switch supports a virtual connection. Tables are maintained by the switch that tell the switch the physical port on which an incoming frame must be transmitted. For users terminating on the same switch, the frames are directly sent to the destination by checking the address and determining which physical port needs to receive the data. For users terminating on two different switches, the data must be sent over the appropriate trunk to the destination node, for ultimate delivery. Centralized administration of the backbone network routing tables and the natural port sharing and multiplexing attributes of frame relay make network growth manageable and simple.

As noted earlier, frame relay networks can be private, public or hybrid. A network consists of (1) user equipment that supports the frame relay interface, (2) one or more frame relay switches owned by the user or a carrier, and (3) communication links between the users and the switches and between the processors (links between the switches are owned by the carrier in a public network). The user equipment typically consists of appropriately configured LAN routers. The switches interpret the frame and transmit it (using cells, or in some cases, frames), making the concept of frame relay a reality. Frames traverse a fixed PVC path through the network, although transmission resources (including bandwidth) are not dedicated to each virtual connection. The PVC approach implies the allocation of *some* resources—such as table entries—regardless of the real-time user traffic condition. Since the PVC is established at subscription time, there is no need for real-time *signaling* in this type of service (there may be status signaling, but this is unrelated to the establishment of the channel). Given the need for any-to-any connectivity, SVC services may yet evolve.

In a connectionless service, such as IP, each data unit is independently routed to the destination; no connection-establishment activities are required, since each data unit is independent of the previous or subsequent one. Connectionless-mode service provides for unit data transfer without regard to the establishment or maintenance of connections. This is advantageous in interenterprise applications. Each unit of data contains the addressing information and the data itself. The responsibility for assurance that the message gets to the other hand is shifted up from the Data Link Layer to higher layers, where the integrity check is done only once, instead of being done at (every) lower layer. In the frame relay environment, the VCs are used by the router as a logical point-to-point connection between it and one or more remote routers.

Transmission Mechanism across a Frame Relay Network

Every network needs to ensure that traffic is forwarded reliably from the source to the destination. In a frame relay network, forwarding of the frames from the various routers is determined by the DLCI of the frame on a given user-network interface. Nodes use the DLCI to determine the frame's destination. The DLCI is not an address of the destination, since it may change as the frame travels through the network (i.e., the DLCI has local significance only). Instead, it identifies the logical connection between an element in the network and the next element in the network (i.e., endpoint and switch, and switch and endpoint; routing between switches is accomplished through the VCI). The forwarding table entries for permanent virtual circuit service are populated via the network management system and routing is *not* determined on a per-call basis.

When using the frame relay interface, the router on a LAN selects the required remote router by specifying the permanent virtual circuit via a DLCI contained in the frame relay frame it builds prior to transmitting the data. If the system is well designed, there should be no segmentation of the LAN frames into multiple frame relay frames, although this could happen in theory, adding delay and overhead. The switch accepts the frame it receives on one of its incoming ports, segments it into cells while appending a sequence number for remote-switch cell-to-frame reassembly, and delivers it over the trunk connecting to that remote switch. Initially, trunk interfaces used a packet-like protocol; more recently, products are moving in the direction of ATM cells standards. The switch must segment incoming frame relay frames for delivery through the cell format, because these frames can be long, while cells are much shorter. Switches do, however, check the frame check sequence (FCS) code of a received frame. If the frame is found to be in error, it is dropped without further processing.

The switches do not have to read the variable-length frame to achieve switching; instead, the DLCI is sufficient to allow the edge processors to make the necessary routing decisions. The DLCI may be reused by virtual circuits that do not share one or both end-points. In modern ATM-based frame relay networks there is an interplay between DLCI, the cell's VCI (or equivalent vendor-proprietary indicator), and the ultimate trunks. Three aspects of Layer 2 routing exist:

- Association between the locally significant DLCI and the cell's VCI (and the other way around). This occurs at origination and destination switches.
- Remapping of a VCI to another VCI. This occurs whenever there are ATM switching points or cross-connect nodes (a specific VCI has no end-to-end significance if the virtual channel connection is switched; the VCI could remain the same end-to-end if the virtual connection is provided on a semipermanent basis). This occurs at intermediate nodes.
- Association between a local DLCI and a DLCI of a user connected to the same switch.

Error Treatment

In frame relay, error correction and retransmission are done only in the user end-system equipment, where a TCP entity is found. The network can detect errors, but the correction is relegated to the end systems. Error conditions include lost, duplicated, misdelivered, discarded, and out-of-sequence frames; recovery from these error conditions must be performed by the user's equipment, which must be appropriately configured to support these tasks. This does not require any additional functionality than what most intelligent equipment, such as LAN routers, has today. Furthermore, with today's higher-quality digital transmission facilities and the migration to fiber, it is unlikely that many frames will be received in error, requiring end-to-end retransmission. Error-prone circuits of the past necessitated complex error checking and recovery procedures at each node of a network.

Since error correction and flow control are handled at the endpoints, frame relay expedites the process of forwarding PDUs through a series of switches to a remote location by eliminating the need for each switch to check each packet and correct those in error. This error treatment increases performance and reduces bandwidth requirements, which in turn can reduce communication costs.

In the past when transmission errors were common, it was not efficient to require the Transport Layer (whose job is to guarantee ultimate end-to-end reliability) to keep track of unacknowledged PDUs. Instead, the Data Link Layer, closer to where the problem had its roots, was responsible for the correction task. It turns out that, in the final analysis, when the probability of error over a link is relatively high, it is better to do error correction on a link-by-link basis (i.e., at the Data Link Layer), as measured by the amount of network bandwidth required to successfully send a PDU (although it may, in fact, have been faster to do it end to end). When the probability of error is low, it is better to do error correction end to end—that is, at the Transport Layer. In other words, for the same amount of network bandwidth, the PDU gets delivered faster by doing the error management end to end; in addition, the switches can be cheaper since they need to undertake fewer tasks.

Congestion Management

Congestion management is important, particularly for voice applications. Frame relay has (in principle) a way to manage and control congestion. However, this control is not explicitly tied to a QoS mechanism (in terms of meeting a stipulated service-level agreement). The frame relay network comprising the switches, private or public, attends to this by first using congestion notification strategies and then by selectively discarding frames when needed to relieve congestion. Congestion control mechanisms are used to treat users fairly and to protect the network and users by localizing the congestion within the network.

The congestion notification takes place when a network node determines that it is becoming congested. It sets the Forward Explicit Congestion Notification (FECN) bit in the frames as it sends them to the destination router. It also sets the Backward Explicit Congestion Notification (BECN) bit in the frames destined for the source router. Upon receipt of these frames, the source and destination routers are expected to initiate procedures to throttle back the traffic offered to the network. If congestion continues to increase despite using congestion notification, the network will begin to discard eligible frames and will put the congestion localization procedures into effect. The network of switches selects frames for discard by looking at the Discard Eligibility (DE) bit in each frame to see if it has been set by the router. If it is set, then the network discards the associated frame. See Table 2.6. These procedures continue until the congestion subsides. These techniques are also known as *congestion avoidance* techniques.

One issue, however, is whether and how the router can enforce throttling back to the PCs originating the traffic. Hence, the important question to ask about a frame relay router, a switch, and a carrier service, is whether the full congestion control apparatus specified by the standard is implemented in each of these devices.

Congestion Control Issues for Public Networks　As indicated, in frame relay the entire bandwidth up to the maximum access speed can be made available to a single user during peak periods. A problem may arise in the network if many users require this bandwidth simultaneously, as might be the case when LANs from multiple organizations (or departments within an organization) are terminated on the network. The frame relay network must be able to detect any overload condition and quickly initiate corrective actions.

Congestion control (also known as *flow control*) is already needed in traditional public packet networks, but in a frame relay network its need is more critical because of the performance objec-

Table 2.6　Congestion Management Elements

Discard Eligibility Indicator

A field in the frame set by the user's equipment to indicate that the frame can be discarded if needed in case of congestion, in order to maintain the committed throughput.

Backward Explicit Congestion Notification Indicator

A bit in the frame set by the network to notify the user's equipment that congestion avoidance procedures should be initiated, so as to limit the amount of traffic injected into the network or sent to the switch. The field is set in a frame going in the opposite direction of the congestion (i.e., it is sent to the origination). It is similar to a "slowdown" signal.

Forward Explicit Congestion Notification Indicator

A field in the frame set by the network or switch to notify downstream equipment and/or the destination equipment that congestion avoidance procedures should be initiated. The field is set in a frame in the direction of the destination. It is similar to a "holdon" signal for received frames, as well as a destination "slowdown" signal for traffic from the destination.

tives of the latter and the greater access speed. In X.25 networks, the access speed is normally much lower than the speed and capacity of the backbone; hence, it is unlikely that a single device would ever monopolize the backbone. In a LAN interconnection/frame relay environment, the routers seen as an ensemble may transmit a combined rate that exceeds the capacity of the backbone itself. A single router may flood the backbone; this in turn will starve other circuits of bandwidth.

Temporary conditions of overload occur in any well-utilized network. Networks that never experience temporary overloads may, in fact, be underutilized. Overengineering, however, is not a desirable way to handle congestion control because such an approach is not cost-effective; ignoring the issue of congestion is also undesirable since, in effect, it means not capitalizing on the full potential of frame relay. On the other hand, not controlling congestion can have disastrous consequences. In private networks, transmission costs are a major component of any design evaluation, and most of the benefits of frame relay technology are lost if implementing it demands the leasing of excessive amounts of bandwidth. The challenge is not how to preclude any temporary congestion, but how to react to it when it occurs. Overengineering or, better yet, relying on statistical averaging to obtain the most efficient utilization of deployed resources may be an approach that is viable in a public network environment, given the large population of potential users.

The frame relay standards specify explicit congestion control notification bits and a congestion notification control message. The important fields in the address portion of the frame relay format are the FECN, BECN, and DE, described earlier. In the ANSI standard, each of the individual virtual circuits in a frame relay connection (if the user and/or topological implementation calls for multiple PVCs over a physical link) can be independently throttled back. To be fair, the sources that contribute the most to the congestion should be slowed down the most, while sources contributing less traffic should be slowed down less. Hence, the network must be able to identify which PVCs over a physical link or beyond the access portion in the network are responsible for monopolizing resources.

Both the user's equipment and the switch should be able to respond to congestion control actions implied by the congestion control fields. For example, during periods of heavy load, the network could signal the user's equipment by setting the congestion bit to reduce the traffic arrival rate; when the overload situation dissipates, the opposite action could be achieved by setting the congestion bit back to normal. In some situations, the user's equipment could be overloaded; for example, a LAN gateway may be servicing another user and may not be able to absorb heavy loads of traffic coming from the network. Here, the user's equipment must be able to throttle the network.

The standards also provide a mechanism to discard some frames if the initial congestion control actions do not correct the situation. The network should not be designed to discard frames indiscriminately: It is fairer to discard frames from the users who contributed the most to the congestion. If the implementation supports the DE field, this can be accomplished equitably, since the user's equipment can indicate which frames should be discarded first. The DE capability makes it possible for the user to temporarily send more frames than it is allowed on the average. The network will forward these frames if it has the capacity to do so, but if the network is overloaded, frames with the DE bit set will be discarded first.

Implicit congestion notification (to the Transport layer of the ultimate user equipment—i.e., the PC) occurs when the user's end-to-end protocol determines that data have been lost. Actions to deal with implicit congestion notifications usually take higher priority than explicit congestion notifications. The former is normally handled by the ultimate equipment; the latter is handled first by the router and subsequently by the ultimate equipment. The network may indicate to the user's router that the data may be about to traverse a congested path by the FECN/BECN bits previously discussed. The user response to these congestion notifications is dependent on the type of notification and the frequency in which they are received.

Class-of-Service Parameters   Many are familiar with frame relay's *committed information rate.* It specifies the amount of bandwidth "guaranteed" to a user, between any two points; CIR can be as high as the access rate. If the CIR is exceeded, the frame relay device can send the information, but it should set the DE bit to indicate that the data can be discarded if necessary. Otherwise, the carrier may set the bit on behalf of the user. Carriers are specifying various class-of-service parameters for frame relay service. These include:

- *Committed burst size* (CBS; also called Bc). This is the maximum amount of user data (in bits) that the network agrees to transfer, under normal conditions, during one second.
- *Excess burst size* (EBS; also called Be). This represents the maximum amount of uncommitted data exceeding the CBS that the network will attempt to deliver during one second.
- *Committed information rate* (CIR). As noted, this represents the user's throughput that the network commits to support under normal network conditions. CIR is measured in bits per second.
- *Committed rate measurement interval* (CRMI; also called T). This is the time interval during which the user is allowed to send information at the CBS rate or at the CBS + EBS rate. Hence T = CBS/CIR.

These quantities are important because they are the basis of the services the carriers provide and for the supporting tariffs. Frame relay carriers will enforce the subscribed CBS, EBS, and CIR in the network in order to meet the grade of service. The user must allocate some minimum CIR to every possible device-to-device relationship (i.e., PVC); this implies that frame relay service, as currently available, is not the optimal solution to interenterprise applications.

As data is received over time interval *T*, a determination is made as to whether the frame is under the committed burst size, over the committed burst size but under the excess burst size, or over the burst size.

Recently, some vendors (e.g., Cascade/Ascend) have suggested that ATM-like classes of service should also be added to frame relay, in order to better handle time-sensitive traffic. They support:

- *Guaranteed packets:* Packets to be delivered according to some time constraint and with high probability.
- *Best effort packets:* Packets to be delivered to the best of the network's ability after meeting the requirement for delivering guaranteed packets.

Cascade/Ascend uses colors green, amber, and red to describe and categorize packet frames for monitoring and enforcement. (Note that these are not FRF constructs at this time.) Here, if the number of bits received during the current time interval, including the current frame, is less than CBS, then the frame is designated as a green frame. Green frames are never discarded by the network, except under extreme congestion conditions. If the number of bits received during the current time interval, including the current frame, is greater than CBS but less than EBS, the frame is designated as an amber frame. Amber frames are forwarded with the DE bit set, and are eligible for discard if they pass through a congested switch. If the number of bits received during the current time interval, including the current frame, is greater than EBS, the frame is designated as a red frame. Red frames are forwarded with the DE bit set when Cascade's special Graceful Discard is enabled and are dropped when the feature is not enabled (as would be the case under the baseline FRF specifications).

Cell Relay Usage in Frame Relay

A cell is a fixed-length packet of user data (payload) plus an over-head—usually small, 53 bytes or less. Cell relay (covered more extensively later) is a high-bandwidth, low-delay switching and multiplexing packet technology, which is *required to implement a frame relay network in an efficient manner*, particularly for mixed-media and multimedia applications. With cell relay, information to be transferred is packetized into fixed-size cells. Vendors tend to use the term *cell relay switch* (or node) when their equipment does not implement the ITU-T ATM standard, but a proprietary standard. If the ITU-T standard is implemented, they typically refer to the equipment as an *ATM switch*. At this time, most vendors implement the ITU-T standards, but this was not always the case.

Cells are identified and switched by means of a VCI/VPI label in the header. A number of functions of the Layer 2 protocol are removed to the edge of the backbone, while "core capabilities" are supported directly by the cell switches, in addition to Layer 1 functions (clocking, bit encoding, physical medium connection). Cells allocated to the same connection may exhibit an irregular recurrence pattern, since cells are filled according to the actual demand. Cell relay allows for capacity allocation on demand, so the bit rate per connection can be chosen flexibly. In addition, the actual channel mix at the interface can change dynamically. The cell header (such as the ATM's header) typically contains a label and an error detection field; error detection is confined to the header. The label is used for channel identification, in place of the positional methodology for assignment of octets, inherent in the traditional TDM T1/T3 systems. Cell relay is similar to packet switching but with the following differences: (1) Protocols are simplified, and (2) cells (packets) have a fixed and small length, allowing high-speed switching nodes. Switching decisions are straightforward and many functions are implemented in hardware. Cell relay is critical to the large-scale deployment of frame relay, and only those switches that implement it give the users the full advantages of the new technology.

It is important that a frame relay switch support a dynamic view of the data being transferred through it; otherwise, the user will not obtain the full benefit possible with the technology. Without a cell-based switch, dynamic bandwidth allocation is not easily achievable. Frame relay to ATM interworking is defined in ITU-T I.555 and FRF.8. The planner should note, however, that the edge frame relay switch typically buffers the incoming frame until it is totally received. This allows the switch to determine if the frame should exit from the same card (which could, for example, support 28 DS1s on a DS3 access card, or 672 DS0s, and/or many virtual channels), where there would be no cellularization involved, or if the frame must be segmented to be put onto the internal bus to reach another card that is also connected on the local side (this segmentation may or may not be ATM-based; e.g., it could be into 64-byte words), or if it is meant for remote (NNI) delivery. Only in the latter case would the I.555 mechanism come into play. Note that this has buffering delay implications.

Voice Considerations

As noted, there is considerable interest in integrated access solutions in general and voice over frame relay support in particular. The frame relay VCs enable the delivery of frames across a WAN in the proper order, and error checking prevents delivery of errored frames. However, frame relay service does not provide any intrinsic mechanisms for higher grades of service. In other words, there is no explicit method for establishing frame-level performance priorities, as are needed for voice. The only way to get any different traffic treatment is:

1. Set up different PVCs from the router/FRAD to the other end, over the WAN.
2. Administratively inform the carrier that certain PVCs carry "higher priority traffic."
3. Hope that the carrier has a switch that has some level of different-grade-of-service treatment
4. Hope that the carrier does not greatly overbook the bandwidth.
5. Hope that there are not too many hops in the network.
6. Acquire a CPE (router or FRAD) that can itself handle different inputs (LAN segment, PBX, etc.) differently (according to some priority scheme).

In 1997, the Frame Relay Forum ratified a standard called FRF.11 for interoperable voice over frame relay networks (see Table 2.7).

Table 2.7 FRF Press Release on FRF.11 (http://www.frforum.com)

The Frame Relay Forum today announced in May 1997 the ratification of FRF.11, an Implementation Agreement (IA) providing for Voice over Frame Relay (VoFR) communications.

Specifically, FRF.11—entitled "Voice over Frame Relay"—provides for bandwidth efficient networking of Voice and Group 3 fax communications over Frame Relay, as well as defining multiplexed Virtual Connections (VCs). This latter function allows for up to 255 voice and data sub-channels to be carried over a single VC through a Frame Relay network. Transparent relay of Group 3 fax communications is provided for in the IA by "spoofing" of the fax protocol, and transmission of fax traffic as a low-bit rate digital stream.

Two classes of voice compliance are supported, for maximum flexibility and worldwide applicability. Class 1 compliance calls for use of G.727 EADPCM typically at 32 Kbps (2:1 compression). Class 2 compliance specifies G.729/G.729A CS-ACELP at 8 Kbps (8:1 compression). In order to maximize use of bandwidth, it is possible to carry multiple voice samples in a single frame, further minimizing overhead.

The new IA is significant in that it is the first step for true multi-vendor interoperability of voice and fax over Frame Relay. Already offering a streamlined, compatible method for interoperability of data applications over the wide area, the new IA bolsters Frame Relay's ability to support the full complement of corporate LAN and legacy data, voice, fax and packetized video communications.

Prior to that, users had to rely on vendor-specific solutions. Implementation plans are unclear at this time; frame relay service providers have cautioned companies against implementing voice over frame relay, most ostensibly because these carriers also stand to lose voice traffic revenues. Secondarily, it may be that their networks are unable to support the QoS required for voice. However, it was expected that equipment suppliers would implement the standard by early 1998.

To support voice, it is necessary to support priorities in the switch (organization- or carrier-owned). Hence, in looking at switch technology (either for one's own network or to assess the strength of the carrier supplying the service), one needs to ascertain how the priorities are allocated and managed. With top-of-the-line switches, such as Ascend/Cascade B-STDX 9000, Newbridge 36170, Cisco IGX-32 or BPX, Nortel Passport 160, Telematics NCX-1E6, and Sentient Ultimate 1000/2000, the frame relay priorities are supported via ATM priorities and qualities of service. Hence, a good understanding of the latter is needed. The bottom line is, however, that since ATM has strong quality-of-service capabilities, it has become possible to support priorities in frame relay, thereby making the support of voice over frame relay possible. Some switches support 2 frame relay priorities; others, 4 or 8 priorities; others, yet as much as 32 priorities (these are assigned by administrative provisioning of the PVC). Some older and/or smaller switches do not support sophisticated priority mechanisms to handle PVCs in different ways (at the queue level). However, the difference with ATM is that even when the priorities are implemented by the switch, the QoS is not "guaranteed," as would be the case in the former.

Although frame relay is popular for its flexible bandwidth, its popularity has given rise to congestion in some networks, because carriers may not properly engineer their networks (in order to maximize their profitability), or carriers have had difficulty keeping up with the demands for new service. Given just the demand for higher bandwidth as additional organizations subscribe, it is a relatively simple step for the public carriers to add switches and capacity to the backbone to accommodate the growing demand. But now customers are requesting lower-latency service for their carriers, so that voice and fax can be carried over frame relay. There is a perception that many carriers are struggling in their efforts to increase capacity to meet this demand and/or to replace older switches with new ones that are ATM-based and support quality of service at the PVC level.

Carriers, central office switch manufacturers, and customer premises equipment vendors are addressing the voice over frame relay opportunity simultaneously. Customer premises equipment (CPE) manufacturers have recently seen a growing interest in voice over frame relay and have followed up with fast-paced research and the development of voice-capable frame relay access devices. It is hoped that FRF.11-conformant equipment will become available in the immediate future. However, although the equipment choices may soon be numerous, many of the carriers do not provide adequate support; only two companies as of now, for example, provide service-level guarantees for voice over frame relay.

Chapter 6 treats the topic of voice over frame relay at length.

2.3 ATM Networking: An Overview

Single Network Solution

ATM[6] is a connection-oriented switching and multiplexing technology that provides a high-speed and efficient method of transferring information between users, irrespective of the nature of the traffic. ATM represents a major change in the way future networks will be built.

ATM derives its name from the method of transferring information across a network. Traffic is broken into short packets, known as *cells*. Incoming cells are queued by the ATM switch until bandwidth is available on an outgoing link. Depending on network traffic, variable delays can be experienced, hence the term *asynchronous* (within the ATM name).

ATM uses a 53-byte, fixed-length cell. This fixed length provides two benefits. First, it allows network cell delay to be predicted and controlled. Second, it allows very fast ATM switches to be designed, where data is switched at the hardware level, improving the throughput previously achieved by slower, software-based equipment. While ATM has some additional overhead in cell headers, this cost is outweighed by the system's ability to statistically multiplex traffic and operate continuously with network trunks running at very high capacity.

As a result, ATM is as adept at handling real-time traffic, such as voice and video, and bursty LAN traffic. It is scaleable from the currently available T1/E1 narrowband rates to full optical speeds, such as OC-12 (622 Mbps).

The capability that makes ATM unique is its ability to combine the benefits of efficient statistical data multiplexing—as used by frame relay and other packet switching technologies—and the high-performance and predictable delivery characteristics of time division multiplexing (TDM) solutions.

This combination of capabilities means that ATM is the first technology capable of delivering or carrying *all* forms of traffic over a single network infrastructure, ultimately providing significant improvements in network flexibility, efficiency, and price performance.

A review of the operating costs of typical networks reveals that personnel and bandwidth costs far outweigh equipment capital costs, as seen in Figure 2.2.

ATM directly addresses these costs:

- Bandwidth cost is reduced by allowing the statistical traffic multiplexing at all levels of the network, eliminating bandwidth lost to idle network segments.
- Personnel costs are reduced by allowing a single network to deliver all services.

Commercially viable carrier-class ATM WAN solutions enable users to realize these two benefits. The ability to perform reliably, when carrying a variety of traffic, and to operate under heavy loads *separates* early ATM LAN solutions *and* many of today's ATM WAN switches from true carrier-class ATM WAN solutions.

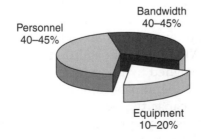

Figure 2.2
Networking costs.

LAN Interconnect

LANs have become the standard solution for provisioning in-building networks since their introduction in the early 1980s. There has been dramatic growth in the number of LAN installations and the traffic they carry.

As business becomes more global in its outlook and the virtual workgroup concept becomes accepted, there will be a significant growth in the requirement for interoffice communications. Given the predominance of the LAN, this has led to a demand for high-performance LAN interconnect solutions. ATM switches now have a number of mechanisms that the service provider can deploy to deliver LAN interconnect services. ATM-based LAN interconnect options include:

- Direct ATM LAN
- Frame relay and routers
- Connectionless server and LAN emulation services

Direct ATM LAN

ATM LANs can be directly connected to an ATM network (at the switch). The ATM LAN switch in these networks typically provides ATM WAN connections with appropriate routing capability and a high-performance solution, as shown in Figure 2.3. This approach

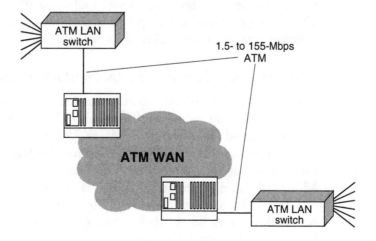

Figure 2.3
Support of ATM LANs.

provides a simple, protocol-independent, high-performance solution that will meet the needs of emerging LAN communities.

A Network Service Provider (NSP) can sell a simple ATM virtual path (VP) or virtual channel (VC) service with the appropriate QoS. Any subscriber with appropriate LAN equipment can connect directly. Tariffs are normally fixed rate, based on connection capacity and QoS. As ATM SVC services become available, a usage-based tariff can be implemented to provide a more flexible service offering.

Advanced ATM networks support both offerings. Advanced traffic management in the ATM switch enables a range of differing QoS services to be defined, each optimized for a different range of customers. Traffic management also provides a traffic firewall between various virtual LAN communities, ensuring that the activities of one set of subscribers cannot impact the service offered to the others.

Frame Relay and Routers

This approach allows for customer-located router equipment to be directly connected to an ATM network. The NSP can sell a frame relay service interface, where customers connect their own equipment. Alternatively, a complete LAN interconnect service also can be offered, providing customer-located equipment.

Figure 2.4 shows a typical implementation utilizing a frame relay–based access concentrator with transport across a multiservice ATM network. In this implementation, customer premise equipment provides a variety of services, including IP LAN interconnect. The switch provides a high-performance frame relay over an ATM solution through frame relay network interworking.

Connectionless Server and LAN Emulation Solutions

A third approach utilizes a connectionless server solution. LAN emulation and Switched Multi-megabit Data Service/Connectionless Broadband Data Service (SMDS/CBDS) services are included in this solution. The SMDS Data Service Unit (DSU) recognizes the connectionless mode of LAN operation where each frame is addressed and no permanent connections exist.

The ATM network provides a high-performance, connection-oriented network where fixed connections can be established between endpoints. Connectionless servers are added to the net-

Figure 2.4
Support of frame relay over an ATM network.

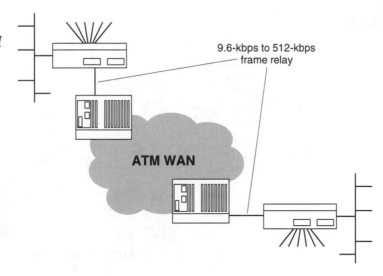

9.6-kbps to 512-kbps frame relay

ATM WAN

work to route connectionless datagrams on established ATM connections.

Figure 2.5 shows the SMDS version. This utilizes SDMS DSUs that convert SMDS frames into ATM cells. The ATM cells then are mapped onto VP/VCs according to their SMDS address. At this point SMDS services and applications are on the decline.

This solution can be used to interconnect high-speed metropolitan area networks (MANs) over an ATM bearer network or, as shown in Figure 2.5, to provide high-speed interconnect to host or server systems. It is typically tariffed on a usage basis, allowing users to utilize a high-speed access link without incurring the cost penalty of a high-speed leased circuit.

ATM provides solutions for the LAN interconnect service requirement. These solutions are:

- High performance to reduce network latency and improve LAN performance
- Variety of service interfaces to meet all applications
- Connectionless or connection-oriented interface options
- Tariff options that allow economic access to high-speed interconnect
- Allowance of statistical multiplexing of users traffic, enabling maximum revenue from deployed equipment

Figure 2.5
*Support of SMDS
over ATM.*

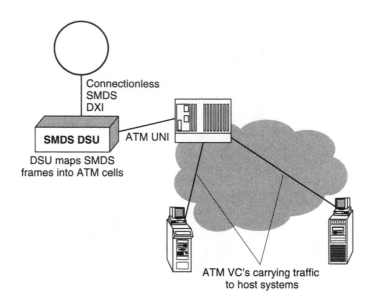

Connectionless
SMDS
DXI

SMDS DSU   ATM UNI

DSU maps SMDS
frames into ATM cells

ATM VC's carrying traffic
to host systems

Network Consolidation

Today, multiple networks are used to provide wide-area communications. It is not uncommon to have a TDM network for voice and low-speed data services, a second network delivering LAN services, and often a third network delivering packet services.

Each network requires its own access equipment, operations staff, and bandwidth, resulting in increased maintenance, equipment, and staff costs. Each network must include sufficient spare capacity to cover usage peaks, even though other networks may have capacity that could be used to cover the demand. Where a single service uses several of these networks, fault resolution becomes extremely complex, as several management systems can be used to reconcile information from each system, lengthening repair times.

An ATM switch provides a solution to all these problems. By implementing an ATM core network or supporting existing networks with an ATM service layer, traffic from the existing networks can be carried over a common bandwidth set (see Figure 2.6).

This solution enables a common infrastructure to be deployed to support all services. Shared management reduces personnel costs. The ability to share bandwidth among all services reduces the requirement for spare capacity, and thus total bandwidth cost.

Figure 2.6
ATM's multiservice support.

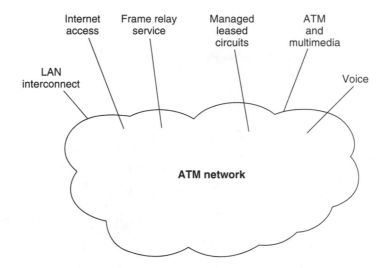

Additionally, this approach enables a network to respond to user demands through faster provisioning of new services on an existing infrastructure. Each new service shares access points, bandwidth, equipment, and staff. As service usage changes and existing services decline, staff and bandwidth can be redeployed, reducing long-term operating cost. NSP long-term profitability is improved as revenues taper in maturing services and are smoothly replaced with revenue from newer services.

Integrated Access

ATM also can provide an integrated access solution, as shown in Figure 2.7. ATM access multiplexers are capable of integrating traffic from a number of sources onto a single ATM access link. This can be either a T1/E1 TDM link or a higher-speed ATM link. The edge concentrator demultiplexes the access traffic, adapts the traffic to ATM if required, and routes each traffic stream to its appropriate destination.

This approach assists service marketing and customer or account control, as an access multiplexer can be deployed for an initial service requirement. As additional services are sold to the customer, the same equipment and access link can be used to backhaul customer traffic to the ATM switch at the local point of presence. The availability of an ubiquitous service network will enable new services to be added at low marginal cost.

Figure 2.7
Use of edge ATM concentrators.

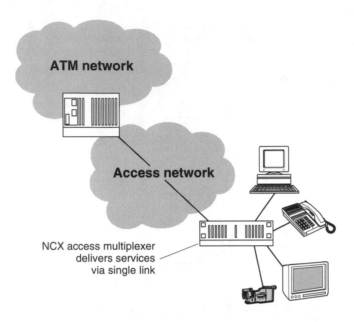

ATM network

Access network

NCX access multiplexer
delivers services
via single link

Video Networking

ATM is ideally suited to provisioning video services, either video-conferencing or video on demand. Figure 2.8 depicts an example.

Network systems will be available that can deliver broadcast or studio-quality pictures with significantly lower data rates than current technology, using variable-bit-rate encoding schemes. Video codec components will take advantage of the variable-bit-rate capability of ATM networks, enabling statistical traffic gain and delivering more traffic for a given network capacity than current fixed-data-rate solutions. Through ATM QoS capabilities, low network delay also will be guaranteed.

ATM provides a wide range of application solutions, each characterized by providing a more economic solution to the delivery of current services or offering the network operator greater flexibility in the delivery of new services, or often both benefits at the same time.

ATM Cells

The ATM cell is 53 bytes long and is divided into two distinct elements: the *header* that is 5 bytes long and the *information field* that is 48 bytes long. See Figure 2.9.

Figure 2.8
Example of video support over ATM.

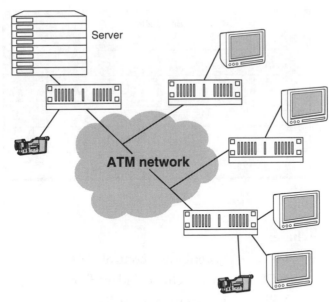

The use of fixed-size, relatively short cells ensures that network transit delays and delay variance are kept to a minimum, while not imposing excessive overhead. It is these attributes that enable ATM to effectively handle delay-sensitive traffic such as voice or video, as well as more traditional, less sensitive, bursty data traffic.

ATM Cell Header

The header contents are interpreted by the network and are used to establish connections and manage data flow. Header contents vary depending on whether the cell is being transmitted across a User-to-Network Interface (UNI) or a Network Node Interface (NNI). The UNI header is shown in Figure 2.10.

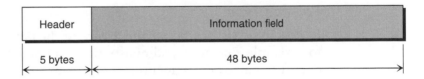

Figure 2.9
ATM cell.

Figure 2.10
ATM header.

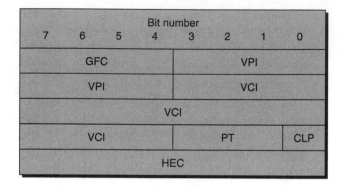

where:

GFC	generic flow control
VCI	virtual channel identifier
VPI	virtual path identifier
PT	payload type
CLP	cell loss priority
HEC	header error control

Generic Flow Control

Generic flow control (GFC) is used to control data flow across the UNI.

Virtual Path Identifier and Virtual Channel Identifier

The virtual path is an address, identified by a number in the virtual path identifier (VPI) field. Inside the virtual path are multiple virtual channels, also identified by a number in the virtual channel identifier (VCI) field.

The virtual channel is a connection between communicating ATM devices that can consist of a number of hops across the network.

Payload Type

Payload type (PT) indicates the nature of the data in the payload, for example, operations, administration, and maintenance (OA&M) data. The payload type identifier consists of three bits as follows:

- *Bit 1:* Carried transparently across the network and used by AAL 5 to distinguish the trailing cell in a sequence.
- *Bit 2:* The congestion-experienced bit is used in some systems to signify that a cell experienced congestion at some point in its virtual circuit. There are no specific rules covering its use.
- *Bit 3:* Used to discriminate between OA&M cells and data cells.

Cell Loss Priority

If the cell loss priority (CLP) bit is set, the network can discard the cell, if congestion is experienced.

Header Error Control

The header error control (HEC) field is used as an error detector for the contents of the header only. It is not used for data error detection within the information field.

Making a Connection

ATM defines two levels of connection and addressing identification: virtual channel (VC) and virtual path (VP). High-end switches provide VP and VC switching. VC switching allows any cell arriving on any circuit on any link of a switch to be switched to any circuit of any other link, as shown in Figure 2.11.

Virtual Channel

A VC is a connection between communicating ATM devices and can involve a number of hops across the network. Each VC has an associated QoS profile that defines the service offered to the user.

Figure 2.11
VP/VC switching.

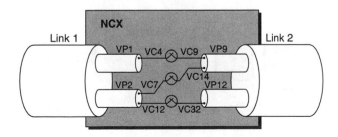

Virtual Path

A VP is a group of VCs that share the same QoS parameters. Typical ATM switches can support a mix of VPs and VCs on any input/output card (IOC), up to a maximum of 2048 connections. By grouping VCs into VPs, the administrative overhead is reduced during network configuration. *Soft VC* mechanisms allow connections to be established and terminated between any two or more points across the network, without having to administratively hard-code the path (see Figure 2.12). In case of transmission facility failures, these soft VCs are automatically rerouted. These connections are typically made possible by the use of a proprietary out-of-band signaling system.

Cells only are transmitted on a connection when there is data to be sent. This ensures that idle time in a channel is available to other network users. Recovery of this idle time, which in other transmission systems is locked up by permanent bandwidth allocation, allows the NSP to make significant gains in efficiency.

Information Field

Where header contents are interpreted by the network to establish and manage connections, the information field—sometimes referred to as the *payload*—is used for transferring the customer's data across the ATM network. See Figure 2.13.

An ATM switch receives user data that already can be in the ATM format or be non-ATM traffic such as voice, data, or fax. ATM data requires no conversion to fit into the information field, but non-ATM traffic needs to be converted. This conversion process is known as *segmentation and reassembly* (SAR).

Depending on the SAR method used, a portion of the information field can be used to carry control information. In this case, the full 48 bytes are not available for carrying customer data.

Figure 2.12
Automatic generation of soft VCs.

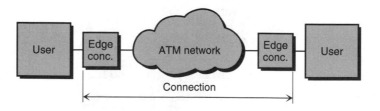

Figure 2.13
Information field of ATM cell.

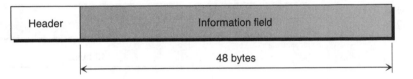

Header | Information field

48 bytes

Segmentation and Reassembly

SAR is handled by the Adaptation Layer service of the ATM switch. The Adaptation Layer maps services from their native format— variable-length frames for SMDS/Connectionless Network Access Protocol (CLNAP)—into the fixed-size, 48-byte ATM cell information field.

Segmentation is carried out at the transmitting end of the user connection, called the *ingress point* in the ATM network. Reassembly is accomplished at the receiving end of the user connection, called the *egress point* in the ATM network.

ATM provides different Adaptation Layer services to accommodate different native information formats. Five services have been defined or allocated for later definition: ATM Adaptation Layer 0 (AAL 0), ATM Adaptation Layer 1 (AAL 1), ATM Adaptation Layer 2 (AAL 2), ATM Adaptation Layer 3/4 (AAL 3/4), and ATM Adaptation Layer 5 (AAL 5).

AAL 2 is intended to support time-sensitive variable-bit-rate services, such as video. It is not currently defined. AAL 3/4 is largely covered by the capabilities of AAL 5 but is still used by some SDMS DSUs.

The basic functionality of these Adaptation Layer services is described in the following pages.

ATM Adaptation Layer 0

AAL 0 is a Null Adaptation Layer. AAL 0 is used for cell relay services that are inherently cell based and therefore require no adaptation. With AAL 0, the full 48 bytes are available for user data, or payload. See Figure 2.14.

Figure 2.15 shows an example of a PC with ATM capability accessing the ATM network through the ATM switch.

Figure 2.14
AAL 0 payload.

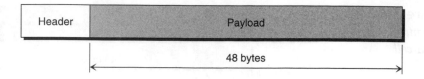

ATM Adaptation Layer 1

AAL 1 segments incoming user data from its native format into a format that can be accommodated by an ATM cell. AAL 1 separates the information field of an ATM cell into three fields:

- Sequence number (SN)
- Sequence number protection (SNP)
- Payload

See Figure 2.16. The remaining 47-byte payload field is used for carrying user data.

AAL 1 uses the SN and SNP fields to provide clock recovery, sequence checking, and loss of signal detection. If the transmitted user data exceeds 47 bytes, the remaining data is sent in 48-byte payload cells with SN and SNP fields omitted.

AAL 1 is typically used for circuit emulation, voice, and video applications, as shown in Figure 2.17. The Adaptation Layer at the receiving end of this connection reverses the process and reassembles the user data into its original format.

These issues are revisited in later chapters.

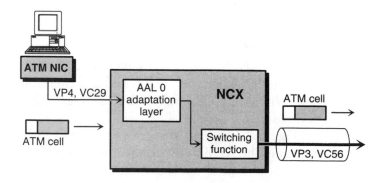

Figure 2.15
AAL 0 adaptation.

Figure 2.16
AAL 1 header.

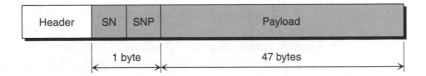

ATM Adaptation Layer 3/4

AAL 3/4 originally was defined as two distinct Adaptation Layers, AAL 3 and AAL 4. AAL 3 was intended to support connection-oriented, variable-bit-rate data, requiring no end-timing transfer. AAL 4 was similar, but for connectionless data. The two were merged to AAL 3/4, as it was determined that the distinction between connection-oriented and connectionless data transfer made no difference to the Adaptation Layer.

AAL 3/4 provides extensive error correction capabilities on data as a whole and content of each cell. For example, a cyclic redundancy check (CRC) is performed on each cell, as well as the entire AAL 4 protocol data unit. It also provides for multiple sessions to be carried over a single virtual circuit, enabling additional user cost saving.

Each data element supplied to AAL 3/4 can be up to 65,535 bytes in length. The element first is given a 4-byte header and a 4- or 8-byte trailer to facilitate overall error checking. This larger data unit then is divided into 44-byte segments, the last segment being padded to 44 bytes, if it is shorter.

Figure 2.17
A view of voice support via AAL 1 adaptation.

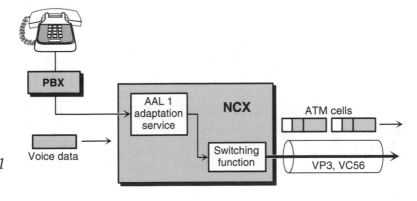

Each segment then is given a 2-byte header known as a *multiplex ID* and a 2-byte CRC trailer. The multiplex ID, sometimes known as the message ID, allows for multiple sessions to be carried on a single VC. Each session is identified by a different multiplex ID value. See Figure 2.18.

AAL 3/4 is used primarily for SMDS services because it is specifically called for SMDS over ATM transfer standards. Other forms of variable-bit-rate transfer use the simpler AAL 5.

ATM Adaptation Layer 5

AAL 5 segments incoming user data from its native format into one that can be accommodated by an ATM cell. AAL 5 uses the information field as follows:

A frame received from a frame relay device has an 8-byte trailer added, and the total is segmented into the smallest possible number of 48-byte ATM cells. Any remaining space is filled with padding characters.

For example, a 128-byte frame will be segmented into three 48-byte ATM cells. Two ATM cells will be completely filled with user data. The third cell will contain the remaining 32 bytes of user data and the 8-byte trailer, leaving 8 bytes to be filled with padding. See Figure 2.19. The trailing cell is identified by setting bit 1 of the

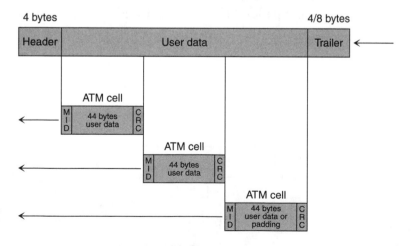

Figure 2.18
AAL 3/4 arrangement.

Figure 2.19
AAL 5.

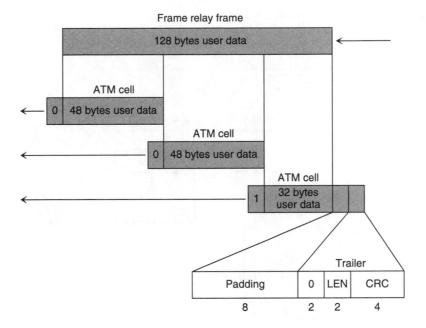

payload-type field in the cell header. The trailer field contains protocol management information that provides both sequencing protection and error detection.

AAL 5 typically is used for carrying variable-rate bitsync protocols such as X25, SDLC, or frame relay, as shown in Figure 2.20.
The Adaptation Layer at the receiving end of the user connection—
network egress—reverses the above process and reassembles the
user data into its original frame relay format.

Traffic Management

The ITU and the ATM Forum define a number of concepts to
enable NSPs to deal with traffic contention and management. These
fall into two areas:

- Parameters defined to characterize the traffic
- Measures available to ensure compliance of traffic streams to
  standards

Figure 2.20
AAL 5 application.

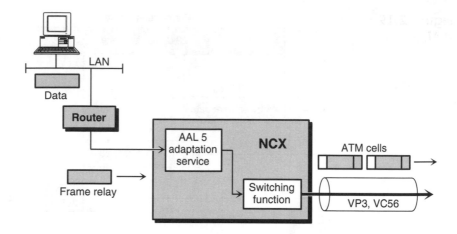

Usage Parameters

The set of parameters available to characterize a traffic stream includes:

- *Peak cell rate* (PCR)—The peak rate of data flow
- *Sustained cell rate* (SCR)—The long-term sustained rate of information flow
- *Cell delay variation tolerance* (CDVT)—The parameter that, together with the PCR, defines the maximum burst at line rate
- *Maximum burst size* (MBS)—The maximum number of cells that can be sent at the peak cell rate

These parameters provide a statistical view of the data flow in any cell stream and allow a network to determine the resource necessary to support that flow.

Parameter Control

The measures a network can take to ensure cell stream compliance to its agreed parameters are traffic shaping and usage parameter control (UPC). These capabilities are often referred to as *policing* or *UPC policing.*

Traffic shaping typically is applied on the egress of a network switch system. Shaping limits the flow rate through the use of a buffer to ensure that the traffic leaving the network is compliant to a given Service Level Agreement (SLA). It ensures that information flow is made predictable by minimizing cell loss as a result of downstream policing actions.

UPC policing is applied by a network switch at network ingress. Policing is the process of measuring traffic flow and discarding—or marking for later possible discard—cells that exceed the SLA traffic flow parameters. Policing uses a class of algorithm know as *leaky buckets*, shown in Figure 2.21.

Management Provisions

The ATM Forum and the ITU also have made a number of provisions for ATM network management by network elements and network manager(s). These include:

- Definition of a standard SNMP MIB for an ATM interface
- Definition of an Interim Link Management Interface (ILMI)
- Definition of in-band OA&M data flows

ILMI

The ILMI defines a standard VC and an SNMP-based interface protocol to enable a user to query the network about the state of the interface. This capability is expected to greatly simplify network configuration by allowing subscription information to traverse this interface.

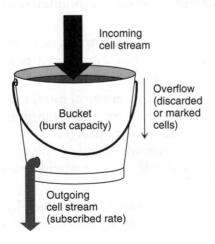

Figure 2.21
UPC.

OA&M Flows

OA&M flows are cells inserted into the cell stream, distinguished from user data by bit 3 of the payload type. These flows are used to provide the following:

- Alarm information that aids in identifying a point of failure
- Injection of monitoring cells for measuring transit delay or cell loss on a sample basis
- Control of local and remote data path loops

OA&M flows are defined by ITU-T I.610.

Notes

[1] This term is a colloquialism used to refer to communication where the information is packaged in blocks (packets, frames, or cells) and is transferred through the network at a higher access and delivery speed than it would be in a traditional packet network.

[2] Q.922/LAP-F (ISDN Data Link Layer Specification for Frame Mode Bearer Services) is a full Data Link Layer protocol on its own merit; it was adopted in 1991. Frame relay uses a the subset called LAP-F Core. LAP-F functions such as windowing and error correction are not included in the core subset.

[3] Eventually, users will have to migrate to ATM directly to achieve broadband campus-to-campus (building-to-building) connectivity.

[4] Instead of using cell relay on the trunk side, some switches use frame relay. In the long run, most switches will probably migrate to the cell relay NNI.

[5] Packet switching and other statistical multiplexing schemes do fulfill the role of supporting error-free transmission of asynchronous traffic from dumb terminals (or devices and PCs emulating dumb terminals) that have no error protection of their own—a frame relay service would be a mismatch in this environment.

[6] This section has been prepared and supplied by Roy D. Rosner, ECI-Telematics. The company is dedicated to providing com-

munications equipment and solutions to network service providers (NSPs) and large end users around the world. ECI's vision is to provide high-performance, low-cost network solutions that enable telecommunications users to increase capacity, improve quality, and maximize overall communications infrastructure effectiveness. ATM products include the NCX 1E6 ATM switch and the NCX Access Multiplexer.

CHAPTER 3

Pulse Code Modulation and Related Digitization Methods[1]

3.1 Introduction

Voice digitization techniques can be broadly categorized into two classes: those digitally encoding analog waveforms as faithfully as possible and those processing waveforms to encode only the perceptually significant aspects of speech and hearing processes. The first category is representative of the general problem of analog-to-digital and digital-to-analog conversions and is not restricted to speech digitization. The three most common techniques used to encode a voice waveform are pulse code modulation (PCM), differential PCM (DPCM), and delta modulation (DM). Except in special cases, digital telephony in the public-switched telephone network uses these techniques. Thus, when studying the most common digital speech encoding techniques, we are, in fact, investigating the more general realm of analog-to-digital conversion.

The second category of speech digitization is concerned primarily with producing very-low-data-rate speech encoders and decoders for narrowband transmission systems or digital storage devices with limited capacity. A device from this special class of

71

techniques is commonly referred to as a *vocoder* (voice coder). Vocoder technology is now beginning to be deployed, particularly for voice over frame relay and over IP.

This chapter covers some of the important analytical methods that are applicable to voice digitization.

3.2 Pulse Amplitude Modulation

The first step in digitizing an analog waveform is to establish a set of discrete times at which the input signal waveform is sampled. Prevalent digitization techniques are based on the use of periodic, regularly spaced sample times. If the samples occur often enough, the original waveform can be completely recovered from the sample sequence using a low-pass filter to interpolate or "smooth out" between the sample values. These basic concepts are illustrated in Figure 3.1. A representative analog waveform is sampled at a constant sampling frequency $f_s = 1/T$ and reconstructed using a low-pass filter. Notice that the sampling process is equivalent to amplitude modulation of a constant-amplitude pulse train. Hence the technique represented in Figure 3.1 is usually referred to as a *pulse amplitude modulation* (PAM).

Nyquist Sampling Rate

A classical result in sampling systems was established in 1933 by Harry Nyquist when he derived the minimum sampling frequency required to extract all information in a continuous, time-varying waveform. This result—the Nyquist criterion—is defined by the relation

Figure 3.1
Pulse amplitude modulation.

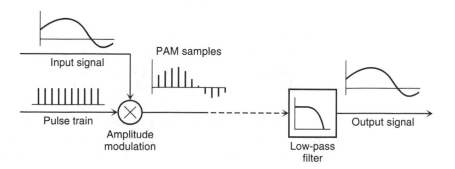

$$f_s > 2 \cdot \text{BW}$$

where f_s = sampling frequency
      BW = bandwidth of the input signal

The derivation of this result is indicated in Figure 3.2, which portrays the spectrum of the input signal and the resulting spectrum of the PAM pulse train. The PAM spectrum can be derived by observing that a continuous train of impulses has a frequency spectrum consisting of discrete terms at multiples of the sampling frequency. The input signal amplitude modulates these terms individually. Thus a double sideband spectrum is produced about each of the discrete frequency terms in the spectrum of the pulse train. The original signal waveform is recovered by a low-pass filter designed to remove all but the original signal spectrum. As shown in Figure 3.2, the reconstructive low-pass filter must have a cutoff frequency that lies between BW and f_s – BW. Hence, separation is possible only if f_s – BW is greater than BW (i.e., if $f_s > 2 \cdot \text{BW}$).

Foldover Distortion

If the input waveform of a PAM system is undersampled ($f_s < 2 \cdot \text{BW}$), the original waveform cannot be recovered without distortion. As indicated in Figure 3.3, this output distortion arises because the fre-

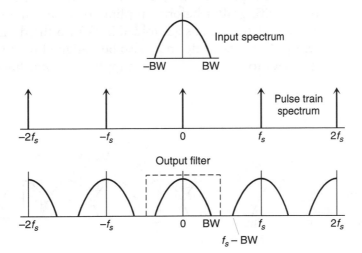

Figure 3.2
Spectrum of pulse amplitude modulated signal.

quency spectrum centered about the sampling frequency overlaps the original spectrum and cannot be separated from the original spectrum by filtering. Since it is a duplicate of the input spectrum "folded" back on top of the desired spectrum that causes the distortion, this type of sampling impairment is often referred to as *foldover distortion*.

In essence, foldover distortion produces frequency components in the desired frequency band that did not exist in the original waveform. Thus another term for this impairment is *aliasing*. Aliasing problems are not confined to speech digitization processes. The potential for aliasing is present in any sample data system. Motion picture taking, for example, is another sampling system that can produce aliasing. A common example occurs when filming moving stagecoaches in old Westerns. Often the sampling process is too slow to keep up with the stagecoach wheel movements, and spurious rotational rates are produced. If the wheel rotates 355° between frames, it looks to the eye as if it has moved backward 5°.

Figure 3.4 demonstrates an aliasing process occurring in speech if a 5.5-kHz signal is sampled at an 8-kHz rate. Notice that the sample values are identical to those obtained from a 2.5-kHz input signal. Thus after the sampled signal passes through the 4-kHz output filter, a 2.5-kHz signal arises that did not come from the source. This example illustrates that the input must be bandlimited, *before sampling*, to remove frequency terms greater than $f_s/2$, even if these frequency terms are ignored (i.e., are inaudible) at the destination. Thus a complete PAM system, shown in Figure 3.5, must include a bandlimiting filter before sampling to ensure that no spurious or source-related signals get folded back into the desired signal bandwidth. The input filter may also be designed to cut off very low frequencies to remove 60-cycle hum from power lines.

Figure 3.3
Foldover spectrum produced by undersampling an input.

 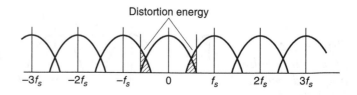

Figure 3.4
Aliasing of 5.5 kHz signal into a 2.5 kHz signal.

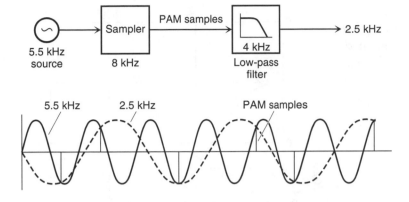

Figure 3.5 shows the signal being recovered by a sample-and-hold circuit that produces a staircase approximation to the sampled waveform. With use of the staircase approximation, the power level of the signal coming out of the reconstructive filter is nearly the same as the level of the sampled input signal. The response of the reconstructive filter, in this case, must be modified somewhat to account for the spectrum of the wider staircase samples.

As indicated in Figure 3.2, when the sampling frequency f_s is somewhat greater than twice the bandwidth, the spectral bands are sufficiently separated from each other that filters with gradual roll-off characteristics can be used. As an example, sampled voice systems typically use bandlimiting filters with a 3-dB cutoff around 3.4 kHz and a sampling rate of 8 kHz. Thus the sampled signal is sufficiently attenuated at the overlap frequency of 4 kHz to adequately reduce the energy level of the foldover spectrum. Figure 3.6 shows a filter template designed to meet ITU-T recommendations for out-of-band signal rejection in PCM voice coders. Notice that 14 dB of attenuation are provided at 4 kHz.

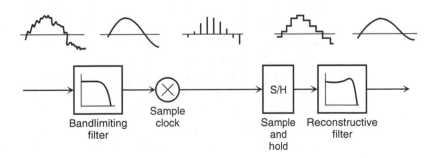

Figure 3.5
End-to-end pulse amplitude modulated system.

Figure 3.6
Bandlimiting filter template designed to meet ITU-T recommendations for PCM voice coders.

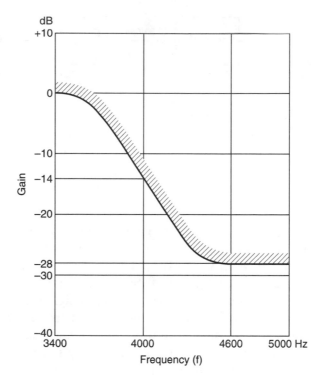

3.3 Pulse Code Modulation

The preceding section describes pulse amplitude modulation, which uses discrete sample times with analog sample amplitudes to extract the information in a continuously varying analog signal. Pulse code modulation (PCM) is an extension of PAM wherein each analog sample value is quantized into a discrete value for representation as a digital code word. Thus, as shown in Figure 3.7, a PAM system can be converted into a PCM system by adding an analog-to-digital (A/D) converter at the source and a digital-to-analog (D/A) converter at the destination. Figure 3.8 depicts a typical quantization process in which a set of quantization intervals are associated in a one-to-one fashion with a binary code word. All sample values falling in a particular quantization interval are represented by a single discrete value located at the center of the quantization interval. In this manner, the quantization process introduces a certain amount of error or distortion into the signal samples. This error, known as *quantization noise,* is minimized by establishing a large number of small quantization intervals. Of course, as the number of quantization intervals increases, so must the number of bits increase to uniquely indentify the quantization intervals.

Quantization Noise

A fundamental aspect of the design and development of an engineering project is the need for analytical measures of systems performance. Only then can a system be objectively measured and its cost effectiveness compared to alternate designs. One of the measures needed by a voice communication engineer is the quality of speech delivered to the listener. Measurements of speech quality are complicated by subjective attributes of speech as perceived by a typical listener. One subjective aspect of noise or distortion on a speech signal involves the frequency content, or spectrum, of the disturbance in conjunction with the power level.[2]

Successive quantization errors of a PCM encoder are generally assumed to be distributed randomly and uncorrelated to each other. Thus the cumulative effect of quantization errors in a PCM system can be treated as additive noise with a subjective effect that is similar to bandlimited white noise. Figure 3.9 shows the quantization noise as a function of signal amplitude for a coder with uniform quantization intervals. Notice that if the signal has enough time to change in amplitude by several quantization intervals, the quantization errors are independent. If the signal is oversampled, that is sampled much higher than the Nyquist rate, successive samples are likely to fall in the same interval causing a loss of independence in the quantization errors.

The quantization error or distortion created by digitizing an analog signal is customarily expressed as an average noise power relative to the average signal power. Thus the *signal-to-quantizing noise*

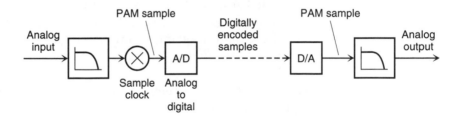

Figure 3.7
Pulse code modulation.

Figure 3.8
Quantization of analog samples.

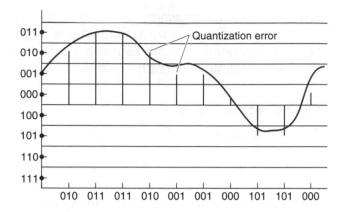

ratio SQR (also called a *signal-to-distortion ratio* or a *signal-to-noise ratio*) can be determined as

$$SQR = \frac{E\{x^2(t)\}}{E\{[y(t) - x(t)]^2\}}$$ **(3.1)**

where $E\{\cdot\}$ = expectation or averaging
    $x(t)$ = analog input signal
    $y(t)$ = decoded output signal

In determining the expected value of the quantization noise, three observations are necessary:

1. The error $y(t) - x(t)$ is limited in amplitude to $q/2$, where q is the height of the quantization interval. (Decoded output samples are ideally positioned at the middle of a quantization interval.)
2. A sample value is equally likely to fall anywhere within a quantization interval—implying a uniform probability density of amplitude $1/q$.
3. Signal amplitudes are assumed to be confined to the maximum range of the coder. If a sample value exceeds the range of the highest quantization interval, *overload distortion* (also called *peak limiting*) occurs.

If we assume (for convenience) a resistance level of 1 Ω, the average quantization noise power is

Figure 3.9
Quantization error as a function of amplitude over a range of quantization intervals.

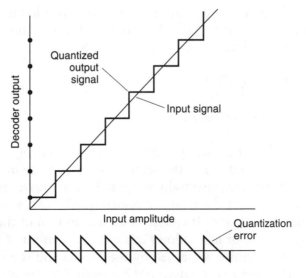

Quantized output signal

Input signal

Decoder output

Input amplitude

Quantization error

$$\text{Quantization noise power} = \frac{q^2}{12} \tag{3.2}$$

If all quantization intervals have equal lengths (uniform quantization), the quantization noise is independent of the sample values and the signal-to-quantization ratio is determined as[3]

$$\text{SQR (dB)} = 10 \log_{10}\left(\frac{v^2}{q^2/12}\right)$$

$$= 10.8 + 20 \log_{10}\left(\frac{v}{q}\right) \tag{3.3}$$

where v is the rms amplitude of the input. In particular, for a sine wave input the signal-to-quantizing noise ratio produced by uniform quantization is

$$\text{SQR (dB)} = 10 \log_{10}\left(\frac{A^2/2}{q^2/12}\right)$$

$$= 7.78 + 20 \log_{10}\left(\frac{A}{q}\right) \tag{3.4}$$

where A is the peak amplitude of the sine wave.

Thus, 13 quantization intervals are needed for each polarity for a total of 26 intervals. The number of bits required to encode each sample is determined as

$$N = \log_2 (26)$$
$$= 4.7$$
$$= 5 \text{ bits per sample}$$

When measuring quantization noise power, the spectral content is often weighted in the same manner as noise in an analog circuit. Unfortunately, spectrally weighted noise measurements do not always reflect the true perceptual quality of a voice encoder/decoder. If the spectral distribution of the quantization noise more or less follows the spectral content of the speech wave-form, the noise is masked by the speech and is much less noticeable than noise uncorrelated to the speech. On the other hand, if the quantization process produces energy at voiceband frequencies other than those contained in particular sounds, they are more noticeable.

High-quality PCM encoders produce quantization noise that is evenly distributed across voice frequencies and independent of the encoded waveforms. Thus, quantization noise ratios defined in Equation 3.4 are good measures of PCM performance. In some of the encoders discussed later (vocoders in particular), quantization noise power is not very useful. Other measures of encoder speech quality provide better correlations to quality as perceived by a listener.

Idle Channel Noise

Examination of Equations 3.3 and 3.4 reveals that the SQR is small for small sample values. In fact, as shown in Figure 3.10, the noise may actually be greater than the signal when sample values are in the first quantization interval. This effect is particularly bothersome during speech pauses and is known as *idle channel noise.* Figure 3.11 depicts one method of minimizing idle channel noise in PCM systems by establishing a quantization interval that straddles the origin. In this case all sample values in the central quantization interval are decoded as a constant zero output. PCM systems of this type use an odd number of quantization intervals since the encoding ranges of positive and negative signals are usually equal.

Figure 3.10
Idle channel noise produced by midriser quantiza-tion.

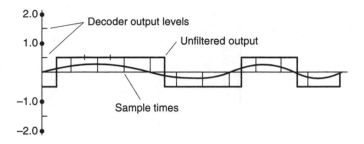

The quantization characteristics required to produce the output waveforms shown in Figures 3.10 and 3.11 are shown in Figures 3.12 and 3.13, respectively. The first characteristic (midriser) cannot produce a zero output level. The second characteristic (midtread) decodes low signals into constant, zero-level outputs. However, if the signal amplitude is comparable to the size of the quantization interval, or if a DC bias exists in the encoder, idle channel noise is a problem with midtread quantization also.

Noise occurring during speech pauses is more objectionable than noise with equivalent power levels during speech. Thus idle channel noise is specified in absolute terms separate from quantization noise, which is specified relative to the signal level.

Uniformly Encoded PCM

An encoder using equal length quantization intervals for all samples produces code words linearly related to the analog sample values. That is, the numerical equivalent of each code word is proportional to the quantized sample value it represents. In this manner a uniform PCM system uses a conventional analog-to-digital converter to generate the binary sample codes. The number of bits required for

Figure 3.11
Elimination of idle channel noise by midtread quanti-zation.

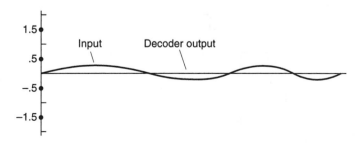

Figure 3.12
*Midriser quantizer
characteristic.*

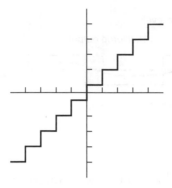

each sample is determined by the maximum acceptable noise power. Minimum digitized voice quality requires a signal-to-noise ratio in excess of 26 dB.

For a uniform PCM system to achieve a signal-to-quantization ratio of 26 dB, Equation 3.4 indicates that $q_{max} = 0.123A$. For equal positive and negative signal excursions (encoding from $-A$ to A), this result indicates that just over 16 quantization intervals or 4 bits per sample are required.

In addition to providing adequate quality for small signals, a telephone system must be capable of transmitting a large range of signal amplitudes referred to as a *dynamic range*. A typical minimum dynamic range is 30 dB. Thus signal values as large as 31 times A must be encoded without exceeding the range of quantization intervals. Assuming equally spaced quantization intervals for uniform coding, the total number of intervals is determined as 496, which requires 9-bit code words.

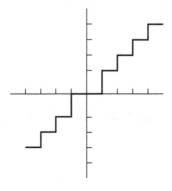

Figure 3.13
*Midtread quan-
tizer characteristic.*

The performance of an *n*-bit uniform PCM system is determined by observing that

$$q = \frac{2A_{max}}{2^n}$$

(3.5)

where A_{max} is the maximum (unoverloaded) amplitude.

Substituting Equation 3.5 into Equation 3.4 produces the PCM performance equation for uniform coding:

$$SQR = 1.76 + 6.02n + 20 \log_{10}\left(\frac{A}{A_{max}}\right)$$

(3.6)

The first two terms of Equation 3.6 provide the SQR when encoding a full-range sine wave. The last term indicates a loss in SQR when encoding a lower-level signal. These relationships are presented in Figure 3.14, which shows the SQR of uniform PCM system as a function of the number of bits per sample and the magnitude of an input sine wave.

Companding

In a uniform PCM system, the size of every quantization interval is determined by the SQR requirement of the lowest signal level to be encoded. Larger signals are also encoded with the same quantiza-

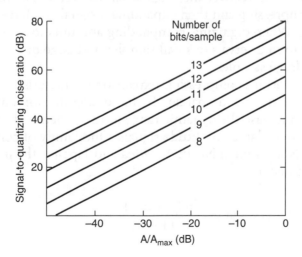

Figure 3.14
Signal-to-quantizing noise of uniform PCM coding.

tion interval. As indicated in Equation 3.6 and Figure 3.14, the SQR increases with the signal amplitude A. For example, a 26-dB SQR for small signals and a 30-dB dynamic range produces a 56-dB SQR for a maximum amplitude signal. In this manner, a uniform PCM system provides unneeded quality for large signals. Moreover, the large signals are the least likely to occur. For these reasons, the code space in a uniform PCM system is very inefficiently utilized.

A more efficient coding procedure is achieved if the quantization intervals are not uniform but allowed to increase with the sample value. When quantization intervals are directly proportional to the sample value, the SQR is constant for all signal levels. With this technique, fewer bits per sample provide a specified SQR for small signals and an adequate dynamic range for large signals. When the quantization intervals are not uniform, a nonlinear relationship exists between the code words and the samples they represent.

Historically, the nonlinear function was first implemented on analog signals using nonlinear devices such as specially designed diodes. The basic process is shown in Figure 3.15, where the analog input sample is first compressed and then quantized with uniform quantization intervals. The effect of the compression operation is shown in Figure 3.16. Notice that successively larger input signal intervals are compressed into constant-length quantization intervals. Thus the larger the sample value, the more it is compressed before encoding. As shown in Figure 3.15, a nonuniform PCM decoder expands the compressed value using an inverse compression characteristic to recover the original sample value. The process of first compressing and then expanding a signal is referred to as *companding*. When digitizing, companding amounts to assigning small quantization intervals to small samples and large quantization intervals to large samples.

Various compression-expansion characteristics can be chosen to implement a compandor. By increasing the amount of compression, we increase the dynamic range at the expense of the signal-to-noise ratio for large-amplitude signals. One family of compression characteristics used in North America and Japan is the μ-law characteristic defined as

$$F_\mu(x) = \text{sgn}\,(x)\,\frac{\ln\,(1 + \mu|x|)}{\ln\,(1 + \mu)} \qquad\qquad\qquad \textbf{(3.7)}$$

Figure 3.15
Companded PCM with analog compression and expansion.

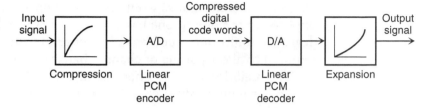

where x is the input signal amplitude $(-1 \leq x \leq 1)$, sgn(x) is the polarity of x, and μ is a parameter used to define the amount of compression.

Because of the mathematical nature of the compression curve, companded PCM is sometimes referred to as *log-PCM*. A logarithm compression curve is ideal in the sense that quantization intervals and, hence, quantization noise are proportional to the sample amplitude. The inverse or expansion characteristic for a μ-law compandor is defined as

$$ F_{\mu}^{-1}(y) = \text{sgn}(y) \left(\frac{1}{\mu} \right) [(1 + \mu)^{|y|} - 1] \qquad (3.8) $$

where y is the compressed value $= F_{\mu}(x)$ $(-1 \leq y \leq 1)$, sgn (y) is the polarity of y, and μ is the companding parameter.

When the D2 channel bank was being developed, digital switching was recognized as a coming technology—implying that

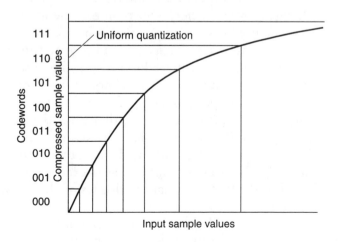

Figure 3.16
Typical compression characteristic.

telephony channel banks would be paired on a dynamic basis as opposed to the one-to-one basis in T-carrier systems. Thus a greater degree of uniformity in companding characteristics would be required to allow pairing of channel banks on a nationwide basis.

The main features incorporated into the D2 channel bank (and ensuing channel banks such as D3, D4, and D5) to achieve the improved quality and standardization are:

1. Eight bits per PCM code word
2. Incorporation of the companding functions directly into the encoder and decoder
3. A new companding characteristic ($\mu255$)

The original D1 channel bank used 1 bit per timeslot for signaling and 7 bits for voice. Thus a signaling rate of 8 kbps is established, which is more than necessary for basic voice service. In order to provide a higher data rate for voice, signaling between D2, D3, D4, D5 channel banks[4] is inserted into the least significant bit position of 8-bit code words in every sixth frame. Thus every sixth $\mu255$ PCM code word contains only 7 bits of voice information, implying that the effective number of bits per sample is actually $7\frac{5}{6}$ bits instead of 8. When common channel signaling is established, however, the associated T-carrier systems no longer need to carry signaling information on a per-channel basis, and a full 8 bits of voice can be transmitted in every timeslot of every frame.

Most signal processing functions (such as attenuating a signal or adding signals together) involve linear operations. Thus, before processing a log-PCM voice signal, it is necessary to convert the compressed transmission format into a linear (uniform) format.

To simplify the conversion process, the particular companding characteristic with $\mu = 255$ was chosen. This companding characteristic has the property of being closely approximated by a set of eight straight-line segments. Furthermore, the slope of each successive segment is exactly one-half the slope of the previous segment. The first four segments of a $\mu255$ approximation are shown in Figure 3.17. The overall result is that the larger quantization intervals have lengths that are binary multiples of all smaller quantization intervals.

As shown in Figure 3.17, each major segment of the piecewise linear approximation is divided into equally sized quantization

Figure 3.17
First four segments of straight-line approximation to µ255 compression curve.

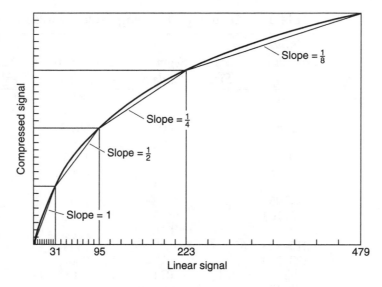

intervals. For 8-bit code words the number of quantization intervals per segment is 16. Thus an 8-bit µ255 code word is composed of 1 polarity bit, 3 bits to identify a major segment, and 4 bits for identifying a quantizing interval within a segment. Table 3.1 lists the major segment endpoints, the quantization intervals, and the corresponding segment and quantization interval codes.

The quantization intervals and decoded sample values in Table 3.1 have been expressed in terms of a maximum amplitude signal of 8159 so that all segment endpoints and decoder outputs are integers. Notice that the quantizing step is doubled in each of eight successive linear segments. It is this property that facilitates the conversion to and from a linear format.

The straight-line approximation of the µ255 companding curve is sometimes referred to as a 15-segment approximation. The 15 segments arise because, although there are 8 positive segments and 8 negative segments, the 2 segments nearest the origin are colinear and therefore can be considered as one. When viewed in this manner, the middle segment contains 31 quantization intervals with one segment straddling the origin (from −1 to +1 in Table 3.1). Code words for this middle quantization interval arise as a positive value less than +1 or a negative value greater than −1. There are, in effect, a positive zero and a negative zero. As represented in Table 3.1, these values are encoded as 00000000 and 10000000, respectively.

Table 3.1   Encoding/Decoding Table for μ255 PCM*

Input Amplitude Range	Step Size	Segment Code S	Quantization Code Q	Code Value	Decoder Amplitude
0–1	1		0000	0	0
1–3			0001	1	2
3–5	2	000	0010	2	4
⋮			⋮	⋮	⋮
29–31			1111	15	30
31–35			0000	16	33
⋮	4	001	⋮	⋮	⋮
91–95			1111	31	93
95–103			0000	32	99
⋮	8	010	⋮	⋮	⋮
215–223			1111	47	219
223–239			0000	48	231
⋮	16	011	⋮	⋮	⋮
463–479			1111	63	471
479–511			0000	64	495
⋮	32	100	⋮	⋮	⋮
959–991			1111	79	975
991–1055			0000	80	1023
⋮	64	101	⋮	⋮	⋮
1951–2015			1111	95	1983
2015–2143			0000	96	2079
⋮	128	110	⋮	⋮	⋮
3935–4063			1111	111	3999
4063–4319			0000	112	4191
⋮	256	111	⋮	⋮	⋮
7903–8159			1111	127	8031

* This table displays magnitude encoding only. Polarity bits are assigned as 0 for positive and 1 for negative. In transmission, all bits are inverted.

However, μ255 PCM channel banks invert all code words for transmission. The smaller amplitude signals, with mostly "0" segment codes, are most probable and would therefore cause less than 50 percent pulses on the transmission line. The density of pulses is increased by inversion of the transmitted data, which improves the timing and clock recovery performance of the receiving circuitry in the regenerative repeaters. Thus the actual transmitted code words corresponding to a positive zero and a negative zero are respectively, 11111111 and 01111111, indicating strong timing content for the line signal of an idle channel.

In the interest of ensuring clock synchronization in the T1 repeaters, D2, D3, D4, and D5 channel banks alter the transmitted data in one other way. As indicated in Table 3.1, a maximum amplitude negative signal is all 1s, which would normally be converted to all 0s for transmission. Instead, for the all-0s code word only, the second least significant bit is set to 1 so that 00000010 is transmitted. In effect, an encoding error is produced to preclude an all-0s code word. Fortunately, maximum amplitude samples are extremely unlikely so that no significant degradation occurs. (If the least significant bit were forced to a 1, a smaller decoding error would result. However, in every sixth frame this bit is "stolen" for signaling purposes and therefore is occasionally set to 0 independently of the code word. To ensure that all-zero code words are never transmitted, the second least significant bit is forced to a 1 when necessary.)

Syllabic Companding

A significant attribute of the companding techniques described for PCM systems is that they instantaneously encompass the entire dynamic range of the coder on a sample-to-sample basis. Thus μ-law and *A*-law companding is sometimes referred to as *instantaneous companding*. However, because the power level of a speech signal remains fairly constant for 100 or more 8-kHz samples, it is wasteful of code space to be able to encode very low level signals adjacent to very high level signals. In other words, it is unnecessary to allow for instantaneous changes in the dynamic range of a signal. One technique of reducing the amount of transmission bandwidth allocated to dynamic range is to reduce the dynamic range of the signal at the source before encoding and then restore the original dynamic range of the signal at the receiver after decoding. When the adjustments to the dynamic range occur on a periodic basis that more or less corresponds to the rate of syllable generation, the technique is referred to as *syllabic companding*.

Syllabic companding was first developed for use on noisy analog circuits to improve the idle channel noise. As shown in Figure 3.18 the power level of low-level syllables is increased (compressing the dynamic range) for transmission but attenuated upon reception (expanding the dynamic range). The process of attenuating the received signal restores the low-power syllable to its original level, but attenuates any noise arising on the transmission link. Thus the

SNR for transmission link noise is improved for low-level signals. The amount of amplification applied at the source is dependent on the short-term (syllabic) power level of the signal. Similarly, the compensating attenuation applied at the receiving terminal is determined from the short-term power level of the received signal.

Syllabic companding on digital systems provides the same basic improvement in signal-to-quantizing noise ratios as it does on noisy analog transmission links. When the digital encoders and decoders are considered as part of the transmission link, the process of amplifying low-level signals before encoding and attenuating them after decoding effectively reduces the quantization noise with no net change in signal level. In practice, syllabic companding, as implemented in digitized voice terminals, does not amplify the signal at the source and attenuate it at the destination. Instead, an equivalent process of controlling the step sizes in the encoder and decoder is used. As far as the transmitted bit stream is concerned, it makes no difference whether the signal is amplified and encoded with fixed quantization or the signal is unmodified but encoded with smaller quantization intervals. Thus syllabic compandors in digital voice terminals typically reduce the quantization intervals when encoding and decoding low-power syllables but increase the quantization intervals for high-power syllables.

Although syllabic companding can be used in conjunction with any type of voice coding, the technique has been applied most often to differential systems. In many of the applications, the adap-

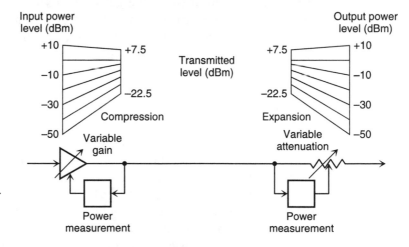

Figure 3.18
Syllabic companding of an analog signal.

tation time has been reduced to 5 or 10 msec, which is somewhat shorter than the duration of a typical syllable (approximately 30 msec). The technique is still generally referred to as syllabic companding, however, to distinguish it from the instantaneous variety.

To adjust the step sizes in the decoder in synchronism with adjustments made in the encoder, some means must be established to communicate the step size information from the source to the destination. One method explicitly transmits the step size information as auxiliary information. As mentioned when discussing forward gain control, this approach has several shortcomings. A generally more useful approach is to derive the step size information from the transmitted bit stream. Thus, in the absence of channel errors, the decoder and the encoder operate on the same information. This procedure is analogous to syllabic companded analog systems in which the receiver determines its attenuation requirements from the short-term power level of the received signal. In a digital system the bit stream is monitored for certain data patterns that indicate the power level of the signal being encoded. Indications of high power level initiate an increase in the step size, whereas indications of low levels cause a decrease.

Determining the step size information from the transmitted bit stream is generally better than explicitly transmitting the step sizes for the following reasons. Because there is no explicit transmission of step size, the transmission of sampled speech information is never interrupted, and the speech sample rate is equal to the transmission rate. Also, the bit stream does not have to be framed to identify step size information separately from the waveform coding. Furthermore, if the step size adjustments are made on a more gradual basis, the individual increments are small enough that occasional incorrect adjustments in the receiver caused by channel errors are not critical. However, on transmission links with very high error rates (one error in a hundred bits or so), better decoded voice quality can be obtained if the step size is transmitted explicitly and redundantly encoded for error correction.

A-Law Companding

The companding characteristic recommended by ITU-T for Europe and most of the world is referred to as an *A*-law characteristic. This characteristic has the same basic features and implementation advantages as does the μ-law characteristic. In particular, the *A*-law characteristic can also be well approximated by straight-line segments to facilitate direct or digital companding and can be easily converted to and from a linear format. The normalized *A*-law compression characteristic is defined as

$$F_A(x) = \text{sgn}\ (x) \left(\frac{A|x|}{1 + \ln (A)} \right) 0 \le |x| \le \frac{1}{A}$$

$$= \text{sgn}\ (x) \left(\frac{1 + \ln |Ax|}{1 + \ln (A)} \right) \frac{1}{A} \le |x| \le 1 \qquad \textbf{(3.9)}$$

The inverse or expansion characteristic is defined as:

$$F_A^{-1}\ (y) = \text{sgn}\ (y) \frac{|y|[1 + \ln (A)]}{A} \qquad 0 \le |y| \le \frac{1}{1 + \ln (A)}$$

$$= \text{sgn}\ (y) \frac{\left(e^{|y|[1 + \ln(A)] - 1} \right)}{A} \qquad \frac{1}{1 + \ln (A)} \le |y| \le 1 \qquad \textbf{(3.10)}$$

where $y = F_A\ (x)$ and $A = 87.6$.

Notice that the first portion of the *A*-law characteristic is linear by definition. The remaining portion of the characteristic ($1/A \le |x| \le 1$) can be closely approximated by linear segments in a fashion similar to the μ-law approximation. In all, there are eight positive and eight negative segments. The first two segments of each polarity (four in all) are colinear and therefore are sometimes considered as one straight-line segment. Thus the segmented approximation of the *A*-law characteristic is sometimes referred to as a *13-segment approximation*. For ease in describing the coding algorithms of the segmented companding characteristic, however, a 16-segment representation is used—just as in the case of the segmented μ-law characteristic.

The segment endpoints, quantization intervals, and corresponding codes for an 8-bit segmented *A*-law characteristic are shown in Table 3.2. The values are scaled to a maximum value of 4096 for integral representations. Figure 3.19 displays the theoretical performance of the *A*-law approximation where it is compared to the performance of a μ-law approximation. Notice that the *A*-law characteristic provides a slightly larger dynamic range. However, the *A*-law characteristic is inferior to the μ-law characteristic in terms of small signal quality (idle channel noise). The difference in small signal performance occurs because the minimum step size of the *A*-law standard is 2/4096, whereas the minimum step size of μ-law is 2/8159. Furthermore, notice that the *A*-law approximation does not define a zero-level output for the first quantization interval (i.e., uses a midriser quantizer). However, the difference between midriser and midtread performance at 64 kbps is imperceptible.

Table 3.2   Segmented *A*-Law Encoding/Decoding*

Input Amplitude Range	Step Size	Segment Code S	Quantization Code Q	Code Value	Decoder Amplitude
0–2			0000	0	1
2–4		000	0001	1	3
⋮			⋮	⋮	⋮
30–32			1111	15	31
	2				
32–34			0000	16	33
⋮		001	⋮	⋮	⋮
62–64			1111	31	63
64–68			0000	32	66
⋮	4	010	⋮	⋮	⋮
124–128			1111	47	126
128–136			0000	48	132
⋮	8	011	⋮	⋮	⋮
248–256			1111	63	252
256–272			0000	64	264
⋮	16	100	⋮	⋮	⋮
496–512			1111	79	504
512–544			0000	80	528
⋮	32	101	⋮	⋮	⋮
992–1024			1111	95	1008
1024–1088			0000	96	1056
⋮	64	110	⋮	⋮	⋮
1984–2048			1111	111	2016
2048–2176			0000	112	2112
⋮	128	111	⋮	⋮	⋮
3968–4096			1111	127	4032

*In transmission, every other bit is inverted.

Figure 3.19
Signal-to-quantizing noise of A-law PCM coding with sine wave inputs.

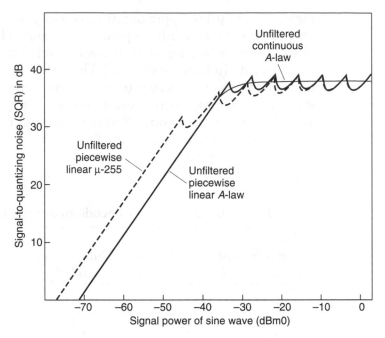

Adaptive Gain Encoding

A process that adjusts all signals to a standard value is referred to as *automatic gain control* (AGC). AGC is traditionally used on carrier transmission systems to adjust all received signals to a standard value—thereby removing variations in propagation attentuation. AGC cannot be applied to a source voice signal with allowances for speech pauses when there is no signal present. Otherwise, idle channel noise would be amplified to the average level of active voice. Notice that with AGC there is no residual information in the power level of the encoded signal as there is in syllabic companding. To ascertain the original power level, AGC must be augmented with *adaptive gain encoding* (AGE) as indicated in Figure 3.20.

There are two basic modes of operation for gain encoding depending on how gain factors are measured and to which speech segments the factors are applied. One mode of operation, as implied in Figure 3.20, involves measuring the power level of one segment of speech and using that information to establish a gain factor for ensuing speech segments. Obviously, this mode of operation relies on gradually changing power levels. This mode of operation is sometimes referred to as *backward estimation*.

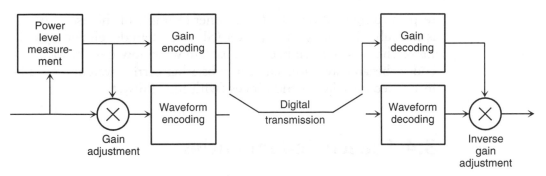

Figure 3.20
Adaptive gain encoding.

Another mode of operation involves measuring the power level of a speech segment and using the gain factor thus derived to adapt the encoder to the same segment. This approach, referred to as *forward estimation*, has the obvious advantage that the encoder and decoder use gain factors specifically related to the speech segments from which they are derived. The disadvantage is that each speech segment must be delayed while the gain factor is being determined. Although the availability of digital memory has made the cost of implementing the delay insignificant, the impact of the delay on echos and singing in a partially analog network must be considered.

Adaptive gain control with explicit transmission of gain factors is not without shortcomings. First, when the periodic gain information is inserted into the transmitted bit stream, some means of framing the bit stream into blocks is needed so gain information can be distinguished from waveform coding. Second, periodic insertion of gain information disrupts information flow, causing higher transmitter clock rates that might be inconveniently related to the waveform sample clock. Third, correct reception of gain factors is usually critical to voice quality—indicating a need to redundantly encode gain information.

A modified form of PCM using forward estimation of gain factors is referred to as *nearly instantaneously companded PCM*. The need for transmitting speech segments in blocks is not a disadvantage in, say, a mobile telephone because repetitive bursts with error checking are used as a means of overcoming short-lived multipath fading. This system provides a bit rate reduction of 30 percent with respect to conventional PCM. Another example of the use of AGE is the subscriber loop multiplexer (SLM) system developed by Bell Labs. The SLM system became obsolete when low-cost PCM codecs became available and the subscriber carrier systems could be integrated into digital end offices (with SLC 96 systems).

3.4 Speech Redundancies

As mentioned in the previous sections, a conventional PCM system encodes each sample of the input waveform independently from all other samples. Thus a PCM system is inherently capable of encoding an arbitrarily random waveform whose maximum frequency component does not exceed one-half the sampling rate. Analyses of speech waveforms, however, indicate there is considerable redundancy from one sample to the next. In fact, the correlation coefficient (a measure of predictability) between adjacent 8-kHz samples is generally 0.85 or higher. Hence, the redundancy in conventional PCM codes suggests that significant savings in transmission bandwidths are possible through more efficient coding techniques. All of the digitization techniques described in the rest of this chapter are tailored, in one degree or another, to the characteristics of speech signals with the intent of reducing the bit rate.

In addition to the correlation existing between adjacent samples of a speech waveform, several other levels of redundancy can be exploited to reduce encoded bit rates. Table 3.3 lists these redundancies. Not included are higher-level redundancies related to context-dependent interpretations of speech sounds (phonemes), words, and sentences. These topics are not covered because techniques that analyze speech waveforms to extract only information content eliminate subjective qualities essential to general telephony.

Nonuniform Amplitude Distributions

As mentioned in the introduction to companding, lower amplitude sample values are more common than higher amplitude sample values. Most low-level samples occur as a result of speech pauses in a conversation. Beyond this, however, the power levels of active speech signals also tend to occur at the lower end of the encoding range. The companding procedures described in the previous sec-

Table 3.3   Speech Redundancies

Time Domain Redundancies

1. Nonuniform amplitude distributions
2. Sample-to-sample correlations
3. Cycle-to-cycle correlations (periodicity)
4. Pitch interval–to–pitch interval correlations
5. Inactivity factors (speech pauses)

Frequency Domain Redundancies

6. Nonuniform long-term spectral densities
7. Sound-specific short-term spectral densities

tion provide slightly inferior quality (i.e., lower signal-to-noise ratios) for small signals compared to large signals. Thus the average quality of PCM speech could be improved by further shortening of lower-level quantization intervals and increasing of upper-level quantization intervals. The amount of improvement realized by such a technique, however, probably would not justify the additional complexities, particularly if the linearizability of contemporary compandors was compromised.

The most beneficial approach to processing signal amplitudes in order to reduce encoder bit rates involves some form of adaptive gain control as discussed earlier.

Sample-to-Sample Correlation

The high correlation factor of 0.85 mentioned previously indicates that any significant attempt to reduce transmission rates must exploit the correlation between adjacent samples. In fact, at 8-kHz sampling rates, significant correlations also exist for samples two to three samples apart. Naturally, samples become even more correlated if the sampling rate is increased.

The simplest way to exploit sample-to-sample redundancies in speech is to encode only the differences between adjacent samples. The difference measurements are then accumulated in a decoder to recover the signal. In essence, these systems encode the slope or derivative of a signal at the source and recover the signal by integrating at the destination. Digitization algorithms of this type are discussed at length in later sections.

Cycle-to-Cycle Correlations

Although a speech signal requires the entire 300- to 3400-Hz bandwidth provided by a telephone channel, at any particular instant in time, certain sounds may be composed of only a few frequencies within the band. When only a few underlying frequencies exist in a sound, the waveform exhibits strong correlations over numerous samples corresponding to several cycles of an oscillation. The cyclic nature of a voiced sound is evident in the time waveform shown in Figure 3.21. Encoders exploiting the cycle-to-cycle redundancies in speech are markedly more complicated than those concerned only with removing the redundancy in adjacent samples. In fact, these encoders more or less represent a transition from the relatively high-rate, natural-sounding waveform encoders to the relatively low-rate, synthetic-sounding vocoders.

Pitch Interval–to–Pitch Interval Correlations

Human speech sounds are often categorized as being generated in one of two basic ways. The first category of sounds encompasses *voiced* sounds, which arise as a result of vibrations in the vocal cords. Each vibration allows a puff of air to flow from the lungs into the vocal tract. The interval between puffs of air exciting the vocal tract is referred to as the *pitch interval* or, more simply, the rate of excitation is the *pitch*. Generally speaking, voiced sounds arise in the generation of vowels and the latter portions of some consonants. An example of a time waveform for a voiced sound is shown in Figure 3.21.

The second category of sounds includes the *fricatives* or *unvoiced* sounds. Fricatives occur as a result of continuous air flowing from the lungs and passing through a vocal tract constricted at some point to generate air turbulence (friction). Unvoiced sounds correspond to certain consonants such as f, j, s, x. An example of a

Figure 3.21
Time waveform of voiced sound.

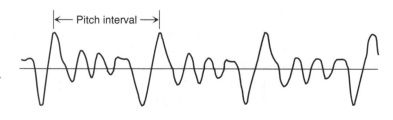
|← Pitch interval →|

time waveform of an unvoiced sound is shown in Figure 3.22. Notice that an unvoiced sound has a much more random waveform than a voiced sound.

As indicated in Figure 3.21, a voiced sound not only exhibits the cycle-to-cycle redundancies mentioned previously, but the waveform also displays a longer-term repetitive pattern corresponding to the duration of a pitch interval. Thus one of the most efficient ways of encoding the voiced portions of speech is to encode one pitch interval waveform and use that encoding as a template for each successive pitch interval in the same sound. Pitch intervals typically last from 5 to 20 msec for men and from 2.5 to 10 msec for women. Since a typical voiced sound lasts for approximately 100 msec, there may be as many as 20 to 40 pitch intervals in a single sound. Although pitch interval encoding can provide significant reductions in bit rates, the pitch is sometimes very difficult to detect. (Not all voiced sounds produce a readily identifiable pitch interval as in Figure 3.19.) If the pitch gets encoded erroneously, strange sounds result.

An interesting aspect of pitch interval encoding is that it provides a means of speeding up speech while maintaining intelligibility. By deleting some percentage of pitch intervals from each sound (phoneme) the rate of sound generation is effectively increased in a manner analogous to more rapid word formation. The pitch of the sounds remains unchanged. In contrast, if the rate of reconstruction is merely increased, all frequencies including the pitch increase proportionately. Moderate speedups produce obvious distortion while greater speedups become unintelligible. Devices designed to simulate faster word formation have demonstrated that we are capable of assimilating spoken information much faster than we normally generate it.

Inactivity Factors

Analyses of telephone conversations have indicated that a party is typically active about 40 percent of a call duration. Most inactivity

Figure 3.22
Time waveform of unvoiced sound.

occurs as a result of one person listening while the other is talking. Thus a conventional (circuit-switched) full-duplex connection is significantly underutilized. Time assignment speech interpolation (TASI) is an old technique to improve channel utilization on international analog links. Digital speech interpolation (DSI) is a term used to refer to a digital circuit counterpart of TASI. In essence, DSI involves sensing speech activity, seizing a channel, digitally encoding and transmitting the utterances, and releasing the channel at the completion of each speech segment.

Digital speech interpolation is obviously applicable to digital speech storage systems where the duration of a pause can be encoded more efficiently than the pause itself. In recorded messages, however, the pauses are normally short since a half-duplex conversation is not taking place. DSI principles and methods are now common.

Nonuniform Long-Term Spectral Densities

The time domain redundancies described in the preceding sections exhibit certain characteristics in the frequency domain that can be judiciously processed to reduce the encoded bit rate. Frequency domain redundancies are not independent of the redundancies in the time domain. Frequency domain techniques merely offer an alternate approach to analyzing and processing the redundancies.

A totally random or unpredictable signal in the time domain produces a frequency spectrum that is flat across the bandwidth of interest. Thus a signal that produces uncorrelated time domain samples makes maximum use of its bandwidth. On the other hand, a nonuniform spectral density represents inefficient use of the bandwidth and is indicative of redundancy in the waveform. Figure 3.23 shows the long-term spectral density of speech signals averaged across two populations: men and women. Notice that the upper portions of the 3-kHz bandwidth passed by the telephone network have significantly reduced power levels. The lower power levels at higher frequencies are a direct consequence of the time domain sample-to-sample correlations discussed previously. Large amplitude signals cannot change rapidly because, on the average, they are predominantly made up of lower-frequency components.

A frequency domain approach to more efficient coding involves flattening the spectrum before encoding the signal. The flattening

Figure 3.23

Long-term power spectral density of speech.

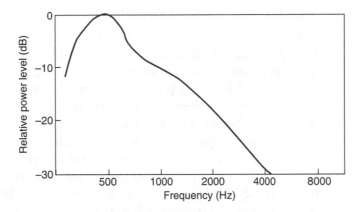

process can be accomplished by passing the signal through a high-pass filter to emphasize the higher frequencies before sampling. The original waveform is recovered by passing the decoded signal through a filter with a complementary, low-pass characteristic. An important aspect of this process is that a high-pass filter exhibits time domain characteristics similar to a differentiator and a low-pass filter has time domain characteristics analogous to an integrator. Thus the spectrum-flattening process essentially means the slope of the signal is encoded at the source, and the signal is recovered by integrating at the destination—the basic procedure described for sample-to-sample redundancy removal in the time domain.

In studying Figure 3.23 it is natural to think that the remarkably low levels of signal energy at the higher frequencies (2 to 3.4 kHz) mean that more bandwidth is being allocated to a voice signal than is really necessary. The error in such a conclusion, however, lies in the distinction between energy content and information content of the voice frequency spectrum. As any beginning computer programmer soon learns, the meaning of a program variable can be retained even though it is shortened by deleting all of the vowels. In speech, the vowels require most of the energy and occupy primarily the lower portion of the frequency band. The consonants, on the other hand, contain most of the information but use much less power and generally higher frequencies. Hence, merely reproducing a high percentage of the original speech energy is an inadequate goal for a digital speech transmission or storage system.

Short-Term Spectral Densities

The speech spectrums shown in Figure 3.23 represent long-term averages of the spectral densities. Over shorter periods of time, the spectral densities vary considerably and exhibit sound-specific structures with energy peaks (resonances) at some frequencies and energy valleys at others. The frequencies at which the resonances occur are called *formant frequencies*, or simply *formants*. Voiced speech sounds typically contain three to four identifiable formants.

Frequency domain voice coders provide improved coding efficiencies by encoding the most important components of the spectrum on a dynamic basis. As the sounds change, different portions (formants) of the frequency band are encoded. The period between formant updates is typically 10 to 20 msec. Instead of using periodic spectrum measurements, some higher-quality vocoders continuously track gradual changes in the spectral density at a higher rate. Frequency domain vocoders often provide lower bit rates than the time domain coders, but typically produce more unnatural-sounding speech.

3.5 Differential Pulse Code Modulation

Differential pulse code modulation (DPCM) is designed specifically to take advantage of the sample-to-sample redundancies in a typical speech waveform. Since the range of sample *differences* is less than the range of individual *samples*, fewer bits are needed to encode difference samples. The sampling rate is often the same as for a comparable PCM system. Thus the bandlimiting filter in the encoder and the smoothing filter in the decoder are basically identical to those used in conventional PCM systems.

A simple means of generating the difference samples for a DPCM coder is to store the previous input sample directly in a sample-and-hold circuit and use an analog subtractor to measure the change. The change in the signal is then quantized and encoded for transmission. The DPCM structure shown in Figure 3.24 is more complicated, however, because the previous input value is reconstructed by a feedback loop that integrates the encoded sample differences. In essence, the feedback signal is an estimate of the input signal as obtained by integrating the encoded sample differences. Thus the feedback signal is obtained in the same manner used to reconstruct the waveform in the decoder.

The advantage of the feedback implementation is that quantization errors do not accumulate indefinitely. If the feedback signal drifts from the input signal as a result of an accumulation of quantization errors, the next encoding of the difference signal automatically compensates for the drift. In a system without feedback, the output produced by a decoder at the other end of the connection might accumulate quantization errors without bound.

As in PCM systems, the analog-to-digital conversion process can be uniform or companded. Some DPCM systems also use adaptive techniques to adjust the quantization step size in accordance with the average power level of the signal.

These adaptive techniques are often referred to as *syllabic companding,* in accordance with the time interval between gain adjustments. Syllabic companding is discussed in conjunction with delta modulation systems, where it is most often used. Typically, DPCM systems provide a full 1-bit reduction in code word size. The larger savings is achieved because, on average, speech waveforms have a lower slope than an 800-Hz tone. (See Figure 3.23.)

A more general viewpoint of a DPCM encoder considers it a special case of a linear predictor with encoding and transmission of the prediction error. The feedback signal of a DPCM system represents a first-order prediction of the next sample value, and the sample difference is a prediction error. Under this viewpoint, the DPCM concept can be extended to incorporate more than one past sample value into the prediction circuitry. Thus the additional redundancy available from all previous samples can be weighted

Figure 3.24
Functional block diagram of differential PCM.

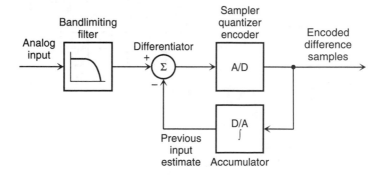

and summed to produce a better estimate of the next input sample. With a better estimate, the range of the prediction error decreases to allow encoding with fewer bits. For systems with constant predictor coefficients, results have shown that most of the realizable improvement occurs when using only the last three sample values. The basic implementation of a linear predictive coder using the last three sample values is shown in Figure 3.25.

As mentioned in this section, analysis of differential PCM systems with first-order predication typically provides a 1-bit-per-sample reduction in code length relative to PCM systems with equivalent performance. Extended DPCM systems utilizing third-order prediction can provide reductions of 1½ to 2 bits per sample. Thus a standard DPCM system can provide 64-kbps PCM quality at 56 kbps, and third-order linear prediction can provide comparable quality at 48 kbps. However, subjective evaluations often indicate that somewhat higher bit rates are needed to match 64-kbps PCM quality.

Although the DPCM techniques described here can provide worthwhile reductions in transmission bit rates, they have not been used extensively in public telephony for two reasons. First, the 64-kbps PCM systems are well entrenched and accepted as being able to provide the desired quality. The same is true for ADPCM as well as the other vocoding techniques discussed in follow-up chapters. These techniques, however, are finding applications in voice over data network environments.

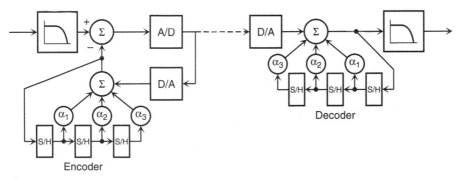

Figure 3.25
Extension of DPCM to third-order prediction.

3.6 Delta Modulation

This section describes other techniques that have been used or proposed in the past decade. Currently, these techniques seem to be eclipsed by ADPCM and the new G.723.1, G.728, and G.729 methods described in the chapters that follow. These techniques are covered here for pedagogical reasons.

Delta modulation (DM) is another digitization technique that specifically exploits the sample-to-sample redundancy in a speech waveform. In fact, DM can be considered as a special case of DPCM using only 1 bit per sample of the difference signal. The single bit specifies merely the polarity of the difference sample and thereby indicates whether the signal has increased or decreased since the last sample. An approximation to the input waveform is constructed in the feedback path by stepping up one quantization level when the difference is positive (one) and stepping down when the difference is negative (zero). In this way, the input is encoded as a sequence of ups and downs in a manner resembling a staircase. Figure 3.26 shows a DM approximation of a typical waveform. Notice that the feedback signal continues to step in one direction until it crosses the input, at which time the feedback step reverses direction until the input is crossed again. Thus, when tracking the input signal, the DM output bounces back and forth across the input waveform, allowing the input to be accurately reconstructed by a smoothing filter.

Since each encoded sample contains a relatively small amount of information (1 bit), delta modulation systems require a higher sampling rate than PCM or multibit DPCM systems. In fact, the sampling rate is necessarily much higher than the minimum (Nyquist) sampling rate of twice the bandwidth. From another viewpoint, oversampling is needed to achieve better prediction from one sample to the next.

Figure 3.26
Waveform encoding by delta modulation.

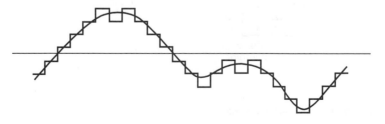

The main attractions of DM is its simplicity. Figure 3.27 shows a basic implementation of a DM encoder and decoder. Notice that the A/D conversion function is provided by a simple comparator. A positive difference voltage produces a 1, and a negative difference voltage produces a 0. Correspondingly, the D/A function in the feedback path, and in the decoder, is provided by a two-polarity pulse generator. In the simplest form, the integrator can consist of nothing more than a capacitor to accumulate the charge from the pulse generator.

In addition to these obvious implementation simplicities, a delta modulator also allows the use of relatively simple filters for band-limiting the input and smoothing the output. As discussed in Section 3.2, the spectrum produced by a sampling process consists of replicas of the sampled spectrum centered at multiples of the sampling frequency. The relatively high sampling rate of a delta modulator produces a wider separation of these spectrums, and, hence, foldover distortion is prevented with less stringent roll-off requirements for the input filter.

Slope Overload

The conceptual operation of a delta modulator shown in Figure 3.24 indicates that the encoded waveform is never much more than a step size away from the input signal. Sometimes, however, a delta modulator may not be able to keep up with rapid changes in the input signal and thus may fall more than a step size behind. When this happens, the delta modulator is said to be experiencing *slope overload*. A slope overload condition is shown in Figure 3.28.

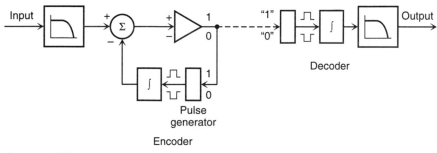

Figure 3.27
Delta modulation encoder and decoder.

Figure 3.28
Slope overload and granular noise of delta modulation system.

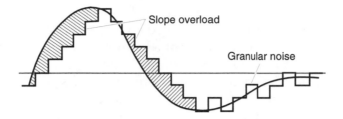

Basically, slope overload occurs when the rate of change of the input exceeds the maximum rate of change that can be generated by the feedback loop. Since the maximum rate of change in the feedback loop is merely the step size times the sampling rate, a slope overload condition occurs if

$$\left| \frac{dx(t)}{dt} \right| > q f_s \qquad\qquad (3.11)$$

where $x(t)$ = input signal
$\quad\quad q$ = step size
$\quad\quad f_s$ = sampling frequency

The design of a delta modulator necessarily involves a trade-off between two types of distortion: the more or less random quantization noise, sometimes referred to as granular noise, and the slope overload noise. As indicated in Figure 3.28, granular noise is a predominant consideration for slowly changing signals, whereas slope overload is dominant during rapidly changing signals. Obviously, granular noise is small if step sizes are small, but small step sizes increase the likelihood of slope overload.

The perceptual effects of slope overload on the quality of a speech signal are significantly different from the perceptual effects produced by granular noise. As indicated in Figure 3.28, the slope overload noise reaches its peaks just before the encoded signal reaches its peaks. Hence, slope overload noise has strong components identical in frequency and approximately in phase with a major component of the input. Distortion that is correlated in this manner to the speech signal is effectively masked by the speech energy and therefore is less noticeable than uncorrelated distortion. In fact, overload noise is much less objectionable to a listener than random or granular noise at an equivalent power level. Hence, from the point of view of perceived speech quality, the optimum mix of granular and slope overload noise is difficult to determine.

Slope overload is not a limition of just a delta modulation system, but an inherent problem with any system, such as DPCM in general, that encodes the difference in a signal from one sample to the next. A difference system encodes the slope of the input with a finite number of bits and, hence, a finite range. If the slope exceeds that range, slope overload occurs. In contrast, a conventional PCM system is not limited by the rate of change of the input, only by the maximum encodable amplitude. Notice that a differential system can encode signals with arbitrarily large amplitudes, as long as the large amplitudes are attained gradually.

Linear Delta Modulation

The simplest delta modulator uses a constant step size for all signal levels and is therefore referred to as a *uniform* or *linear delta modulator* (LDM). The design of a linear delta modulator is fundamentally concerned with selecting a fixed step size and a sampling rate to satisfy two criteria. First, the signal-to-granular noise ratio must be some minimum value for the lowest-level signal to be encoded. Second, the signal-to-slope overload distortion ratio must be some minimum for the highest-level signal to be encoded.

A convenient procedure for satisfying the slope overload criterion is to use Equation 3.11 and design the system so that slope overload is just on the verge of occurring at the highest level of input. Thus the step size for the highest-level signal is not optimum in a perceptual sense or even in terms of minimizing the sum of granular noise and overload distortion. Nevertheless, when only granular noise is present, a delta modulator's SQR performance can be appropriately compared to the SQR performance of a PCM system. Comparing the two encoding methods under other conditions—for example, when overloads occur in either system—requires listener evaluations.

$$\text{LDM noise power} = K \left(\frac{f_c}{f_s} \right) q^2 \tag{3.12}$$

The basic drawback of linear delta modulation, like uniform PCM, is that low-level signals and high-level signals are both encoded with the same step size. Thus, high-level signals are encoded with excess quality at an expense in data rate. The solution, of course, is to vary the step size in some manner dependent on the magnitude of the input slope. Commonly, the step size is adjusted gradually based on a short-term average of the slope amplitude.

A significant consideration in the implementation of a delta modulator is maintaining equal positive and negative steps in the encoder and decoder. If a step size imbalance exists in the decoder, the reconstructed waveform accumulates a DC offset that may lead to circuit saturations. As discussed in the next section, modest step size imbalances in the decoder are relatively easy to accommodate. On the other hand, step size imbalances in the encoder are more troublesome and therefore require close attention.

When a delta modulator encodes the signal of an idle channel (speech pause), the output data ideally alternates between a 1 and a 0. When alternation does occur, the output filter of the decoder eliminates the relatively high-frequency sampling noise. However, if an imbalance in step sizes exists, as shown in Figure 3.29, two 1s or two 0s occasionally occur together. Since double 0s or double 1s occur relatively infrequently, they produce low-frequency distortion, which is not filtered out, and idle channel noise results. Idle channel noise is a particular problem in delta modulators because of the relatively large quantization intervals. One means of balancing the step sizes in the encoder is to subtract an offset obtained by low-pass filtering (integrating) the feedback signal over a long time period.

Adaptive Delta Modulation

Numerous researchers have proposed and studied a large variety of algorithms for adapting the step size of a delta modulator. Basically, all algorithms increase the step size when the onset of slope overload

Figure 3.29
Effect of imbalance in positive and negative step sizes in a delta modulator with a zero-level input.

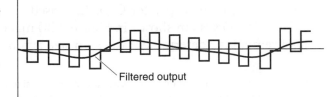

Filtered output

is detected and reduce the step size as the input slope decreases. Some of the algorithms measure the input slope directly and transmit explicit step size information. Other algorithms derive the step size information from the transmitted bit stream for both the encoder and decoder. The rate of adaptation is sometimes instantaneous in that adjustments are made on a sample-to-sample basis, but more often syllabic in that significant changes in the step size occur only once every 10 msec or so. All of the basic algorithms appear to provide approximately the same voice quality, but some algorithms have certain features, making them more attractive than others in specific applications. In particular, the algorithms vary in terms of their channel error sensitivity, transmission format, interconnectability with other coders, and amenability to digital signal processing.

This section describes the basic operation of one particular type of adaptive delta modulation (ADM) generally referred to as *continuously variable slope delta* (CVSD) *modulation*. The basic CVSD encoding algorithm was first described by Greefkes and de Jager in 1968. A subsequent design by Greefkes and Riemens incorporated what is referred to as *delta modulation with digitally controlled companding*. This particular type of adaptive delta modulation is chosen because it is simple and embodies many generally desirable features. Furthermore, the basic algorithm is available from several manufacturers as a single integrated circuit.

Digitally controlled companding, as the name implies, derives its step size information from the transmitted bit stream. As shown in Figure 3.30, the adaptation logic monitors the transmitted data to detect the occurrence of four successive ones or four successive zeros.* A string of ones indicates that the feedback signal is probably not rising as fast as the input, while a string of zeros indicates the feedback is probably not falling as fast as the input. In either case, all ones or all zeros implies that slope overload is occurring and the step size should be increased. Thus the all-ones and all-zeros signals are "or"-ed together to control a pulse generator. During overload, the pulse generator is enabled so that the step size voltage, as stored on capacitor C_1, is increased.

The CVSD system shown in Figure 3.30 makes no explicit measurements to determine if the step size is too large and there-

---

*The number of successive ones or zeros causing a step size increase is reduced to three on lower-rate delta modulators to improve the response time.

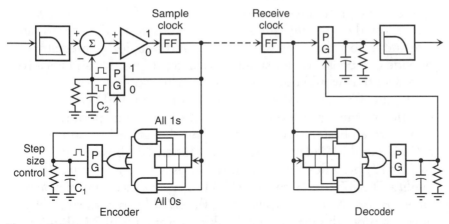

Figure 3.30
Continuously variable slope delta modulation with digitally controlled companding.

fore should be reduced. Instead, a resistor is connected to capacitor C_1 to allow the step voltage to decay with time. Thus, in the absence of explicit increases, the step size automatically becomes smaller through exponential decay. Eventually the step size decays to a minimum value or to a point at which overload is detected, causing the step size to increase again.

The resistor-capacitor combination is sometimes referred to as a *leaky integrator*, implying that the capacitor integrates the input pulses but the resistor allows the accumulated step size voltage to leak off. Besides providing an automatic way to reduce the step size, the leaky integrator also eliminates the long-term effects of channel errors in the receiving terminal. If "perfect" integration were used, an erroneous increment in the step size would be retained indefinitely. With leaky integration, however, the duration of an erroneous increment (or lack of increment) is limited to a few time constants of the leaky integrator.

Notice that leaky integration is also used to reconstruct the input signal at the output of the decoder and, correspondingly, in the feedback path of the encoder. Thus an offset in the output of the receiving terminal, caused by a channel error, naturally decays in time and is effectively eliminated within a few time constants of the second leaky integrator. Elimination of an offset in the output signal is not so important from a listener's point of view since a fixed offset is inaudible, but is useful for preventing saturation in the decoder. If "perfect" integration were used, a large excess of positive or negative errors would eventually cause the electronics in the decoder to saturate and distort the voice waveform. In addition, leaky integrators provide compensation for small imbalances in positive and negative step sizes that would otherwise lead to saturation also.

Figure 3.31 shows the performance of two CVSD codecs as a function of the input level of a 1-kHz test tone. The performance curves were obtained from specification sheets for Motorola's MC3417 and MC3418 CVSD codecs. Then 16-kbps codec (MC3417) provides what is referred to as *general communications quality*. The 37.7-kbps codec (MC3418) provides *commercial telephone quality*. Notice, however, that the 37.7-kbps performance does not meet the D3 channel bank requirements of 33-dB minimum signal-to-noise ratio (SQR) across 30-dB dynamic range. Recall that the D3 specification arose out of a need for higher quality because of the possibility of multiple conversions. Thus, although a CVSD at 37.7 kbps provides acceptable end-to-end quality, the data rate must be increased for tandem coding applications. The idle channel noise of the CVSD is also inferior if step size imbalances exist.

The performance curves shown in Figure 3.31 do not completely reflect the output quality when applied to an input speech signal. Since the 1-kHz tone is a steady state input, it does not test the adaptive aspects of the codec. In particular, adaptive delta modulators are generally noted for a certain lack of crispness in the speech output. The lack of crispness occurs at the beginning of

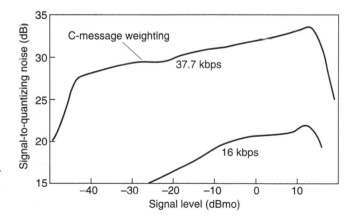

Figure 3.31
Signal-to-quantizing noise ratios of CVSD.

words and relatively strong syllables that experience temporary slope overloads.

In conclusion, it should be mentioned again that numerous varieties of delta modulation algorithms have been proposed and implemented. A CVSD codec is described here because it is currently the most popular type and represents a very basic form of delta modulation.

3.7 Adaptive Predictive Coding

The differential systems described in the previous sections (DPCM, ADPCM, ADM) operate with lower data rates than PCM systems because they encode a difference signal that has lower average power than the raw input signal. The ratio of the input signal power to the power of the difference signal is referred to as the *prediction gain*. Simple DPCM systems (first-order predictors) provide about 5 dB of prediction gain. ADPCM provides greater levels of prediction gain depending on the sophistication of the adaption logic and the number of past samples used to predict the next sample. The prediction gain of ADPCM is ultimately limited by the fact that only a few past samples are used to predict the input and the adaption logic only adapts the quantizer—not the prediction weighting coefficients.

Adaptive predictive coding (APC) provides greater levels of prediction gain by adapting the prediction coefficients to individual speech segments and, in most cases, using higher orders of prediction (e.g., up to 12). If the coefficients are determined from past history and used to predict subsequent speech segments (backward estimation) 13 dB of prediction gain is possible. If speech segments are delayed so predictor coefficients can be used on the same speech segments from which they were derived (forward estimation), 20 dB of prediction gain is possible.

A block diagram of a basic APC encoder/decoder is shown in Figure 3.32. The input to the encoder and the output from the decoder are assumed to be uniform PCM—most likely representing conversions from and to log PCM. The transmitted data stream is necessarily composed of blocks containing three types of information: (1) the encoded difference signal (residual), (2) a gain factor, and (3) the predictor coefficients. The most significant difference

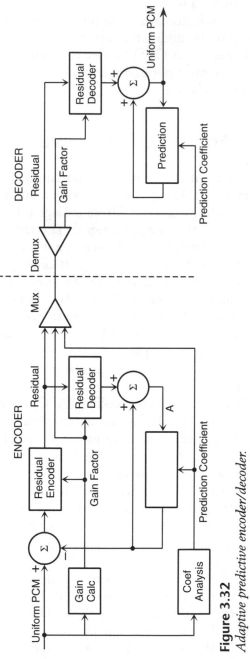

Figure 3.32
Adaptive predictive encoder/decoder.

114

between this coder and a DPCM or ADPCM coder involves the periodic determination and transmission of the predictor coefficients. Notice that the integrated residual signal at point A is identical to the input signal delayed by one sample (except for residual quantization error). Thus the corresponding point in the decoder is the reconstructed PCM output.

An APC encoder of this type can provide as much as 20 dB of improvement over a PCM system. The large amount of computation required to determine the pitch period and the predictor coefficients is becoming less of a drawback as integrated circuit technology continues to advance.

Notes

[1] This chapter is reprinted by permission in an abridged form from *Digital Telephony* by John Bellamy, © 1991 John Wiley & Sons.

[2] For discussion of these effects of noise as a function of frequency, see Bellamy, Chapter 1.

[3] The signal-to-quantization noise ratios commonly compare unfiltered decoder outputs to unfiltered quantization errors. In actual practice, the decoder output filter reduces the power level of both the signal and the noise. The noise power experiences a greater reduction than the signal power, since the uncorrelated noise samples have a wider spectrum than the correlated voice samples. Thus filtered signal-to-noise ratios are usually higher than the values calculated here by 1 to 2 dB.

[4] Today, most of the channel banks are of the D4/D5 type.

CHAPTER 4

Adaptive Differential Pulse Code Modulation

Initial implementations of voice over ATM tended to utilize PCM or ADPCM methods (with newer compression-based schemes and AAL 2 expected to enter the market in the immediate future), while frame relay has tended to use ADPCM or proprietary compression schemes (with standardized compression-based schemes expected to enter the market in the immediate future). Given the role of ADPCM—although such a role is expected to be somewhat less important as technology develops—this chapter discusses this technology.

4.1 Introduction

As discussed in the preceding chapter, there are two classes of methods to digitize voice: *waveform coding* and *vocoding*. Waveform coding attempts to code and then reproduce the analog voice curve by modeling its physical shape. With this method, the number of bits per second required to represent the voice is high: 64, 32, 16, or at least 9.6 kbps, depending on the technology. Vocoding attempts to reproduce the analog voice curve by performing a mathematical analysis that identifies abstractly the type of curve; a small set of parameters describing the nature of the curve is transmitted. The number of bits per second needed to represent the voice with this method is low: 9.6, 4.8, or 2.4 kbps, or even 1200 bps, depending on the technology (See Table 4.1). However, voice quality is increasingly degraded as the digitization rate becomes smaller. In spite of the fact that an extensive body of research on vocoding methods has evolved in the past 25 years, historically, the technology has not experienced major deployment, although that is poised to change with the deployment of voice over IP networks.

As noted in Chapter 3, Nyquist theory specifies that, to properly code an analog signal of bandwidth W with basic PCM techniques, $2W$ samples per second are needed. For voice, bandlimited to a nominal 4000-Hz bandwidth, 8000 samples per second are needed (the actual telephony frequency range used is 300 to 3400 Hz). The dynamic range of the signal (and ultimately the signal-to-noise ratio) dictates the number of quantizing levels required. For telephonic voice, 256 levels suffice, based on psychoacoustic studies conducted in the 1950s and early 1960s; it follows that 8 bits are needed to uniquely represent these many levels. In turn, this implies that 64,000 bps are needed to encode telephonic human speech in digital form. PCM does not require sophisticated signal

Table 4.1 Speech Digitization Methods and Some Illustrative Examples

Method	*Aspect*
Waveform coders	*Utilize algorithms to produce an output that approximates the input waveform*
PCM	Standard telephony method for toll-quality voice. Typically used at 64 kbps.
ADPCM	Adaptive coding for rates of 40, 32, 24, and 16 kbps. Uses a combination of adaptive quantization and adaptive prediction.
Vocoding	*Digitizes a compact description of the voice spectrum in several frequency bands, including extraction of the pitch component of the signal*
Adaptive subband coding	Supports rates of 16 and 8 kbps. Speech is separated into frequency bands and each is coded using different strategies. The strategies are selected to suit properties of hearing and some predictive measure of the input spectrum.
(*Hybrid*) Multipulse linear predictive coding (LPC)	Supports rates of 8 and 4 kbps. A suitable number of pulses is utilized to optimize the excitation information for a speech segment and to supplement linear prediction of the segments.
Stochastically excited linear predictive coding	Supports rates of 8 to 2 kbps. The coder stores a repository of candidate excitations, each a stochastic sequence of pulses, and the best is matched.

processing techniques and related circuitry; hence, it was the first method to be employed and is the prevalent method used today in the telephone plant. PCM provides excellent quality. This is the method used in modern compact disc (CD) music recording technology, although the sampling rate is higher and the coding words are longer, to guarantee a frequency response to 22 kHz. The problem with PCM is that it requires a fairly high bandwidth (64 kbps) to represent a voice signal.

Sophisticated voice coding methods have become available in the past decade as a result of the evolution of Very Large Scale Integration (VLSI) technology. Coding rates of 32 kbps and 16 kbps, and even vocoder methods requiring 4800 bps, 2400 bps, and even less, have evolved. There is interest in pursuing these new coding schemes, since the implication is that the voice-carrying capacity of the network can be doubled or quadrupled in place without the introduction of new transmission equipment. The ADPCM scheme provides toll-quality voice with minimal (voice) degradation at 32 kbps. As noted in the preceding chapter, the problem with this voice coding method is that, if the input analog signal varies rapidly between samples, the DPCM technique is not able to represent with sufficient accuracy the incoming signal. Just as in the PCM technique, clipping can occur when the input to the quantizer is too large; in this case, the input signal is the change in signal from the previous sample. The resulting distortion is known as *slope overload distortion*. In *adaptive* DPCM, the coder can be made to adapt to slope overload by increasing the range represented by 4 bits. In principle, the range implicit in the 4 bits can be increased or decreased to match different situations. This will reduce the quantizing noise for large signals, but will increase noise for normal signals; so when the volume drops, the range covered by the 4-bit signal drops accordingly. These adaptive aspects of the algorithm give rise to its name.

In practice, the ADPCM coding device accepts the PCM coded signal and then applies a special algorithm to reduce the 8-bit samples to 4-bit words using only 15 quantizing levels. These 4-bit words no longer represent sample amplitudes; instead, they contain only enough information to reconstruct the amplitude at the distant end. The adaptive predictor predicts the value of the next signal based on the level of the previously sampled signal. A feedback loop ensures that voice variations are followed with minimal deviation. The deviation of the predicted value measured against the actual signal tends to be small and can be encoded with 4 bits. In the event that successive samples vary widely, the algorithm adapts by increasing the range represented by the 4 bits through a slight increase in the noise level over normal signals.

ADPCM begins with the analog-to-digital conversion of the voiceband signal into the μ-law PCM format. This is converted into uniform PCM and a difference signal is obtained by subtracting an estimate of the immediately previous sample of the input signal from the current sample of the input signal. The difference signal is then assigned 4 binary bits by a 15-level adaptive quantizer. To make an estimate of the previous signal, the 4-bit quantizer output is passed through an inverse adaptive quantizer, an adaptive predictor, and a reconstructed-signal calculator, which are used to form the estimate. The 4-bit binary word of the adaptive quantizer output (1 bit for sign and 3 for magnitude) is the signal to be transmitted [1].

Low-bit-rate voice methods such as ADPCM reduce not only the capacity needed to transmit digital voice but also that needed for voiceband data (e.g., fax). As noted, low bit rates are realized by methods that reduce the redundancies in speech, provide adaptive quantization and pitch extraction, and then code the processed signal in a perceptually optimized manner. However, quality, bit rate, complexity, and delay are all impacted by the processing and coding. Quality is negatively impacted as the bit rate goes down, but this effect can be decreased to some degree by adding complexity of processing (at increased cost, however); in turn, processing increases the delay. In general, as the bit rate decreases by a binary order of magnitude, the complexity of the vocoder increases by approximately a decimal order of magnitude (except for LPC). At the same time, the delay increases and the quality deteriorates. Figure 4.1 (based partially on Reference 1) depicts the MOS and other factors for various coding schemes.

This chapter provides a description of ADPCM encoding methods, which can be utilized in ATM and frame relay environments. Vocoding is now used more prevalently in IP-based voice (although it can also be used in frame relay environments); hence, it is covered more extensively in the companion text, *Delivering Voice over IP Networks* [2]. Table 4.2 depicts some of the key standards relevant to voice over data networks.

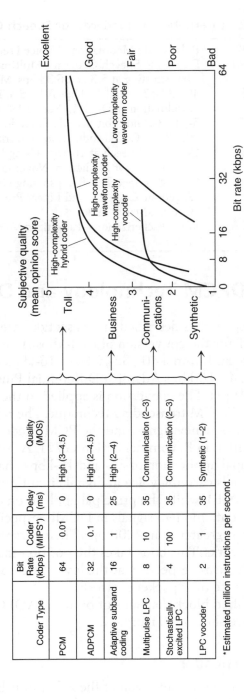

Figure 4.1
Complexity versus quality versus bit rate versus delay in voice processing/compression.

121

Table 4.2   International Standards for Speech Compression

ITU G.711	Pulse Code Modulation of Voice Frequencies, 1988
ITU G.723.1	Dual Rate Speech Coder for Multimedia Communications Transmitting at 5.3 and 6.3 kbps, March 1996
ITU G.726	40-, 32-, 24-, and 16-kbps Adaptive Differential Pulse Code Modulation (ADPCM), March 1991
ITU G.727	5-, 4-, 3-, and 2-bit Sample Embedded Adaptive Differential Pulse Code Modulation, November 1994
ITU G.728	Coding of Speech at 16 kbps Using Low-Delay Code Excited Linear Prediction, November 1994
ITU G.729	Coding of Speech at 8 kbps Using Conjugate Structure–Algebraic Code Excited Linear Predictive (CS-ACELP) Coding, March 1996
ITU G.764	Voice Packetization—Packetized Voice Protocol, December 1990

4.2 ADPCM Technology and Details

The characteristics described in this section[1] are recommended by the ITU-T for the conversion of a 64-kbps *A*-law or μ-law PCM channel to and from a 40-, 32-, 24-, or 16-kbps channel in G.726, 40-, 32-, 24-, 16-kbps Adaptive Differential Pulse Code Modulation (ADPCM) [3]. The conversion is applied to the PCM bit stream using an ADPCM transcoding technique. The relationship between the voice frequency signals and the PCM encoding/decoding laws is fully specified in Recommendation G.711. As stated by the ITU-T, the principal application of 24- and 16-kbps channels is for overload channels carrying voice in digital circuit multiplication equipment (DCME), while the principal application of 40-kbps channels is to carry data modem signals in DCME, especially for modems operating at greater than 4800 bps. Their perspective was still for TDM networks. This book takes the position that these compression mechanisms, especially at the lower rate, can be used, equally well, for voice over packet networks.

Simplified block diagrams of both the ADPCM encoder and decoder are shown in Figure 4.2.

ADPCM Encoder

Subsequent to the conversion of the *A*-law or μ-law PCM input to *uniform* PCM, a difference signal is obtained by subtracting an esti-

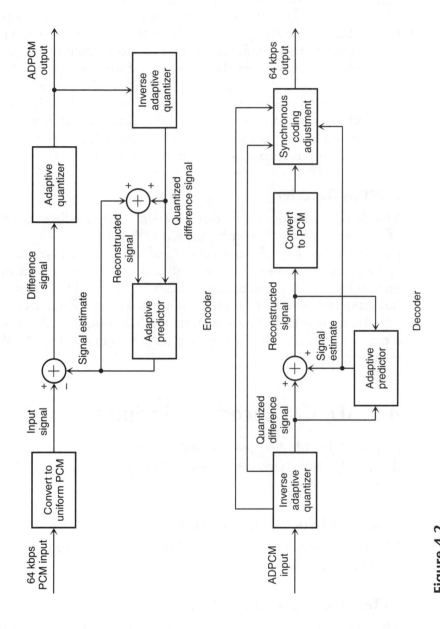

Figure 4.2
Simplified block diagrams for ADPCM (ITU-T G.726) [3].

mate of the input signal from the input signal itself. An adaptive 31-, 15-, 7-, or 4-level quantizer is used to assign five, four, three, or two binary digits, respectively, to the value of the difference signal for transmission to the decoder. An inverse quantizer produces a quantizer difference signal from these same five, four, three, or two binary digits, respectively. The signal estimate is added to this quantized difference signal to produce the reconstructed version of the input signal. Both the reconstructed signal and the quantized difference signal are operated upon by an adaptive predictor, which produces the estimate of the input signal, thereby completing the feedback loop.

ADPCM Decoder

The decoder includes a structure identical to the feedback portion of the encoder, together with a uniform PCM to A-law or μ-law conversion and a synchronous coding adjustment. The synchronous coding adjustment prevents cumulative distortion from occurring on synchronous tandem codings (ADPCM-PCM-ADPCM, etc., digital connections) under certain conditions. The synchronous coding adjustment is achieved by adjusting the PCM output codes in such a manner as to eliminate quantizing distortion in the next ADPCM encoding stage.

4.3 ADPCM Encoder Principles

Figure 4.3 is a block schematic of the encoder. For each variable described, k is the sampling index and samples are taken at 125-μs intervals.

Input PCM Format Conversion

This block converts the input signal $s(k)$ from A-law or μ-law PCM to a uniform PCM signal $s_l(k)$.

Difference Signal Computation

This block calculates the difference signal $d(k)$ from the uniform PCM signal $s_l(k)$ and the signal estimate $s_e(k)$:

$$d(k) = s_l(k) - s_e(k)$$

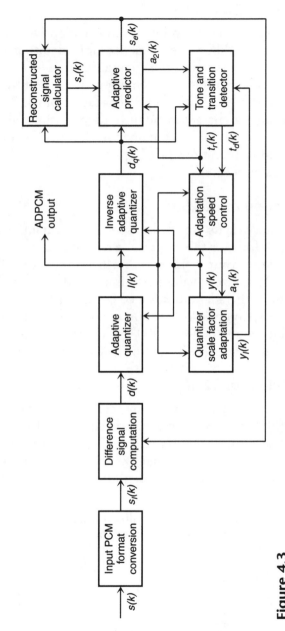

Figure 4.3
Encoder block schematic (ITU-T G.726) [3].

Adaptive Quantizer

A 31-, 15-, 7-, or 4-level nonuniform adaptive quantizer is used to quantize the difference signal $d(k)$ for operating at 40, 32, 24, or 16 kbps, respectively. Prior to quantization, $d(k)$ is converted to a base-2 logarithmic representation and scaled by $y(k)$, which is computed by the scale factor adaptation block. The normalized input/output characteristic (infinite precision values) of the quantizer is given in tables contained in the specification, one for each of the various operations (40, 32, 24, or 16 kbps). Table 4.3 illustrates 24-kbps operation.

Operation at 40 kbps

Five binary digits are used to specify the quantized level representing $d(k)$, four for the magnitude and one for the sign. The 5-bit quantizer output $I(k)$ forms the 40-kbps output signal; $I(k)$ takes on one of 31 nonzero values. $I(k)$ is also fed to the inverse adaptive quantizer, the adaptation speed control, and the quantizer scale factor adaptation blocks that operate on a 5-bit $I(k)$ having one of 32 possible values. $I(k) = 00000$ is a legitimate input to these blocks when used in the decoder, due to transmission errors.

Operation at 32 kbps

Four binary digits are used to specify the quantized level representing $d(k)$, three for the magnitude and more for the sign. The 4-bit quantizer output $I(k)$ forms the 32-kbps output signal; it is also fed to the inverse adaptive quantizer, the adaptation speed control, and the quantizer scale factor adaptation blocks. $I(k) = 0000$ is a legiti-

Table 4.3   Quantizer Normalized Input/Output Characteristic for 24-kbps Operation

Normalized quantizer input range $\log_2 \mid d(k) \mid - y(k)$	$\mid I(k) \mid$	Normalized quantizer output $\log_2 \mid d_g(k) \mid - y(k)$
$[2.58, +\infty)$	3	2.91
$[1.70, 2.58)$	2	2.13
$[0.06, 1.70)$	1	1.05
$(-\infty, -0.06)$	0	$-\infty$

Note: "[" indicates that the endpoint value is included in the range, and "(" or ")" indicates that the endpoint value is excluded from the range.

mate input to these blocks when used in the decoder, due to transmission errors.

Operation at 24 kbps

Three binary digits are used to specify the quantizer level representing $d(k)$, two for the magnitude and one for the sign. The 3-bit quantizer output $I(k)$ forms the 24-kbps output signal, where $I(k)$ takes on one of several nonzero values. $I(k)$ is also fed to the inverse adaptive quantizer, the adaptation speed control, and the quantizer scale factor adaptation blocks, each of which is modified to operate on a 3-bit $I(k)$ having any of the eight possible values. $I(k) = 000$ is a legitimate input to these blocks when used in the decoder, due to transmission errors.

Operation at 16 kbps

Two binary digits are used to specify the quantized level representing $d(k)$, one for the magnitude and one for the sign. The 2-bit quantizer output $I(k)$ forms the 16-kbps output signal; it is also fed to the inverse adaptive quantizer, the adaptation speed control, and the quantizer scale factor adaptation blocks. Unlike the quantizer for operation at 40 kbps, at 32 kbps, and at 24 kbps, the quantizer for operation at 16 kbps is an even-level (four-level) quantizer. The even-level quantizer for the 16-kbps ADPCM has been selected because of its superior performance over a corresponding odd-level (three-level) quantizer.

Inverse Adaptive Quantizer

A quantized version $d(k)$ of the difference signal is produced by scaling, using $y(k)$ and specific values selected from the normalized quantizing characteristic given in the specification tables (e.g., the one shown earlier), and then transforming the result from the logarithmic domain.

Quantizer Scale Factor Adaptation

This block computes $y(k)$, the scaling factor for the quantizer, and the inverse quantizer. The inputs are the 5-, 4-, 3-, and 2-bit quantizer output $I(k)$ and the adaptation speed control parameter $a_1(k)$.

The basic principle used in scaling the quantizer is bimodal adaptation:

- Fast for signals (e.g., speech) that produce difference signals with large fluctuations
- Slow for signals (e.g., voiceband data, tones) that produce difference signals with small fluctuations

The speed of adaptation is controlled by a combination of fast and slow scale factors. The fast (unlocked) scale factor $y_u(k)$ is recursively computed in the base-2 logarithmic domain from the resultant logarithmic scale factor $y(k)$:

$$y_u(k) = (1 - 2^{-5})y(k) + 2^{-5} \, W[I(k)]$$

(note that $1.06 \leq y_u(k) \leq 10.00$), where the function $W[I(k)]$ is described by point specifications in the standard for 40, 32, 24, and 16 kbps; for example, see Figure 4.4.[2] The slow (locked) scale factor $y_l(k)$ is derived from $y_u(k)$ with a low pass-filter operation:

$$y_l(k) = (1 - 2^{-6})y_l(k - 1) + 2^{-6}y_u(k)$$

The fast and slow scale factors are then combined to form the scale factor:

$$y(k) = a_l(k)y_u(k - 1) + [1 - a_l(k)]y_l(k - 1)$$

($0 \leq a_l(k) \leq 1$ and is defined below)

Adaptation Speed Control

The controlling parameter $a_l(k)$ can assume values in the range [0, 1]. It tends toward unity for speech signals and toward zero for voiceband data signals. It is derived from a measure of the rate of change of the difference signal values.

$$d_{ms}(k) = (1 - 2^{-5})d_{ms}(k - 1) + 2^{-5}F[(I(k)]$$

$|I(k)|$	15	14	13	12	11	10	9	8
$W[I(k)]$	43.50	33.06	27.50	22.38	17.50	13.69	11.19	8.81

$|I(k)|$	7	6	5	4	3	2	1	0
$W[I(k)]$	6.25	3.63	2.56	2.50	2.44	1.50	0.88	0.88

Figure 4.4
Definition of $W[I(k)]$.

and

$$d_{ml}(k) = (1 - 2^{-7})d_{ml}(k - 1) + 2^{-7}\, F[(I(k)]$$

where the function $F[I(k)]$ is described by point specifications in the standard for 40, 32, 24, and 16 kbps; see Figure 4.5. $d_{ms}(k)$ is a relatively short-term average of $F[I(k)]$, and $d_{ml}(k)$ is a relatively long average of $F[I(k)]$. Using these averages, the variable $a_p(k)$ is defined as follows:

$$a_p(k) = \begin{cases} (1 - 2^{-4})a_p(k - 1) + 2^{-3} & \text{if } |d_{ms}(k) - d_{ml}(k)|^3 2^{-3}d_{ml}(k) \\ (1 - 2^{-4})a_p(k - 1) + 2^{-3} & \text{if } y(k) < 3 \\ (1 - 2^{-4})a_p(k - 1) + 2^{-3} & \text{if } t_d(k) = 1 \\ 1 & \text{if } t_r(k) = 1 \\ (1 - 2^{-4})a_p(k - 1), & \text{otherwise} \end{cases}$$

Thus, $a_p(k)$ tends toward the value 2 if the difference between $d_{ms}(k)$ and $d_{ml}(k)$ is large (average magnitude of $I[k]$ is changing) and $a_p(k)$ tends toward the value 0 if the difference is small (average magnitude of $I[k]$ relatively constant). $a_p(k)$ also tends toward 2 for idle channel (indicated by $y[k] < 3$) or partial band signals (indicated by $t_d[k] = 1$ as described below). Note that $a_p(k)$ is set to 1 upon detection of a partial band signal transition (indicated by $t_r[k] = 1$).

Given these definitions, one can obtain the value $a_l(k)$ referred to earlier, as follows:

$$a_l(k) = \begin{cases} 1, & \text{if } a_p(k - 1) > 1 \\ a_p(k - 1), & \text{if } a_p(k - 1)^2\, 1 \end{cases}$$

This asymmetrical limiting has the effect of delaying the start of a fast-to-slow state transition until the absolute value of $I(k)$ remains constant for some time. This tends to eliminate premature transitions for pulsed input signals such as switched carrier voiceband data.

Figure 4.5
$F[I(k)]$ for 40-
kbps ADPCM.

$|I(k)|$	15	14	13	12	11	10	9	8
$F[I(k)]$	6	6	5	4	3	2	1	1

$|I(k)|$	7	6	5	4	3	2	1	0
$F[I(k)]$	1	1	1	0	0	0	0	0

Adaptive Predictor and Reconstructure Signal Calculator

The primary function of the adaptive predictor is to compute the signal estimate $s_e(k)$ from the quantized difference signal $d_q(k)$. Two adaptive predictor structures are used, a sixth-order section that models zeros and a second-order section that models poles in the input signal. This dual structure caters to the variety of input signals that might be encountered. The signal estimate is computed as follows:

$$
\begin{aligned}
s_{ez}(k) = {} & b_1(k-1)d_q(k-1) + b_2(k-1)d_q(k-2) \\
& + b_3(k-1)d_q(k-3) + b_4(k-1)d_q(k-4) \\
& + b_5(k-1)d_q(k-5) + b_6(k-1)d_q(k-6).
\end{aligned}
$$

The reconstructed signal is defined as follows:

$$
s_r(k-i) = s_e(k-i) + d_q(k-i)
$$

Both sets of predictor coefficients are updated using a simplified gradient algorithm, one for the second-order predictor and one for the sixth-order predictor, as shown in the following:

Second-order predictor:

$$
a_1(k) = (1 - 2^{-8})a_1(k-1) + (3 \cdot 2^{-8})\, \text{sgn}\,[p(k)]\, \text{sgn}\,[p(k-1)],
$$

$$
\begin{aligned}
a_2(k) = {} & (1 - 2^{-7})a_2(k-1) + 2^{-7}\,\{\text{sgn}\,[p(k)]\text{sgn}\,[p(k-2)] \\
& -f[a_1(k-1)]\, \text{sgn}\,[p(k)]\, \text{sgn}\,[p(k-1)]\}
\end{aligned}
$$

where

$$
p(k) = d_q(k) + s_{ez}(k),
$$

$$
f(a_1) = \begin{cases} 4a_1, & |\,a_1\,| \le 2^{-1} \\ 2\,\text{sgn}\,(a_1), & |\,a_1\,| > 2^{-1} \end{cases}
$$

and sgn $[0] = 1$, except sgn $[p(k-i]$ is defined to be 0 only if $p(k-i) = 0$ and $i = 0$; with the stability constraints:

$$
|\,a_2(k)\,| \le 0.75 \text{ and } |\,a_1(k)\,| \le 1 - 2^{-4} - a_2(k)
$$

If $t_r(k) = 1$, then $a_1(k) = a_2(k) = 0$.

Sixth-order predictor:

$$b_i(k) = (1 - 2^{-8})b_i(k-1) + 2^{-7} \text{ sgn} [d_q(k)] \text{ sgn} [d_q(k-i)]$$

for $i = 1, 2, \ldots, 6$.

Tone and Transition Detector

In order to improve performance for signals originating from frequency shift keying (FSK) modems operating in the character mode, a two-step detection process is defined. First, partial band signal (e.g., tone) detection is invoked, so that the quantizer can be driven into the fast mode of adaptation:

$$t_d(k) = \begin{cases} 1, \text{ if } a_2(k) < -0.71875 \\ 0, \text{ otherwise} \end{cases}$$

In addition, a transition from a partial band ID defined so that the predictor coefficients can be set to zero and the quantizer can be forced into the fast mode of adaptation:

$$t_r(k) = \begin{cases} 1, \text{ if } a_2(k) < -0.71875 \text{ and } |d_q(k)| > 24 * 2y_l(k) \\ 0, \text{ otherwise} \end{cases}$$

4.4 ADPCM Decoder

Figure 4.6 is a block schematic of the decoder [3]. The key functions are:

- Inverse adaptive quantizer
- Quantizer scale factor adaptation
- Adaptation speed control
- Adaptive predictor and reconstructed signal calculator
- Tone and transition detector
- Output PCM format conversion (this block converts the reconstructed uniform PCM signal $s_r[k]$ into an *A*-law or µ-law PCM signal $s_p(k)$ as required)
- Synchronous coding adjustment, to prevent cumulative occurrences on synchronous tandem coding

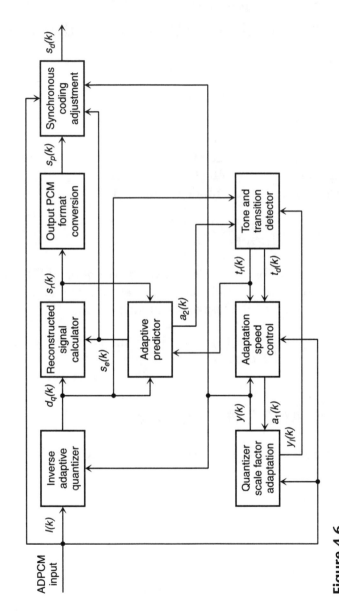

Figure 4.6
Decoder block schematic (ITU-T G.726).

132

4.5 G.727 Version of ADPCM

ITU-T G.727, 5-, 4-, 3-, and 2-bit Sample Embedded Adaptive Differential Pulse Code Modulation (ADPCM), contains the specification of an embedded ADPCM algorithm with 5, 4, 3, and 2 bits per sample. The recommendation describes the conversion of 64-kbps *A*-law or μ-law PCM channels to or from variable rate-embedded ADPCM channels. Applications where the encoder is aware and the decoder is not aware of the way in which the ADPCM code word bits have been altered, or when both the encoder and decoder are aware of the ways in which the code words are altered, or where neither the encoder nor the decoder are aware of the ways in which the bits have been altered, can benefit from other embedded ADPCM algorithms.

The embedded ADPCM algorithms specified here are extensions of the ADPCM algorithms defined in ITU-T recommendation G.726 and are recommended for use in packetized speech systems operating according to the Packetized Voice Protocol (PVP) specified in G.764. PVP is able to relieve congestion by modifying the size of a speech packet when the need arises. Utilizing the embedded property of the algorithm, the least significant bit(s) of each code word can be disregarded at packetization points and/or intermediate nodes to relieve congestion. This provides for significantly better performance than does dropping packets during congestion [4].

Embedded ADPCM algorithms are variable-bit-rate coding algorithms with the capacity of bit dropping outside the encoder and decoder blocks. They consist of a series of algorithms such that the decision levels of the lower-rate quantizers are subsets of the quantizer at the highest rate. This allows bit reductions at any point in the network without the need of coordination between the transmitter and the receiver. In contrast, the decision levels of the conventional ADPCM algorithms, such as those in recommendation G.726, are not subnets of one another; therefore, the transmitter must inform the receiver of the coding rate of the encoding algorithm [4].

Embedded algorithms can accommodate the unpredictable and bursty characteristics of traffic patterns that require congestion relief. Because congestion relief may occur after the encoding is performed, embedded coding is different from the variable-rate coding where the encoder and decoder must use the same number of bits in each sample. In both cases, the decoder must be told the number of bits to use in each sample.

Embedded algorithms produce code words that contain enhancement bits and core bits. The *feed-forward* (FF) path utilizes enhancement and core bits, while the *feedback* (FB) path uses core bits only. The inverse quantizer and the predictor of both the encoder and decoder use the core bits. With this structure, enhancement bits can be discarded or dropped during network congestion. However, the number of core bits in the FB paths of both the encoder and decoder must remain the same to avoid mistracking.

Also see Reference 2 for more discussion.

References

1. Bellcore. *Telecommunications Transmission Engineering*, vol. 2. Red Bank, NJ: Bellcore, 1990.
2. D. Minoli and E. Minoli. *Delivering Voice over IP Networks.* New York: Wiley, 1998.
3. ITU-T. 40, 32, 24, 16 kbps Adaptive Differential Pulse Code Modulation (ADPCM). Geneva, Switzerland, 1990.
4. ITU-T. 5-, 4-, 3-, and 2-bit Sample Embedded Adaptive Differential Pulse Code Modulation (ADPCM). Geneva, Switzerland, 1990.

Notes

[1] This section is based on the ITU-T G.726 recommendation. This material is for pedagogical purposes only. Developers, engineers, and readers requiring more information should acquire the recommendation directly from the ITU-T. The document is 57 pages long, small print.

[2] The factor $(1 - 2^{-5})$ introduces finite memory into the adaptive process so that the states of the encoder and decoder converge following transmission errors.

CHAPTER 5

Traditional Voice and Voice Signaling Systems

5.1 Introduction

This chapter provides background material in the area of voice switching and signaling. In particular, it covers central office and private branch exchange switching. Also, it covers general as well as T1 channel-associated signaling (CAS). This material is intended to help the discussion of the chapters that follow. In covering this material, the presentation contains more than a bare minimum treatment that might suffice for the rest of the text.

Switches[1] are a fundamental component of the telephone network. They allow a subscriber to connect with any remote subscriber on the network by specifying to the switch the address of the remote destination. The switch (and the subtending network) will then establish a temporary path to the destination, to enable information exchange. At a high level, a modern switch consists of (1) the switching matrix, (2) the common control, (3) subscriber line cards, (4) trunk line cards, and (5) maintenance channels. Switching matrix technology can be analog, including crossbar and reed relay systems, and digital, based on time division multiplexing techniques. Stored program control (SPC) methods allow the use of computer software to control the switching matrix, rather than performing this function in hardware, as was the case until the early

135

1960s. In the United States, the majority of switches are now digital, both in terms of the switching matrix and the control.

Signals are messages pertaining to call management generated by the user or by network elements. Signaling is the act of transferring this information among remote entities. Early switching systems employed signaling that consisted of DC levels. Later, between the 1930s and 1960s, single- and multiple-frequency tones were used, both in an in-band fashion (within the spectrum of the voice) and out of band (beyond the spectrum of the voice, but below 4000 Hz). Since the mid-1970s, signaling networks for *interoffice applications* have begun to employ a separate dedicated data communications network, where this could be proved in economically; here the signaling is both *out of band* and over a *common channel*[2] (common channel signaling is becoming critical for the provision of advanced services). On the *user-to-network side*, there has been a movement toward formal signaling methods, notably Q.931 for ISDN, Q.933 for frame relay, and Q.2931 for ATM. Many PBXs today use T1-based ABCD signaling, although ISDN Primary Rate Interfaces may eventual prevail. These PBX signaling methods will have to be supported by voice over data networks hardware.

The rest of this chapter addresses these issues in more detail.

5.2 Voice Switching Systems

Brief Introduction to Switching Technology

The public switched telephone network (PSTN) is designed so that any user can be directly connected to any other user on the network. In order to achieve these connections in an economical and practical way, switching systems (switches) are used. Switching systems are designed to concentrate many users onto relatively few distribution paths and to provide a connection over the distribution path to the destination called party. The terms *concentration, distribution*, and *expansion* relate to functions that must be performed in order to connect any inlet over a path to any outlet. A circuit-switched (voice) call comprises three formal phases. These phases are carried out through the services of the switch. The phases occur in the following order: *call request, information transfer*, and *call clearing.* These call phases that are to be supported by the switch are defined as follows:

- *Call request phase:* A call with specific parameters is requested by the calling party. This call request is processed by and routed through the network, unless it cannot be accepted by the network. The request is then delivered to and processed by the called party. Acceptance of the call is reported by the calling party, unless this party does not accept the call. Final arrangements are made through the network for that call. The call confirmation is returned to the calling party.
- *Information transfer phase:* Voice and voiceband information can be exchanged between calling and called parties in accordance with the characteristics of the applicable call type.
- *Call clearing phase:* Any network or party involved in a call has the ability to clear that call in any phase of the call. At the time a call is cleared, any network involved in the call would immediately abort the current phase and report the call clearing to the adjacent network or party, unless they were already informed of that clearing. Once call clearing is completed, any resource used for that call can be reused by the network for other calls.

Common Control

Telephone switches now employ *common control*. A common control system can determine the existence of a path through the switching matrix, for connecting available inlets and outlets, before actually trying to commit resources for the path between them. This activity is in support of the call phases just described. In this environment, the system control can, if desired, look ahead to the output switching resources of the switch; this avoids tying up machine resources and paths for an outlet (destination) that may already be busy. The common control works in conjunction with a connection-switching matrix (analog or digital). The control can be assigned to an incoming call as required. It takes in the dialed digits and then sets up the path through the switching matrix according to stored program rules. These rules provide for variation in the handling of local and long distance calls, for choosing an alternate route for an interoffice call in case the first route chosen is busy, and for trying the call again automatically in cases of blocking or faults in the switching path, for both interoffice and intraoffice calls.

Figure 5.1 depicts some internals of a common control/stored program control switch. It is representative of a switch such as Lucent's #2 ESS. More modern switches (like AT&T's #5 ESS) have a distributed architecture that places some of the functions (if needed) in remote switching modules.

Space Division Switching

Space division switching was originally developed for the analog environment and has been carried over into digital technology by a number of manufacturers of early digital equipment, since the fundamental switching principles are the same whether the switch is used to carry analog or digital signals. A space division switch is one in which the signal paths are physically separate from one another (*divided*, i.e., separated in space). Each connection requires the establishment of a physical path through the switch that is dedicated to the transfer of signals between the two endpoints. The basic module of this type of switch is a metallic crosspoint or semiconductor gate that can be enabled and disabled by a control unit.

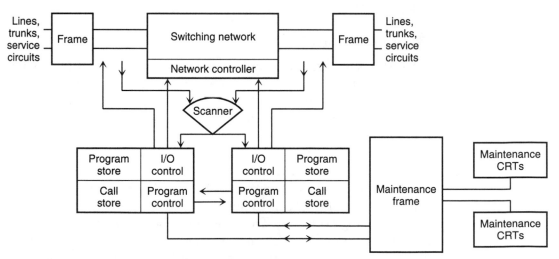

Figure 5.1
Common control/SPC switch.

To establish a path in a single-stage network, it is only necessary to enable the gate.

This space switching methodology has a number of limitations:

1. The number of crosspoints grows with the square of the number of input ports N; this can be costly for large N and results in high capacitive loading on any message path.
2. The crosspoints are inefficiently utilized (at most, N out of N^2).
3. The loss of a crosspoint prevents connection between the two devices involved.

(The failure described in point 3 would generally not be seen by an end user, unless the user was actually engaged in a conversation at the time of the failure.)

To ameliorate these limitations, multiple-stage switches are employed. N input lines are broken up into N/m groups of m lines. Each group of lines goes into a first-stage matrix. The outputs of the first-stage matrices become inputs to a group of second-stage matrices, and so on. The last stage has N outputs; thus each device attaches its input line to the first stage and its output line to the last stage. One has j second-stage matrices, each with N/m inputs and N/m outputs. The number of second-stage matrices is a design decision. Each first-stage matrix has j outlets so that it connects to all second-stage matrices. Each second-stage matrix has N/m outputs so that it connects to all third-stage matrices. See Figure 5.2 as an example. In a multistage network, a free path through all the stages must be determined and the appropriate gates enabled.

As indicated in point 2 above, a direct crosspoint matrix to interconnect 100 inlets to 100 outlets would require 10,000 crosspoints. Figure 5.2 shows that 3000 crosspoints are sufficient in the multistage arrangement shown (there are $10 \times 10 = 100$ crosspoints in each of the ten building blocks in each of the three stages, for a total of 3000).

While a multistage network requires a more complex control scheme, this arrangement has the following advantages over a single-stage matrix:

1. The number of crosspoints is reduced, increasing crossbar utilization.

Figure 5.2
A multiple-stage switch (example). Note: In general, given modules of i *(*i = N/m*) inlets, it will require* 2i − 1 *(i.e.,* 2N/m − 1*) midstage modules to achieve non-blocking. However, fewer midstages may be employed. In this example, 19 midstages lead to nonblocking.*

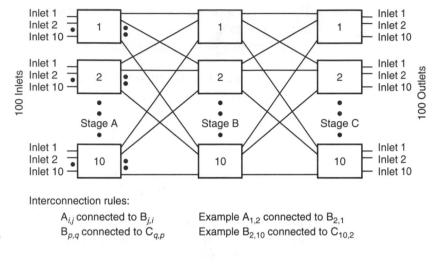

Interconnection rules:

$A_{i,j}$ connected to $B_{j,i}$ Example $A_{1,2}$ connected to $B_{2,1}$
$B_{p,q}$ connected to $C_{q,p}$ Example $B_{2,10}$ connected to $C_{10,2}$

2. There is more than one path through the network to connect two endpoints, increasing reliability.

Crossbar switches are electromechanical space division switching devices that make connections in a telephone system by moving parts. The first major crossbar switching system (No. 1 Crossbar) was introduced in 1938. Some electromechanical crossbar switching was still in use in the United States, and it is common in other parts of the world. As the name suggests, a lattice of crossed bars is involved. Each vertical bar carries a set of contacts that are connected to those carried on a horizontal bar when magnets are activated to move the two bars. Contact is made where the two bars cross—hence the name *crossbar.* Its contacts will latch; that is, they will stay attached after the magnets are deactivated, and contacts can be made elsewhere by the other bars. Of course, when the communication is over, the contacts can be disconnected.

Time Division Switching

With the advent of digitized voice (particularly PCM) and synchronous time division multiplexing techniques, both voice and data can be transmitted using digital signals. This has led to a major change in the design and technology of switching systems. Modern digital systems rely on computerized control of space and time division elements.

Voice switches manufactured today use digital time division techniques for establishing and maintaining communication paths and are based on the use of synchronous time division multiplexing (TDM). Time division switching involves the partitioning of a lower-speed bit stream into pieces that share a higher-speed stream with other bit streams. The slots are manipulated by control logic to route information from input to output. Synchronous TDM permits multiple low-speed bit streams to share a high-speed line. A set of inputs is sampled in turn. The samples are organized serially into slots to form a recurring frame of N slots. A slot may be a bit, a byte, or a larger block. In synchronous TDM, the source and destination of the information in each timeslot are known. Therefore, there is no need for address bits in each slot. There is interest, however, in using ATM techniques at least at the trunking level to achieve statistical gain in transport (the internals of the voice switch, however, would continue to be TDM-based, at least until such time as PCM methods are used in the PSTN rather than some other compression technique, such as described in Chapter 8).

Three methodologies are employed in time division switching, which are described next [1].

TDM Bus Switching

In this arrangement, all lines are connected to a bus. Time on the bus is divided into slots. A path is created between two lines by assigning repetitive timeslots. This is the simplest form of time division switching. The size of the switch is limited by the data rate on the bus. This architecture is common for small and medium-sized PBXs. PBXs are customer premises equipment (CPE)-based switches for intrapremises voice communication; they also provide user access to the public network. (PBXs are treated in more detail later in the chapter.) Each input line deposits data in a buffer; the multiplexer scans these buffers sequentially, taking fixed-size groups of data from each buffer and sending them out on the line. One complete scan produces one frame of data. For output to the lines, the reverse operation is performed, with the multiplexer filling the output line buffers one by one.

Timeslot Interchange (TSI)

In this arrangement, all lines are connected to a synchronous TDM multiplexer and a synchronous TDM demultiplexer. A path is created by the interchange of timeslots within a time division multiplexed frame. The size of the switch is limited by the speed of the control memory. TSI can be used as a building block in multistage switches. A TSI unit operates on a synchronous TDM stream of timeslots, or channels, by interchanging pairs of slots to achieve full-duplex operation. See Figure 5.3. The input lines of N devices are passed through a synchronous time division multiplexer to produce a TDM stream with N slots. To achieve the interconnection of two devices, the slots corresponding to the two inputs are interchanged; the resulting stream is demultiplexed to the outputs of the N devices. This results in a full-duplex connection between pairs of lines. A real-time data store, whose width equals one timeslot of data and whose length equals the number of slots in a frame, is used. An incoming TDM frame is written sequentially, slot by slot, into the data store. An outgoing TDM frame is created by reading slots from memory in an order dictated by an address store that reflects the existing connections.

TSI is a simple way of switching TDM information. However, the size of such a switch, in terms of number of connections, is limited by the memory access speed. In order to keep pace with the

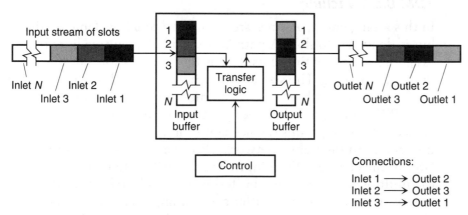

Figure 5.3
Timeslot interchange.

input, data must be read into and out of memory as fast as it arrives. So, for example, if 12 sources are operating at 64 kbps each and the slot size is 8 bits, the arrival rate would be 96,000 slots per second. For each timeslot, both a read and a write are required. In this example, memory access time would need to be $1/(96,000 \times 2)$ seconds, or about 5.2 ms. A TSI unit can support only a limited number of connections. Also, as the size of the unit increases, for a fixed access speed, the delay at the TSI unit increases.

Time Multiplex Switching (TMS)

This arrangement is a form of space division switching in which each input line is a TDM stream. The switching configuration may change for each timeslot. It is used in conjunction with TSI units to form multistage switches. A small increase in delay is caused by the use of multiple stages, but this allows much larger capacity. To work around the bandwidth and delay problems of TSI, multiple TSI units must be used. To connect a channel on one TDM stream (going into one TSI) to a channel on another TDM stream (going into another TSI), some form of interconnection of the TSI units is needed. The purpose of the interconnection is to allow a slot in one TDM stream to be interchanged with a slot in another TDM stream. Multiple-stage networks can be built up by concatenating TMS and TSI stages. TMS stages, which move slots from one stream to another, are referred to as S (space), and TSI stages are referred to as T (time). See Figure 5.4.

This discussion should make it clear that current voice switches are ill equipped to handle sub-DS0 voice applications.

5.3 Loop Plant Switch Interfaces

There is a need to effectively interconnect the multitude of end-user loops to a switch. This is done via *digital loop carriers*. A remote device will aggregate loops in a *carrier serving area* (CSA) and deliver them, multiplexed, over a physical link. Today that link is generally fiber-based, and the central office demultiplexing terminal is built into the switch.

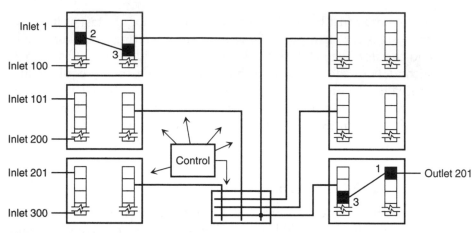

Figure 5.4
Time-space-time switching.

Overview

Bellcore Technical Reference TR-TSY-00303 (referred to in the telecom industry as TR-303) defines a set of generic interface requirements that permit digital switches from one vendor to interface with access systems (such as digital loop carriers or hybrid fiber/coax residential broadband systems) from another vendor.[3] See Figure 5.5. TR-08, the previous generic interface standard, was designed to support the installed base of existing access equipment. In contrast, TR-303 is a modern interface, designed to support the full range of services and operations capabilities typical of modern access systems.

Figure 5.5
TR-303 defines a generic interface that ensures flexible and economical integration of a digital switch and a remote digital terminal.

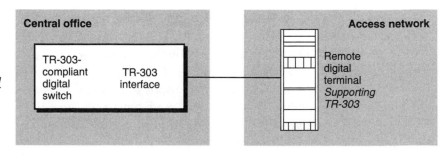

TR-08 opened the door to multivendor capability and greater flexibility in telecom networks. In turn, TR-303 delivers significant advantages over TR-08 (see Table 5.1). Technology developers make the case that more flexible networking, more efficient concentration, distributed network intelligence, improved OAM&P (operations, administration, maintenance, and provisioning), and support for ISDN and other next-generation capabilities promise an improvement in network planning ease, performance, and cost efficiency for carriers. TR-303 is being positioned by developers as an enhancement that allows service providers to deliver voice, data, and multimedia capabilities over a single common feeder-plant facility. With TR-303, network providers can address residential broadband and narrowband telephony service needs. This issue is important to voice over frame and ATM because it is expected that ATM switch vendors implement this interface.

Interface Description

TR-08 was originally designed to support the large installed base of access devices that populated the telecom landscape in the early

Table 5.1 TR-303 versus TR-08 at a Glance

TR-303	*TR-08*
Large concentration groups—2048 lines/668 DS0 channels per group, for a 3:1 ratio; engineerable ratios of up to 9:1.	Relatively small concentration groups—48 lines/ 24 DS0 channels per group, for a maximum 2:1 ratio.
Enhanced data link and signaling capability, with standard Open Systems Interconnection (OSI) protocols and separate links for call control and OAM&P.	No dedicated data link or signaling capability.
64 kbps available for both call-control messages and remote OAM&P.	1.2 kbps for call-control messages; 0.4 kbps for remote OAM&P.
Supports a wide range of advanced services, including ISDN and wideband (DS1).	No ISDN or wideband support; limited support for other advanced services.
Supports remote provisioning for numerous services, including ISDN.	No remote provisioning.
Supports extensive remote maintenance and testing.	Limited remote maintenance/testing.
Supports sophisticated remote surveillance, including comprehensive event reporting and filtering.	Limited event reporting only. No filtering capability.

1980s. In line with the limited intelligence in access network devices of the era, TR-08 supported a limited number of configurations, services, and remote capabilities. In contrast, TR-303 was designed from the ground up to provide the flexibility and bandwidth required by evolving telecommunications systems. It supports a spectrum of features such as ISDN, dynamic timeslot interchange for concentration and remote provisioning, as well as useful maintenance, testing, and surveillance capabilities.

Figure 5.6 shows the basic architecture assumed by TR-303. An integrated digital loop carrier (IDLC) system consists of a remote digital terminal (RDT) located in the outside plant and an integrated digital terminal (IDT) located in the switch. Figure 5.6 also shows that segment of the access network governed by TR-303. The local digital switch (LDS) is the switching system located in the central office that provides switched services—such as Plain Old Telephone Service (POTS)—to subscriber lines on one or more RDTs. The IDT is the switch resource used to manage and support a single RDT. The IDT interfaces with the RDT to coordinate OAM&P functions of the RDT, including facility terminations, control data links, and other functions. The RDT is a network element in an access system located in the outside plant or at a customer site. The RDT's main function is to multiplex traffic from a number of subscriber line interfaces onto a high-speed transmission facility for transport to the central office and vice versa. TR-303 defines a maximum of 2048 access lines per RDT.

The TR-303 interface is composed of up to 28 DS1 facilities (see Figure 5.7). Most of them carry end-user traffic between the IDT at the central office and the RDT. However, two of these DS1 facilities carry data link control channels (for both primary signaling and protection). The first facility carries the primary embedded

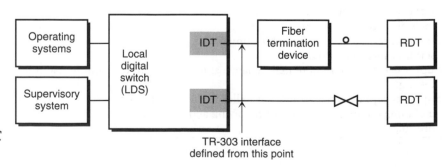

Figure 5.6
The TR-303 IDLC basic architecture.

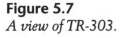

Figure 5.7
A view of TR-303.

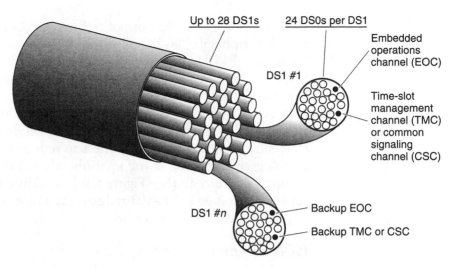

operations channel (EOC) and the primary signaling channel in DS0 channels 12 and 24, respectively. The EOC channel carries all OAM&P-related messaging, while the signaling channel is responsible for call processing and supervision messaging. The signaling channel can consist of either the timeslot management channel (TMC) or the common signaling channel (CSC). A separate DS1 facility is used to carry the redundant EOC and TMC/CSC in a hot-spare configuration.

TR-303 requirements for IDLC systems specify two signaling options: hybrid signaling and out-of-band signaling. The hybrid signaling method uses ABC&D robbed-bit signaling (RBS) for call supervision and the timeslot management channel for timeslot assignment. The out-of-band signaling method uses the common signaling channel for both call supervision and timeslot assignment (signaling is covered in more detail in the next section).

TR-303 Economic Benefits

The economic advantages of the TR-303 interfaces derive from three main factors: larger concentration groups, inherent ISDN support, and comprehensive OAM&P capabilities.

Larger Concentration Groups

TR-303 interfaces deliver direct equipment savings over TR-08-based networks by supporting larger concentration groups to effectively carry a specific amount of traffic over fewer facilities and switch peripherals. TR-303 allows 2048 DS0 subscriber lines coming into an RDT to be mapped into as many as 668 DS0 channels. See Figure 5.8. While TR-08 systems have a maximum concentration ratio of 2:1, TR-303 systems can achieve concentration ratios as high as 9:1 with normal traffic levels, using facilities far more efficiently while maintaining typical grade-of-service parameters. Large concentration groups enable carriers to reduce DS1 interfaces by up to 80 percent and both switch peripherals and network interfaces by up to 75 percent. (See Figure 5.9.) In addition, the greater line capacity specified in TR-303 reduces the number of RDTs required to provide service in a given area.

ISDN Equipment Savings

TR-303 specifies the signaling and OAM&P capabilities needed to support ISDN. This eliminates the costly TR-08 workarounds that require extra switch peripherals. For ISDN, TR-303 supports B-channel concentration and provides a special multiplexing scheme that allows a 4:1 decrease in the bandwidth required to carry D-channels. The target market for these ISDN services is residential Internet access.

Operations Expense Reduction

TR-08 was based on technologies developed almost three decades ago and assumes a very simple remote terminal with no built-in

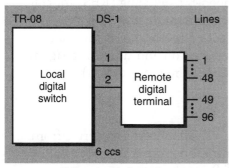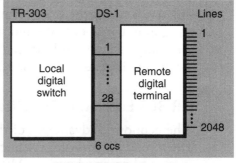

Figure 5.8
The TR-303 specification supports larger line concentration groups while maintaining grade of service.

Figure 5.9
With TR-303's greater concentration capacities versus TR-08, the greater the line size, the more DS-1 facilities are saved.

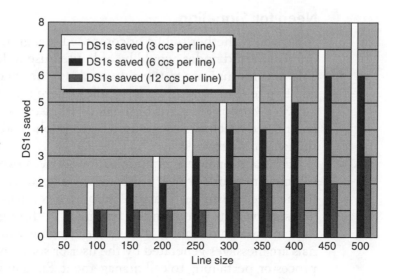

intelligence. In contrast, TR-303 assumes a high degree of intelligence in the remotes. TR-303 supports remote provisioning; for example, card parameters can be automatically downloaded from the particular operations system in question, typically eliminating the need for remote site visits to plug in the correct circuit card and/or manually set the appropriate options. TR-303 simplifies RDT administration, because its remote provisioning capabilities allow line cards to be installed in the RDT without restriction on slot location or service type. The large concentration groups reduce the recurring engineering and traffic monitoring (for load balancing) activities required with multiple, small concentration groups. TR-303 supports remote maintenance and testing, allowing faults to be remotely verified and isolated. TR-303 also delivers more precise surveillance capability than TR-08; unlike the binary event reports of TR-08, TR-303 reports contain a great deal of information about the nature and service impact of an event.

Ultimately (by 2005?), a new version of TR-303 *could* support compressed voice over IP, for the ultimate concentration and SNMP/CMIP capabilities for network management.

5.4 Signaling

This section focuses on the important issue of signaling.

Need for Signaling

A network, whether public or composed of a group of privately interconnected nodes, would be of limited use unless the user is able to communicate to the network his or her needs for service. In addition to this user-network signaling, there is a need for signaling between various elements of the network itself. Signaling systems and related mechanisms are used by all public and private telecommunications networks.

For traditional telecommunication services over the public switched network or over a private voice network, signaling refers to the mechanism necessary to establish a connection, to monitor and supervise its status, and to terminate it, through the transmission and switching fabric of the underlying network. Formally, signals are messages generated by the user or some internal network processor, pertaining to call management. Signaling is the function of transferring this information among remote entities. The *signaling network* is the collection of physical transport facilities, which carry the signals. The signaling equipment performs the functions of alerting, addressing, supervising, and providing status in both private and common carrier networks. Methods and technology supporting voice over data networks must successfully address signaling issues if PBXs and/or public switches are to be supported. PBXs are gateways to the local users; central office switches are gateways to the world.

Even early networks had some kind of signaling. For example, in the early days of telephony (1880s to 1900s) a ringer with a crank attached to the telephone set was used to inform a central human processor—the operator—that the user wanted some service; the operator would orally obtain instructions from the user—typically a destination name—and then proceeded manually to render the required service by electrically connecting the two parties. Eventually this human switch was replaced by an automatic switch. In this environment the user would inform the system that he or she required a connection to a local party by lifting the handset, while the destination address was coded by way of the dialed number. Long-distance service, however, continued to be manual with respect to addressing and connection until the introduction of direct distance dialing (DDD) in the early 1950s.

Traditionally, POTS consisted of establishing an end-to-end transparent path between the user and some remote party (circuit switching). Recently, more sophisticated services have emerged (800/888 service, credit card calling, remote call forwarding, and 500 service, to list a few public services). In the future, a host of new services will begin to emerge and be available, both in the public network as well as from privately configured networks. Today, a network totally dedicated to signaling is being deployed for the PSTN: the Common Channel Signaling System No. 7 network.

Signaling Functions

Signals can be classified by three methods: *topologically*, in the sense of where (or to what types of facilities) they apply; *functionally*, in the sense of what they are intended to do; and *physically*, in the sense of an actual network implementation.

The topological category includes:

- *Customer line signaling:* Interaction between the customer and the switching system serving that customer.
- *Interoffice trunk signaling:* Exchange of call-handling information between switching processors in the network.

The functional category includes:

- *Supervising:* Monitoring the status of a line or circuit to determine its state (busy, idle, etc.). In a metallic loop, supervisory signals are indicated by the on-hook/off-hook status of the loop. These supervisory signals allow designated equipment at the central office or at the CPE switch to recognize origination and termination of a call. Often, loops are implemented over IDLCs (say, connected to the switch over TR-303); hence, a way to interwork the two signaling domains—traditional (i.e., metallic) and T1-based—is needed. Some PBXs still support traditional line-side signaling.
- *Addressing:* Transmitting routing and destination signals over the network. These signals are generally dial pulses and tone pulses over local loops and trunks. More recently, with common channel interoffice signaling, these signals can also be data streams over the associated signaling links.

- *Alerting:* Advising the addressee of the arrival of an incoming call. Ringer currents can be used to drive audible bells, tones, and/or lights.

The physical category includes:

- *In-band signaling:* In addition to traditional residential loops, we include here channel-associated signaling for T1 links.
- *In facility but out of band:* For example, Basic Rate Interface or Primary Rate Interface in ISDN, where the D- (delta) channel is carried in the same facility but in a separate logical channel[4] (this is also called *common channel signaling* in ATMF documents).
- *Out of band:* For example, over Common Channel Signaling System No. 7.

Table 5.2 provides a summary of signaling environments in the public switched network [2].

Table 5.2   Signaling, a Perspective

Functional perspective
Supervision Addressing
Topological perspective
Customer loop Interoffice trunks Special services (including PBX trunks and tie lines)
Signaling systems
Facility dependent
DC Out of band (e.g., obsolete *N*1 carrier) Digital (T1 CAS)
Facility independent

In-band tones
    Single frequency (SF)—supervision, addressing, or both
    Multifrequency (MF)—addressing over interoffice trunks
    Dual-tone multifrequency (DTMF)—addressing in POTS customer loop
Functional signaling (ISDN customer loop)
Common Channel Signaling System No. 7

Functional versus Stimulus Signaling

This signaling method implied by the audible tones is geared to communication with humans. When computer equipment started to be connected to the plant in the mid-1960s, it had to "learn" to "hear" ring tones, busy tones, and so forth. The reception of tones implies what is called *stimulus signaling*, whereby actions have to be deduced from certain stimuli—for example, a current flowing or a tone that is present for a length of time. Functional signaling allows a data packet to be passed back to the computer with a coded message that explains what happened or is happening to a call, rather than having to rely on tones.

In *functional signaling*, a device is instructed what to do by a data packet, which actually contains the instructions in message form. Common channel signaling (CCS), discussed below, provides another example of functional signaling. In functional signaling, appropriate interconnection rules and procedures that allow two entities to exchange information must be defined by a formal protocol, rather than by electrical/acoustical levels. Obviously, a voice system ultimately requires that a signaling protocol with the user exist, using tones. However, under functional signaling, the entire system can operate with data messages, which are then converted to a tone at the point closest to the user, *if the user is human*. This can be done as far away from the network as the phone set; the set may receive a data packet that instructs it to apply a locally generated busy tone, or a dial tone, or the like.

Functional signaling has existed for years in (packet) data networks; since the mid-1980s it is being incorporated in the telecommunications environment. Only with functional signaling of the type specified in Q.931 [3], complemented with appropriate application-level messages, can advanced, new datacom/telecom services be realized. ABC&D signaling used in DS1 lines is a hybrid: it is not a stimulus method, nor is it a totally functional method whereby complex messages are composed by the CPE (e.g., an ISDN SETUP message) and sent across the interface. Instead, 16 states (b1b2b3b4) are indicated via the exchange of 4-bit code words.[5]

In-Band and Out-of-Band Signaling

Traditional in-band signaling places supervisory and address instructions in the same stream as the actual user information. The signaling is not independent of the voice channel itself: not only is there the possibility of unwanted interaction between the two (called a *talk-off*, where the voice signal becomes confused with signaling tones and can cause a disconnect), but there is also the possibility of fraud [4]. (When the user's voice contains enough vocal energy at 2600 Hz to actuate the tone-detecting circuits in the signaling set, interference will occur—people with high-pitched voices may encounter this problem.) For data applications, in-band signaling has been a nuisance: Equipment (modems, in particular) had to be engineered to avoid certain portions of the spectrum where various signaling tones are placed. The one-to-one relationship between information channel and supervisory channel meant the provision of a signaling mechanism for every voice channel; because of the required number, such a mechanism has to be simple and inexpensive. In turn, this leads to an inflexible system implementation and low signaling capacity in terms of supervisory interexchanges, and it is expensive to evolve in parallel with network technology and architecture.

Another problem is known as *glare*. It occurs when both ends of a circuit are seized, as a result of propagation and processing delays. The way around this problem is to use one-way signaling on trunks; however, on small trunk groups this solution is uneconomical. When glare occurs, the equipment is unable to complete the connection; the circuit must time out (which is quite inefficient) and a reorder (fast busy tone to indicate equipment or trunk unavailability) is issued to the user [5]. Glare can affect some CPE networks—notably, privately networked PBXs that use traditional tie-line technology. (Glare is also possible with out-of-band and/or common channel systems, but is more prevalent with in-band signaling.) This issue affects ATM-to-ISDN interworking, as noted in Chapter 10.

Table 5.3 summarizes the signaling methods of interest in voice over data networks environments.

Traditional Signaling Mechanisms

Signaling occurs on the trunk and on the loop side. This section addresses both aspects.

Trunk Side

Trunk signaling[6] (i.e., per-trunk signaling between switches) for the public telephone network occurs in four ways (as contrasted to common channel signaling, discussed below; see Figure 5.10):

Table 5.3 **Signaling Methods Relevant to Voice over Data**

T1/E1 Signaling

Channel-associated signaling (CAS, see below)
Common channel signaling (CCS, see below)
Proprietary systems

Channel-Associated Signaling (CAS)

Uses some of the bits in each of the 125-μs multiframes to transmit signaling
  information.
Supervision is sent using channel-associated signaling.
Address information is sent as PCM-encoded tone signaling
  DTMF
  MF

Common Channel Signaling (CCS)

Signaling information for all of the channels is transmitted on a separate time
  slot.
Supervision and address information may be sent using CCS.
Implementation examples:
  E1—32 channels at 64 kbps
  ISDN (2B+D) or 23B+D)
  CCSS7—the CCS par excellence

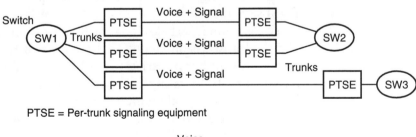

PTSE = Per-trunk signaling equipment

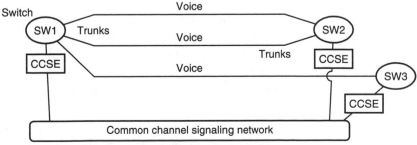

CCSE = Common channel signaling equipment

Figure 5.10
*Per-trunk versus
common channel
signaling.*

- DC (direct current) signaling
- In-band pulse signaling
- Out-of-band pulse signaling
- Internal digital signaling, such as the T1 signaling mechanism

DC Signaling   DC signaling is accomplished through the use of two electrical states called *on-hook* and *off-hook*.* A third state may sometimes exist as a transition state. In a DC signaling arrangement, the supervisory or address signaling is done by superimposing one or more DC states on the same conductors that are used for voice transmission. There are currently two types of per-circuit in-band trunk supervisory signaling methods: loop reverse battery (based on subscriber line signaling methods) and E&M signaling.

The first method is applicable to trunks that require call origination/seizure at only one end (one-way trunks—for example, direct outward dialing trunks). The method employs open and closure signals from the originating end, and reversal of battery/ground from the terminating end. At the originating end, on-hook is indicated by an open circuit, and off-hook by a bridged circuit. At the terminating end, on-hook is indicated by a ground on the tip lead and −48 V on the ring lead of the circuit, and off-hook is indicated by −48 V on the tip lead and ground on the ring lead [6].

On two-way trunks (call origination possible at both ends), E&M signaling is required. The E&M interface has been one of the most common interfaces for signaling between a switching system and the transmission facility that connects it to another switching system. A number of variations of E&M signaling exist. The Regional Bell Operating Companies (RBOCs) have standardized four E&M lead signaling interfaces arrangements and have tentatively standardized a fifth. The three types used in the United States are known as Type I, Type II, and Type III. The basic method (Type I) provides for signaling from the switch toward the transmission facility over the M-lead by presenting a ground (0 V) for on-hook and −48 V for off-hook. The signaling from the transmission facility to the switch occurs over the E-lead, with an open circuit for on-hook, and ground for off-hook [6].

*Although this method is still used on the line side, it is no longer employed, at the practical level, on the trunk side. Note, however, that PBXs-to-public-network interfaces use line-side signaling.

DC signaling for *interoffice applications* has been reduced in an evolution involving first AC signaling and then common channel signaling. In interoffice applications it is relatively easy to upgrade the signaling: It only necessitates replacing the old signaling equipment at two ends with new signaling equipment (two pieces of equipment).

AC Signaling   Carrier systems started to appear in the early 1920s, typically in the trunk side of the telephone system; *carrier* refers to the multiplexing of several channels over a single transmission system. Digital loop carriers are now prevalent in the local loop plant (but naturally now use modern signaling methods). A 1000-Hz tone interrupted 20 times a second was initially used to convey signaling information [7]. The use of this single-frequency tone for signaling is called *single-frequency* (SF) signaling. Automatic switching machines were widely deployed in the 1920s and 1930s, putting an end to operator-established local calling. Automatic local dial spread fairly rapidly by the early 1940s. However, all toll calls were placed by operators until the 1950s. Originally it took from 1 to 7 minutes to establish a call; a need for faster processing was the driving factor for the introduction of direct distance dialing (DDD). DDD service began in 1951 and spread fairly rapidly; by 1960 over 50 percent of the users had this capability. DDD was generally available by the late 1960s.

Single frequency eventually utilized a 2600-Hz tone. SF can provide both supervisory and dial-pulse addressing. Since a single frequency is available (on-hook being presence of tone, and off-hook absence of tone), addressing must be exchanged by pulse-type interruption of the signal (one interruption represents the digit 1, two interruptions represent the digit 2, and so on). This interruption process is slow, with ten interruptions a second being the maximum speed. Also, time delays must be allocated for tone recognition, to allow for distortion caused by facility noise or transmission degradation, and to prevent false signaling possibly introduced by talk-off (interference with speech) [2].

N-carrier analog systems for short-haul applications were introduced in the late 1940s and 1950s. Some continued to be deployed in the early 1960s. In the initial design, a tone at 3700 Hz was used for signaling; this out-of-band tone provided complete protection against talk-off. Later, in some *N*-carrier systems, in addition to single-frequency supervision, multifrequency (MF) address signals were sent by a selection of two frequencies in the range from 700 to 1700 Hz [7]. This technology is obsolete, but it is mentioned here as an example of out-of-band signaling.

Multifrequency pulses convert addressing digits (initially input by the subscriber, in most applications) by coding them with combinations of two-out-of-six fixed frequencies between 700 and 1700 Hz. The six frequencies are 700, 900, 1100, 1300, 1500, and 1700 Hz. Fifteen combinations are possible when picking two items out of six: ten combinations are for the digits and five combinations are used for auxiliary status codes. For example, the digit 1 is coded by a 700- plus a 900-Hz tone, the digit 2 is coded by a 700- plus an 1100-Hz tone, and so on. MF is used only for interoffice signaling. MF signals are used for called number address signaling, calling number identification, ring-back, and coin control [6]. Digits are sent on interoffice trunks at the rate of *seven digits per second*, compared to dual-tone multifrequency (DTMF), used for addressing in customer loops (as discussed in the next section), and SF signaling, both of which are transmitted at a lower speed. (DTMF signaling over the local loop takes place at a lower speed due to the potentially noisy condition of the loop.) Therefore, MF signaling used for addressing, in the process of setting up a call, requires substantially less time than would be required with SF signaling. It should be noted that MF tones do not encounter the talk-off problem (so that special selection of the frequencies was not critical), since voice transmission from the calling party is inhibited during MF signaling.

Signaling on Digital Systems   Digital carrier systems (notably T1s) have used a different type of signaling, involving *framing* and *VF robbed bits* (also called CAS) to achieve the desired signaling. Appropriately configured line cards on the carrier equipment (and now on PBXs) have provided the necessary interface between the digital signaling method internal to the carrier equipment and other types of signaling external to the carrier system. These line cards have also provided for special signaling arrangements required for special services applications. This topic is treated in Section 5.5.

Loop Side

Subscriber Line Signaling over Metallic Facilities   At present, the largest majority of local loops (for residential applications) still involve a metallic segment. The feeder portion has employed carrier for a number of years and is now being complemented with fiber, but the distribution plant (the segment of the plant closest to the user) has continued to use copper because of the requirement of the installed phone sets to employ DC signaling. (The only exception has been for large commercial customers, for which fiber local loops have been installed to provide the appropriate bandwidth.)

DC signaling is mandated not by the fact that the transmission facility is metallic, but by the fact that the receiving station can operate only with DC signaling. To upgrade signaling on the local loop would require replacing equipment for a large number of customers (approximately 100,000,000 in the United States). This is fairly expensive and may occur only gradually under ISDN, if the customer can be induced to buy a new phone set in exchange for the ability to obtain new services.

With DC signaling, taking the phone off the hook closes the electrical path between the tip and ring leads, allowing current to flow. This arrangement is also called *loop start* and is indeed used on all subscriber loops that terminate in actual phone sets. Metallic loop signaling provides for continuous application of a direct current voltage, nominally at 48 V, from a power supply (referred to as a *battery*), together with a current-sensing mechanism at the central office (or carrier system). When the loop is implemented on a carrier feeder system, the user's station equipment is connected by a pair of wires to the carrier's remote terminal (near the user), rather than to the CO; it is the responsibility of the carrier system to provide for the metallic loop signaling protocol. It should be noted that, in these digital loop carrier applications, the switch will employ metallic loop signaling to the CO-based carrier terminal; the terminal will convert the signaling into internal digital signaling and reconvert it to DC signaling in the proximity of the user [2].

When coded with dial pulses, the address information consists of short, on-hook pulses occurring as interruptions in the normal off-hook loop supervision current, at a rate of ten pulses per second; the number of dial pulses in a stream equals the value of the intended addressing digits (ten pulses, by exception, signals the number 0). This loop signaling technique is clearly slow.

DTMF   The addressing portion of the signaling handshake between the user station and the switch uses either dial pulses or DTMF. (The supervisory portion of the loop signaling over the distribution plant will continue to use DC, until the deployment of ISDN.) In the latter case, translation equipment is required at the CO switch to convert the tones to interoffice addressing signals. All modern switches are capable of receiving DTMF. Addressing signals are in turn transmitted over interoffice trunks as SF dial pulses, MF codes, or common channel signals.

Push-button dialing was introduced to accelerate call setup; it became available in 1963. This made voice frequency in-band signaling a feature of the local loop plant, as it had been for some time for the interoffice trunk plant. The coding of digits with tones is called *dual-tone multifrequency* and is used for part of the subscriber loop signaling (the addressing portion). The differences between DTMF and MF are:

- DTMF is used only on customer loops or PBX trunks to the central office; MF is used interoffice.
- The sets of frequencies are different.
- The speeds at which the pulses are sent are different.

With push-button DTMF, the dial digits are encoded as a combination of two sinusoidal tones selected out of eight tones. The tones are 697, 770, 852, 941, 1209, 1336, 1477, and 1633 Hz; the first four are considered to be a frequency group and the second four in another frequency group; all digits are represented with a frequency from the first group and a frequency from the second group. For example, the digit 1 is coded by a 697- combined with a 1209-Hz tone, the digit 2 is coded by a 697- combined with 1336-Hz tone, and so on. Special selection of these base frequencies was undertaken with the aid of harmonic analysis to minimize the interference with voice and the talk-off problem and to differentiate them from MF.

Dual-tone multifrequency allows 16 combinations, as seen in Figure 5.11. The states A, B, C, and D[7] are reserved for future use [6]. The top row of frequencies in Figure 5.11 is called *high group frequencies;* the column of frequencies is called *low group frequencies.*

All switching systems that interface with end users require 20-Hz ring generators supplying 90 V to the loop. Other audible tones are also required. Some of the common audible tones used to communicate with the end user are shown in Table 5.4 [8].

Other   The E&M method and the CAS method described in the previous subsection also apply to the line side, especially for PBXs, as described in Section 5.6.

Observation   In voice over frame or voice over ATM applications, the user-to-CO mechanism will likely be an overlay T1 or T3

Figure 5.11
Dual-tone multi-frequency plan.

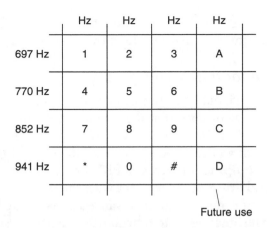

line (not connected with the public switched telephone network). Where the signaling takes place is (a) between the PBX and the branch-location ATM/frame concentrator, and (b) between the Central Office ATM/frame equipment and the voice switch. What we discussed above applies to case (b); that is why support of TR-303 is so important.

Common Channel Signaling

Beginning in the late 1970s, an improved system of segregating the signaling mechanism over its own dedicated supervisory (data) network has begun to be deployed in the public U.S. telephone network. It is being deployed to support interoffice trunk-side signaling. Common channel signaling is a signaling method in which a single channel conveys, by means of labeled messages, signaling information relating to a multiplicity of circuits, or other information, such as that used for network management. This migration to out-of-band signaling is only the beginning of a major network evolution with regard to signaling, which will culminate in widespread

Table 5.4 Analog Signaling Tones

Dial tone	350 Hz + 440 Hz	continuous
Station busy	480 Hz + 620 Hz	0.5 s on; 0.5 s off
Network busy	480 Hz + 620 Hz	0.2 s on; 0.3 s off
Audible ring return	440 Hz + 480 Hz	2.0 s on; 4.0 s off
Off-hook alert	Multifrequency howl	1.0 s on; 1.0 s off
Recording warning	1400 Hz	0.5 s on; 15.0 s off
Call waiting	440 Hz	0.3 s on; 9.7 s off

deployment of ISDN in the late 1990s and broadband ISDN (B-ISDN) during the first decade of the new century [9].

The Need for Improved Signaling

Until 1976, signaling in the U.S. plant was almost entirely on a per-trunk basis, as discussed in the previous sections. The disadvantages of in-band signaling were not overwhelming when the only users of the network were humans. When sophisticated high-speed/high-capacity equipment (such as a PBX or a computer) is interconnected and attempts to interact with the network with the objective of obtaining some advanced service, the limitations of a traditional signaling system become evident. These limitations have been the motivation for the development and introduction of common channel signaling in the telephone plant. Another motivation for the establishment of a common channel was to reduce the possibility of fraud [4].

Although initial voice over data networks may be for on-net applications only, eventually there will be a need to interwork with the PSTN. Hence, some understanding of CCS is useful.

Common Channel Signaling Architecture

Common channel signaling involves a separate high-speed network (the *common channel*) to transfer supervisory signaling information in an out-of-band fashion; this separate network carries signaling information from a large number of different users, in a multiplexed fashion, employing packet switching technology. The separation of the signaling from the information channel, as well as the greater repertoire of command message formats, allows a more methodical migration of the network to advanced architectural configuration; this follows from the fact that changes can be made without the high cost associated with physical replacement or modification of hardware.

Because supervisory instructions are coded as messages instead of some sequence of tones, and because of the higher bandwidth available for signaling, more detailed information about a call, in terms of desired network treatment, call origin, and so on, can be exchanged across the network. In turn, this implies more sophisticated services. The talk-off problem is totally eliminated with the separate signaling facilities. Another advantage of CCS is that signals can be sent in both directions simultaneously and during the conversation, if necessary; this last feature is very valuable for some advanced services. Business-case analyses also proved CCS on the merits of saving network equipment and trunks with faster signaling.

Common channel signaling allows access to many points in the network, not just switches. Advanced voice and data services may depend on remote databases, processors, and facilities. Thus CCS provides direct local office-to-local office signaling connectivity and local office-to-service node signaling connectivity.

Common channel signaling is reliable and fast. CCS replaces both the SF and the MF signaling equipment and methods; addressing digits are converted to data messages (packets). All modern digital switches can be equipped with CCS capabilities; the CCS interface is an electronic device that interprets incoming data messages and transfers the translated signal to the common control/call processor.

There are three signaling modes that must be considered:

1. *Associated mode.* In this mode the messages relating to a particular signaling relation between two adjacent points are conveyed over a link directly interconnecting these signaling points.

2. *Nonassociated mode.* In this mode the messages relating to a particular signaling relation are conveyed over two or more links in tandem passing through one or more signaling points other than those that are the origin and the destination of the messages.

3. *Quasi-associated mode.* This mode is a subcase of the nonassociated mode. Here, the path taken by the messages through the network is predetermined and, at a given point in time, fixed.

A direct plant implementation of fully associated CCS would require a point-to-point signaling link between any two switches. Switches equipped with CCS interfaces can be interconnected with direct data links, if the traffic volume of these signaling messages is high enough. Most switches are, however, connected to packet switches that act in their traditional data communications role. The nonassociated signaling is then implemented over a network that employs signal transfer points (STPs) operating as packet switches; this topology obviates the need for a large number of point-to-point links. See Figure 5.12. Signals are sent between offices by two or more links and one or more STPs in tandem. Connectionless packet

Figure 5.12
Links to the common channel signaling network.

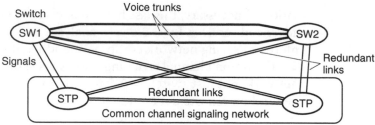

STP = Signal transfer point (packet switch)

switching techniques are employed. The function of the STPs is to route signaling messages between the various constituent links without altering the message. The only functions are, thus, the Layer 2 error detection/correction task on signaling message content and the Layer 3 network routing function.

The signal transfer points are packet switches that handle the routing of the signaling messages. As such, these nodes provide for concentration and ensuing efficiency: few switching offices in the interLATA or intraLATA (local access transport area) network have trunk groups large enough to justify direct connection of the signaling channels between offices in question (*associated* or *direct-connected* links). STPs may be redundant to ensure availability and reliability. While normally operating in a load-sharing mode, one STP can take over if the other fails. In most cases, signaling messages are routed over one or two STPs. CCS was introduced in the United States in the mid-1970s [4].

Not all switches in the United States are currently connected to a carrier's common channel signaling system. This is an evolutionary deployment; while inroads have been made in the 1980s, ubiquitous deployment will likely occur by the year 2000.

ITU-T Signaling System No. 7

The goal of ITU-T's Signaling System No. 7 (ITU-T SS7) is to provide an international standard for common channel signaling suitable for stored program control exchanges, computers, and PBXs. It operates on digital networks with DS0 channels (64 kbps), and it accommodates low-speed analog links if desired. While ITU-T No. 6 lived up to its promise of providing improved call management and facilitating some new services, it was not totally adequate to a digital environment. Hence, the need to define a more comprehensive common channel signaling system; this gave rise to ITU-T SS7 [10, 11].

The ITU-T SS7 meets the requirements of call control signaling for telecommunications services such as POTS, ISDN, and circuit-switched data transmission services. It can also be used as a reliable transport system for other types of information transfer between exchanges and specialized centers in telecommunications networks (e.g., for management and maintenance purposes) [4, 12].

The signaling system uses signaling links for transferring messages between switches or other nodes in the telecommunications network served by the system. Arrangements are provided to ensure reliable transfer of signaling information in the presence of transmission disturbances or network failures. The system includes redundancy of signaling links and functions for automatic rerouting of signaling traffic to alternative paths in case of link failure.

ITU-T SS7 supports the associated and quasi-associated signaling modes described above. The fundamental principle of the SS7 structure is the division of functions into a *message transfer part* (MTP) and separate *user parts* (UPs) (see Figure 5.13). The term *user* refers to any functional entity that utilizes the transport capability provided by MTP (in this context, the user *is not* the ultimate customer of the network). The MTP does not include a resequencing mechanism to handle the dynamic message routing arising in the general nonassociated environment. The parts are as follows:

- *Message transfer part* contains the necessary mechanism to ensure reliable transmission of functional signaling messages, with maximum network availability.

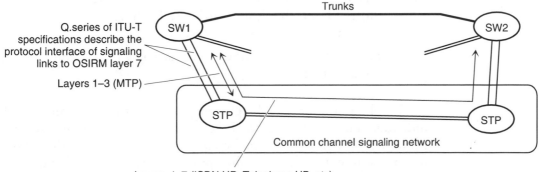

Figure 5.13
SS7 interfaces.

- *User parts* provide criteria for service management. Individual user parts are being introduced for a number of services—for example, operating procedures for interexchange signaling in the telephone network (ISDN-UP).

Message Transfer Part.   Level 1 specifies the physical, electrical, and functional characteristics of a signaling link (type A, B, or C); this has to do, for example, with the channel plug characteristics, voltages required to identify a bit, and so on.

Level 2 defines the functions and procedures for the transfer of signaling messages over a link in an error-free and reliable manner. This has to do with message blocking and retransmissions. Messages are transmitted using signal units that follow the framing conventions of the high-level data link control (HDLC) procedure. This bit-oriented protocol allows transparency and variable signal units. This is accomplished with a single (reserved) flag character 01111110 and zero insertion. Zero insertion assures that a sequence 01111110 in the data stream will not be confused with a synchronizing HDLC flag: the transmitting station over a link will insert a 0 after five consecutive 1s in the data stream; the receiving station will apply the reverse process.

There are three types of messages, or signal units, which are transacted by the signaling network in a link-by-link fashion [13, 14]:

1. *Fill-in signal units* (FISUs). These are transmitted over the link when there are no other signal units to be sent; basically, they maintain the link connection in the absence of real traffic.
2. *Link status signal units* (LSSUs). These consist of status information (establishing or de-establishing a connection), checking alignment, and related functions.
3. *Message signal units* (MSUs). These carry the content of the signaling message.

Level 3 defines networking (transport) functions common to all individual links in the end-to-end circuit. It provides the means to multiplex on a single physical link several logical links. In the signaling environment this implies the ability to carry on one channel call control information about several calls. ITU-T Q.701 to Q.707 specify the MTP.

The collection of these three layers constitutes the message transfer part, because they have to do with the physical movement of signaling information. This provides a service similar (but not identical) to a traditional packet network (MTP provides a connectionless packet service).

User Parts   The OSI Reference Model specifies four upper layers, which are, in order, Transport, Session, Presentation, and Application Support. SS7 user parts correspond to these higher layers, though the clean segmentation suggested by the OSI model is not followed in the upper four layers. This is because, when SS7 was being developed, the higher OSI layers were not yet fully defined; there is an ongoing effort to migrate SS7 protocols to the OSI model. These higher layers have to do with the content and coding of the signaling messages. The original SS7 architecture had monolithic user protocols. Some of the message types are:

- Call establishment messages for alerting, call proceeding, connect, and setup
- Call disestablishment messages for disconnect and release
- Intracall information messages for suspending, resuming, and other user information
- Miscellaneous messages

The parameters to be included in these messages for the purpose of call management is a function of the type of call: voice, data, circuit-switched, channel-switched, video, ISDN call, and so on.

The ISDN-UP encompasses signaling functions required to provide switched services and user facilities for voice and data applications in ISDN (it is also suited for applications in dedicated telephone and circuit-switched data networks, and in mixed analog/digital networks). This series of recommendations defines the ISDN signaling messages, their encoding, and cross-office performance.

5.5 Digital Transmission and DS1 Signal Format

Today many PBXs utilize T1/DS1 lines to connect to the CO switch. Therefore, even for on-net applications, the PBXs utilize the same interface cards (PBXs are described in more detail in Section 5.6). Consequently, voice over data networks will have to utilize these facilities.

This section describes the DS1 signal format—for example, how 24 voice channels are arranged so that they can be placed simultaneously (multiplexed) onto a single high-speed T1 transmission facility. The following list identifies aspects associated with defining the DS1 format, particularly from a telephony perspective [15, 16].

Channel numbering. This refers to how the 24 channels are arranged as they appear in the combined bit stream. In the modern scheme, channels are numbered sequentially in one-to-one correspondence with the sequence of 8-bit timeslots; older schemes employed different numbering methods. The 8 bits being discussed arise from the PCM sampling process for each voice channel.

Information bits. The information bits in each timeslot are used in a variety of ways. In most instances, the 8 bits are used in a similar fashion in all 24 timeslots, but there are exceptions where two or more usages are intermixed in the 24 timeslots. There are three ways to utilize the information bits: voice, data, and transparency.

Channel-associated signaling bits. Channel-associated signaling bits are used for per-channel supervision and addressing. There are three ways to signal: A, B signaling, network control, and ABC&D signaling.

Code substitutions. Under a number of conditions, a fixed code must be substituted for the contents of a particular timeslot; three substitutions are zero-suppression codes, unassigned and idle channels codes, and alarm codes.

Framing bits. The framing bit (F-bit) in each frame allows the receiving equipment to synchronize (frame) on the incoming DS1 signal.

Framing method. Framing (also called *synchronization*) is needed for identification of digital information. It can be handled by a number of schemes, all involving, in one way or another, the F-bit.

Yellow code. The yellow code provides an alarm indicating a failure in the outgoing direction. There are a number of ways to achieve this alerting.

DS1 data links. Within the DS1 signal format, a number of alternatives exist to provide a control/management data link of a few kbps.

Many of these key topics are treated in more detail in the sections that immediately follow.

Framing and Framing Bit

One of the challenges of any multiplexing technique is to establish the boundary of the octets within the overall combined stream of bits. As indicated, a common approach is to have the 24 channels arranged in a round-robin fashion: each channel is transmitted in turn, in a linear sequence. Each channel is represented by 8 bits (an octet or a byte) in turn, corresponding to the PCM-sample word. For the receiving equipment to interpret the 24 octets properly, the receiving hardware needs a way to distinguish the beginning and end of each frame, after which the position and, hence, the content of each octet can be determined. This is called *frame-level synchronization.*

A unique sequence of bits, known as the *starting delimiter* or *flag,* could be located at the beginning of each frame of 24 octets, to identify the beginning of the frame. For example, the sequence 100011011100 could designate the beginning of the frame. When the receiving hardware locates this string, the offsets for the individual octets can be easily computed. See Figure 5.14, top. In this fashion, the receiving equipment can make a firm decision at the end of each frame. With this scheme, a single flag will allow synchronization; put differently, a single frame suffices to recover the synchronization.

A 12-bit flag every 192 bits of payload, however, represents an overhead of approximately 5 percent. Specifically, if a 12-bit framing pattern were included in each frame, the total number of bits would be 204 bits (192 plus 12), and the line rate would have to be (increased to) 1.932 Mbps in order to retain the 8-kHz PCM sampling rate. The designers of the carrier systems in the early 1960s decided that this overhead was too high. Instead, they decided to sprinkle the flag over 12 frames, thus putting only one of the framing bits (in turn) at the end of a frame. See Figure 5.13, bottom.

In this situation, by simply looking at one frame, it is not possible to determine the position of the synchronization point, since

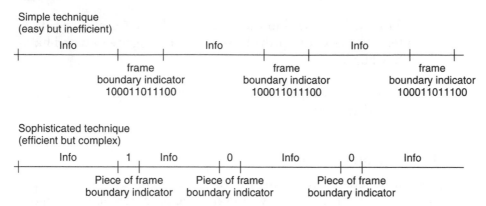

Figure 5.14
Frame boundary.

that bit will simply be a 0 or a 1, which does not tell much. Instead, the receiving equipment must buffer the entire 12 frames (12 × 192 = 2316) bits. The termination hardware is constantly looking for frame boundaries. A framing-pattern-sequence detector is employed to accomplish this. The equipment postulates the frame boundary at a bit x (assuming that bit was 1), then looks at 193 bits beyond that one to see if the new bit was a 0, then looks 193 bits beyond that one to see if the new bit was a 0, and so on, across the 12 frames, until the entire 100011011100 flag is registered. If at any point an unexpected bit is found, the equipment "realizes" that the postulated boundary was, in fact, not correct. The hardware then postulates the boundary at bit $x + 1$ and repeats the process. If the flag is recovered, then the boundary has been found; otherwise the process repeats at $x + 2, \ldots, x + j, j \leq 192$, until the boundary is located. Hence, in its search for the true boundaries, the hardware postulates a certain boundary and then checks to see if the expected framing bits are found in the appropriate location in the stream (for example, if it has tracked the 10011 part of the word, 193 bits later it should be able to find a 0, etc.). Once the boundary is located, the decoding of all octets for the preceding 12 buffered frames can be accomplished.

More algorithmically than described above, the synchronization process carried out by typical equipment connected to a T1 line involves nine steps [17]:

Step 1: Compare assumed frame bit with locally generated frame bit. Go to Step 2.

Step 2: Determine whether there have been two errors in the last four frames. If NO, go to Step 1, and the system is in-frame. If YES, go to Step 3 (to determine new framing).

Step 3: Store 8 PCM bits starting after last frame bit. Declare out-of-frame. Change phase relationship of timing generator and PCM by 1 bit. Go to Step 4.

Step 4: Store comparison of real-time PCM bits and 8 stored bits. Store the 8 real-time bits used above. Go to Step 5.

Step 5: Determine whether assumed frame bit is in error (check of comparisons). If NO, go to Step 6. If YES, go to Step 7.

Step 6: Determine whether assumed frame bit has been corrected for nine checks. If NO, go to Step 4. If YES, go to Step 8.

Step 7: Change phase relationship by 1 bit. Go to Step 9.

Step 8: Resynchronize timing generator and declare in-frame. Go to Step 1.

Step 9: Determine if 8 bits have been processed without loading in 8 new PCM bits. If NO, go to step 5. If YES, go to Step 4.

The framing bit in each frame permits the receiving terminal to frame on the incoming DS1 signal, once these F-bits are accumulated over a horizon. A problem could arise if the signal in the channel provides a sequence that closely or identically resembles the framing word. This can happen when the DS0 channels carry data [17, 18]. The synchronization hardware may lock on this spurious word and declare synchronization at the wrong place. In this case, the Data Link Layer protocol of the end-user system receiving the data would have to correct the ensuing errors; however, for voice, such a mechanism is not available. Termination hardware is such that, in the absence of channel noise errors, the maximum average reframing time will be less than 50 ms (maximum average reframe time is the average time to reframe when the maximum number of bit positions must be examined for the framing pattern [19]). One of the challenges in ATM's circuit emulation service is to retain synchronization to minimize frame slips to the user of the emulated T1 line (e.g., PBX).

Two framing formats have been used in the United States: *superframe format* (SF), also known as *D4 format* or *D4 framing* (named after AT&T's model D4 channel bank), and *extended super-frame format* (ESF).

The superframe format uses a 12-frame superframe horizon and divides the F-bits of each individual frame into alternating frame bits F_t and signaling bits F_s. F_t bits occur in the odd frames and alternate between 1 and 0. The F_s bits occur in even frames and carry the pattern 000111 . . . , which identifies frames 6 and 12. These frames include voice-frequency (VF) signaling bits. This same F-bit sequence is repeated in every 12-frame superframe. SF was the original T1 format (the frames corresponding to the above pattern are the 12th, 2nd, 4th, 6th, 8th, and 10th). This technology has now by and large been replaced in the United States by ESF-based technology.

The extended superframe format uses a 24-frame superframe horizon and subdivides the F bits among a framing pattern sequence that identifies the location of frames 1 to 24 and other channels discussed later. ESF was developed in the early 1980s.

Superframe Format

In SF, there is a framing bit after every 192 payload bits. The 192 bits correspond to 24 conversations sampled with PCM methods generating 8-bit words (acoustical amplitude values being quantized at 256 discrete, but not equally spaced, intervals); the combined signal is *byte-interleaved*, providing 1 frame. The superframe is a repeating sequence of 12 frames; see Figure 5.15. One frame corresponds to 125 µs; one superframe is therefore 1.5 ms in duration. Each superframe contains a 12-bit flag, made up of individual bits coming from each of the 12 frames. The 12-bit flag, 100011011100, is used for synchronization and for identifying frames numbers 6 and 12, which contain VF channel signaling bits. Carrier equipment (channel banks in particular) minimizes the bandwidth spent on VF signaling by putting information only every 6th frame. The VF signaling method consists of *time-sharing* the least significant bit in the 6th and the 12th frames, providing what are referred to as 7⅚ *bits* for encoding the voice signal.

The SF DS1 superframe format grew out of the 1960s, based on the then-available technology. Given the repeater technology of the 1960s, at least 1 bit in 15 bits of the combined stream (information plus signaling) had to be a 1, and at least 3 bits in 24 bits of the

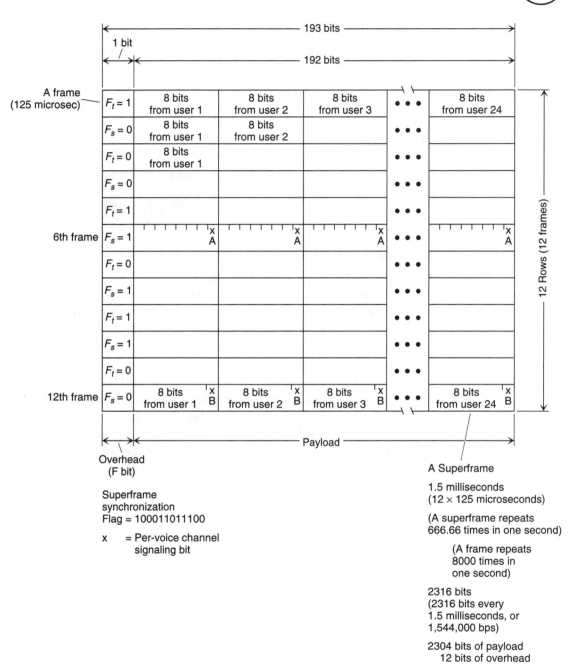

Figure 5.15
Bit layout in DS1 SF format (from top left to bottom right).

stream had to be a 1. This is required by the channel banks to keep track of the clocking and, ultimately, the frame structure.

In SF, the F_t bits alternate every frame, providing the sequence 101010. The receiving channel bank or PBX can identify this unique sequence in the incoming digital stream to maintain or reestablish frame boundaries. Frame 6 is identified by the fact that it occurs when the F_s is 1, preceded by 3 F_s bits that were 0; frame 12 is identified by the fact that it occurs when the F_s is 0, preceded by 3 F_s bits that were 1; the receiving channel bank can easily identify this sequence, in the absence of severe line errors or impairments, and thus identify the desired frames that contain VF signaling information.

Extended Superframe Format

The basic challenge of DS1 transmission, as discussed earlier, is that of preserving bit and word synchronization. To do this with SF methods, 24 eight-bit words (corresponding to samples for 24 conversations) are followed by one bit (the 193rd bit) for frame tracking. The hardware of the early 1960s was relatively unsophisticated and required 8000 bps to synchronize the channel. Modern hardware has progressed to the point where only 2000 bps are required for frame synchronization. This implies that the other 6000 bps become available for other service-related purposes.

There is a strong OAM&P-based desire for the introduction of intelligent (automated) network surveillance functionality, to monitor the plant in a proactive mode in order to detect impaired conditions before they result in a total facility outage. Equipment providing this functionality will use this newly freed up bandwidth to communicate with the appropriate centralized computers, which can dispatch staff or take other corrective measures. The future is one of automation for the purpose of reduced labor in the management of the telephone plant. The reason for this is not strictly an economic one: Today's technology has progressed to the point where a fully automated plant is indeed possible and just around the corner.

During the 1980s, a new framing format, the extended superframe format, was introduced. Most carriers have introduced equipment supporting ESF. ESF benefits the end user by providing a more reliable digital service. The present SF format will continue to be supported to protect the embedded base of equipment.

Figure 5.16 provides a detailed view of the ESF framing format. The key difference is that the new superframe format is composed of a sequence of 24 frames, rather than 12 (the 193rd bits are now being looked at as an ensemble of 24-bit words). There are 6 bits in the frame synchronization word, rather than 12. Substantial progress has occurred in the VLSI area in the past decade, so that modern carrier equipment keeps timing more accurately; this implies that fewer bits are required for this housekeeping function. The D-bit facility represents a link-level data channel to support telemetry associated with automated network surveillance. The C-bit facility handles error checking and monitoring functions. Of course, this means that the channel banks and other network equipment need to be upgraded or replaced to benefit from this enhanced functionality. Similarly, user equipment must be appropriately configured.

ESF Properties

The properties of the ESF format are as follows [18].

All previous functionality, including the VF-level signaling rules, remains available; no new bits from the 1.544-Mbps signal are taken away from the user. Twenty-four frames have to be examined by the termination equipment to establish synchronization and extract other channel information. This means that, in case of total loss of synchronization, it takes longer under ESF to regain synchronization; however, with more sophisticated clocking mechanisms, this situation should occur rarely if a facility is operating correctly.

A 4000-bps data link, also called *embedded operations channel* or *facility data link* (FDL), used for maintenance information, supervisory control, and other future needs, becomes available.

A 6-bit cyclic redundancy check (CRC) code is provided. The CRC is used for monitoring transmission quality of the DS1 facility; additional functions include false-framing protection and other performance functions. The CRC-6 is generated from the bits of the preceding frame (for the calculation, the framing bits of that frame are considered to be equal to 1). This will allow the carrier equipment to inform the appropriate agency in the network that something appears to be degrading; the problem may thus be fixed before total failure occurs. The CRC-6 will detect 100 percent of all errors of 6 bits or less and 98.4 percent of errors of more than 6 bits.

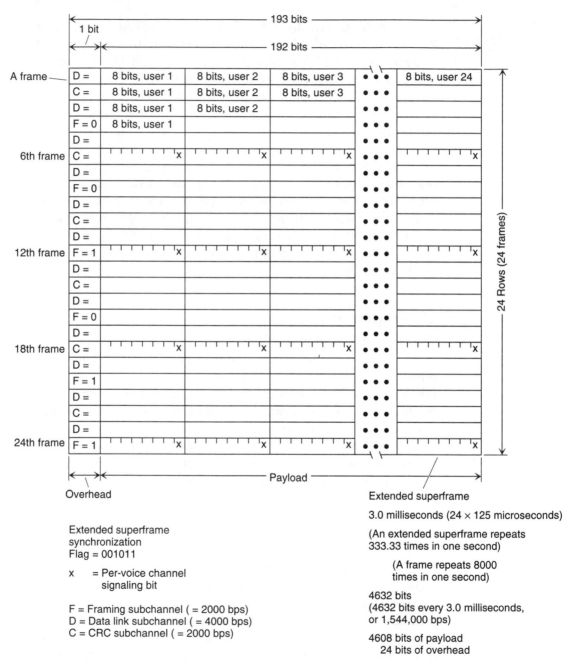

Figure 5.16
Bit layout in DS1 ESF format (from top left to bottom right).

The CRC-6 will also provide false-frame protection. This follows from the fact that if the wrong synchronization boundary is selected by the channel bank hardware, the CRC will not calculate correctly; assuming the channel was not experiencing intrinsic problems, the hardware can assume that the wrong boundary was selected and resume the search.

In addition to the increased functionality just described, and implemented "outside" the user's signal—namely in the 193rd bit area—new VF-level signaling capabilities become available under ESF. Two additional robbed signaling bits become available to allow representation of up to 16 states. The bits are known as C and D, and complement the A and B bits of the regular superframe format. Options are available (out of these 16 codes) for transparency (no robbed signaling bits), 2-states signaling (A bit only), 4-states signaling (A and B bits), or 16-states signaling (A, B, C, and D bits are used).

In the transparent signaling option, all 8 bits within a frame within the extended superframe are given to the user for his or her data. When the A-signaling mode is employed, the least significant bit of every sixth signaling frame is robbed to show the desired bit. When the A, B signaling mode is employed, the first and third signaling frames are robbed to carry the A bits; the second and fourth signaling frames are robbed to carry the B bits. When the A, B, C, D signaling mode is employed, the desired bits are obtained by robbing the first, second, third, and fourth signaling frames, respectively.

These channel-associated signaling bits are further discussed below. Table 5.5 depicts the voice signaling capability carried within the user data, via bit robbing. This 16-state voice signaling method is not consistent with the ISDN view of explicit message-oriented signaling and it is not clear if it will be implemented in a widespread fashion.

The ESF signaling bits follow the sequence shown in Table 5.6. In summary, the 8000-bps overhead bits are now reallocated as follows:

1. 2000 bps for framing (6 bits distributed over 24 framing bits; there are 333 such 24-bit words per second).
2. 2000 bps for CRC error and performance determination (6 bits distributed over 24 framing bits).

Table 5.5   Voice Signaling Options with ESF

Frame	Information bits, all users	VF signaling bit, all users	2 state	4 state	16 state
1	1–8	—			
2	1–8	—			
3	1–8	—			
4	1–8	—			
5	1–8	—			
6	1–7	8	A	A	A
7	1–8	—			
8	1–8	—			
9	1–8	—			
10	1–8	—			
11	1–8	—			
12	1–7	8	A	B	B
13	1–8	—			
14	1–8	—			
15	1–8	—			
16	1–8	—			
17	1–8	—			
18	1–7	8	A	A	C
19	1–8	—			
20	1–8	—			
21	1–8	—			
22	1–8	—			
23	1–8	—			
24	1–7	8	A	B	D

In 2-state signaling, only 1 bit, bit A, leading to two signaling states 0 or 1, is available. The two signal messages can be sent at a rate of 1333 times per second per user.

In 4-state signaling (most common), 2 bits, bits A and B, leading to four signaling states 00, 01, 10, 11, are available. The four signal messages can be sent at a rate of 667 times per second per user.

In 16-state signaling, 4 bits, bits A, B, C, and D, leading to 16 signaling states 0000, 0001, . . . , 1111, are available. The 16 signal messages can be sent at a rate of 333 times per second per user.

3. 4000 bps for telemetry and facility management and reconfiguration (12 bits distributed over 24 framing bits). With clear channel capability, 2000 bps are used to undertake this function, leaving only 2000 for telemetry.

Information Bits

Having discussed the synchronization framing formats, we can look at the payload bits within the frame. The 8 bits in each timeslot

Table 5.6   ESF Frame Overhead Structure

Frame	*Bit number*	*FAS*	*FDL*	*CRC*
1	0	—	D1	—
2	193	—	—	C1
3	386	—	D2	—
4	579	F=0	—	—
5	772	—	D3	—
6	965	—	—	C2
7	1158	—	D4	—
8	1351	F=0	—	—
9	1544	—	D5	—
10	1737	—	—	C3
11	1930	—	D6	—
12	2123	F=1	—	—
13	2316	—	D7	—
14	2509	—	—	C4
15	2702	—	D8	—
16	2895	F=0	—	—
17	3088	—	D9	—
18	3281	—	—	C5
19	3474	—	D10	—
20	3667	F=1	—	—
21	3860	—	D11	—
22	4053	—	—	C6
23	4246	—	D12	—
24	4439	F=1	—	—

FAS: frame alignment signal (F1 to F6)
FDL: facility data link (D1 to D12)
CRC: cyclic redundancy check-6 (C1 to C6)

within a frame (SF or ESF) can be used in a variety of ways. The three schemes for information bit use from a telephony perspective, are as follows.

Voice, Nearly 8 Bits

This traditional scheme for T1 lines was shown in Figure 5.14. To accommodate signaling requirements, while still maintaining 8 (or nearly 8) bits of information in each timeslot, the least significant bit is robbed and used for channel-associated signaling every sixth frame (b1 is the most significant bit and b8 is the least significant bit). This leaves only 7 bits for the coded voice circuit in that particular timeslot. This scheme results in five out of six frames containing 8 bits, with the sixth frame containing only 7 information bits. This is often referred to as *robbed-bit signaling, 7⅞ bit voice coding,* or *nearly 8-bit voice coding.* The framing bits in this superframe are used alternatively as terminal framing bits F_t, and signaling framing bits F_s. The coded voice channel normally contains 8 bits—except in those frames following a transition in the F_s bit. In the 24-frame ESF, the framing bits contain a framing pattern sequence that identifies the frames from 1 to 24; the coded voice channel contains 8 bits except in frames 6, 12, 18, and 24.

Data, 23 Timeslots

This traditional frame format is used by a telecommunications carrier to transmit low-speed digital data. This framing technique has been used by Digital Data Service (DDS) network multiplexers and in office channel units data ports. Data transmission must be accommodated over a T1 format, which evolved principally to carry voice streams. The scheme uses a 12-frame superframe and shares the F-bit between alternating F_s and F_t bits. In this format, the first 23 timeslots contain data bytes of either 6 or 7 bits, and the 24th timeslot contains a 6-bit fixed framing pattern, a yellow alarm bit, and a remote signaling bit. The 8 bits in each timeslot are numbered sequentially. For 7-bit data bytes, bits b1 through b7 form a 56-kbps channel. For 6-bit data bytes, bits b2 through b7 form a subrate data channel (less than 56 kbps), with bit b1 used as a subrate synchronization bit. For both 6- and 7-bit data bytes, b8 in each slot is used for network control. This bit identifies whether the channel carried in that timeslot is passing customer data (bit 8 set to 1) or network control codes (bit 8 set to 0). This approach is now becoming obsolete.

Eighth-Bit Transparency

This scheme allows switching of 8-bit data bytes through a digital switching machine. In this scheme, the signaling bits are not inserted into the DS1 signal, which permits full 8-bit data bytes. This is commonly called *64-kbps clear channel capability.*

Channel-Associated Signaling Bits

The topic of signaling associated with the individual channels of a DS1, particularly in support of traditional voice applications, has already been introduced in the context of the identification of the

6th and 12th frames. This section focuses directly on this type of signaling. The 193rd F-bit signaling, described in some detail above, deals with synchronization and/or management of the DS1 facility itself. Each individual voice channel requires its own signaling information to indicate, for example, call setup or call completion. These signaling bits are contained in a small fraction of the timeslots and are used for per-channel supervision and addressing. Because the 8th bit of every 6th timeslot in a voice call is robbed to transmit signaling information, the terminology used is *robbed-bit signaling*. Three schemes, already briefly discussed, are as follows.

A, B Signaling

This signaling scheme employed by the PBX uses the 12- or 24-frame structure and "steals" the eighth (b8) bit of each timeslot in every 6th frame for signaling purposes. The two signaling channels in the SF format are designated A and B. The 6th bit is also called the A bit and the 12th the B bit. These two VF signaling channels provide a four-state signaling capability for each voice channel, at a rate of 0.667 kbps (8 kbps, divided by 12) per signaling channel. The use of the signaling bits is equipment-dependent. These combinations of bits will allow the end-user station equipment to carry out its signaling protocol, which involves indicating events such as idle, busy, ringing, no-ringing, and loop open. For data applications, the A, B signaling has no relevance; however, other types of in-band signaling may be required. The signaling information must be transmitted along with the PCM samples; to achieve this, the channel bank will rob or share the least significant bit (b8) from the user data stream; consequently, this bit alternatively carries information or signaling data. For five frames, b8 will contain voice bits; on the sixth, it will contain a signaling bit. Thus the sequence of bits for a given voice/data channel will be:

b8=v; b8=v; b8=v; b8=v; b8=v; b8=s; b8=v; b8=v; b8=v; b8=v; b8=v; b8=s

(v=voice, s=signal).

ABC&D Signaling

The four signaling channels in the ESF format are designated as A, B, C, and D, as previously discussed. When needed, the four signaling channels provide 16-state signaling capability for each voice channel at a rate of 0.333 kbps per signaling channel (8 kbps divided by 24). The equipment may also be configured for only A, B signaling, in which case the bits are equivalent to A and B bits for the SF format.

Network Control Signaling

This signaling scheme is used for data transmission in the DS1 format by a telecommunications carrier (it is not the method used by a CPE multiplexer). The last bit, b8, in each data timeslot of every frame is used as a network control bit. This bit transmits channel status information; it is a 1 if data is being sent over the channel and a 0 in the control mode. In the control mode, an abbreviated ASCII character may be transmitted in the remaining bits. This network signaling technique has been used for DDS. This approach is now becoming obsolete.

5.6 Private Branch Exchanges: Technology and Networking

To position the discussion of support of voice via ATM and Frame Relay, this section provides a basic review of PBX technology.

Overview

PBXs are stored program control customer premises equipment that provide a switching function for voice services. PBXs allow the user to switch on-net calls at a given location without requiring the services of the central office. Signaling to the network remains a major issue, because until ISDN (Q.931) becomes widely available, PBXs must rely on stimulus or CAS signaling rather than on functional signaling.

Voice over data networks probably will have two manifestations in the short term: voice over ATM and voice over frame relay. Both scenarios likely will involve the use of PBXs at the end of the virtual channels. Voice over IP may initially be more PC/CTI based, but may eventually also be PBX (or next-generation PBX) based.

PBXs have gone through three major generations, with the evolving fourth generation being the emerging client/server-, ATM-,

CTI-based technology alluded to in Chapter 1. Many of the modern features found on a PBX are a result of the computerized capabilities of SPC, originally developed for switches, as well as of the switching fabric. The PBX can be analog (switching through a mechanical matrix) or digital (switching through TDM techniques); contemporary technology is exclusively digital. PBXs offer a flexible numbering plan for intrapremises communication. Features easily obtainable with a PBX include restriction of stations from dialing specified numbers (900 lines, etc.), routing of outgoing calls to use the least expensive service available, and generation of detailed management billing and traffic reports.

PBXs are similar to telephone switches, except that they do not include many of the operations and administration functions. PBXs often omit line protection and redundancy found in CO switches. A PBX is generally smaller than a CO switch in terms of served stations. Tandem switches generally do not terminate subscriber line circuits; hence, many of the loop management functions are omitted (customer line powering, customer line voltage protection, etc.). PBXs do terminate stations, but the loops are much shorter, so many of the loop management functions found in CO local switches are omitted. On the other hand, local switches and tandem switches have substantial trunk interface and signaling requirements; PBXs are involved with a smaller number (both in terms of quantity and variety).

Generations of PBXs

As indicated, four generations of PBXs have evolved in the past 30 years. Rapid evolution has resulted in PBXs that have numerous features and capabilities.

The early PBXs were scaled-down central office switches. The PBXs of the 1920s established paths between callers through a central matrix of operator-run *cordboards*. All PBX lines and trunks terminated in switchboard jacks; the PBX attendant connected two stations or a station and a trunk manually with a jumper cord circuit. The attendant monitored lamp signals to recognize requests for connections. The next improvement was the dial PBX (commercialized in the early 1930s), which automated intercom calling and outgoing call placement using step-by-step technology. The most well-known models were the 701 and 740 types. During the 1950s and 1960s, step-by-step PBXs were enhanced to provide new features. In the 1950s, new PBXs based on crossbar technology started to appear. These systems used consoles rather than switchboards. Enhancement of this technology continued into the early 1970s. The more well-known models were the 756 (handling up to 60 lines), the 757 (up to 200 lines), and the 770 (up to 400 lines) [20].

Second-generation systems emerged in the 1970s and started to incorporate software (stored program control) that switched calls automatically, thus replacing operators and electromechanical switches. These systems also began carrying some data traffic in addition to the voice traffic. Fully digital PBXs appeared in 1975. These second-generation systems were engineered to handle relatively low levels of traffic, and the data capabilities were very primitive. Data was handled through add-on techniques such as port doubling, submultiplexing, alternate use ports, and dedicated data ports.

Since the 1980s, third-generation PBXs have carried both voice and data transmissions without blocking the voice calls (second-generation systems gave callers high numbers of busy signals because of the high holding time of the data calls). The third-generation systems incorporated integrated voice and data as part of the original design, rather than as an afterthought as in the second-generation systems. Direct digital switching is a capability that has become available with the third-generation. Second-generation systems used modems to translate digital bit streams from terminals into analog waves. The new systems reverse this process by digitizing analog voice signals so that they can interchangeably travel with computer data along the PBX's digital bus. Third-generation and fourth-generation PBXs can also exploit economies made available by VLSI components, thus permitting more PBX intelligence at a lower cost. The third-generation was sold on the basis of money-saving voice features such as call accounting (for intracompany cost control) and automatic route selection (to exploit less expensive long-distance services). Increasingly these PBXs use ISDN access, or if not ISDN, then T1 access.

Fourth-generation systems may utilize client/server technology over LANs, perhaps using IP for in-band movement of voice frames, or perhaps using a derivative of the IEEE 802.9 standard on Integrated Voice Data LAN (IVDLAN) for more direct support of voice in a separate logical circuit. The various voice servers could then be interconnected using ATM. CTI principles could also be used at the desktop. Wireless handsets (also with internal cell/external cell integration) could also be supported. It is still too early to tell if traditional PBXs will give way to this kind of technology, or if what we have described will be a flash in the pan. See Table 5.7 for a summary of PBX generations.

ATM-Based PBXs

Lucent (Definity) and Nortel (Meridian) announced ATM-based next-generation PBXs that were expected to be available by press time, while Siemens and NEC were reported to be planning to deliver ATM interfaces or provide ATM solutions in other product lines. Specifically, Lucent and Nortel were planning to introduce ATM switch fabrics in their larger systems, while Siemens and NEC plan to provide cell-based interfaces to ATM networks and separate product lines that incorporate ATM switching. Buyers will have to decide whether ATM-based PBX technology represents a technical curiosity or something that can deliver useful functionality at a reasonable price (see Table 5.8 [21]).

Table 5.7   PBX Generations

First-generation systems

Hardwired electromechanically switched. (1930–1950s).

Second-generation systems

Computer-controlled, programmable switches that offer substantially more features, but have limited capacity due to the blocking nature of the devices. Voice/data integration on second-generation products is generally the result of capability that has been added to the original design. (1960s and 1970s).

Third-generation devices

Nonblocking architecture capable of creating a completely digital system with digital telephones to convert vocal conversation from analog to digital at the source; third-generation systems integrate voice and data by design, not as an add-on capability. They also employ a distributed architecture in which modules offload some of the work of the central processing unit. (1970s and 1980s).

Fourth-generation products

Client/server-, IP-, ATM-, CTI-, and wireless-based systems. (1990s and 2000s)

Table 5.8   Challenges for ATM-Based PBXs

Functionality: PBX-based ATM capability needs to be delivered in a useful fashion and, no matter how it's packaged, it has to work.
Cost effectiveness: Must demonstrate value. It is hoped that there will not be a repeat of the integrated voice/data PBX action in the 1980s.
Security/reliability: Industrial-strength tools needed for local data services.
Manageability: Besides delivering bits from one port to another, ATM-based switches must also collect traffic statistics and provide configuration support and testing capabilities.

PBX vendors already tried to enter the data market in the 1980s. As noted above, once PBX design shifted from analog to digital switching, another data communications capability became available: Voice was converted into a 64-kbps digital format on the line card, and the connection through the switch was made using a digital representation of the voice. The bit stream could be connected directly to a digital transmission system or converted back into analog form for transmission over an analog interface. When the analog-to-digital conversion was moved from the line card out to the station set, a new series of digital telephone sets with enhanced user interface features was introduced [21].

During the late 1980s LANs saw rapid deployment in North America. While LANs supported high-speed communication (10 or 16 Mbps), the PBX vendors were proposing that users invest considerable per-port money to get fixed-rate digital connections. In effect, they were proposing a traditional telephone solution to a datacom problem that did not exist, in the view of practitioners—namely, connecting dial-up 64-kbps terminals.

ATM may reduce the cost and increase the capacity of one significant element of the PBX—that is, the switching matrix. Rather than using a traditional bus-based timeslot interchange process for the connecting users, an ATM PBX would use a matrix built on ATM hardware switching elements. However, observers note that it will not be easy for the PBX designers to integrate the new hardware switching components with existing hardware and software elements, all the while protecting the customer's investment in station equipment, system add-ons, and, it is hoped, line cards, cabinets, and other system resources. When all is said and done, the user will have a telephone switching system that does as much as it did before the addition of ATM [22]. Another approach is to incorporate an IP gateway into the PBX.

At face value, given the cost of the switching hardware relative to the other hardware elements and the software that make up a PBX, it is not clear that ATM technology is going to have a major impact on the overall system cost. An ATM PBX can, however, support ATM cell-based campus connections and legacy LANs. ATM's quantum impact could be the interface to the desktop—namely, a shared, cell-based interface supporting multimedia workstations. Several ATM connections can be supported simultaneously with the interface. The ATM specifications for campus applications define interface rates from 25 to 155 Mbps over Electronics Industry Association (EIA) category 5 cable. Currently, however, none of the PBX vendors has announced desktop ATM support.

Internetworking PBXs

Large corporate users that have office facilities in several buildings within a city or in several cities statewide or nationwide have, at times, found it useful to create a private network of PBXs (referred to hereafter as *PBX networks*) to interconnect each site into a cohesive, closed user group network. Some PBXs also have remote switching modules endowed with some, but not all, of the PBX capabilities. A number of traditional interconnection techniques exist. The choice is affected by distance and costs (in addition to internodal traffic); in turn, the choice affects the type of internode service and grade of service that the network user receives. Interconnection can be direct or via tandem intermediary nodes [22, 23]. It is in this scenario that voice over data networks may play a near-term role. For this reason it is important to understand what PSTN signaling is in the context of PBXs, how the network deals with it, and how this impacts PBX network users. This section applies some of the signaling techniques discussed in the previous chapter.

If the distance between nodes is very short (typically 5000 to 50,000 feet) and/or the designer is willing to pay the cost, the interconnection may consist of a dedicated umbilical fiber link. In this case the users of the PBX network will probably enjoy full service capabilities regardless of the location; this is because the PBX can transact the full repertoire of necessary signaling information across the large unconstrained digital bandwidth, employing a pertinent hardware-dependent scheme.

If the distance is long and/or the user is unwilling to pay the cost of specially dedicated facilities, then the user will have to employ carrier-provided trunks. Three approaches are available: (1) use of aggregated DS1/T1 links, (2) use of individual two- or four-wire voice trunks, and (3) use of the switched public network (particularly when the internodal traffic is low). The traditional PSTN network, whether for dedicated lines or over switched facilities, has not carried end user–to–end user signaling beyond basic alerting; this in turn limits the type of functionality and services derivable by remote users of the private PBX network. User-to-user signaling under ISDN should remedy this situation, as discussed later.

There are situations, particularly where there is a large number of PBX nodes, in which the direct networking of these nodes with point-to-point inter-PBX (tie) links becomes impractical. In this case the designer finds it useful to deploy one or more tandem switches, to which the PBXs are in turn connected. When the number of network nodes is small, nodes are interconnected with direct point-to-point trunks; as the number of nodes increases, the number of links and the complexity of the arrangement increases exponentially. To keep the cost down, a hierarchical topology is often employed. When a user needs to communicate intra-PBX, he or she only needs the switching services of the PBX node (the first level); when the user needs to communicate inter-PBX, he or she needs the switching services of the first-level switch, plus the services of the second-level (tandem) switch. In this scenario, end-node PBXs connect directly to end-user stations, and they usually switch traffic between their own users internally. Internode traffic is routed up the switching hierarchy to a tandem node that services internode traffic. If the designer were in such a predicament, he or she would have to employ signaling techniques that closely resemble or are identical to the signaling methods employed in the telco plant. In the most sophisticated case, the designer may opt to go all the way in terms of signaling sophistication and employ a private common channel signaling system.

Full interconnection, which provides point-to-point links between each node and every other node, requires approximately $N^2/2$ internode links, given N PBXs in the network. This approach would be followed when the nodal traffic matrix is fairly balanced, the individual matrix entries are not trivial (that is, they involve at least several erlangs of traffic at the busy hour), the number of

PBXs is small, and the airline radius of the network is not excessive (say up to 100 miles). Full interconnection becomes expensive and complex for networks with many nodes (generally over half a dozen), due to the large number of links and the associated cost. For this reason, internode tandem switches are often used to interconnect a large number of nodes.

Partial interconnection, which provides less than the full number of point-to-point links between nodes, is feasible when the amount and distribution of traffic can be characterized fairly accurately in advance; nodes that exchange a large amount of traffic are connected directly to one another, while the traffic between nodes with low point-to-point requirements is routed through intermediary (tandem) nodes. For both on-net and off-net applications, a dedicated path need not always be provided. A low traffic node can connect to the rest of the system via a dial-up arrangement and/or virtual network service. In other cases, the traffic between two nodes can be fairly high. At this time, PBXs tend to use digital T1/fractional T1 interconnections.

Drawbacks of tandem networks include long dial sequences with intermediary dial tones and, in the absence of digital trunking, accumulated distortion due to transmission limitations in subsequent stages. Out-of-band signalization of recent PBXs and T1 interfaces, as well as ISDN signaling, should facilitate tandem design.

Several of the more recently designed PBXs utilize a fully distributed architecture. In this case, each node is a standalone entity, at an equal level in the hierarchy with all other nodes. Distributed nodes may be fully or partially interconnected [22–24].

PBXs can be equipped to serve as tandem switches, for pass-through purposes. Large customers may even find that a telco-grade tandem switch (such as AT&T's No. 5 ESS or NTI's DMS 500) is required. Tandem switches are generally four-wire switches that can deal with trunks (these being four-wire as compared to two-wire subscriber lines). The digital switches can interface directly with DS1 lines without requiring channel banks to break down the signal into analog conversations. Private voice application tandem switches afford the same type of functionality as PSTN machines, while at the same time providing a number of features unique to private use. In particular, private tandem switches aim at maximizing the efficiency of trunk management, for cost-control reasons. In large sophisticated networks employing tandem machines, several other advanced cost-control and security features are incorporated, as a service to the end user; this includes least cost routing (LCR), queuing, and code blocking (denying access to 900 numbers, for example). Tandems are invoked by dialing an access code in a PBX application where the PBX is directly trunked to the tandem switch. Transmission issues have to be considered when designing a PBX network with tandems, particularly for remote access, where a user off premises can dial a local telco number to access the tandem in order to use the private network to make a long-distance call. Loss problems may be encountered.

This discussion should make it clear that if an integrated solution can be found (see Figure 5.17), it would be advantageous.

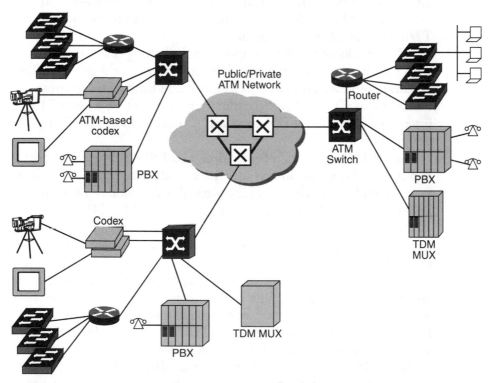

Figure 5.17
Integrated voice/data applications.

Traditional PBX and Key System Signaling

The network aspect of signaling is of interest to PBX users because (1) PBX may have to coexist or interact with that signaling system, particularly under ISDN; (2) a private network is a microcosm of a larger network—the methods and techniques employed in large scale in the latter can apply to the former on a reduced scale, particularly in a case involving private tandem nodes; (3) advanced services, either in the public network or via the PBX (or in conjunction) are possible only with a sophisticated signaling system; and (4) development of an integrated ATM/frame voice/data network depends on being able to support signaling. In addition to the network aspects of signaling, issues pertaining strictly to PBX networking deserve attention, as these will ultimately determine how cohesive and transparent the PBX network will look to the corporate users. PBX tie trunks and large private switched voice networks require essentially all the signaling capabilities of the telephone network. Connection of PBXs to voice-supportive FRADs and ATM-adaptation equipment will need to support signaling.

PBXs interface to remote entities through a variety of signaling interfaces, depending on what the remote entity is. All switching systems are equipped with circuits to interconnect the system with stations, trunks, and other service/maintenance/telemetry circuits. PBX applications are considered special services. Analog PBX trunks employ a ground-start format for central office trunks, and automatic or ringdown signaling for nondial tie trunks. E&M is employed for PBX dial tie trunks or carrier systems. The M-lead is for sending signals (an analogy with the mouth), and the E-lead is for receiving signals (an analogy with the ear); a caller's M-lead communicates with the called party's E-lead and vice versa. Dial-repeating trunks are used with those PBXs that are capable of routing tie trunk calls without attendant intervention, but require dial-pulse address information. The E&M lead interface for tie trunks is virtually identical to that used in interoffice trunks and is able to pass the dial pulse of DTMF addressing information.

Dial pulses or DTMF tones are used between PBXs and their serving offices. The CO furnishes the dial tone to the PBX when it is ready to accept addressing information, coded in dial pulses or DTMF. Traditionally, PBXs have been designed to terminate on the line side of a CO switch; they must therefore use line signaling methods (loop or ground-start signaling with dial or DTMF pulses). This is beginning to change with digital interfaces and ISDN in particular (for comparison note that CO switches connect to each other on the trunk side, and so can employ trunk signaling or, if equipped, common channel signaling). If ISDN Primary Rate Interface service is not available, then ABC&D signaling will have to be supported over the T1 trunks that are most likely employed.

Until the advent of T1 access (with CAS signaling), or the ubiquitous introduction of ISDN-based technology, PBXs connect to the central office for off-net access over trunks equipped with two-way signaling. This can lead to glare, particularly with loop start signaling. In this type of simple signaling, the only indication that the PBX has regarding an incoming call is the ringing signal, with a pulse every 6 seconds (20 Hz). During those first 6 seconds (from the time the CO switch seizes the trunk and the first pulse), the PBX is oblivious to the possibility of an incoming trunk seizure and may itself grab the same circuit for outgoing traffic [5]. It should be noted that, although T1 facilities have gone down in price in recent years and are expected to continue to do so because of Symmetric Digital Subscriber Line (SDSL), some SOHO locations may have only a key system and not require a full T1.

In addition to segregating the incoming trunks (direct inward dial, or DID, trunks) from the outgoing trunks (direct outward dial, or DOD, trunks), *ground-start signaling* must be used on analog PBX trunks. In this mode, the CO switch grounds the tip side of the line immediately upon seizure by an incoming call. By detecting the tip ground, the PBX is immediately able to recognize line seizure before the ringing pulse is actually received. When a local user of the PBX dials an access code (typically the digit 9), the PBX will seize an idle DOD trunk and pass the station's addressing information on to the CO.

Although many PBXs have already moved to T1 access (and CAS), and even to ISDN, key systems (smaller 10-50 stations with 1-10 trunk lines for SOHO applications) still employ analog lines. This is because there is no need for all of the trunks to the CO that a T1 line or ISDN Primary access would make available (some high-end key systems can grow to digital interfaces if needed).

Signaling capabilities and compatibilities are important factors to consider when purchasing voice over packet network equipment. Compatibility with CO line equipment is important to maximize the functionality of the PBX for both on-net and off-net applications. The equipment available at the CO may be a function of the CO and may not always be state-of-the-art digital in nature, though the conversion to total digital switching is expected by the end of the decade. ISDN access will greatly streamline the PBX-CO and PBX-PBX signaling.

Traditional PBX-CO Signaling

Central Office–PBX Trunks with Loop-Start Signaling   In this configuration, the tip lead at the CO as well as at the PBX has a 0-V potential in an idle state; the ring lead has a −48-V potential at the CO and at the PBX. When the PBX wishes to place an outgoing call, the tip-and-ring (T/R) circuit at the PBX (more specifically at the PBX trunk interface card) is closed by inserting a resistor. The current flow is detected by the CO, signaling the switch for a request for dial tone. On the reverse path, the CO signals the PBX of an incoming call by modulating (adding) to the ring-lead voltage, normally at −48 V DC, an AC component alternating at 20 Hz. Thus the ring lead presents to the PBX a voltage that varies from −98 V to +2 V; this alternation is interpreted by the PBX's ring detector as an incoming call, which is acknowledged by the PBX by attaching a 600-ohm load to the T/R circuit, in turn completing the process by generating a current flow to the CO switch.

Central Office–PBX Trunks with Ground-Start Signaling   In this configuration, the ring lead has a −48 V at the PBX because it is connected to a battery at the CO; the tip lead has a −48 V on it, applied by the PBX. In an idle state, no current flows since the circuit is open in two places: the tip lead is open at the CO and the ring lead is open at the PBX. The PBX signals the request of a dial tone by momentarily grounding the ring side of the line (namely changing the −48 V normally present to 0 V). When the PBX grounds the ring lead, the change in potential is detected by the central office switch. The switch will in turn signal the PBX by grounding the tip lead with a 0-V potential, which can be detected by the PBX. After the ground start has been thus signaled to the PBX, the PBX will remove the ground previously applied to the ring lead, and it will close its side of the ring-lead circuit. The CO will also remove the ground and close the loop so that current can flow. At this stage the PBX will be able to send dial pulses. For an incoming call, the tip lead from the central office is connected to ground, while the ring lead receives the 100-V AC ring voltage, again modulated on its –48-V potential [25].

DID Central Office–PBX Signaling   Direct inward dial trunks are employed to reduce the number of channels between the PBX and the central office; they are one-way trunks. A PBX perceives the DID trunk as one of its single-line phones and can interpret four-digit dialing. Outside callers dialing a station on a DID-configured PBX inform the CO switch to signal the PBX for service. An available DID trunk is activated by the CO by causing a current to flow; the PBX detects the current flow, but rather than responding with a dial tone (which it would have done if it really considered this loop to be a true station-to-PBX loop), it gives the CO a wink-start signal. The wink informs the CO that the PBX has been able to allocate resources (notably, registers) to receive the incoming addressing information. The wink signals the CO switch to repeat the last four digits dialed by the distant user, from which the PBX can complete the connection. (The wink is a quarter-of-a-second reversal of the polarity of the current that the CO had previously caused to flow; the CO had placed a load across the PBX line, and the PBX forced a current through it, as if the loop was a station line with a phone on it that had gone off-hook.) At the end of the 250 ms, the polarity is restored to its initial state. After the pulses have been received by the PBX and the desired station has answered the call, the PBX must signal the central office to initiate billing; the PBX does this by reversing the polarity of the current as it had done for the wink-start signal, but at this juncture it will leave the polarity reversed for the entire duration of the call. When the call is finally disconnected, the DID facility returns to its idle state.

Traditional PBX-to-PBX Tie Trunk Signaling

Signaling over traditional PBX-to-PBX tie trunks is generally of the E&M type. In this configuration there are two "wires" used for signaling only, as well as two or four "wires" for the voice path. The two signaling leads, the E-lead and the M-lead, are not carried end to end as separate transmission facilities, but are multiplexed at the E&M interface card with the voice path. *Logically*, they can be considered as independent of the voice. The E&M interface converts the voice and the signaling information into a stream that is compatible with the transmission medium.

When the caller's PBX puts a request signal on the M-lead for a dial tone from the remote PBX, the remote PBX will detect the request on its E-lead, and in response to this will provide battery (−48 V) on its M-lead. The remote E&M interface card will appropriately encode this event so that the receiving E&M interface can render this −48-V signal to the local PBX, on the E-lead. The caller's PBX thus receives an acknowledgment that the remote PBX is able to receive addressing information (this being similar to the wink on DID trunks discussed above). In turn, an auditory dial tone will be returned to the end user on the voice path, to initiate entry of addressing information. Since the E&M signaling is essentially dichotomous, it cannot handle DTMF addressing over the E&M leads; hence, while rotary dial pulses are passed over the E&M leads, DTMF addressing digits are transmitted directly in the voiceband.

Three common signaling methods used by various E&M systems are [25]:

1. Immediate-start E&M signaling
2. Wink-start E&M signaling
3. Delay-dial E&M signaling

Immediate-Start E&M Signaling   In this mode the caller's E-lead is at −48 V in an idle state and the M-lead is grounded. The same is true for the called party's leads. A request for service is indicated by changing the state of the M-lead from 0 to −48 V. The called party's E-lead would register a change in its state from −48 V to 0 V. The far end is thus responding to the request for service with this change on the E-lead; at the same time it provides a dial tone to the calling party over the voice path. The addressing information (pulses) is placed on the M-lead of the sender and is received as inverted pulses on the called party's E-lead; the remote station is signaled with a ringing voltage, and an auditory copy of the ring is sent back to the originating PBX over the voice path. When the destination answers the call, the remote PBX connects the voice path to the remote station. The remote PBX informs the local PBX of what has occurred by changing the state of its M-lead (which so far had been at 0 V) to −48 V. This condition is maintained for the duration of the call. When either party hangs up, the closest M-lead is brought back to the idle state of 0 V grounded.

The other end will receive this notification on its E-lead and will release all resources associated with the call, as did the first PBX.

Wink-Start E&M Signaling   This is similar to wink start on DID trunks, but does not involve the reversal of the loop current; instead, a wink (momentary change in the status of the signal) is applied to the appropriate lead (E- or M-lead, depending on the direction). The wink occurs when the remote PBX is ready to receive the addressing digits. The local PBX can start accepting and transferring the addressing information from the caller after the wink is over.

Delay-Dial E&M Signaling   In delay-dial, the status of the caller's E-lead is changed immediately when the called PBX recognizes a request for service and is changed back to its normal state as soon as a register is found to accept the addressing information. As soon as the E-lead returns to the idle state, the caller can start entering the addressing information. In the wink-start mode, dialing can begin only after the wink is over. It is conceivable that a register is found sooner than the 250 ms required to complete the wink, which in turn expedites the call setup process [25].

Signaling on T1 Links

Most modern digital PBXs are capable of direct DS1 interface, and ISDN Primary Rate interfaces are becoming available. By the year 2000, ISDN Primary Rate Interface (PRI) service will be the de facto method to connect large PBXs. If available and cost effective from a transmission point of view, T1 facilities and associated signaling are superior to analog facilities with ground- or loop-start signaling. Digital signaling methods and related equipment are relatively simple and inexpensive. As discussed earlier, VF-level signaling is achieved by literally robbing some real bits every 6th and 12th frame of each DS0 channel. This is also called *DS1 ABC&D signaling* or *CAS signaling*. Older DS1 systems and PBXs may support only two of the bits (four states); this is called *AB signaling*.

Interest in T1 signaling in a PBX environment arises because DS1-based systems have been used extensively for metropolitan interoffice applications and T1-based digital loop carrier systems servicing the feeder part of the loop (and sometimes right up to the customer building) have become quite prevalent. Until the general availability of ISDN, the digital feeder plant has to be interfaced to an analog distribution plant and existing station equipment, which requires traditional electrical currents to carry out their signaling.* Furthermore, with the establishment of DS1-rate PBX interfaces, the signaling aspects of T1 have to be dealt with, since PBXs now generally have DS1/T1 interfaces that can be used to interconnect two PBXs in a network [26]. These interfaces are a migration step toward the ISDN primary rate PBX interface of the late 1990s. However, industry practitioners indicate, as noted, that ISDN PRI will soon be the norm for PBX interconnection.

During the 1980s, a variety of proprietary (digital) networking techniques were developed by manufacturers of large PBXs for inter-PBX signaling. This approach employs DS1 lines to carry on-net voice, data, and signaling between the PBX nodes in a network. The first generation of DS1 connections to PBXs performed the analog functions of a D3 channel bank, thus providing tie-line connections with 24 digital PCM channels. As was the case with the analog tie lines that the DS1 link replaced, these DS1 interfaces used on-hook/off-hook signaling bits and in-band tones in each channel to establish connections and pass numbering information between networked PBXs. The need to implement a uniform set of PBX features across the network soon stretched the limits of in-band signaling to deliver the more complex information between network nodes. Most current DS1-networking options use some type of common channel signaling implementation to carry digital messages between PBX nodes; this occurs either over a dedicated separate data connection or one that is shared with voice and data channels. Messages needed for the call processing and management of a group of connected channels are generated by the software of each networked PBX [27].

As recently as the early 1990s, the majority of DS1-based, inter-PBX, common channel systems in use were proprietary. It should be noted, as implied in passing above, that call control involves Layer 1–to–Layer 7 Open Systems Interconnection Reference Model (OSIRM) functionality. To interwork two PBXs from two different vendors, a consistent protocol at each of the seven OSIRM layers is needed, plus a standardized language above Layer 7 is needed to manage the remote PBX resources. A consistent Layer 1 (Physical), Layer 2 (Data Link Control), Layer 3 (packetization) set of protocols is necessary, plus upper-layer consistency for end-to-end integrity, session, character set representation, and application-

*As of 1998, only 1 percent of the U.S. loops (that is, 1,000,000) used ISDN.

support functions. In addition, as indicated, it is necessary to standardize the functional procedures (for example, how to complete the transfer of a call, how to connect to the central attendant, how to fetch remote traffic data). The ABC&D signaling only really covers Layer 1 functionality. ISDN PRI signaling does cover the seven layers plus call control–level functions.

ISDN and Its Impact on User-to-Network Signaling

In ISDN, a separate *user-to-network signaling* channel is provided for both the basic (2B+D) and the primary (23B+D) interfaces. The key relevant specifications are shown in Table 5.9. Notice that the user-to-network Q.931-based signaling is known as *Digital Subscriber Signaling System No. 1* (DSS1).

ISDN is finding commercial success in applications between the PBX and the network (the PBX may, if desired, continue to use pre-ISDN methods to the stations on the PBX). The D-channel for out-of-band signaling employs a three-layer protocol stack for user-to-network signaling. This allows functional signaling, whereby messages are exchanged between the CPE and the network [28, 29]. It should be noted that the signaling path terminates at the *exchange terminator* (ET) at the CO; the *protocol partner* of the user is at the ET. The ET will remap the signaling requests over the SS7 network, for both user-to-network and user-to-user signaling.

ISDN also provides methods of transferring *end-to-end user-to-user signaling* using the D-channel in conjunction with SS7 [30]. Fields are now provided in the SETUP message and in the Initial Address Message of SS7 that allow a certain amount of user signaling bytes to be carried end to end during the call setup phase. Clearly, this can be beneficial to a PBX network arrangement over the public switched network (for example, in a software-defined network) to pass administrative information. An application might be to display the extension of the calling party from the distant PBX; this could already be done if one employed a proprietary umbilical link between some of the more well-known PBXs, but not across a normal link facility such as a T1 trunk or an analog trunk.

User-to-user signaling (UUS)[8] with call control (UUSCC) is a service that allows user equipment to exchange user information in the call request phase, call confirmation phase, and/or in the call clearing phase of a call.[9] This feature is applicable for point-to-point, on-demand, circuit-switched, and packet-mode calls. In all

Table 5.9   Key ISDN Standards Relevant to the Service and ATM-to-ISDN Interworking

ITU-T I.251.1 (rev. 1)-1992, Integrated Services Digital Network (ISDN)—General Structure and Service Capabilities—Direct-Dialing-In

ITU-T I.251.2 (rev. 1)-1992, Integrated Services Digital Network (ISDN)—General Structure and Service Capabilities—Multiple Subscriber Number

ITU-T I.251.3 (rev. 1)-1992, Integrated Services Digital Network (ISDN)—General Structure and Service Capabilities—Calling Line Identification Presentation

ITU-T I.251.4 (rev. 1)-1992, Integrated Services Digital Network (ISDN)—General Structure and Service Capabilities—Calling Line Identification Restriction

ITU-T I.251.5-1995, Integrated Services Digital Network (ISDN)—Service Capabilities—Connected Line Identification Presentation

ITU-T I.251.6-1995, Integrated Services Digital Network (ISDN)—Service Capabilities—Connected Line Identification Restriction

ITU-T I.251.8 (rev. 1)-1992, Integrated Services Digital Network (ISDN)—General Structure and Service Capabilities—Subaddressing Supplementary Service

ITU-T I.257.1-1995, Integrated Services Digital Network (ISDN)—Service Capabilities—User-to-User Signaling (UUS)

ITU-T I.411-1993, Integrated Services Digital Network (ISDN); ISDN user-network interfaces; ISDN User-Network Interface—Reference Configuration

ITU-T I.413-1993, Integrated Services Digital Network (ISDN); ISDN User-Network interfaces; B-ISDN User-Network Interface

ITU-T I.580-1995, General Arrangements for Interworking between B-ISDN and 64-kbp/s-Based ISDN

---

these phases, the UUS is transmitted by inclusion of the information in the appropriate end-to-end call control message [30]. During any of the three call phases, the calling party may send an integral number of octets (up to 128) of user information to the called party. For a circuit-switched call request, the calling party requests UUS for the call by sending to the switch a SETUP message that contains the user-user information element. The user-user information element may, but is not required to, contain user information. If the UUS request is accepted by the switch and the circuit-switched call is interswitch, an SS7 user-to-user information (UUI) parameter, with any user information sent by the calling party, is contained in the outgoing SS7 initial address message. The SETUP message is used to request UUS for a circuit-switched call. Five other ISDN messages can be used in UUS: CONNect, DISConnect, RELease, RELease COMplete, and PROGress.

References

1. W. Stallings. *ISDN: an Introduction*. New York: MacMillan, 1989.

2. R. F. Rey, ed. *Engineering and Operations in the Bell System*, 2nd ed. Murray Hill, NJ: AT&T, 1984.

3. ITU-T Recommendation Q.931/I.451. ISDN User-Network Interface Layer 3 Specification. Blue Book. Geneva, Switzerland, 1988.

4. R. Eward. *The Deregulation of International Telecommunications*. Dedham, MA: Artech House, 1985.

5. J. H. Green. *The Dow Jones-Irwin Handbook of Telecommunications*. Homewood, IL: Dow Jones-Irwin, 1986.

6. "Signaling, LATA Switching Systems Generic Requirements, Section 6." TR-TSY-000506, Issue 2 (July 1987). Livingston, NJ: Bellcore.

7. E. F. O'Neil, ed. *A History of Engineering and Science in the Bell System—Transmission Technology (1925–1975)*. Murray Hill, NJ: AT&T, 1985.

8. E. B. Carne. *Modern Telecommunications*. New York: Plenum Publishing, 1985.

9. P. Distler and F. Faller. "Towards an ISDN Signalling System Paving the Way for the Future," *XIII International Switching Symposium*. Stockholm, Sweden, May 27–June 1, 1990.

10. D. Minoli. "Common Channel Signaling System Number 7." *DataPro Report* MT30-320-201 (November 1988).

11. W. Stallings. "Demystifying SS7 Architecture." *Telecommunications* (March 1989): 41–47.

12. Recommendations Q.700 to Q.716. ITU-T Blue Books. Geneva, Switzerland, 1989.

13. M. G. Walker. "Get inside ITU-T Signaling System No. 7." *Telephony* (March 10, 1986).

14. W. C. Roehr. "Inside SS No. 7: A Detailed Look at ISDN's Signaling System Plan." *Data Communications* (October 1985).

15. "Systems Interface." TR-TSY-000510, Issue 2 (July 1987). Livingston, NJ: Bellcore.

16. Miscellaneous LSSGR. TR-TSY-000530 (July 1987). Livingston, NJ: Bellcore.

17. *The Bell System Technical Journal*, Special Issue on the D4 Channel Bank Family (November 1982).

18. W. Freyer. "Performing DS1 Signal Testing with a User-Configured Test Set." *Communications News* (December 1984).

19. Bell System Technical Reference PUB 43801 (November 1982).

20. J. W. Falk, Bellcore. Personal communication. June 1990.

21. M. Finneran. "Voice/Data PBX Rides Again." *Business Communications Review* (July 1997): 18 ff.

22. D. Minoli. "Engineering PBX Networks Part 3: Signaling." *DataPro Report* MT30-315-301 (April 1987).

23. D. Minoli. "Engineering PBX Networks Part 1: Design Models." *DataPro Report* MT30-315-120 (September 1986).

24. T. C. Bartee, ed. *Data Communications, Networks, and Systems.* Indianapolis: Howard W. Sama, 1985.

25. M. L. Gurrie and P. J. O'Connor. *Voice/Data Telecommunications Systems—An Introduction to Technology.* Englewood Cliffs, NJ: Prentice-Hall, 1986.

26. E. E. Mier. "PBX Trends and Technology Update: Following the Leaders." *Data Communications* (September 1985).

27. R. L. Koenig. "How to Make the PBX-to-ISDN Connection." *Data Communications* (May 1989): 91 ff.

28. D. Minoli. "ISDN Bodes Improvements." *ComputerWorld* (January 13, 1986).

29. D. Minoli. "ISDN Stands at the Threshold." *ComputerWorld.* (January 20, 1986).

30. "User-to-User Signaling with Call Control." TR-TSY-000845, Issue 1 (December 1988). Livingston, NJ: Bellcore.

Notes

[1]The material on switching and signaling is based on D. Minoli's *Telecommunications Technology Handbook*, (Norwood, MA: Artech House, 1991) and on D. Minoli's *Enterprise Networking: Fractional T1 to SONET, Frame Relay to BISDN* (Norwood, MA: Artech House, 1993).

[2]In telephony, the term *common channel signaling* usually refers to a separate packet switched network, known as Common Channel Signaling System No. 7. In the ATMF literature (Chapter 12), the term has a more limited meaning. Specifically it refers to a dedicated timeslot on a DS1-level facility that carries signaling for the other timeslots, particularly for the 24th DS0, which is the D channel in an ISDN Primary Rate Interface (23B+D structure).

[3]This material is based on promotional literature provided by Nortel, manufacturer of high-end switching and transmission systems (Reference 50042.08/0896, Issue 1).

[4]Theoretically, the D-channel on a Primary Rate Interface could be carried in a separate facility, but this is rarely if ever supported in practice.

[5]ITU-T G.704 defines the framing structure for the channel-associated signaling bits for E1 and DS1. The channel associated signaling for DS1 is ear and mouth (E&M) supervisory signaling and DTMF address signaling as specified in ANSI/TIA/EIA-464-B.

[6]PBXs connected to the public network are not allowed to use trunk signaling. A PBX connected in a private network may use trunk signaling over the private interconnection medium (over a logical tunnel).

[7]Do not confuse this with ABC&D signaling, which is used on DS1/T1 lines connected to PBXs.

[8]For example, see ITU-T I.257.1-1995, Integrated Services Digital Network (ISDN)—Service Capabilities—User-to-User Signalling (UUS).

[9]However, many carriers do not actually support this ISDN function, although it is in the specification.

CHAPTER 6

Voice over Frame Relay

6.1 Introduction

This chapter focuses on voice over frame relay. The majority of the chapter addresses the Frame Relay Forum Implementation Agreement for Voice over Frame Relay (FRF.11, May 1997), on which the discussion is directly based.

Background and Approaches

By the late 1980s, many companies realized that they (1) needed high-capacity digital connectivity to support access to critical business information and (2) needed to reach all company locations, including dispersed branch offices. This led to a transition away from dedicated point-to-point transmission facilities, such as T1/DS1 lines, and to the introduction of switched services, such as frame relay. However, until recently, planners did not see frame relay as supporting corporate voice requirements on an extensive basis for mission-critical applications. This is because frame relay technology was initially developed to support data applications, particularly for router interconnections and for the movement of SNA traffic (see Chapter 2). Four key problems impacted voice delivery over a frame relay network: (1) lack of standards for voice over frame relay, (2) lack of QoS support in frame relay, (3) poor voice quality and limited equipment availability, and (4) high overbooking of bandwidth on the part of carriers; further impacting quality achievable over a wide area network (WAN). However, all of these areas have seen improvement in the recent past, now making voice over frame relay in the corporate enterprise network a practical and cost-effective possibility. In particular, industry agreements have been reached.

On the *plus side* is the cost effectiveness of this technology, particularly for integrated delivery of voice and data services to the small office/home office (SOHO) segment. Voice over frame relay eliminates the need for multiple distinct facilities to and from remote locations. Integrated access technology for SOHO support is playing an ever more important role in the networking solutions that corporate planners are seeking to deploy at this time. Consequently, frame relay is being positioned as the answer to organizations searching for an integrated service offering that will allow them to consolidate data, voice, and fax services into a single *WAN-access* mechanism (thus eliminating the access charges that have to be paid to Regional Bell Operating Companies for traditional voice services between remote offices), as well as into a single *WAN*. On the *minus side* are continued concerns about the quality of the resulting voice, particularly for public frame relay networks and especially those not based on ATM at the core. Also, the agreement supports several voice-encoding schemes, so that some degree of interoperability concern will remain until a de facto consensus on the encoding choice is reached.

Voice over frame relay makes sense over an enterprise network (even if implemented with public carrier services), rather than for generic off-net applications. It makes the most economic sense for voice requirements between a company's domestic and international sites. Voice over public frame relay networks is still at an early stage, although end users' demand for integrating voice networks with data via frame relay has been picking up speed: The number of announcements from carriers recently means that customers are pushing them for voice over frame relay services. Ameritech recently joined MCI and AT&T by announcing voice over frame relay service.

As covered in Chapter 2, frame relay—being based on statistical frame-based multiplexing with the associated possibility for frame-to-frame delay variation, frame loss, and jitter—needs to be carefully deployed if reasonable voice quality is to be secured. Although frame relay is popular for its flexible bandwidth, its popularity has given rise to congestion in some public networks, because carriers may not properly engineer their networks (in order to maximize their profitability). Carriers also have had difficulty keeping up with the demand for new service.

Initially, frame relay networks were separate overlay networks, but today an increasing number of carriers' frame relay networks are integrated with ATM. This means that the switch supports a frame relay user-to-network interface to the user side, but internally it is an ATM switch. So input frames are cellularized (typically on the input card using ITU-T I.555 and FRF.8), and the ATM quality of service and traffic/buffer management mechanisms are used to handle the resulting cells. On the output side, cells are either converted back to frames for immediate delivery or are passed up to another switch for wide area coverage. At the destination switch, cells are converted back to frames (having thereby achieved network interworking) or are delivered directly over an ATM link to the user (achieving service interoperability). The user can in turn convert those cells back to frame relay. The advantage of this approach is that a high-speed link—for example, 45 Mbps or 155 Mbps—can be used, rather than just a T1 link as would be the case in a frame relay NNI. It should be noted from a QoS point of view that frame relay was not designed to support voice, while ATM has been developed from the beginning for this type of traffic mixing. The use of ATM at the core at least provides some of the desired QOS.

To produce a viable voice offering, carriers must eliminate significant delays, jitter, and loss through the backbone. Only the carriers that have replaced older frame relay switches and carefully planned their network from a capacity-planning point of view will find this task possible. Upgrading older switches to higher-end second-generation equipment is not a trivial undertaking, but doing so allows the carrier to support prioritization techniques (traffic-based permanent virtual channels), advanced bandwidth management, and the congestion control needed to handle the load. The CIR provided by carriers may be of little consequence, particularly if it is low and/or if the carrier overbooks bandwidth excessively, because it is an average, and actual throughput can vary significantly from moment to moment. As of mid-1997, less than 1 percent of most service providers' frame relay traffic was estimated to be voice.

The quality of voice transmission is determined both by perception and by measurement (quantization noise, etc.). Voice transmissions can tolerate at most no more than 250 to 300 ms of delay round-trip; in fact, for traditional commercial applications, that delay has been of the order of 10 to 30 ms. Voice delays in frame relay networks, when using voice compression, can be around 125 to 200 ms, as shown in Table 6.1. For voice over data networks, occasional dropped packets, frames, or cells are not an issue, since the human ear can tolerate small glitches without losing intelligibility. (The retransmission of dropped packets containing voice information often is self-defeating.) Although perceptions of voice quality vary by individual, the mean opinion score (MOS) is a widely accepted measure of voice quality. MOS ratings provide a subjective quality score averaged over a large number of speakers, utterances, and listeners. The following list indicates the value of MOS [1]:

4.0 to 5.0   toll quality

3.0 to 4.0   communication quality

Less than 3.0   synthetic quality

The end-to-end voice service including the network and the compression algorithm must produce an MOS of 3.0 to 4.0.

Voice carriage over frame relay does not generally rely on PCM techniques, although these are not excluded. The conversion from analog to digital transmission in the early 1960s began an era of enhanced telephone communications quality and significant improvements in network utilization. As demand for telephone lines increased, even more efficient methods of using the existing

Table 6.1   Various Voice Delays

Traditional telephony networks	20–30 ms
Satellite networks	250 ms
Frame relay	125–193 ms
	Input buffer: 24 ms
	Compression: 20 ms
	Access queues: 0–24 ms (depending on network complexity)
	Network latency: 5–25 ms (depending on network complexity)
	Far-end queue: 0–24 ms (depending on network complexity)
	Jitter buffer: 72 ms
	Voice decoder: 4 ms

Figure 1.1 depicted some of the key voice over packet technologies available. The protocol stack approximately represents the kind of functionality to be available in the FRAD.

transmission facilities were needed. The original standard algorithm for 64-kbps digital transmission was pulse control modulation (PCM). ADPCM eventually improved efficiency to 32 kbps for each voice call, allowing twice as much traffic to be transmitted. PCM and ADPCM are currently used by telephone carriers worldwide to transport circuit-switched voice traffic [1].

Early approaches for voice over frame relay service assumed a PCM model where voice encoding and transmission take place in real time. This model imposed a need to preserve timing in frame delivery and playback, which can be accomplished with time stamping. Time stamping involves having each frame depict when it was originated; this enables the receiver to play back the frames with the same relative timing. This works in conjunction with a per-connection priority mechanism in the CPE/switch, so that voice frames receive higher priority and more predictable end-to-end delay variation. Several mechanisms for time stamping voice frames have been proposed to the Frame Relay Forum and the ITU. The ITU has adopted a procedure for sending ADPCM over packet networks (G.764). The goal of these efforts was to maintain the locked-timing environment that evolves naturally from PCM transmission over a synchronous channel. Chapter 4 covered the newly introduced voice compression methods that are likely to see commercial introduction in the voice over frame relay market.

The FRF.11 specification supports both the compressed and the PCM/ADPCM method. At the commercial level, it is likely that the compression methods will see greater deployment, because many networks in the United States still utilize only DS0 access for frame relay, especially for SOHO applications. The compressed/packetized model of voice transmission separates the time scales for encoding, transmission, and playback. Hence, preserving synchronous timing is no longer necessary: Improvements in encoding algorithms and faster and cheaper hardware have changed the paradigm. At this juncture, most voice encoding uses some kind of prediction technique at the receiving end. Predictions are based on the most recently received information. Therefore, if a frame is lost, the newly arriving frame will show that the receiver's prediction is not current (since the receiver was not updated by the missing frame). It follows that the output will not be correct, which results in distorted voice. Hence, the performance is related to both delay and loss in the frame relay network. The issue is how much time is needed for the receiver to catch up with the arriving frames and get current, so that the voice output will be as intended. State-of-the-art voice compression algorithms of the early 1990s could require several seconds to synchronize after a loss of bits. Newer algorithms are able to self-synchronize within the length of a single frame; this makes each frame effectively independent. Since human ears can compensate for the loss of 20 ms of sound, an occasional lost frame does not disrupt communications (however, if every other frame were lost, then there would be a serious problem).

The assumptions underlying the FRF development work of the mid-1990s were as follows:

1. Preferably, voice over frame relay should be compressed 8:1 compared to 64-kbps PCM. Most access/transmission lines operate much faster than the voice-encoding rate of 8 or 16 kbps (e.g., at 8 kbps, a 40-ms interval of voice-encoded speech is 320 bits, which can be transmitted across a DS1 link in about 0.2 ms).

2. Voice should be supported for both the new (compression) techniques and the traditional PCM/ADPCM techniques. While PCM does not allow or have a need for the storing of voice, frame relay buffers voice segments at intermediate switching points.

3. The receiver should be able to buffer frames in sequence and need not play them back immediately.

4. To the extent possible, voice must be carried over existing frame relay networks, particularly without modification to the existing standards.

5. Silence suppression is desirable.

6. Integral echo cancellation and delay compensation will be used to preserve voice quality (low compression/decompression delay helps prevent voice collisions between speakers who start talking at the same time).

To ensure reliable voice packet delivery, the integrated voice/data FRAD must be designed to minimize congestion at the edge of the network (since there likely will already be congestion in the network). Fragmenting data packets allows voice packets to traverse the network within acceptable delay parameters. Configuring network buffers to reasonably small depths permits rapid transmission of voice across many network-level queues [1]. Many vendors offer FRADs with advanced techniques to overcome delay problems. These techniques include:

- Payload generation and transfer syntax
- Transport of compressed voice within the payload of a frame relay frame, with a vendor-proprietary or preferably a standardized method (specifically, FRF.11)
- Voice compression

As already noted, ITU G.729 (CS-ACELP) is an international standard that compresses the standard 64-kbps PCM streams as used in typical voice transmission to a low as 8 kbps. ITU G.728 (called LD-CELP) is an international standard that compresses to 16 kbps. Generic PCM (ITU-T G.711) and ADPCM (G.726) will be supported, as will the Discard-Eligible Embedded Adaptive Differential Pulse Code Modulation (EADPCM, ITU-T G.727). In the past, many vendors offered proprietary algorithms that dropped the rate as low as 2.4 kbps.

Echo Cancellation ITU G.165 defines a method of dealing with echo, which occurs when delays cause voice traffic to be reflected back to the transmission point. Echo becomes perceptible when the delay exceeds 15 to 20 ms.

Traffic Management Traffic prioritization algorithms in the CPE can place voice frames at a higher priority than data frames and can tune the size of the data frames to reduce delays for voice traffic.

Continuity Algorithms These are designed to intelligently fill the void of missing or erroneous voice frames.

Purpose of the FRF.11 Specification

As discussed above, there is interest in supporting voice over frame relay. Until now the problem has been that users were forced to use proprietary vendor solutions. This has limited the scope of penetration and the cost effectiveness of the technology. The publication of the standard, along with the deployment of frame relay services that support some level of QoS, will go a long way to popularize voice over data networks capabilities.

Specification FRF.11 (May 1997) extends frame relay application support to include the transport of digital voice payloads. The

implementers' agreement [2] describes frame formats and procedures required for voice transport. FRF.11 provides for bandwidth-
efficient networking of voice and Group 3 fax communications
over frame relay. Up to 255 voice and data subchannels can be carried over a single virtual channel (VC) through a frame relay network. Two classes of voice compliance are supported, for maximum
flexibility and worldwide applicability. Class 1 compliance calls for
use of G.727 EADPCM typically at 32 kbps (2:1 compression).
Class 2 compliance specifies G.729/G.729A CS-ACELP at 8 kbps
(8:1 compression). In order to maximize use of bandwidth, it is
possible to carry multiple voice samples in a single frame, further
minimizing overhead. The specification addresses the following
requirements:

- Transport of compressed voice within the payload of a frame
  relay frame
- Support of a diverse set of voice compression algorithms
- Effective utilization of low-bit-rate frame relay connections
- Multiplexing of up to 255 subchannels on a single frame relay
  DLCI
- Support of multiple voice payloads on the same or a different
  subchannel within a single frame
- Support of data subchannels on a multiplexed frame relay
  DLCI

Transport of compressed voice is provided with a generalized
frame format that supports multiplexing of subchannels on a single
frame relay DLCI. Support for the unique needs of the different
voice compression algorithms is accommodated with algorithm-
specific *transfer syntax* definitions. These definitions establish
algorithm-specific frame formats and procedures. Transport of supporting information for voice communication, such as signaling
indications (e.g., ABCD bits), dialed digits, and facsimile data, is
also provided through the use of transfer syntax definitions specific
to the information being sent. However, the requirements for
implementation of voice interfaces themselves are beyond the
scope of the FRF.11 implementation agreement.

This chapter describes the FRF.11 specification with which
implementers are now developing equipment and is in large part

based on the specification itself. This material is for informative purpose only. Protocol specialists and developers should refer directly to the specification text.

Overview of Agreement

A description of the reference model and service description for the voice over frame relay (VOFR) service is provided in Section 6.2, along with the concept of a voice frame relay access device (VFRAD). Specification of the frame formats and procedures is provided in Section 6.3. Transfer syntax definitions for individual voice compression algorithms as well as generic information (e.g., dialed digits) are provided in Annex sections, which are only briefly discussed herewith. Figure 6.1 illustrates some of the transfer syntax definitions used for voice over frame relay [3–12].

Voice Frame Relay Access Device (VFRAD)

A voice frame relay access device supports voice services. Typically, a VFRAD may be positioned between a PBX or key set and the frame relay network. Alternatively, the VFRAD may be integrated into an end system that directly supports telephony applications and frame relay, or it may be an end system. The VFRAD multiplexes voice and fax traffic along with data traffic from a variety of services/sources into a common frame relay connection.

6.2 Reference Model and Service Description

Frame Relay Access

VFRAD uses the frame relay service at the user-to-network interface (UNI) as a transmission facility for voice, voice signaling, and

Figure 6.1
Transfer syntax examples covered by FRF.11.

Vocoders					Other			
G.729 CS-ACELP	G.728 LD CELP	G.723.1 MP-MLQ	G.726/ G727 ADPCM	G.711 PCM	Dialed Digits	CAS	Data Transfer	Fax Relay

data. The reference model for voice over frame relay is shown in Figure 6.2. Using the VOFR service, it is possible for any type of VFRAD on the left-hand side of Figure 6.2 to exchange voice and signaling with any type of VFRAD on the right-hand side of Figure 6.2. A VFRAD connects to a frame relay UNI via physical interfaces as defined in Reference [2]. Three types of devices are shown in Figure 6.2. The top layer shows end-system devices similar to telephones or fax machines. The middle layer shows transparent multiplexing devices similar to channel banks. The bottom layer shows switching system devices similar to PBXs.

End-System Devices

The top left device in Figure 6.2 could be a PC with fax or telephony application software, using a frame relay network port for connectivity to other VFRAD devices. Such an end system could use the VOFR protocol stack on a frame relay connection to another end system (top right). It could also use the VOFR protocol stack on a connection to a transparent channel bank into a private network (middle right) or to a PBX (bottom right).

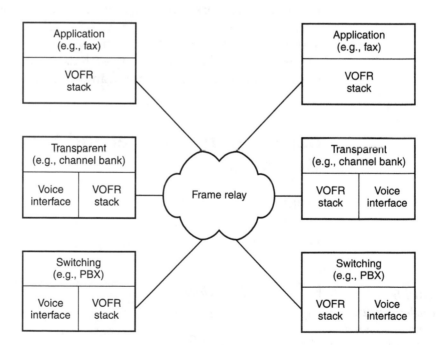

Figure 6.2
Voice over frame relay network reference model.

Transparent Multiplexing Devices

The middle left device in Figure 6.2 could be a channel bank connected via analog trunks to an external PBX (not shown). Such a multiplexing device could use the VOFR protocol stack on a frame relay connection to an end system (top right), another channel bank (middle right), or a PBX (bottom right).

Switching System Devices

The bottom left device in Figure 6.2 could be a PBX using a frame relay network for connection to off-premise extensions (end systems) or as trunks to other PBX devices. Such a switching system device could use the VOFR protocol stack on a frame relay connection to an end system (top right), a channel bank (middle right), or another PBX (bottom right).

Note: The capabilities of FRF.11 are initially directed toward on-net (PBX-to-PBX) applications. To connect to off-net customers, the frame relay provider (which may not even be a Local Exchange Carrier [LEC] or Competitive LEC [CLEC]) would have to have an interworking unit that connected both the user plane and the control plane of the voice switch to the frame relay switch (see Figure 6.3). Although the VFRAD functionality would be required at the central office, additional capabilities would be required to connect in a reliable, efficient, and secure manner to the voice switch (including TR-303 support).

Voice over Frame Relay Service Description

FRF.11 defines formats and procedures that support a VOFR service. Elements of the VOFR service support various types of service users that may be performing any of the following voice applications:

1. Call origination and termination, for an end system
2. Transparent interworking between individual subchannels on a VOFR interface and subchannels on another type of voice interface
3. Call-by-call switching, for a switching system to terminate an incoming call and originate a call on another voice interface

Figure 6.3
On-net/off-net infrastructure.

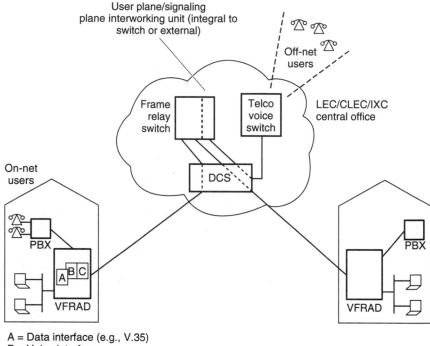

A = Data interface (e.g., V.35)
B = Voice interface
C = VOFR stack

To support the VOFR service, the underlying protocol stack must provide a full-duplex transport service. The service users can use the following service elements to operate a voice connection. The service elements support the transport of two types of payloads: primary payloads and signaled payloads. Payload types are discussed in Section 6.3.

Primary Payloads

Encoded Voice   This service element conveys voice information supplied by the service user. The voice information is packaged according to the rules specified by a voice transfer syntax. Voice transfer syntax definitions for various voice compression schemes are described in the annexes of the FRF.11 specification.

Encoded Fax or Voiceband Modem Data   The service users can exchange digital data in a baseband format suitable for remodulation into a fax or analog modem signal. The VOFR service transports this information between the two service users. The transmitting service user may locally detect the presence of a fax or voiceband modem signal for the voice connection and demodulate it before sending it. The receiving service user can detect arriving packets that contain demodulated data and can reconstruct the original modulated signal instead of reconstructing a speech signal. The encoded fax or voiceband data payload format is within the scope of FRF.11, but the algorithms used for demodulation and remodulation of fax and/or voiceband data are outside the scope of the IA.

Data Frames   This service element conveys data frames supplied by the service user. The frames are packaged according to the rules specified in the IA. The content of the data frames is transparent to the VOFR service. One application of the data frame service element enables transparent tunneling of common channel signaling messages between two compatible endpoints (e.g., PBX interfaces). Common channel signaling message formats and procedures are beyond the scope of FRF.11 (see Chapter 5 for an overview).

Signaled Payload

Dialed Digits   This service element transparently conveys DTMF, pulse, or other dialed digits supplied by the service user. These digits may be sent during the voice call setup or following call establishment to transfer in-band tones.

Signaling Bits (Channel-Associated Signaling)   This service element transparently conveys signaling bits supplied by the service user. These bits may indicate seizure and release of a connection, dial pulses, ringing, or other information in accordance with the signaling system in use over the transmission facility.

Fault Indication   The service users can use this service to convey an alarm indication signal across the VOFR service.

Message-Oriented Signaling (Common Channel Signaling)   Refer to the section entitled "Data Frames," above.

Encoded Fax   Refer to the section entitled "Encoded Fax or Voiceband Modem Data," above. Encoded fax may be transmitted on a subchannel that utilizes a primary payload for encoded voice. In this case, the subframes containing the encoded fax must be sent as a signaled payload.

Silence Information Descriptor   Silence information descriptor (SID) subframes indicate the end of a talk spurt and convey comfort noise-generation parameters. These SID indications support voice activity detection (VAD) and silence suppression schemes. When VAD is utilized, a SID subframe may optionally be transmitted following the last encoded voice subframe of a talk spurt. Reception of a SID sub-frame after a voice sub-frame may be interpreted as an explicit indication of end of talk-spurt. In addition, SID subframes may be transmitted at any time during the silence interval to update comfort noise-generation parameters. The SID payload is defined for PCM and ADPCM encoding in the appropriate annexes (the SID payload definition for other voice-encoding algorithms is for further study and can be null). SID subframes should not be sent if VAD is not utilized.

VFRAD Configuration Requirements

VOFR devices compliant with FRF.11 are not required to negotiate operational parameters. Negotiation procedures are for further study. Therefore, at the time of provisioning, the network manager must configure end-to-end configuration parameters (e.g., vocoder). Endpoint devices providing the VOFR service are configured with compatible subchannel assignments, signaling, compression algorithms, and other options.

VOFR Service Block Diagram

The relationship of the voice over frame relay service, VOFR service user, and the frame relay service is shown in Figure 6.4.

Service Multiplexing

The frame relay UNI can support multiple PVCs, each of which can provide VOFR service. The VOFR service supports multiple voice and data channels on a single frame relay data link connection. The VOFR service delivers frames on each subchannel in the order in which they were sent. As shown in Figure 6.5, each instance of the voice/data multiplexing layer can support one or more voice connections and data protocol stacks over a single frame relay PVC. The mechanism for separation of the voice and data connections being supported over a single frame relay PVC is within the scope of the FRF.11 specification. The mechanisms and

Figure 6.4
VOFR service block diagram.

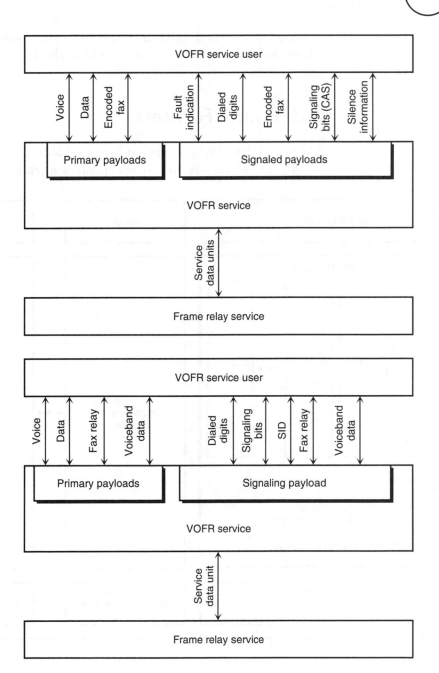

protocol stacks used for data connections are covered in other
Frame Relay Forum IAs and relevant standards.

6.3 Frame Formats

Voice and data payloads are multiplexed within a voice over frame
relay data link connection by encapsulation within the frame for-

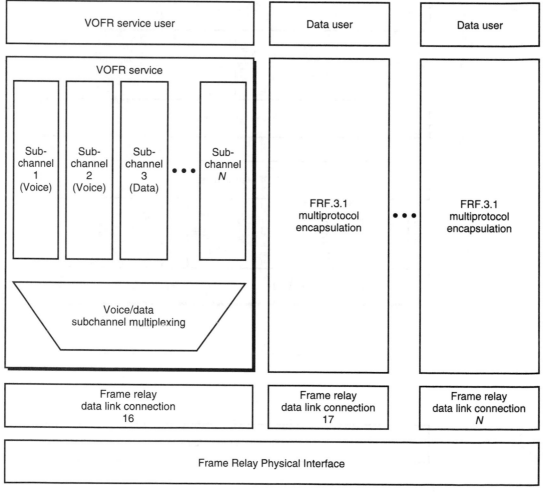

Figure 6.5
Voice over frame relay multiplexing model.

mat specified in Reference 2. Each payload is packaged as a subframe within a frame's information field. Subframes may be combined within a single frame to increase processing and transport efficiencies. Each subframe contains a header and payload. The subframe header identifies the voice/data subchannel and, when required, payload type and length. Refer to Figure 6.6 for an illustration of subframes. In this example, a single DLCI supports three voice channels and one data channel. Three voice payloads are packaged in the first frame and a data packet payload is contained in the second frame.

Payloads

This section describes payloads.

Primary Payload

Each subchannel of a VOFR connection transports a primary payload. A primary payload contains traffic that is fundamental to operation of a subchannel. Other payloads may be sent to support the primary payload (e.g., dialed digits for a primary payload of encoded voice). These additional payload types are differentiated from the primary payload by a signaled encoding in the payload type field of the subframe. A payload type of all zeros always indicates the primary payload.

Three basic types of primary payloads are utilized: encoded voice payloads, encoded fax payloads, and data payloads. Annexes provide descriptions of the transfer syntax that supports these payload types.

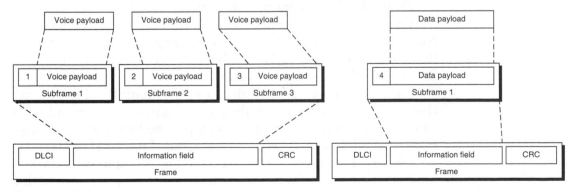

Figure 6.6
Relationship between frames and subframes.

Signaled Payload

Payloads containing in-band information that augments the primary payload flow are indicated using payload type codings. These signaled payloads include information such as channel-associated signaling, dialed digits, in-band encoded fax relay, and fault indications. Refer to the appropriate annex for a description of the service elements that support the signaled payloads.

Subframe Format

Each subframe consists of a variable-length header and a payload. The minimal subframe header is a single octet containing the least significant bits of the voice/data channel identification along with extension and length indications. An extension octet containing the most significant bits of the voice/data channel identification and a payload type is present when the extension indication is set. A payload-length octet is present when the length indication is set. Refer to Figure 6.7 and Table 6.2 for a description of the subframe structure.

Subframe Examples

The figures in this section illustrate some of the possible combinations of subframes.

Figure 6.8 shows a frame that contains a single voice payload for a low-numbered subchannel. Octets 1a and 1b are not required. The payload, a CS-ACELP sample, starts after octet 1.

Figure 6.9 shows a frame that contains a single voice payload for a high-numbered channel (>63). Octet 1a must be included. Note that the payload type is zero, indicating the transfer syntax that has been configured for the channel. In this example, the transfer syntax is the CS-ACELP syntax.

Figure 6.10 shows a frame that contains multiple subframes for channels 5 and 6. In this case, the payload type is nonzero and octet 1a is required to encode the payload type. The first of the two subframes includes octet 1b with the encoding of payload length.

Figure 6.11 shows a frame that contains multiple subframes for channels 5 and 6. In this case, the payload type is zero and the payload length (octet 1b) appears in the first of the two subframes.

Figure 6.7
Subframe format.

Bits

8	7	6	5	4	3	2	1	Octets
EI	LI	Subchannel identification (CID)						1
		(Least significant 6 bits)						
CID (Most significant 2 bits)		0 S p a r e	0 S p a r e	Payload type				1a (Note 1)
Payload length								1b (Note 2)
Payload								p

Notes:
1. When the EI bit is set, the structure of Octet 1a given in Table 6.2 applies.
2. When the LI bit is set, the structure of Octet 1b given in Table 6.2 applies.
3. When both the EI bit and the LI bit are set to 1, both Octet 1a and 1b are used.

6.4 Minimum Requirements for Conformance

The FRF.11 agreement provides support for several optional transfer syntax definitions. Interoperability between VOFR devices is possible only when both devices share support for one or more common transfer syntax definitions. VOFR devices are classified based on the support provided for the common transfer syntax defi-

Table 6.2   Subframe Format

Extension indication (octet 1)

The extension indication (EI) bit is set to indicate the presence of octet 1a. This bit must be set when a subchannel identification value is >63 or when a payload type is indicated. Each transfer syntax has an implicit payload type of zero when the EI bit is cleared.

Length indication (octet 1)

The length indication (LI) bit is set to indicate the presence of octet 1b. The LI bit of the last subframe contained within a frame is always cleared and the payload length field is not present. The LI bits are set for each of the subframes preceding the last subframe.

Subchannel identification (octets 1 and 1a)

The six least significant bits of the subchannel identification are encoded in octet 1. The two most significant bits of the subchannel identification are encoded in octet 1a. A zero value in the two most significant bits is implied when octet 1a is not included in the VOFR header (EI bit cleared). Subchannel identifiers 0000 0000 through 0000 0011 are reserved in both the short and long format.

Payload type (octet 1a)

This field indicates the type of payload contained in the subframe.

4	3	2	1	
0	0	0	0	Primary payload transfer syntax
0	0	0	1	Dialed digit transfer syntax (Annex A/FRF.11)
0	0	1	0	Signaling bit transfer syntax (Annex B/FRF.11)
0	0	1	1	Fax relay transfer syntax (Annex D/FRF.11)
0	1	0	0	Silence Information Descriptor

A zero value for the payload type is implied when octet 1a is not included in the header (EI bit cleared).
Payload length (octet 1b).
Payload length contains the number of payload octets following the header. A payload length indicates the presence of two or more subframes packed in the information field of the frame.

Payload (octet p)

The payload contains octets as defined by the applicable transfer syntax assigned to the subchannel or as indicated by the payload type octet 1a.

Figure 6.8
Frame containing one subframe.

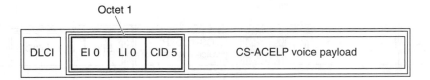

nitions. Class 1–compliant devices support capabilities suitable for high-bit-rate interfaces. Class 2–compliant devices support capabilities that enable optimal performance over low-bit-rate frame relay interfaces. An implementation is compliant with this agreement if the requirements for at least one of the two classes are met.

Class 1 Compliance Requirements

Compliance requirements are as follows.

Frame Formats

1. Support the frame structure described in Section 6.3.
2. Received optional frames may be discarded.

Primary Payload Types

1. Support of G.727 as described in Annex F of FRF.11 is mandatory. Support of other vocoders described in Annex F is optional.
2. A transmit rate of 32 kbps is mandatory.
3. Support for rates of 32 kbps, 24 kbps, and 16 kbps is mandatory at the receiver. Support for other primary payload transfer syntax definitions (e.g., fax) is optional.

Signaled Payload Types

1. Support for the dialed digit signaled payload type is optional.
2. Support for the signaling bits signaled payload type (CAS and AIS) is mandatory.

Figure 6.9
Frame containing one subframe for a high-numbered channel.

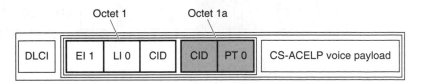

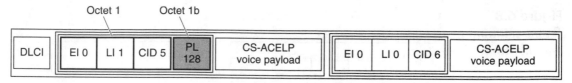

Figure 6.10
Frame containing multiple subframes.

　　　3. Support for the encoded fax signaled payload type is optional.

Class 2 Compliance Requirements

Compliance requirements are as follows.

Frame Formats

　　　1. Support the frame structure described in Section 6.3.
　　　2. Received optional frames may be discarded.

Primary Payload Types

　　　1. Support for Annex E CS-ACELP G.729 or G.729A voice transfer syntax is mandatory.
　　　2. Support for other primary payload transfer syntax definitions (e.g., fax) is optional.

Signaled Payload Types

　　　1. Support for the dialed digit signaled payload type is mandatory.
　　　2. Support for the signaling bits signaled payload type (CAS and AIS) is mandatory.

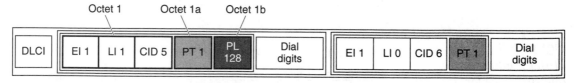

Figure 6.11
Frame containing multiple subframes.

3. Support for the encoded fax signaled payload type is optional.

6.5 Annexes

Table 6.3 identifies the contents of the FRF.11 annexes and the implied functionality of the specification.

6.6 Appendix to Chapter 6: Specification Details for Voice over Frame Relay

This appendix contains minutiae related to the FRF.11 specification. It may be used as a rough take of some of the transfer syntaxes between VFRADs. Implementers should refer directly to the FRF specification.

FRF.11 Annex A—Dialed Digit Transfer Syntax

The Dialed Digit Transfer Syntax comprises the Dialed Digit Payload Format and the Dialed Digit Transfer Procedure.

Dialed Digit Payload Format

At the originating VFRAD, the detected digits are inserted into a dialed digit payload by the dialed digits service element. Payload carrying digits will be identified using the VOFR subframe payload type field codepoint for the Dialed Digit Transfer Syntax. The digits will automatically be associated with the corresponding voice traffic based on the channel ID field.

Each digit payload contains three windows of digit transition (see Figure 6.12). The first window represents the current 20-ms period (0); the second, (−1), is the recent period; and the third, (−2), is the previous period.

Dialed Digit Transfer Procedures

Procedure for Transmission of Dialed Digit Payloads   When the transmitter detects a validated digit or has addressing information

Table 6.3   Contents of the FRF.11 Specification/Functionality

Annex A—Dialed Digit Transfer Syntax

Reference Documents
Transfer Structure
Dialed Digit Payload Format
    Sequence Number
    Signal Level
    Digit Type
    Digit Code
Dialed Digit Transfer Procedures
    Procedure for Transmission of Dialed Digit Payloads
    Procedure for Interpreting Received Dialed Digit Payloads

Annex B—Signaling Bit Transfer Syntax

Reference Documents
Transfer Structure
Payload Format
Procedures for Transmission of Payloads
    Procedures for Interpreting Received Payloads

Annex C—Data Transfer Syntax

Reference Documents
Data Transfer Structure
Data Payload Format
Data Procedures

Annex D—Fax Relay Transfer Syntax

Reference Documents
Fax Transfer Structure
Fax Relay Payload Format
    Modulation Turn-on Payload
    Modulation Turn-off Payload
    T.30 Payload
    T.4 Payload
    Relay Command
    Modulation Type
    HDLC
    Sequence Number
    Time Stamp
    EI1 and EI2
    Frequency LS and MS Bytes
    Data
Fax Relay Transfer Procedures
    Procedure for Transmission of T.30 Data
    Procedure for Transmission of T.4 Data
    Handling of Nonstandard Facilities (NSF) Frame

Table 6.3 *(Continued)*

Annex E—CS-ACELP Transfer Syntax
Reference Document
CS-ACELP Transfer Protocol
CS-ACELP Transfer Structure
Transfer Characteristics
Optional Sequence Number

Annex F—Generic PCM/ADPCM Voice Transfer Syntax
Reference Documents
Voice Transfer Structure
Active Voice Payload
Coding Type
Sequence Number
Silence Information Descriptor (SID) Payload
Reserved
Sequence Number
Noise Level
Transfer Characteristics

Annex G—G.727 Discard-Eligible EADPCM Voice Transfer Syntax
Reference Documents
Voice Transfer Structure
Active Voice Payload
Coding Type
Sequence number
Silence Insertion Descriptor (SID) Payload
Transfer Characteristics

Annex H—G.728 LD-CELP Transfer Syntax
Reference Documents
Voice Transfer Structure
Transfer Protocol
Transfer Characteristics
Optional Sequence Number

Annex I—G.723.1 MP-MLQ Dual-Rate Speech Coder
Reference Document
Transfer Structure
Transfer Protocol
Transfer Characteristics
Optional Sequence Number

Figure 6.12
Dialed digit
payload type.

Bits								Octet
8	7	6	5	4	3	2	1	Octet
Sequence numbers								Octet P
reserved 000			Signal level					P+1
Digit type [0]			Edge location [0]					P+2
reserved 000			Digit code [0]					P+3
Digit type [−1]			Edge location [−1]					P+4
reserved 000			Digit code [−1]					P+5
Digit type [−2]			Edge location [−2]					P+6
reserved 000			Digit Code [−2]					P+7

Sequence number: The sequence field is an 8-bit number that is incremented for every fragment transmitted. The sequence field wraps from all ones to zero in the usual manner of such sequence numbers. Each increment of the sequence represents a period of 20 ms.

Signal level: The power level of each frequency is between 0 and −31 in −dBm0. Power levels above zero dBm0 are coded 00000. In the event that one dialed digit payload contains a transition from one dialed digit to another dialed digit, the signal level field applies to the dialed digit in the "current" 20-ms period. The codes are: −1 dBm0 = 00001; −2 dBm0 = 00010; −3 dBm0 = 00011; etc.; −31 dBm0 = 11111.

Digit type: A 20-ms window is used to encode the edge when a digit is turned on and off. This is the delta time, 0 ms (00000) to 19 ms (10011), from the beginning of the current frame in milliseconds. If there is no transition, the edge location will be set to 0 and the digit type of the previous windows will be repeated.

Code	Digit Type
000	Digit off
001	DTMF on
010-111	Reserved

Digit code: The following DTMF digit codes are encoded when dialed digit type = DTMF ON.

Digit Code	DTMF Digits	Digit Code	DTMF Digits
00000	0	01000	8
00001	1	01001	9
00010	2	01010	*
00011	3	01011	#
00100	4	01100	A
00101	5	01101	B
00110	6	01110	C
00111	7	01111	D
		10000-11111	Reserved

to send, it will start sending a dialed digit payload every 20 ms. Since each payload covers 60 ms of digit on/off edge information, there is redundancy of the edge information. The sequence number is incremented by one in each transmitted payload. When the digit activity is off, the transmitter should continue to send three more dialed digit payloads for 60 ms.

Procedure for Interpreting Received Dialed Digit Payloads When the receiver gets a dialed digit payload or accepts the received addressing information, it will generate digits according to the location of the on and off edges. Silence will be applied to the duration after an off edge and before an on edge. Digits will be generated after an on edge and before an off edge. If the sequence number is one greater than the last received sequence number, the receiver appends the current edge information to the previously received information. If the sequence number is two greater than the last received sequence number, the receiver appends the recent and current edge information to the previously received information. If the sequence number is three greater than the last received sequence number, the receiver appends the previous, recent, and current edge information to the previously received information. If the sequence number is more than three greater than the last received sequence number, the receiver appends the previous, recent, and current edge information to the previously received information. It fills in the gap with the static values based on the previously received payload.

On a given subchannel, if a voice payload is received at any time, an off edge should be appended to the previously received digits' on/off edge information.

FRF.11 Annex B—Signaling Bit Transfer Syntax

Signaling Bit Transfer Syntax comprises payload formats and transfer procedures for alarm indications and channel-associated signaling bits.

Payload Format

Payloads carrying signaling bits will be identified using the payload type field in the VOFR header (see Figure 6.13). The signaling bits will automatically be associated with the corresponding voice traffic based on the Channel ID field.

The first byte following the VOFR header contains a 7-bit sequence number with the most significant bit assigned as an *alarm indicator signal* (AIS) bit: A value of 1 signifies an alarm condition.

The sequence number starts at 0 and increments by 1 up through 127 and rolls over back to 0. The transfer syntax for signaling bits contains 60 ms worth of samples for up to four signaling bits. Each sample has a time resolution of 2.0 ms. Each payload contains ten "new" samples for the current 20-ms time interval and a repetition of the ten samples for each of the two immediately preceding 20-ms time intervals. This will result in 15 bytes of packed signaling bit values.

For 16-state coding, all four bits are independent. For 4-state coding, the A and B bits are repeated in the C and D bit fields, respectively. For 2-state coding, the A bit is repeated in the B, C, and D bit fields.

Procedures for Transmission of Payloads

While there are transitions occurring in the signaling bit values, the transmitter sends a signaling bit payload every 20 ms. Since each payload covers 60 ms of signal bit states, there is redundancy of signal bit information. The sequence number is incremented by one in each transmitted payload. When the signal bit values have been static for 500 ms, the transmitter switches frequency of transmission and sends a signal bit payload only once in every 5 s. During this time, the sequence number is not incremented.

When transitions start occurring again, the transmitter resumes incrementing the sequence numbers by one and sending payloads every 20 ms.

The first such payload contains ten static previous and ten static recent values with ten new current samples. The second such payload contains ten static previous values with the ten previous values that were current in the first payload and ten new current samples. This restarts the overlapping redundancy of information.

The transmitter may debounce the sequence of signaling bit values prior to transmission, but is not required to do so.

	Octet	Bits							
		8	7	6	5	4	3	2	1
					Sequence Number				
Previous	P	AIS							
	P+1	D[t−56ms]	C[t−56ms]	B[t−56ms]	A[t−56ms]	D[t−58ms]	C[t−58ms]	B[t−58ms]	A[t−58ms]
	P+2	D[t−52ms]	C[t−52ms]	B[t−52ms]	A[t−52ms]	D[t−54ms]	C[t−54ms]	B[t−54ms]	A[t−54ms]
	P+3	D[t−48ms]	C[t−48ms]	B[t−48ms]	A[t−48ms]	D[t−50ms]	C[t−50ms]	B[t−50ms]	A[t−50ms]
	P+4	D[t−44ms]	C[t−44ms]	B[t−44ms]	A[t−44ms]	D[t−46ms]	C[t−46ms]	B[t−46ms]	A[t−46ms]
	P+5	D[t−40ms]	C[t−40ms]	B[t−40ms]	A[t−40ms]	D[t−42ms]	C[t−42ms]	B[t−42ms]	A[t−42ms]
Recent	P+6	D[t−36ms]	C[t−36ms]	B[t−36ms]	A[t−36ms]	D[t−38ms]	C[t−38ms]	B[t−38ms]	A[t−38ms]
	P+7	D[t−32ms]	C[t−32ms]	B[t−32ms]	A[t−32ms]	D[t−34ms]	C[t−34ms]	B[t−34ms]	A[t−34ms]
	P+8	D[t−28ms]	C[t−28ms]	B[t−28ms]	A[t−28ms]	D[t−30ms]	C[t−30ms]	B[t−30ms]	A[t−30ms]
	P+9	D[t−24ms]	C[t−24ms]	B[t−24ms]	A[t−24ms]	D[t−26ms]	C[t−26ms]	B[t−26ms]	A[t−26ms]
	P+10	D[t−20ms]	C[t−20ms]	B[t−20ms]	A[t−20ms]	D[t−22ms]	C[t−22ms]	B[t−22ms]	A[t−22ms]
Current	P+11	D[t−16ms]	C[t−16ms]	B[t−16ms]	A[t−16ms]	D[t−18ms]	C[t−18ms]	B[t−18ms]	A[t−18ms]
	P+12	D[t−12ms]	C[t−12ms]	B[t−12ms]	A[t−12ms]	D[t−14ms]	C[t−14ms]	B[t−14ms]	A[t−14ms]
	P+13	D[t−8ms]	C[t−8ms]	B[t−8ms]	A[t−8ms]	D[t−10ms]	C[t−10ms]	B[t−10ms]	A[t−10ms]
	P+14	D[t−4ms]	C[t−4ms]	B[t−4ms]	A[t−4ms]	D[t−6ms]	C[t−6ms]	B[t−6ms]	A[t−6ms]
	P+15	D[t]	C[t]	B[t]	A[t]	D[t−2ms]	C[t−2ms]	B[t−2ms]	A[t−2ms]

Figure 6.13
Signaling bit transfer syntax payload format.

231

Procedures for Interpreting Received Payloads   When the receiver gets a signaling bit payload, it processes the bits based on the sequence number. If the sequence number is one larger than the last received sequence number, the receiver appends the current signal bits to the previously received values. If the sequence number is two larger than the last received sequence number, the receiver appends the recent and current signal bits to the previously received values. If the sequence number is three larger than the last received sequence number, the receiver appends the previous, recent, and current signal bits to the previously received values. If the sequence number is more than three larger than the last received sequence number, the receiver appends the previous, recent, and current signal bits to the previously received values. It fills in the gap with static values based on the previously received payload.

If the sequence number is the same as the last received sequence number, the receiver takes the first value and uses it to set its current values for the signaling bits. (The signal bit values are static.)

The transmitter may or may not have debounced the signal bit values before transmission. If the receiving VOFR service user is interpreting the semantics of the signal bits, it should debounce the sequence of bit values received.

FRF.11 Annex C—Data Transfer Syntax

This annex describes a transfer syntax to support transport of data frames between two voice over frame relay service users. The contents of the frames are transparent to the voice over frame relay service. Typical applications include the transport of common channel signaling messages, RFC1490 packets, and FRF3.1 packets. All data subframes contain the fragmentation header. The payload type is set to primary payload type.

Data Payload Format

Figure 6.14 shows the subframe payload format.

FRF.11 Annex D—Fax Relay Transfer Syntax

The Fax Relay Transfer Syntax comprises the Fax Relay Payload Format and the Fax Relay Transfer Procedure. The fax relay transfer syntax provides a transfer syntax for fax. The Payload Format and

Figure 6.14
Data transfer syntax payload format.

Bits								
8	7	6	5	4	3	2	1	Octet
VOFR subframe header								1
B	E	0	Sequence number (upper 5 bits)					P
Sequence number (lower 8 bits)								P+1
Payload fragment (variable length)								P+2 to P+N

the Procedures are fairly complex. The interested reader is referred to FRF.11.

FRF.11 Annex E—CS-ACELP Transfer Syntax

When the VOFR service user offers a frame of samples speech, it is immediately transmitted using the transfer structure described below.

CS-ACELP Transfer Structure

CS-ACELP (ITU-T G.729/ITU-T G.729 Annex A, Coding of Speech at 8 kbps using Conjugate Structure–Algebraic Code Excited Linear Predictive (CS-ACELP) Coding, March 1996) produces 80 bits for each 10-ms frame of sampled speech. The list of the transmitted parameters used by the CS-ACELP algorithm is provided below. In order to allow the frame relay device to adjust its transmission rate, the CS-ACELP transfer syntax structure will permit multiples of 10-ms frames to be packed into the voice information field. An integer number of 10-ms frames will be packed into the voice information field to form an $M *$ 10-ms payload. For each M * 10 ms of compressed speech, $M *$ 80 bits or M * 10 octets will be produced (packetization time, or frame size, is $M * 10$ ms). Support of $M=2$ is required. A range of 1 to 6 can optionally be supported. See Tables 6.4 and 6.5 and Figure 6.15.

Table 6.4 **List of Transmitted Parameters**

Symbol	Description	Bits
LSP0	Switched predictor index of LSP quantizer	1
LSP1	First-stage vector of LSP quantizer	7
LSP2	Second-stage lower vector of LSP quantizer	5
LSP3	Second-stage lower vector of LSP quantizer	5
P1	Pitch period (delay)	8
P0	Parity check of pitch period	1
C1	Fixed codebook—1st subframe	13
S1	Signs of pulses—1st subframe	4
GA1	Gain codebook (stage 1)—1st subframe	3
GB1	Gain codebook (stage 2)—1st subframe	4
P2	Pitch period (delay)—2nd subframe	5
C2	Fixed codebook—2nd subframe	13
S2	Signs of pulses—2nd subframe	4
GA2	Gain codebook (stage 1)—2nd subframe	3
GB2	Gain codebook (stage 2)—2nd subframe	4
Total	Per 10-ms frame	80

*LSP = line spectrum pair

Transmission of (optional) sequence numbers may be configured on a subchannel basis. When enabled, the voice transfer syntax defined in Figure 6.15 is encapsulated in the voice transfer structure field of the active voice payload shown in Figure 6.17. The sequence number of Figure 6.13 should be incremented every 10 ms. The coding type field of Figure 6.13 should be set to 0000.

Table 6.5 **CS-ACELP Bit Packing Structure for Each Frame**

Octet	MSB	Bit Packing	LSB
1		LSP0, LSP1[7...1]	
2		LSP2[5..1], LSP3[5..3]	
3		LSP3[2,1], P1[7..3]	
4		P1[2,1], P0, C1[13..9]	
5		C1[8..1]	
6		S1[4..1], GA1[3...1], GB1[4]	
7		GB1[3...1], P2[5..1]	
8		C2[13...6]	
9		C2[5...1], S2[4..2]	
10		S2[1], GA2[3..1], GB2[4..1]	

Bits →

7	6	5	4	3	2	1	0	
LSP0	LSP1[7]	LSP1[6]	LSP1[5]	LSP1[4]	LSP1[3]	LSP1[2]	LSP1[1]	Octet F+P+1
LSP2[5]	LSP2[4]	LSP2[3]	LSP2[2]	LSP2[1]	LSP3[5]	LSP3[4]	LSP3[3]	Octet F+P+2
LSP3[2]	LSP3[1]	P1[8]	P1[7]	P1[6]	P1[5]	P1[4]	P1[3]	Octet F+P+3
P1[2]	P1[1]	P0	C1[13]	C1[12]	C1[11]	C1[10]	C1[09]	
C1[08]	C1[07]	C1[06]	C1[05]	C1[04]	C1[03]	C1[02]	C1[01]	
S1[04]	S1[03]	S1[02]	S1[01]	GA1[03]	GA1[02]	GA1[01]	GB1[04]	Frame 1
GB1[03]	GB1[02]	GB1[01]	P2[05]	P2[04]	P2[03]	P2[02]	P2[01]	
C2[13]	C2[12]	C2[11]	C2[10]	C2[09]	C2[08]	C2[07]	C2[06]	
C2[05]	C2[04]	C2[03]	C2[02]	C2[01]	S2[04]	S2[03]	S2[02]	
S2[01]	GA2[03]	GA2[02]	GA2[01]	GB2[04]	GB2[03]	GB2[02]	GB2[01]	Octet F+P+N

. . . .

7	6	5	4	3	2	1	0	
LSP0	LSP1[7]	LSP1[6]	LSP1[5]	LSP1[4]	LSP1[3]	LSP1[2]	LSP1[1]	Octet (M−1)*N+F+P+1
LSP2[5]	LSP2[4]	LSP2[3]	LSP2[2]	LSP2[1]	LSP3[5]	LSP3[4]	LSP3[3]	
LSP3[2]	LSP3[1]	P1[8]	P1[7]	P1[6]	P1[5]	P1[4]	P1[3]	
P1[2]	P1[1]	P0	C1[13]	C1[12]	C1[11]	C1[10]	C1[09]	
C1[08]	C1[07]	C1[06]	C1[05]	C1[04]	C1[03]	C1[02]	C1[01]	
S1[04]	S1[03]	S1[02]	S1[01]	GA1[03]	GA1[02]	GA1[01]	GB1[04]	Frame M
GB1[03]	GB1[02]	GB1[01]	P2[05]	P2[04]	P2[03]	P2[02]	P2[01]	
C2[13]	C2[12]	C2[11]	C2[10]	C2[09]	C2[08]	C2[07]	C2[06]	Octet (M−1)*N+F+P+N−2
C2[05]	C2[04]	C2[03]	C2[02]	C2[01]	S2[04]	S2[03]	S2[02]	Octet (M−1)*N+F+P+N−1
S2[01]	GA2[03]	GA2[02]	GA2[01]	GB2[04]	GB2[03]	GB2[02]	GB2[01]	Octet (M−1)*N+F+P+N

Where: F = Frame relay header (2 octets)
P = Voice packet header size in octets
M = Number of 10-ms frames
N = Number of octets in Voice Information Field = $M*10$

Figure 6.15
CS-ACELP Transfer Structure

FRF.11 Annex F—Generic PCM/ADPCM Voice Transfer Syntax

This section focuses on PCM and ADPCM.

Voice Transfer Structure

Encoded voice samples—G.711 (PCM), G.726 (ADPCM), or G.727 (EADPCM)—should be inserted into the structure defined by Figure 6.16. The transfer of PCM/ADPCM/EADPCM is inspired by ITU-T Recommendation G.764. The following sections define two payload types and the voice transfer structure.

   The voice transfer structure contains blocks arranged according to the significance of the bits. The first block contains the most significant bits (MSBs) of all the encoded samples, the second contains the second MSBs, and so on. Within a block, the bits are ordered according to their sample number. Since the 5-ms encoding interval corresponds to 40 samples, each block contains five octets.

   A particular feature of this structure is that noncritical (enhancement) information is placed in locations where it can easily be discarded, without impacting the critical (core) information. For example, if 32-kbps EADPCM (G.727 (4,2)) is used, then there will be four blocks corresponding to 4 bits of varying significance

Figure 6.16
PCM/ADPCM/ EADPCM voice transfer structure (showing case of M = 1).

Bit number	8	7		1	
MSB block	MSB/S8	MSB/S7	···	MSB/S1	P+5
			•		
	MSB/S40	MSB/S39	···	MSB/S33	
MSB-1 block	(MSB-1)/S8	(MSB-1)/S7	···	(MSB-1)/S1	
			•		
	(MSB-1)/S40	(MSB-1)/S39	···	(MSB-1)/S33	
⋮			⋮		
LSB block	LSB/S8	LSB/S7	···	LSB/S1	
			•		
	LSB/S40	LSB/S39	···	LSB/S33	Octet N

(msb, msb-1, msb-2, 1sb). The least significant blocks (msb-2, 1sb) are the enhancement blocks and may be discarded under congestion conditions (Annex G describes a related way of placing the critical and noncritical information into separate frames, so that the enhancement blocks can be marked with discard eligibility.)

The size of the voice transfer structure depends on the packing factor M and the coding type, as shown in Table 6.6. The packing factor is a multiple from 1 to 12. The value of M is configured identically at transmitter and receiver. It is typically, but not necessarily, the same in both directions. Equipment complying with this transfer syntax shall be configurable to support the default value $M = 1$.

When M is greater than 1, the voice transfer structure contains a first set of blocks, ordered from MSB to LSB, followed by a second set of blocks, ordered likewise, and so on up to the Mth set of blocks.

Active Voice Payload

When the payload type is primary payload, other fields in the subframe are as shown in Figure 6.17.

Coding type (4-bit field)   The coding type field indicates the method of encoding PCM/ADPCM/EADPCM voice samples into the voice transfer structure. The transmitting end system should only encode using algorithms for which there is decode support at

Table 6.6   PCM/ADPCM/EADPCM Transfer Characteristics

Coding Type	Algorithm Name	Reference Document	Compression Bit Rate (kbps)	Voice Transfer Structure (octets)
0000	PCM *A*-law	ITU-T G.711	64	40*M
0001	"	"	56	35*M
0010	"	"	48	30*M
0011	PCM μ-law	"	64	40*M
0100	"	"	56	35*M
0101	"	"	48	30*M
0110	ADPCM	ITU-T G.726	40	25*M
0111	"	"	32	20*M
1000	"	"	24	15*M
1001	"	"	16	10*M
1010	EADPCM (5,2)	ITU-T G.727	40	25*M
1011	(4,2)	"	32	20*M
1100	(3,2)	"	24	15*M
1101	(2,2)	"	16	10*M

Figure 6.17
2 PCM/ADPCM/ EADPCM steady state payload.

Bits								
8	7	6	5	4	3	2	1	Octet
Sequence number				Coding type				P
Voice transfer structure								P+1

the receiving end system. The algorithms supported by the receiver are known by mutual configuration. Values of the coding type field are shown in Table 6.6.

Sequence number (4-bit field)   The sequence number is used to maintain temporal integrity of voice played out by the receiving end system. For PCM/ADPCM/EADPCM, the underlying encoding interval is 5 ms. Voice samples are processed with this periodicity and the sequence number is incremented by 1. After a count of 15 is reached, the sequence number rolls back to 0. The sequence number is incremented every 5 ms, even when there is no active voice to be sent. This would be the case during a silence insertion period, if voice activity detection were operational. The peer end system expects to receive voice samples in sequence and within a certain time period. If voice activity detection is operational and no active voice is received, the peer end system will continue to increment its expected sequence number every 5 ms. When multiple voice samples are packed into and received in a single subframe ($M > 1$), the next expected sequence number is incremented by M.

When the payload type is primary payload with silence insertion, other fields in the subframe are as shown in Figure 6.18. (This payload type should not be sent if voice activity detection is not operational.) Additional subframes of this type may be sent if the noise level changes or may be sent redundantly to increase the probability of being received.

FRF.11 Annex G—G.727 Discard-Eligible EADPCM Voice Transfer Syntax

Here, the voice transfer structure is the same as defined in Annex F.

Active Voice Payload

The G.727 EADPCM compression algorithm outputs core and enhancement information. This information is separately assembled into blocks. Core information is inserted into frames with low dis-

Figure 6.18
*PCM/ADPCM/
EADPCM silence
insertion descriptor
(SID) payload.
Encoding interval:
5 ms
Packing factor:
M = 1 to 12
Support of M = 4
is required. A
range of 1 to 12
can optionally be
supported.*

				Bits				
8	7	6	5	4	3	2	1	Octet
Sequence number				Reserved				P

Noise level (8-bit field) The background noise level is expressed in –dBm0. The receiver can use this field to play out an appropriate level of background noise in the absence of active voice.

card eligibility (DE = 0), and enhancement information is inserted into frames with high discard eligibility (DE = 1). Core and enhancement information, if required by a particular traffic type, may be combined within a single frame with DE = 0. When the payload type is primary payload, other fields in the subframe are as shown in Figure 6.19. The voice transfer structure containing encoded voice samples is defined in Annex F.

Figure 6.19 shows only two subframes, one each for core and enhancement information, but transmitters are explicitly allowed to use the VOFR header to pack multiple subframes of the same kind of information into each frame, with DE = 0 or 1, correspondingly.

Figure 6.19
*Discard-eligible
EADPCM steady
state payload
(showing single
subframes).
Encoding interval:
5 ms
Packing factor:
M = 1 to 12*

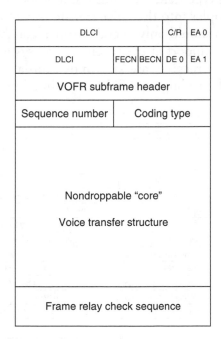
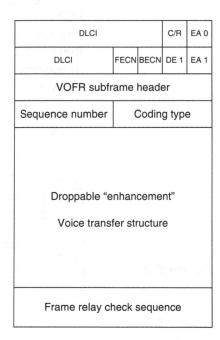

Table 6.7 **Discard-Eligible EADPCM Transfer Characteristics**

Coding Type	Algorithm Name	Type of Information	Compression Bit Rate (kbps)	Voice Transfer Structure (octets)
0000	EADPCM (2,2)	Core	16	10*M
0001	(3,2)	Enhancement	8	5*M
0010	(4,2)	"	16	10*M
0011	(5,2)	"	24	15*M
0100	(3,2)	Combined	24	15*M
0101	(4,2)	"	32	20*M
0110	(5,2)	"	40	25*M
0111	EADPCM (3,3)	Core	24	15*M
1000	(4,3)	Enhancement	8	5*M
1001	(5,3)	"	16	10*M
1010	(4,3)	Combined	32	20*M
1011	(5,3)	"	40	25*M
1100	EADPCM (4,4)	Core	32	20*M
1101	(5,4)	Enhancement	8	5*M
1110	(5,4)	Combined	40	25*M

Note: Encoding interval: 5 ms. Packing factor: M = 1 to 12.

The coding type field indicates the method of encoding EAD-PCM voice samples into the voice transfer structure. The transmitting end system should only encode using algorithms for which there is decode support at the receiving end system. The algorithms supported by the receiver are known by mutual configuration.

Values of the coding type field are defined in Table 6.7.

9			3	2		0
MSB	7-bit shape vector		LSB	MSB	3-bit gain vector	LSB

(MSB) 7 bits of shape vector [0] (LSB)	(MSB) 1 bit of gain [0]		Octet P+1
2 bits of gain [0] (LSB)	(MSB) 6 bits of shape vector [1]		Octet P+2
1 bit of shape vector [1] (LSB)	(MSB) 3 bits of gain [1] (LSB)	(MSB) 4 bits of shape vector [2]	Octet P+3
3 bits of shape vector [2] (LSB)	(MSB) 3 bits of gain [2] (LSB)	(MSB) 2 bits of shape vector [3]	Octet P+4
5 bits of shape vector [3] (LSB)	(MSB) 3 bits of gain [3] (LSB)		Octet P+5
(MSB) 7 bits of shape vector [4] (LSB)	(MSB) 1 bit of gain [4]		Octet P+6
2 bits of gain [4] (LSB)	(MSB) 6 bits of shape vector [5]		Octet P+7
1 bit of shape vector [5] (LSB)	(MSB) 3 bits of gain [5] (LSB)	(MSB) 4 bits of shape vector [6]	Octet P+8
3 bits of shape vector [6] (LSB)	(MSB) 3 bits of gain [6] (LSB)	(MSB) 2 bits of shape vector [7]	Octet P+9
5 bits of shape vector [7] (LSB)	(MSB) 3 bits of gain [7] (LSB)		Octet P+10

Figure 6.20
LD-CELP voice transfer structure (showing case of M = 1).

Where: P = VOFR subframe header and optional transfer protocol octets

FRF.11 Annex H—G.728 LD-CELP Transfer Syntax

Voice samples that are compressed using 16-kbps LD-CELP (G.728) will be inserted into the voice transfer structure defined in Figure 6.20. The LD-CELP compression algorithm produces a 10-bit codeword vector for every five samples of input speech from an 8000-sample/second stream. The 10 bits are reformatted to fit within the octet structure of the voice transfer structure. Every group of five octets contains four 10-bit codewords, resulting in a 2.5-ms-duration subframe. Two of these 2.5-ms groups are combined into a 5-ms block for transmission. The MSB of the first 10-bit codeword is aligned with the MSB of the first octet in the block. Subsequent bits of the codeword are placed in descending bit locations of the first octet with the other bits of subsequent codewords being bit-packed into the remaining octets. Each block consists of eight 10-bit codewords, which are mapped into 10 octets. The size of the voice transfer structure depends on the packing factor M. The packing factor is a multiple from 1 to 12. The value of M is

Table 6.8   List of Transmitted Parameters

Name	Transmitted Parameters	High Rate	Low Rate # Bits
LPC	LSP VQ index	24	24
ACL0	Adaptive codebook lag	7	7
ACL1	Differential adaptive codebook lag	2	2
ACL2	Adaptive codebook lag	7	7
ACL3	Differential adaptive codebook lag	2	2
GAIN0	Combination of adaptive and fixed gains	12	12
GAIN1	Combination of adaptive and fixed gains	12	12
GAIN2	Combination of adaptive and fixed gains	12	12
GAIN3	Combination of adaptive and fixed gains	12	12
POS0	Pulse positions index	20*	12
POS1	Pulse positions index	18*	12
POS2	Pulse positions index	20*	12
POS3	Pulse positions index	18*	12
PSIG0	Pulse sign index	6	4
PSIG1	Pulse sign index	5	4
PSIG2	Pulse sign index	6	4
PSIG3	Pulse sign index	5	4
GRID0	Grid index	1	1
GRID1	Grid index	1	1
GRID2	Grid index	1	1
GRID3	Grid index	1	1

Note: The 4 MSBs of these codewords are combined to form a 13-bit index, MSB position.

configured identically at transmitter and receiver. It is typically, but not necessarily, the same in both directions. Equipment complying with this transfer syntax shall be configurable to support the value $M = 1$ to 12. When M is greater than 1, the voice transfer structure contains multiple blocks, starting with the first encoded voice sample and ending with the last encoded voice sample.

FRF.11 Annex I—G.723.1 MP-MLQ Dual Rate Speech Coder

Voice samples that are compressed using the 6.3-kbps MP-MLQ algorithm (G.723.1 high rate) and 5.3-kbps ACELP algorithm (G.723.1 low rate) yield a frame of packed parameters for every 240 samples of input speech from an 8000-sample/second stream. Some of these parameters are based on an analysis of the entire frame; others are based on the analyses of each of the four compo-

Table 6.9   Octet Packing for the 6.3-kbps MP-MLQ Codec

Transmitted	PARx_By, ...
1	LPC_B5...LPC_B0, VADFLAG_B0, RATEFLAG_B0
2	LPC_B13...LPC_B6
3	LPC_B21...LPC_B14
4	ACL0_B5...ACL0_B0, LPC_B23, LPC_B22
5	ACL2_B4...ACL2_B0, ACL1_B1, ACL1_B0, ACL0_B6
6	GAIN0_B3...GAIN0_B0, ACL3_B1, ACL3_B0, ACL2_B6, ACL2_B5
7	GAIN0_B11...GAIN0_B4
8	GAIN1_B7...GAIN1_B0
9	GAIN2_B3...GAIN2_B0, GAIN1_B11...GAIN1_B8
10	GAIN2_B11...GAIN2_B4
11	GAIN3_B7...GAIN3_B0
12	GRID3_B0, GRID2_B0, GRID1_B0, GRID0_B0, GAIN3_B11...GAIN3_B8
13	MSBPOS_B6...MSBPOS_B0, UB
14	POS0_B1, POS0_B0, MSBPOS_B12...MSBPOS_B7
15	POS0_B9...POS0_B2
16	POS1_B2, POS1_B0, POS0_B15...POS0_B10
17	POS1_B10...POS1_B3
18	POS2_B3...POS2_B0, POS1_B13...POS1_B11
19	POS2_B11...POS2_B4
20	POS3_B3...POS3_B0, POS2_B15...POS2_B12
21	POS3_B11...POS3_B4
22	PSIG0_B5...PSIG0_B0, POS3_B13, POS3_B12
23	PSIG2_B2...PSIG2_B0, PSIG1_B4...PSIG1_B0
24	PSIG3_B4...PSIG3_B0, PSIG2_B5...PSIG2_B3

nent 60-sample subframes. Table 6.8 lists transmitted parameters for both MP-MLQ and ACELP.

For MP-MLQ, the resulting 191-bit frame is formatted to fit within the 24-octet structure of the voice information field (1 bit is unused) as defined in Table 6.9. For ACELP, the resulting 160-bit frame is formatted to fit within the 20-octet structure of the voice information field as defined in Table 6.8. In Table 6.9, each bit of transmitted parameters is named PAR (x)_By:, where PAR is the name of the parameter and x indicates the G.721 subframe index if relevant and y stands for the bit position starting from 0 (LSB) to the MSB.

The expression PARx_By . . . PARx_Bz stands for the range of transmitted bits from bit y to bit z. The unused bit is named UB (value = 0). RATEFLAG_B0 tells whether the high rate (0) or the low rate (1) is used for the current frame. VADFLAG_B0 tells whether the current frame is active speech (0) or nonspeech (1). The combination of RATEFLAG and VADFLAG both being set to 1 is reserved for future use. Octets are transmitted in the order in

Table 6.10   Octet Packing for the 5.3-kbps ACELP Codec

Transmitted Octets	PARx_By, ….
1	LPC_B5…LPC_B0, VADFLAG_B0, RATEFLAG_B0
2	LPC_B13…LPC_B6
3	LPC_B21…LPC_B14
4	ACL0_B5…ACL0_B0, LPC_B23, LPC_B22
5	ACL2_B4…ACL2_B0, ACL1_B1, ACL1_B0, ACL0_B6
6	GAIN0_B3…GAIN0_B0, ACL3_B1, ACL3_B0, ACL2_B6, ACL2_B5
7	GAIN0_B11…GAIN0_B4
8	GAIN1_B7…GAIN1_B0
9	GAIN2_B3…GAIN2_B0, GAIN1_B11…GAIN1_B8
10	GAIN2_B11…GAIN2_B4
11	GAIN3_B7…GAIN3_B0
12	GRID3_B0, GRID2_B0, GRID1_B0, GRID0_B0, GAIN3_B11…GAIN3_B8
13	POS0_B7…POS0_B0
14	POS1_B3…POS1_B0, POS0_B11…POS0_B8
15	POS1_B11…POS1_B4
16	POS2_B7…POS2_B0
17	POS3_B3…POS3_B0, POS2_B11…POS2_B8
18	POS3_B11…POS3_B4
19	PSIG1_B3…PSIG1_B0, PSIG0_B3…PSIG0_B0
20	PSIG3_B3…PSIG3_B0, PSIG2_B3…PSIG2_B0

which they are listed in Tables 6.9 and 6.10. Within each octet shown, the bits are ordered with the most significant bit on the left.

References

1. Act Networks Promotional Material, http://www.acti.com/vofr.html.
2. FRF.1.1, Frame Relay User-to-Network Implementation Agreement, January 1996.
3. FRF.3.1, Multiprotocol Encapsulation Implementation Agreement, June 22, 1995.
4. FRF.12, Frame Relay Fragmentation Implementation Agreement, 1997.
5. ITU G.711, Pulse Code Modulation of Voice Frequencies, 1988.
6. ITU G.723.1, Dual-Rate Speech Coder for Multimedia Communications Transmitting at 5.3 and 6.3 kbps, March 1996.
7. ITU G.726, 40-, 32-, 24-, 16-kbps Adaptive Differential Pulse Code Modulation (ADPCM), March 1991.
8. ITU G.727, 5-, 4-, 3-, and 2-bit Sample Embedded Adaptive Differential Pulse Code Modulation, November 1994.
9. ITU G.728, Coding of Speech at 16 kbps Using Low-Delay Code Excited Linear Prediction, November 1994.
10. ITU G.729, Coding of Speech at 8 kbps using Conjugate Structure–Algebraic Code Excited Linear Predictive (CS-ACELP) Coding, March 1996.
11. ITU G.764, Voice Packetization—Packetized Voice Protocols, December 1990.
12. ITU T.30, Terminal Equipment and Protocol for Telematic Service/Procedure for Facsimile General Switch Networks, March 1993.

CHAPTER 7

Voice over ATM Preliminaries

7.1 Introduction

This chapter provides some additional preliminaries to complement the foundation provided in Chapter 2. It highlights Voice and Telephony Services over ATM (VTOA) efforts and it provides a description of the ATM service classes along with some details of the ATM Adaptation Layer 1 (AAL 1) protocol. The chapter also looks at migrations of corporate networks as well as interworking of ATM voice with the PSTN. The chapters that follow build on this material to provide a more in-depth treatment of these topics. Many of the voice concepts highlighted in 1993 in Reference [1] have been standardized in the ATMF VTOA Implementation Agreements. This chapter looks at these issues from a conceptual point of view, whereas the chapters that follow discuss the exact implementation specifications.

7.2 VTOA Efforts: A Snapshot

ATM was developed to be a multimedia, multiservice, multipoint, QoS-enabled technology. Until the present, however, the practical focus of developers and service providers has been on the data side. Interest exists, however, in supporting integrated corporate networks, because of the economies of scale in transmission, switching, and operations, administration, maintenance, and provisioning (OAM&P) costs. ATM switches have been designed with effective traffic management capabilities (e.g., call admission control, usage parameter control, traffic shaping, cell tagging, cell discard, and per-VC queue management) to support the quality of service and service classes needed for the various applications, including real-time voice.

There have been considerable recent efforts aimed at standardization of voice over ATM UNIs/networks.[1] Currently, circuit emulation service (CES)–based services have been standardized, and AAL 2 approaches are well under development. Voice alternatives of interest include:

1. Voice over ATM with AAL 1/CBR (constant bit rate), AAL 5/VBR (variable bit rate), or the newly introduced AAL 2/VBR
2. ATM-based voice interworked with ISDN, to reach the public at large
3. ATM-based desktop voice

Other areas of interest include:

- Voice over frame relay service interworked to ATM
- Voice over IP carried in an ATM network using one of three available IP-carrying methods (these are not discussed further here; see Reference [2]):
    Classical IP over ATM (CIOA)
    LAN Emulation (LANE)
    Multiprotocols over ATM (MPOA)

At a macro level two technical approaches for voice over ATM are implied in point 1 above: use of constant-bit-rate (CBR) service class and use of AAL 1 to support CES, and use of real-time variable-bit-rate (RT-VBR) service class and the use of AAL 2 or AAL 5. The CBR approach is currently the most common of the two voice approaches and has been around for the longest. One of the advantages is that it provides CES, meaning that it gives a PBX the appearance that a standard T1 tie/trunk line is available to it, while in reality it is an ATM permanent virtual connection (PVC) over an ATM cell flow. The disadvantages of this approach are that (1) there is a need for higher bandwidth to recover a DS1 signal; (2) a mesh of end-to-end, point-to-point emulated circuits is required, generally without (carrier) network participation; (3) signaling and PSTN interworking is only now beginning to be considered (with the publication of appropriate standards); and (4) TR-303 voice switch support is not yet generally available.

In general, voice over ATM is not the least-cost solution at this time, unless an organization already has an ATM-based enterprise network that uses ATM via edge multiplexers and the organization is interested only in on-net voice. Today, the typical access device (edge multiplexer) is actually an ATM-ready router that supports legacy ports on the user side and ATM on the network side. Currently, some large fraction of these devices does not support CES. However, some edge multiplexers now entering the market do support T1 interfaces on the user side, to connect PBXs utilizing signaling-enriched CES. The importance of signaling was discussed in Chapter 5.

The ATM Forum started work on voice transport in 1993, and it was not until April 1995 that the VTOA working group published its first document, which contained the unstructured circuit emulation and the structured circuit emulation specs. Other specifications have followed. Table 7.1 identifies the set of specifications that have recently been issued [3]. Table 7.2 highlights key features in these specifications. Figure 7.1 shows a classification of CBR capabilities being leveraged for voice.

Unstructured circuit emulation maps an entire T1 (1.544-Mbps) circuit to a single ATM virtual circuit, thus limiting it to point-to-point applications. On the other hand, structured circuit emulation allows switches to map individual 64-kbps circuits in a T1 line to ATM VCs, and it can be used for point-to-multipoint connections. See Figure 7.2. Each of these approaches, however, requires voice to be treated as CBR traffic. A problem is that CBR traffic forces customers to reserve bandwidth for voice even when they are not actually sending it. Figures 7.3 and 7.4 show two applications. Figure 7.3 shows both structured and unstructured CES for on-net applications. Figure 7.4 shows how structured CES can be used to accomplish PSTN interworking; the figure also shows the

Table 7.1   VTOA Specifications

Document Number	Approval	Specification and Features
af-vtoa-0078.000	1/97	Circuit emulation service (CES-IS v2.0)
		• Structured and unstructured service
		• Synchronous and asynchronous clock recovery
		• ATM CBR PVC (SPVC) service
af-vtoa-0085.000	7/97	Dynamic bandwidth CES (DBCES)
		• Defines DB IWF based on CES-IS

		• PVC and optional SVC services
		    Idle pattern detection
		    CAS AB bit detection

af-vtoa-0089.000	7/97	Landline trunking over ATM
		• B-ISDN to N-ISDN (public) interworking

		• ISDN CCS support/interpretation
		    Nx64-kbps voice switching
		    (ATM SVCs)

af-vtoa-0083.000	5/97	ATM desktop
		• B-TE to B-ISDN interworking
		• B-ISDN to N-ISDN interworking (public and private)
		• AAL 5 and AAL 1 B-TE options
		• 64-kbps voice switching (ATM SVCs)
		• UNI 4.0 supplementary service

integrated use of ATM on the customer's location. Dynamic bandwidth allocation is a step in the direction of making more efficient use of CBR, and so making the use of ATM for voice (conceivably) more practical. Figures 7.5 and 7.6 depict the protocol stack for unstructured and structured CES. Additional details are provided in the sections that follow.

Sending voice as VBR traffic is the obvious alternative. There is work under way to develop standards for VBR support of voice. Silence suppression and voice compression will be a part of the new specification, providing greater use of bandwidth. AAL 2 is a proposal in ITU-T Study Group 13. Initially, AAL 2 was targeted VBR service for low-bit-rate voice traffic between a wireless base station

Table 7.2   VTOA Features

Transparent transport of channel signaling over ATM
  Channel-associated signaling (CAS) utilizing structured CAS service
  Common channel signaling (CCS) utilizing structured basic or unstructured
  service

Variable cell fill
  Reduces overall network latency

Flexible network timing optimized for reliable TDM voice and video transport
  Synchronous timing
  Asynchronous timing

Dynamic bandwidth allocation
  Detection of idle states
Interworking with PSTN

and a mobile switch center, but it has been parlayed into a new voice standard for more general applications.

ATM Forum work is focused into two areas: VTOA trunking for narrowband services, targeted primarily at applications in private voice networks, and VTOA legacy voice services at a native ATM terminal, targeted at applications in private and public networks, where interworking and interoperation of ATM and non-ATM networks and services for voice are necessary.

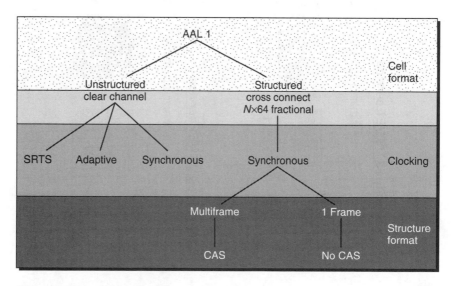

Figure 7.1
Taxonomy of AAL 1 services (CES).

CAS = Circuit-associated signaling

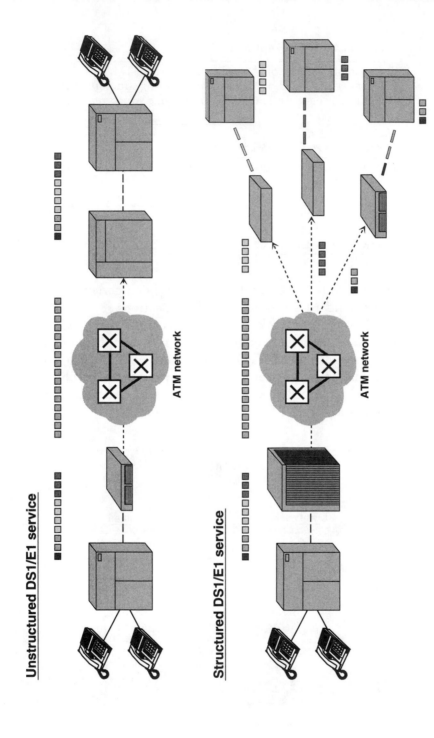

Figure 7.2
Unstructured versus structured CES single point/multipoint capabilities.

250

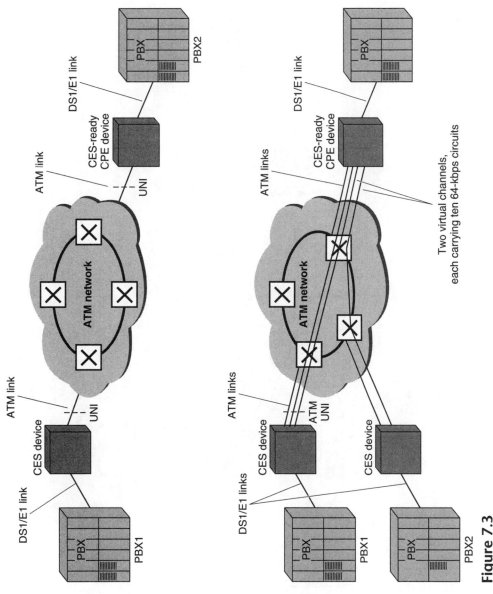

Figure 7.3
CES service (emulates T1 link).

251

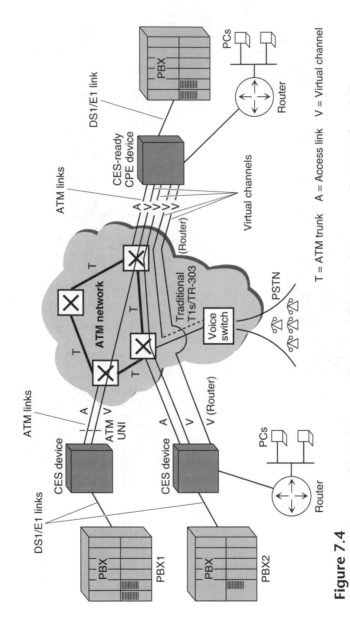

Figure 7.4
Structured CES service within a multiservice ATM environment with PSTN handoff.

252

Figure 7.5
DS1/E1 unstructured service protocol stack.

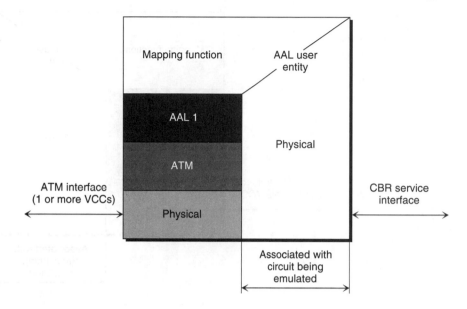

Circuit Emulation Service (CES) Interoperability Specification
This service has a CES and has a dynamic bandwidth CES version. Features are as follows:

- CES:
    Constant bit rate (64-kbps) service
        Structured service for fractional applications (FT1/FE1)
        Unstructured service for DS1/E1/DS3
        Options for carrying channel-associated signaling (CAS)
        Configured bandwidth used regardless of whether there is traffic
    ATM's overhead makes this more costly than TDM solutions
- Dynamic bandwidth CES:
    CES structured service models FT1/FE1
    Bandwidth allocated dynamically based on active channel indication
    Uses CAS or common channel signaling (e.g., ISDN's D channel)

Figure 7.6
*DS1/E1 structured
service protocol
stack.*

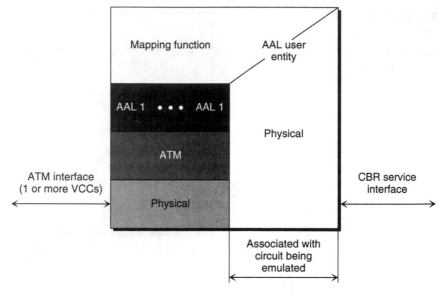

Requires the user to allocate bandwidth for the maximum
number of channels

Trunking for Narrowband Services   This specification is based
on the use of an *interworking function* (IWF) between the ATM network and each interconnected narrowband network. This includes a
Land Line I, a Land Line II, and a mobile trunking specification.

- Land Line I
    Targets ISDN trunking over an ATM network
        Call-by-call routing to make effective use of bandwidth
        Dynamic bandwidth by allowing VCC setup in response
        to call
        64-kbps channels
        No silence suppression
- Land Line II
    Targets access and private trunking applications
        Call-by-call routing to make effective use of bandwidth
        Uses new AAL 2 to multiplex multiple channels in a cell
        Supports compressed voice and silence suppression

Supports switched calls to outgoing trunks

Supports fax

- Mobile Trunking

 Targets cellular networks

 Supports transport between the base station and the mobile service central office

 Efficiently transports voice that is already compressed by mobile handset

 Uses AAL 2 to multiplex multiple channels into a cell

Voice and Telephony over ATM to the Desktop Specification   This document specifies the functions required to provide voice and telephony services over ATM to the desktop. It describes the functions of the IWF and a native ATM terminal. This version covers only the transport of a single 64-kbps *A*-law or μ-law encoded voiceband signal.

Network delays are always an issue in real-time voice delivery. Because there is no voice compression time when using PCM (which is currently the norm), in general, the end-to-end (one-way) delay is around 25 ms. The cell packing delay is from 1 to 6 ms; 1 ms is achieved in the *partial cell fill mode.* See Figure 7.7. Note that this delay is incurred twice, because it is also encountered in the cell disassembly.

Two features emerging from the VTOA specifications that vendors were expected to implement in 1998 are CAS-based cut-through and idle pattern suppression. With CAS-based cut-through in the structured CES, when the on-hook state is detected for a certain set of DS0 channels coming from a PBX, which may be aggregated over a VC, an OAM cell is sent as a keep-alive signal; but when every DS0 in the VC has become idle, the VC is dropped (thereby conserving bandwidth allocation). For this to work, SVC or soft PVC services are needed in the ATM network. In the idle suppression mode, certain well-known idle patterns from TDM multiplexers that may be using the CES connection are tracked, with the goal of dropping the connection if the multiplexer becomes idle.

The issue of bandwidth conservation may make a lot of sense in a private ATM network, but for public ATM networks the value is

Figure 7.7
Variable cell fill.

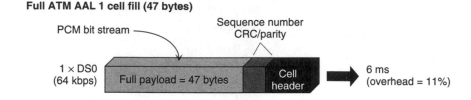

Full ATM AAL 1 cell fill (47 bytes)

PCM bit stream

Sequence number
CRC/parity

1 × DS0
(64 kbps)   Full payload = 47 bytes   Cell header   6 ms
(overhead = 11%)

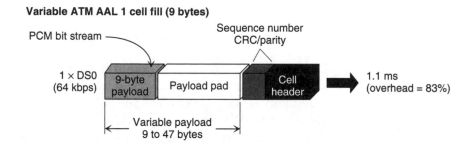

Variable ATM AAL 1 cell fill (9 bytes)

PCM bit stream

Sequence number
CRC/parity

1 × DS0
(64 kbps)   9-byte payload   Payload pad   Cell header   1.1 ms
(overhead = 83%)

Variable payload
9 to 47 bytes

unclear at the practical level. First, there has been relatively little tariffing/pricing activity in the CES market (and in the T1 UNI market for that matter) at the present time; hence, the pricing implications cannot be addressed. Furthermore, unlike frame relay, ATM carriers may not be interested in traffic contract granularity for peak cell rate/sustained cell rate (PCR/SCR) at the $n{\times}D0$ level; some carriers offer granularity at the 1-Mbps range. The key motivation for idle suppression, therefore, seems to be more for access bandwidth conservation than for backbone network bandwidth conservation. Using AAL 1, only about 20 DS0 voice trunks can be supported on a T1 line (due to the AAL 1/ATM overhead); hence, designers have to find a way to support, say, 24 effective trunks on a single ATM T1 rather than requiring two physical links. This is accomplished by statistical gain on the CES access side in over-promising the DS0 slots (say, CES port #1 gets 18 ports and CES port #2 gets 6 ports) and turning down the ones not being used at any particular time (thus, as long as there is a maximum active need for 20 ports, both end systems are led to believe that they have access to the maximum number of slots—that is, 18 and 6, respectively, in the example). Or, if there is only one CES port, then the unclaimed bandwidth secured via the dynamic allocation can be available on the access to other local VBR/UBR/ABR applications.

7.3 Advantages of the Integrated ATM Data/Voice Approach

In principle, the emerging technologies for transmitting voice over data networks present opportunities for organizations to reduce costs and enable new applications. In particular, traditional router vendors see the opportunity to cannibalize the voice traffic by adding features to their routers to support voice. Clearly, if a company uses separate facilities to carry on-net voice (company location–to–company location), there could be additional costs in terms of communication channels, equipment, and carrier charges. However, the fact that voice may be introduced over IP networks (intranets or the Internet) may prove to be cross-elastic with the voice over ATM (and over frame relay) market.

In the past, enterprises justified the cost of a private WAN by the cost savings these networks achieved for the on-net voice traffic. Now bandwidth requirements for data networks are so great that organizations can add voice capabilities to these networks for relatively limited incremental costs. These considerations are primarily true for voice over frame relay and ATM; voice over IP will experience quality degradations. As already implied, voice over ATM is still relatively expensive at this time, in terms of the required CPE. However, it is expected that by 1998 or 1999, these CPE devices will be available for around $2500 to 3500; they are now in the $5000 to 10,000 range.

Figures 7.8 through 7.11 depict some possible migrations of enterprise networks and intranets to make use of integration and voice over ATM. Figure 7.8 shows a late 1980s/early 1990s corporate network that used traditional TDM facilities. Figure 7.9 depicts a mid-1990s situation, where power users within an organization have migrated to ATM to support high-capacity requirements. Figure 7.10 depicts a late 1990s network where ATM is used for backbone/WAN support. Figure 7.11 depicts a contemporary view of networks, where integration advantages are being achieved utilizing ATM.

Implicit in Figure 7.11 is the assumption that the organization is using an ATM carrier that has an overlay ATM network (that is, the ATM network and the voice networks are separate). If that is the case, only on-net voice applications are supported. Note that the organization needs an ATM edge device that supports circuit

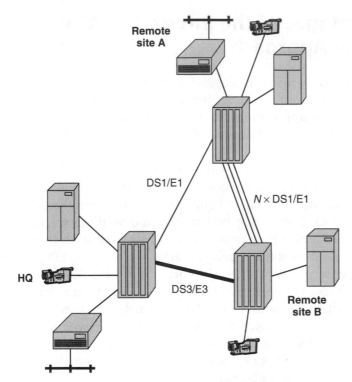

- Physically meshed private line networks
- Primarily low speed facilities (DS1/E1)
- Scalability to high speed, high capacity solutions very expensive (DS3, E3)
- Mostly narrowband applications (<2 Mbps)
- Fixed bandwidth assignment
- Unclear and expensive vendor migration paths
- Single vendor proprietary product solutions

Figure 7.8
Enterprise TDM networks. (Courtesy of Fore Systems, © 1997)

emulation, so that the PBX can be plugged in. In some cases the organization already has an ATM network but it may not support circuit emulation, either at the CPE or the QoS level. This is typically the case when the organization utilizes ATM to interconnected traditional routers. This would then necessitate an upgrade. Fortunately, new routers such as Xylan 3WX support both routing function and circuit emulation. Another option would be for the PBX to develop a direct ATM/AAL 5/VBR connection to the switch, but this may be more popular in a year or two.

There are no voice-quality issues when using circuit emulation, particularly if the number of switched hops is small (say less than three). This configuration makes sense if the organization has an ATM network with (1) a CES-ready edge device and (2) available bandwidth in the network. Note that, although the overlay arrange-

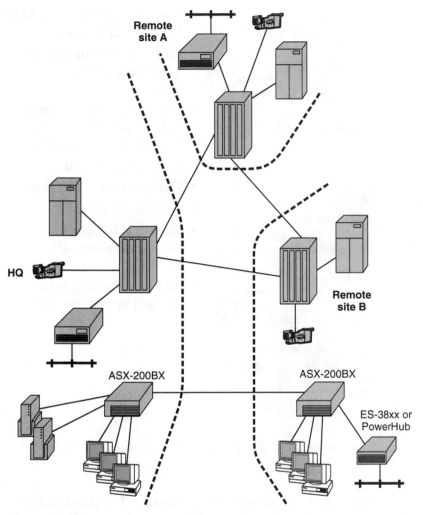

- Isolated high-speed ATM LAN/WAN data-only networks
- Parallel multisite networks
- No traffic aggregation
    ATM LAN
        traffic
    WAN TDM
        MUX traffic
- Increased operational expense of dual WAN networks:
    Recurring line
        costs
    Network
        management
    Operations
    Parts sparing

Figure 7.9
TDM to ATM integration parallel networks. (Courtesy of Fore Systems, © 1997)

ment limits voice access to on-net, one can hope that at some point the carrier would connect the two central office switches, supporting the required connectivity.

When the ATM network is privately owned, rather than being supplied by the carrier (i.e., the "cloud" in Figure 7.11 is composed of dedicated facilities interconnecting the organization's ATM switches), the network planner can (perhaps) better control QoS

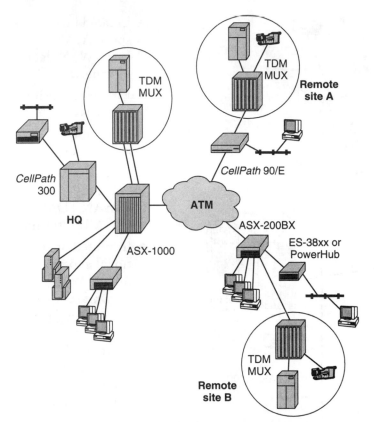

- Common multiservice ATM WAN infrastructure
- Graceful transition from TDM data MUX equipment
- Transparent integration of proprietary TDM MUX functionality across ATM
- Voice compression
- Traffic activity detection
- Subrate connectivity
- Statistical bandwidth assignments through ATM QoS
- Reduced monthly leased line and operations cost

Figure 7.10
TDM to ATM integration, backbone integration. (Courtesy of Fore Systems, © 1997)

and congestion, thereby achieving better quality. The disadvantage of this approach is that this will preclude any off-net voice access. Even if the carrier eventually offers connectivity to the public voice network, the user has no access.

Figure 7.12 depicts an integrated arrangement (not currently offered by any carrier) that allows on-net and off-net voice over ATM services. Although Figure 7.12 shows technical feasibility, the economics and the commercial prospects are unknown. Note that at least in the *User Plane* (the information-carrying plane), interconnection is achieved by putting the interworking function either in the ATM switch or in the voice switch. In the former, the voice switch remains unchanged; in the latter, the voice switch needs to

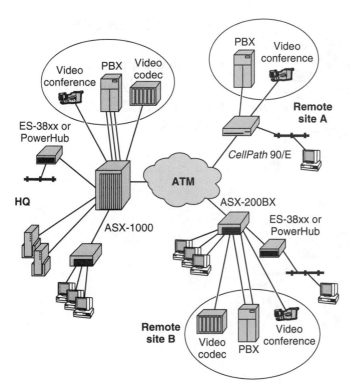

- Integrated multiservice ATM network
- Direct connection of TDM sources to ATM
- Network equipment consolidation
- Statistical bandwidth assignments through ATM QoS
- Unified network management
- Increased network scalability and reliability
- Reduced network costs
- Planned: dynamic CBR bandwidth utilization

Figure 7.11
TDM to ATM integration, network integration. (Courtesy of Fore Systems, © 1997)

be upgraded. Another alternative would be to upgrade the voice switch to support VBR/AAL 5 capabilities, thereby eliminating the need for circuit emulation. The challenge in the design depicted in Figure 7.12 is in the *Control Plane,* to achieve signaling-to-signaling conversion and support. The VTOA specifications do provide a mechanism to achieve this interworking function, but CES only at this time.

Voice and data traffic have different requirements for network services. A voice transmission requires only a small amount of bandwidth, but that bandwidth must be available on a dedicated (continuous basis), with very little delay, delay variation, and loss. Even delays in the millisecond range can give rise to a noticeable echo or gap in the conversation. By contrast, data traffic can adjust to network delay and, with its bursty requirement, can use the amount of

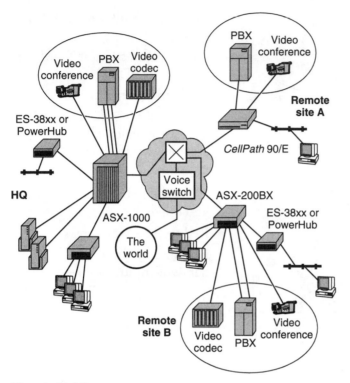

- CO-based interworking with PSTN
- Signaling supported
- Structured/dynamic CES
- Requires LEC/CLEC to support

Figure 7.12
PSTN to ATM integration, network integration. (Courtesy of Fore Systems, © 1997)

bandwidth available in the network at any moment (e.g., TCP can throttle to match the actual throughput of the network).

Proponents offer the argument that, in order for carriers to make ATM ubiquitous and inexpensive, it must support voice and multimedia. Also, for ATM switches to replace T1/T3 multiplexers in private networks, they have to support voice. In fact, a number of ATM switch manufacturers, notably Nortel, Cisco/Stratacom, and GDC, are moving in that direction. Many switches now can carry AAL 1 traffic with the desirable QoS features. One of the good things about this model is that the voice quality is absolutely top of the line (that is, toll quality, with MOS around 4.0 or better). However, it does so only at the T1 level,[2] not the n×DS0 level. Treating the entire T1 PBX-to-PBX tie line connection as a single CBR VC implies that a separate link for voice for each pair of locations of interest is required. Furthermore, there may be limited support for actual PBX interfaces (beyond the basic bit stream and connector type). Also this limits the voice to on-net applications, because there is no connection to the voice switch at the central office (as shown in Figure 7.12). As implied by this discussion, the first step in that direction of increased granularity is to include support for *structured* AAL 1 in the CPE, which allows individual DS0s to be identified (in the early *unstructured* AAL 1, there was no DS0 visibility).

Proponents make the case that the support of voice via AAL 1/circuit emulation is not really practical, and that AAL 2/VBR/compression support is needed. Specifically, four voice processing enhancements are required to make voice over ATM attractive: voice compression, silence suppression, idle channel cell suppression, and signaling support including translation of voice signaling to switched virtual connection (SVC) ATM signaling. This will enable the use of AAL 2 and VBR, which promises to be more bandwidth efficient than CBR/CES methods. Some of these capabilities may appear in the ATM context in the next couple of years.

7.4 ATM Service Classes

This section sets the stage for the AAL 1 discussion of Section 7.5. AALs were briefly covered in Chapter 2; more detailed coverage is provided here.

Background

The ATM Protocol Reference Model applicable to both the User Plane and the Control Plane (see Figure 7.13) is divided into three protocol layers: the *Physical Layer*, the *ATM Layer*, and the *AAL and Service-Specific Layers*.

The Physical Layer provides the ATM Layer with access to the physical transmission medium. Its functions include transmission of bits across the physical medium, timing recovery, line coding, cell delineation, cell scrambling and descrambling, and generation and checking of the header error control.

The ATM Layer provides for the transport of ATM cells between the endpoints of a virtual connection. It is the basis for

Figure 7.13
Protocol reference model.

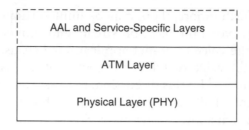

native cell relay service, as well as other services. ATM cells are delivered across the network in the same sequence in which they are received from the CPE.

The AAL maps the upper-layer information, (e.g., voice bits, video bits, video packets, TCP/IP protocol data units) into cells for transport across the network. The Service-Specific Layer performs application-dependent processing and functions (i.e., there are distinct AAL protocols).

This section discusses briefly the Service-Specific Layer, which is not only a classical protocol layer but also a logical partitioning of applications that can run over ATM. Initially, there was a taxonomy of applications into four classes. In effect, these classes have now been extended. In order to minimize the number of AAL protocols, the ITU-T recommendations, specifically ITU-T I.362 (also see Table 7.3), define a service classification for the AAL based on the following requirements:

- Timing relation required/not required between source and destination
- Constant or variable bit rate
- Connection-oriented or connectionless mode

Only a limited number of combinations of the above requirements were foreseen by the ITU. These allowed combinations result in service classes for the AAL termed classes A, B, C, and D, and their specific requirements are indicated in Table 7.4.

Examples of higher-layer services that would fall into these service classes are:

- Class A—DS1 and DS3 circuit emulation
- Class B—packet video

Table 7.3 Relevant AAL-Related Specifications by Various Bodies

UNI 3.1, ATM Forum User-Network Interface (UNI) Specification
af-bici-0013.003, ATM Forum Broadband Intercarrier Interface (B-ICI)
 Specification v2.0
af-vtoa-0078.000, ATM Forum Circuit Emulation Service Interoperability
 Specification v2.0
ANSI T1.630-1993, B-ISDN ATM Adaptation Layer CBR Services
ANSI T1.627-1993, B-ISDN ATM Layer Functionality and Specification
ITU-T I.356-1993, B-ISDN ATM Layer Cell Transfer Performance
ITU-T I.362-1993 B-ISDN ATM Adaptation Layer (AAL) Functional
 Description
ITU-T I.363.1-1996, B-ISDN ATM Adaptation Layer (AAL) Specification,
 Types 1 and 2
ITU-T I.363.5-1996, B-ISDN ATM Adaptation Layer (AAL) Specification,
 Type 5
ETSI ETS 300 353 B-ISDN ATM Adaptation Layer (AAL) Specification
 Type 1
Bellcore GR-1113-CORE, Issue 1, July 1994, Asynchronous Transfer Mode
 (ATM) and ATM Adaptation Layer (AAL) Protocols

- Class C—frame relay
- Class D—switched multimegabit data service (SMDS), a connectionless data service

As noted in Chapter 2, several AAL protocol types have been defined to meet the needs of the above service classes. AAL Type 1 (Figure 7.14) meets the needs of class A services, Type 2 meets class B needs, AAL Type 3/4 (Figure 7.15) meets the needs of classes C and D, and AAL Type 5 (Figure 7.16) meets the needs of class C. However, there is not a strict relationship between the service classes and the protocol types, and other combinations may be used as appropriate. In this context, it is necessary to discuss the traffic parameters that can be used by the end systems to establish VCs or

Table 7.4 ITU-T I.362 ATM Classes

	Class A	*Class B*	*Class C*	*Class D*
Timing relation between source and destination	Required		Not Required	
Bit rate	Constant	Variable		
Connection mode	Connection-oriented			Connectionless

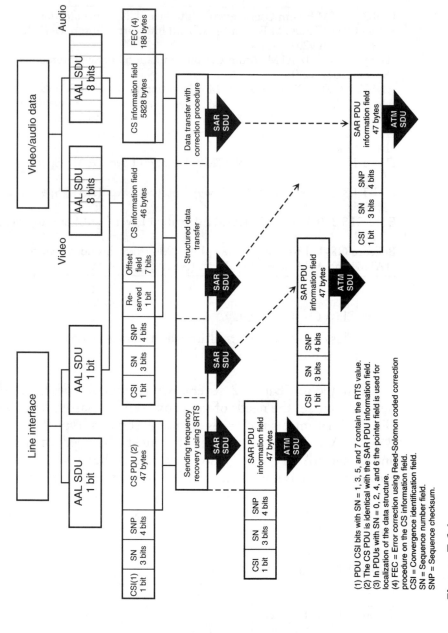

Figure 7.14
A view of AAL 1.

(1) PDU CSI bits with SN = 1, 3, 5, and 7 contain the RTS value.
(2) The CS PDU is identical with the SAR PDU information field.
(3) In PDUs with SN = 0, 2, 4, and 6 the pointer field is used for localization of the data structure.
(4) FEC = Error correction using Reed-Solomon coded correction procedure on the CS information field.
CSI = Convergence identification field.
SN = Sequence number field.
SNP = Sequence checksum.

VPs through the ATM network. These traffic parameters (already identified in Chapter 2) defined for the ATM Layer include the following [4]:

- *Peak cell rate* (PCR)—the cell rate which the source may never exceed.
- *Sustainable cell rate* (SCR)—upper bound on the "average" rate of an ATM connection, over time scales that are generally long relative to those for which the PCR is defined.
- *Maximum burst size* (MBS)—the maximum number of consecutive cells that can be transmitted at the peak cell rate.
- *Minimum cell rate* (MCR)—a rate negotiated between the end system and the network such that the actual cell rate sent by the end system need never fall below the negotiated value. The MCR may be zero. MCR is used only with the available bit rate service category (discussed below).

To ensure that the limits set for traffic parameters are observed, the ATM Layer may perform traffic-shaping functions—for example, spacing out cells transmitted over a particular connection to adhere to a peak cell rate limit. Protocol data units from various traffic sources are multiplexed and shaped for delivery to the Physical Layer. The shaper is intended to provide a smoothing function to the cell flow. It ensures that, at the Physical Layer, the interarrival time between two consecutive cells for a connection is greater than or equal to the inverse of the negotiated value of the peak cell rate traffic parameter [4].

Service Categories

In general, to satisfy the needs of a range of higher-layer applications, only a subset of the traffic and QoS parameters needs to be specified for a connection. Particular combinations of these parameters are referred to as *service categories*. Thus a service category will consist of a set of QoS and source traffic parameters and, in some cases, feedback mechanisms for adjustments to these parameters. The primary motivation for the specification of service categories is that it is anticipated that support of a limited set of such categories will meet the requirements of most applications. In addition, specification of a limited number of service categories can minimize the

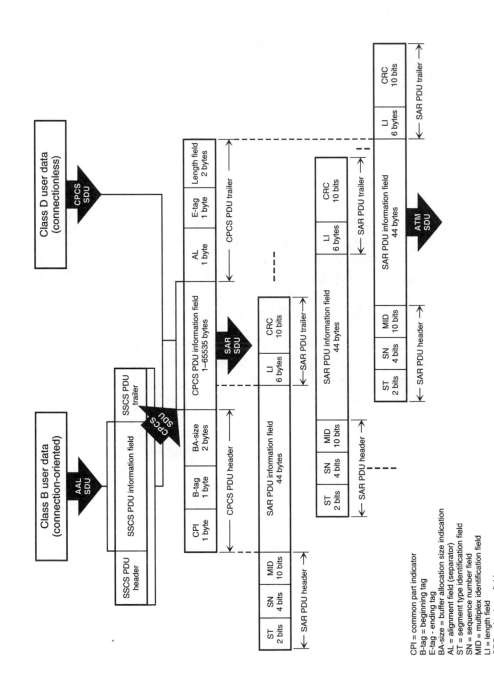

Figure 7.15
AAL 3/4.

CPI = common part indicator
B-tag = beginning tag
E-tag - ending tag
BA-size = buffer allocation size indication
AL = alignment field (separator)
ST = segment type identification field
SN = sequence number field
MID = multiplex identification field
LI = length field
CRC = checksum field

268

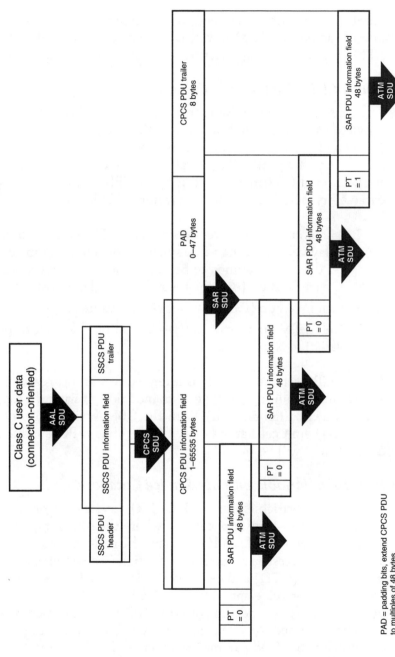

Figure 7.16
AAL 5.

PAD = padding bits, extend CPCS PDU
to multiples of 48 bytes
PT = payload type identification field
0 = beginning/continuation of SAR PDU
1 = end of SAR PDU

number of protocols that need to be defined. Following is a description of each of the ATM service categories currently defined by the ATM Forum and the applications they are intended to support.

Constant Bit Rate Service Category

The constant bit rate (CBR) service category involves connections providing a fixed amount of bandwidth during the lifetime of the ATM connection. The amount of bandwidth provided is defined by the value of the peak cell rate traffic parameter. Table 7.5 depicts an application of CBR methods to support CES. The applicable QoS parameters include the following (refer to Table 7.6).

1. Maximum cell transfer delay (maxCTD)—Cells that are delayed beyond the value specified by a maximum cell transfer delay are assumed to be of significantly reduced value to the application (e.g., they may be considered lost cells).
2. Cell loss ratio (CLR)—A maximum value is specified.
3. Cell delay variation (CDV)—A limit on the peak-to-peak variation is specified.

The CBR service category is intended to support real-time applications requiring tightly constrained delay variation (e.g., voice, video, and circuit emulation). With the CBR service category, the source may emit cells at or below the negotiated PCR and the QoS commitment will be met [4].

Real-Time Variable Bit Rate Service Category

The real-time variable bit rate (RT-VBR) service category is intended for real-time applications, where the source rate is expected to be variable and/or bursty. The real-time nature of the application suggests a requirement for tightly constrained cell transfer delay (CTD) and cell delay variation (CDV), as would be appropriate for voice and video applications. Cells that are delayed by the network beyond a maximum CTD value specified by maxCTD are assumed to be of significantly reduced value to the application. Thus the QoS parameters specified for this category are identical to those of the CBR service category. Traffic parameters specified for this category include PCR, SCR, and MBS (refer again to Table 7.6) [4].

Table 7.5   Scope of the ATMF VTOA Circuit Emulation Service Interoperability Specification, January 1997

The CES-IS specifically covers the following types of CBR service:

1. Structured DS1/E1 $n\times64$-kbps (Fractional DS1/E1) Service
2. Unstructured DS1/E1 (1.544-Mbps, 2.048-Mbps) Service
3. Unstructured DS3/E3 (44.736-Mbps, 34.368-Mbps) Service
4. Structured J2 $n\times64$-kbps (Fractional J2) Service
5. Unstructured J2 (6.312-Mbps) Service

The structured $n\times64$ and unstructured DS1/E1/J2 services offer two ways to connect DS1/E1/J2 equipment across emulated circuits carried on an ATM network. The two techniques can be used to solve different kinds of problems.

The structured DS1/E1/J2 $N\times64$ service is modeled after a Fractional DS1/E1/J2 circuit and is useful in the following situations:

1. The $n\times64$ service can be configured to minimize ATM bandwidth by only sending the time slots that are actually needed.
2. The $n\times64$ service provides clocking to the end-user equipment, so it fits into a fully synchronous network environment.
3. Because it terminates the facility data link, the $n\times64$ service can provide accurate link quality monitoring and fault isolation for the DS1/E1 link between the IWF and the end-user equipment

The unstructured DS1/E1/J2 service provides transparent transmission of the DS1/E1/J2 data stream across the ATM network and is modeled after an asynchronous DS1/E1 leased private line. It allows for the following situations:

1. End-user equipment may use either standard (SF, ESF, G.704, or JT-G.704) or nonstandard framing formats.
2. When end-to-end communication of the facility data link or alarm states is important.
3. When timing is supplied by the end-user DS1/E1/J2 equipment and carried through the network. The end-user equipment may or may not be synchronous to the network.

The unstructured DS3/E3 service provides basic DS3/E3 circuit emulation service and allows for the following situations:

1. Standard or nonstandard framing may be used by the end-user DS3/E3 equipment.
2. End-to-end communication of P-Bit, X-Bit, and C-Bit channels is provided.
3. Timing is supplied by the end-user DS3/E3 equipment and carried through the network. The end-user equipment may or may not be synchronous to the network.

Table 7.6 ATM Service Category Attributes Defined in ATMF UNI 4.0

	ATM Layer Service Category				
Attribute	*CBR*	*rt-VBR*	*nrt-VBR*	*UBR*	*ABR*
	delay-sensitive		*non-delay-sensitive*		
Traffic parameters: PCR and CDVT(4.5)	specified			specified[1]	specified[2]
SCR, MBS, CDVT(4.5)	n/a	specified		n/a	
MCR[3]	n/a			n/a[4]	specified
QoS Parameters: Peak-to-peak CDV	specified		unspecified		
maxCTD	specified		unspecified		
CLR[3]	specified			unspecified	See Note 5
Other attributes: Feedback	unspecified				specified

Notes:

1. May not be subject to CAC and UPC procedures.

2. Represents the maximum rate at which the ABR source may ever send. The actual rate is subject to the control information.

3. These parameters are either explicitly or implicitly specified for PVCs or SVCs.

4. Work is underway in the ATMF to support MCR for UBR.

5. CLR is low for sources that adjust cell flow in response to control information. Whether a quantitative value for CLR is specified is network specific.

Applications that might use the RT-VBR service category would include any real-time application (including those listed above for the CBR service category) that generates traffic at a variable rate. This can allow for more efficient use of network resources through statistical multiplexing. An example would be the transmission of compressed video in a video-on-demand application. Newer voice over ATM applications may also use RT-VBR.

Non-Real-Time Variable Bit Rate Service Category

The non-real-time VBR (NRT-VBR) service category is intended for non-real-time applications that have bursty traffic that can be characterized in terms of the same parameters used for RT-VBR, that is, PCR, SCR, and MBS (see Table 7.6). *Non-real-time* suggests that response time is not critical to the applications. A small value for the CLR parameter is specified.

Examples of applications that might use the NRT-VBR service category are bursty applications that are sensitive to cell loss, but not delays. The NRT-VBR service category is useful for delay-sensitive transfers because use of the SCR parameter causes the allocation of some bandwidth for the connection, as opposed to UBR and ABR (discussed below) where the traffic effectively joins a pool of bandwidth shared by other connections [4].

Unspecified Bit Rate Service Category

The unspecified bit rate (UBR) service category represents a best effort service intended for non-real-time applications not requiring tightly constrained delay or delay variation and tolerant of cell loss. Thus the UBR service category provides no QoS commitments for CTD, CDV, or CLR. UBR traffic may be extremely bursty. The only source traffic attribute specified for UBR connections is PCR (work is under way to also specify MCR).

Examples of applications that might make use of the UBR service category are text, data, and image applications for which best effort is acceptable service. Whatever the applications, they must be tolerant of potentially high cell loss.

Available Bit Rate Service Category

The available bit rate (ABR) service category can be viewed as the UBR service category enhanced for applications that are sensitive to certain QoS parameters (e.g., CTD, CDV, and CLR) and/or that require a minimum bandwidth commitment (refer to Table 7.6). The ABR service category will allow applications to use whatever bandwidth is available at a given point in time up to a maximum value. The ABR service category is distinguished by the incorporation of continuous feedback from the network indicating adjustment of the flow of cells into the network. The ABR flow control mechanism supports several types of feedback conveyed through ATM resource management (RM) cells, identified by the PTI code point in the cell header. This feedback mechanism permits each customer to use the maximum available bandwidth consistent with low cell loss and a notion of "fairness" in sharing the available bandwidth. No QoS commitments are provided for CDV or CTD, although cells admitted to the network are assumed not to be delayed unnecessarily [4].

In the ABR service category, the end system negotiates the PCR and two additional traffic parameters, the minimum cell rate

(MCR) and initial cell rate (ICR), at connection establishment. The bandwidth available to an application may vary, but it does not become less than the MCR nor greater than the PCR. At any given time, an allowed cell rate (ACR) parameter is calculated (based on feedback) to determine the current bandwidth permitted to a connection. It is expected that an end system that adapts its traffic flow in accordance with the feedback will experience a low cell loss ratio and obtain a fair share of the available bandwidth.

The ABR service category is not intended to support real-time applications. Examples of applications that might use the ABR service category would include any UBR application that is willing to trade lower cost for better cell loss performance.

Table 7.6, from the ATMF Traffic Management 4.0 specification, summarizes the service classes, the traffic and QoS parameters, and the map between these.

7.5 AAL 1 Mechanisms—Details

This section[3] focuses on AAL protocols, specifically AAL 1 (ANSI T1-630-1993, ITU-T I.363, and ATFM VTOA af-vtoa-0078.000) used in CES (described at length in Chapter 8). As noted, the AAL performs the functions necessary to adapt the capabilities provided by the ATM Layer to the needs of higher-layer applications. AALs are typically implemented in CPE, as shown in Figure 7.17, but can also (occasionally) be found in the network—for example, for network-supported interworking such as CES-to-PSTN interworking or ATM-to-frame relay interworking at the central office. The functions of the AAL include segmentation and reassembly of the higher-layer data units and mapping them into the fixed-length payload of the ATM cells. Effectively, AAL protocols allow a user with some preexisting application—say, using TCP/IP or voice—to get the benefits of ATM. Three AAL protocol types have been standardized and widely implemented: AAL Type 1, for circuit emulation services, and AAL Type 3/4 and AAL Type 5 for VBR services; AAL 2 is also being developed. In AAL Type 1, 1 octet of the cell payload is reserved for control; the remaining 47 octets are utilized for user information. AAL Type 3/4 reserves 4 octets of each cell payload for control use. AAL Type 5 provides all 48 octets of each cell (except for the last cell of a higher-layer packet) for user information. Figure 7.18 depicts the segmentation process.

Model

Architecturally, the AAL is a layer between the ATM Layer and the *Service Layer* (the Service Layer is shown in Figure 7.19). The purpose of an ATM Adaptation Layer is to provide the necessary functions that are not provided by the ATM Layer to support the Service Layer. The functions provided by the AAL depend upon the service. VBR users may require such functions as PDU delimitation, bit error detection and correction, and cell loss detection. CBR users typically require source clock frequency recovery, detection, and possible replacement of lost cells.

Figure 7.20 depicts the positioning of AAL in the context of the corporate user equipment (as noted, AAL capabilities can also be used at an interworking point in the carrier's network).

The AAL for VBR services consists of two parts: a *common part* (CP) and a *service-specific part* (SSP). The SSP is used to provide those additional capabilities, beyond those provided by the CP, that are necessary to support the user of the AAL. For some applications the SSP may be null; in these cases the user of the AAL utilizes the AAL common part (AALCP) directly. For all AAL types, the AAL receives from the ATM Layer information in the form of a 48-octet ATM service data unit (ATM_SDU). The AAL passes to the ATM Layer information in the form of a 48-octet ATM_SDU.

AAL 1

One of the services possible with an ATM platform is emulation of a dedicated line (typically at 1.544 Mbps or at 45 Mbps). This type of service is also known as Class A or CBR service. To support CBR services, an Adaptation Layer is required in the user's equipment for the necessary functions that cannot be provided by the ATM cell header. Some characteristics and functions that may be needed for efficient and reliable transport of CBR services are identified below.

Ideally, CBR services carried over an ATM-based network should appear to the corporate user as equivalent to CBR services provided by the circuit-switched or dedicated network. Some char-

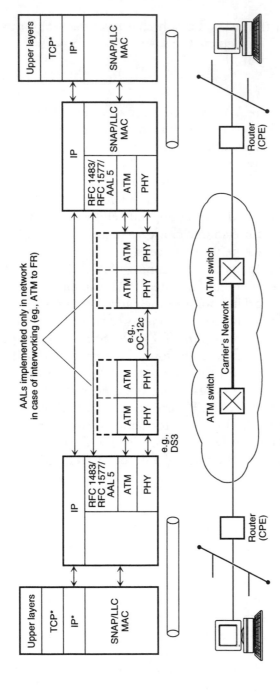

• AAL 1—Supports constant bit rate services (e.g., video on DS1)

• AAL 3/4—Supports connectionless packet services (i.e., SMDS)

• AAL 5—Supports connection oriented data services (e.g., Frame Relay)

*Example transport and network protocols; Transmission Control Protocol (TCP), Internet Protocol (IP) AAL-ATM Adaptation Layer

Figure 7.17
Simplified view of an ATM network.

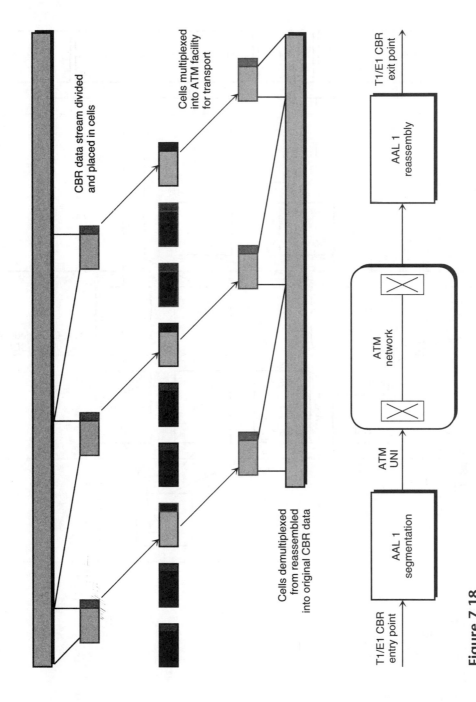

Figure 7.18
Circuit emulation: SAR function.

277

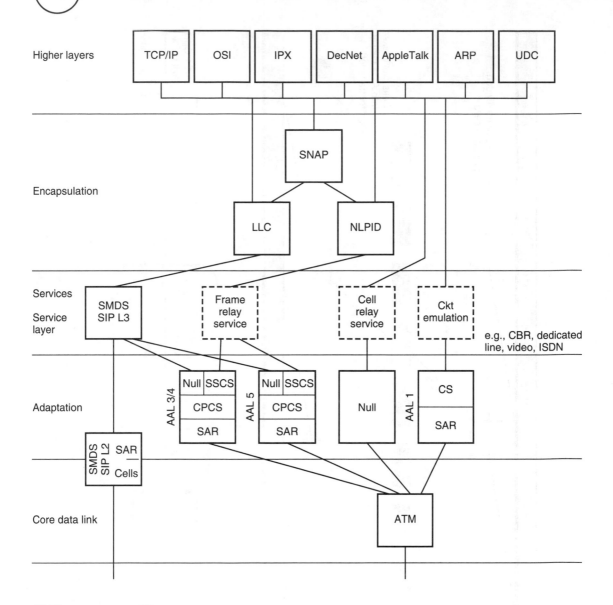

CPCS = common part CS
SSCS = service-specific CS
LLC = logical link control
SNAP = subnetwork access protocol
NLPID = Network Layer Protocol ID

Figure 7.19
Support of user applications.

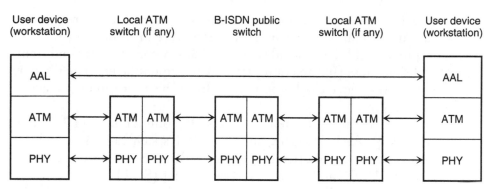

Figure 7.20
The positioning of AAL in CPE.

acteristics of these CBR services are maintenance of timing information, reliable transmission with negligible reframes, and path performance monitoring capability. CBR services with these characteristics can be provided by assigning the following functions for the CBR Adaptation Layer:

- Lost cell detection
- Synchronization
- Performance monitoring

(The above functions may not be required by all the CBR services.)

Therefore, the CBR AAL performs the necessary functions to match the service provided by the ATM Layer to the CBR services required by its service user. It provides for the transfer of AAL service data units (AAL_SDUs) carrying information of an AAL user supporting constant bit rate services. This layer is service-specific, with the main goal of supporting services that have specific delay, jitter, and timing requirements, such as circuit emulation. This layer provides timing recovery, synchronization, and indication of lost information.

The AAL 1 functions are grouped in *segmentation and reassembly* (SAR) functions and in *convergence sublayer* (CS) functions. The SAR is responsible for the transport and bit error detection (and possibly correction). The CS performs a number of related functions: it blocks and deblocks AAL_SDUs, counting the blocks (modulo 8) as it generates or receives them; also, it maintains bit count integrity, generates bit timing information when needed, recovers timing, generates and recovers data structure information (if required), and detects and generates indications of error conditions and signal loss (to the appropriate management layer). The CS may receive reference clock information from the appropriate management layer.

The existing agreements in ITU-T Recommendation I.363, the ANSI CBR AAL Standard, and the ATMF specifications provide two basic modes of operation for the CBR AAL: unstructured data transfer (UDT) and structured data transfer (SDT).

When the UDT mode is operational, the AAL protocol assumes that the incoming data from the AAL user is a *bit stream* with an associated bit clock. When the SDT mode is operational, the AAL protocol assumes the incoming information is *octet blocks* of a fixed length (such as an $n\times64$-kbps channel with 8-kHz integrity) with an associated clock.

CBR AAL Services

This section describes the functions of AAL 1.

AAL Type 1 Services and Functions

The services provided by AAL Type 1 to the AAL user are:

- Transfer of service data units with a constant source bit rate and the delivery of them with the same bit rate
- Transfer of timing information between the source and the destination
- Transfer of structure information between the source and the destination
- Indication of lost or errored information that is not recovered by AAL Type 1, if needed

Specifically, the functions are:

- Segment and reassemble user information
- Handle cell delay variation
- Handle cell payload assembly delay
- Handling of lost and misinserted cells

- Source clock recovery at the receiver
- Recovery of the source data structure at the receiver
- Monitoring of AAL-PCI for bit errors
- Handling of AAL-PCI for bit errors
- Monitoring of user information field for bit errors and possible corrective actions

SAR Functions

The SAR functions are:

- Mapping between the CS_PDU and the SAR_PDU. (The SAR sublayer at the transmitting end accepts a 47-octet block of data from the CS and then prepends a 1-octet SAR_PDU header to each block to form the SAR_PDU.)
- Indicating the existence of CS function. (The SAR can indicate the existence of CS function; the use of the indication mechanism is optional.)
- Sequence numbering. (For each SAR_PDU payload, the SAR sublayer receives a sequence number value from the CS.)
- Error protection. (The sequence number and the CSI bits are protected.)

A buffer is used to handle cell delay variation. When cells are lost, it may be necessary to insert an appropriate number of dummy SAR_PDUs. Figure 7.21 depicts the AAL 1 frame layout.

Convergence Sublayer Functions

The functions of CS are:

- Handling of cell delay variation for delivery of AAL_SDUs to the AAL user at a constant bit rate. (The CS layer may need a clock derived at the S_B or T_B interface to support this function).
- Processing the sequence count to detect cell loss and misinsertion.
- The AAL can provide the mechanism for timing information transfer for AAL users requiring recovery of source clock frequency at the destination end.

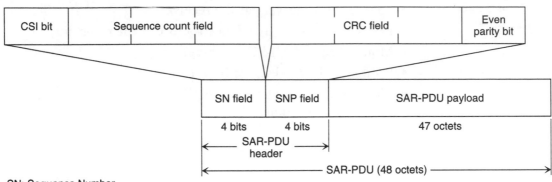

SN: Sequence Number
SNP: Sequence Number Protection
CSI: Convergence Sublayer Indication

Figure 7.21
AAL 1 frame layout.

- Provide the transfer of structure information between source and destination for some AAL users.
- Forward error correction may be supported (particularly for video).

For those AAL users that require transfer of structured data (e.g., 8-kHz structured data for circuit-mode bearer services for 64-kbps-based ISDN), the structure parameter is used.

The structure parameter can be used when the user data stream to be transferred to the peer AAL entity is organized into groups of bits. The length of the structured block is fixed for each instance of the AAL service. The length is an integer multiple of 8 bits. An example of the use of this parameter is to support circuit-mode services of the 64-kbps-based ISDN. The two values of the structure parameter are *Start,* used when the data is the first part of a structured block that can be composed of consecutive data segments, and *Continuation,* used when the value Start is not applicable.

The use of the structure parameter depends on the type of AAL service provided; the use of the parameter is agreed upon prior to or at the connection establishment between the AAL user and the AAL.

I.363 notes that "for certain applications such as speech, some SAR functions may not be needed." For example, I.363 provides the following guidance for CS for voiceband signal transport (which is a specific example of CBR service):

- *Handling of AAL user information:* The length of the AAL_SDU (i.e., the information provided to the AAL by the upper-layer protocols) is 1 octet (for comparison, the SAR_PDU is 47 octets).
- *Handling of cell delay variation:* A buffer of appropriate size is used to support this function.
- *Handling of lost and misinserted cells:* The detection of lost and inserted cells, if needed, may be provided by processing the sequence count values. The monitoring of the buffer fill level can also provide an indication of lost and misinserted cells. Detected misinserted cells are discarded.

P and Non-P Formats

The 47-octet SAR_PDU payload used by CS has two formats called *non-P* and *P formats*, as seen in Figure 7.22. These are used to support transfer of information with structure. Note that in the non-P format, the entire CS_PDU is filled with user information.

Partially Filled Cells

I.363 notes that SAR_PDU payload may be filled only partially with user data in order to reduce the cell payload assembly delay. In this case, the number of leading octets utilized for user information in each SAR_PDU payload is a constant that is determined by the allowable cell payload assembly delay. The remainder of the SAR_PDU payload consists of dummy octets. The advantage of this was discussed earlier in the context of voice delay. Naturally, this increases the effective transport overhead.

CBR Clocking Approaches

Besides UDT/SDT issues discussed earlier, the other basic CBR service attribute that determines the AAL functionality required to support a service is the status of the CBR service clock (see Figure 7.23): either synchronous or asynchronous. Since the service clock is assumed to be frequency-locked to a network clock in the synchronous case, the recovery of the service clock is done directly with a clock available from the network (or a good internal clock). See Figure 7.24.

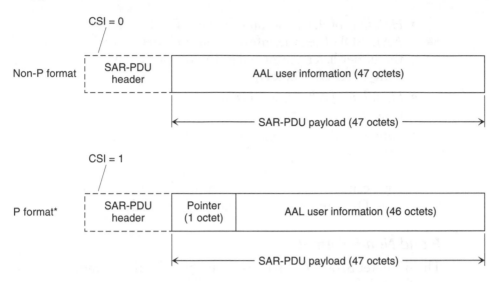

Figure 7.22
Non-P and P formats.

For an asynchronous service clock, the AAL provides a method for recovering the source clock at the receiver. Two methods are available: the *synchronous residual timestamp* (SRTS[4]) method (see Figure 7.25) and the *adaptive clock method* (see Table 7.7). The SRTS method is used to recover clocks with tight tolerance and jitter requirements such as DS1 or DS3 clocks. The adaptive clock recovery method has not been described in enough detail in standards bodies to determine what type of service clocks are supported—presumably less accurate clocks with looser low-frequency jitter (i.e., wander) specifications—or what, if any, added agreements are needed. However, since adaptive clock is in common use in user equipment, this method is assumed to be available.

The support of DS1 and DS3 CBR service uses the entire 47-octet information payload available with the basic CBR AAL protocol; uses the UDT mode of operation; uses the SRTS methods of timing recovery, if the service clock is asynchronous; and maintains bit count integrity by inserting the appropriate alarm indication signal for the service supported as a DS1 and DS3 error control measure.

Figure 7.23
Clocking approaches: (a) synchronous environment—line-derived, network-derived, or internally derived clock; (b) asynchronous environment using adaptive methods; (c) asynchronous environment with SRTS.

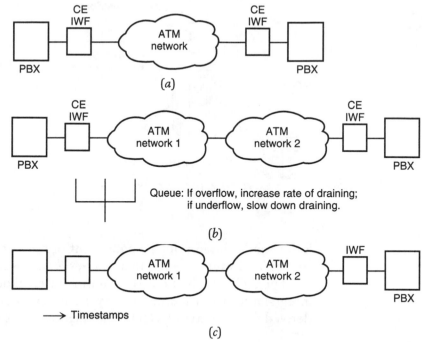

Some information on SRTS follows, based on References [5, 6, and 7].

The synchronous residual timestamp method is used to support asynchronous clock recovery for CBR services with stringent clock specifications, such as those associated with the 1.544-MHz and 44.736-MHz hierarchies. The SRTS method uses a measure that conveys timing information related to the frequency difference between a reference clock and the clock to be recovered, which is referred to as the *source clock*. It requires that SRTS at the CBR AAL transmitter and SRTS at the CBR AAL receiver use synchronized reference clocks. This requirement is necessary to control the jitter in the recovered clock introduced by the ATM transport (particularly, low-frequency jitter known as *wander*).

Since the timing information generation process is related to the timestamp (TS) approach of clock recovery, SRTS supports a range of source clock frequencies with a single reference clock frequency. If the source clocks to be recovered are stable and accurate, then the most significant bits of a TS value convey information that does not impact the clock adjustment at the receiver. Therefore, the

Figure 7.24
Synchronous clocking.

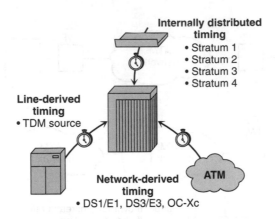

SRTS method transmits the equivalent of the least significant portion of a TS value referred to as the *residual timestamp* (RTS).

The SRTS method measures a time interval defined to be an integral number of source clock cycles in terms of a reference clock derived from a network clock. The measurement generates the

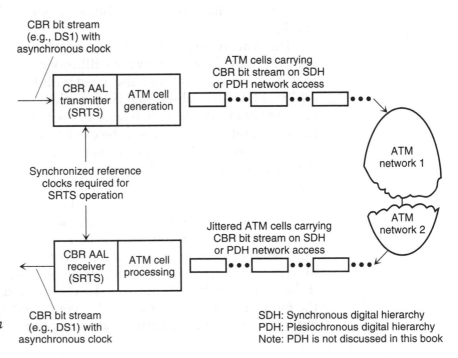

Figure 7.25
Asynchronous clock recovery with SRTS.

Table 7.7   Adaptive Clocking Method

- Monitors cells arriving at destination buffer to derive clock
- Clock speed stepped up or stepped down based on buffer status
- Accurate if network introduces a minimal delay
- ATM Forum Implementation of AAL 1

equivalent of a truncated timestamp value. The following notation is used in the discussion:

f_{nx} = reference clock derived from network clock

f_s = source clock frequency

N = period of RTS in source clock (f_s) cycles

ε = Source clock tolerance in parts per million (ppm)

M(max, nom, min) = minimum, nominal, or maximum number of f_{nx} cycles in an RTS sampling period

Figures 7.26 and 7.27 illustrate the concept and generation of RTS.

The sampling period is measured within the accuracy permitted by the f_{nx} clock. An RTS with size P bits and the f_s clock variation bounds—that is, M(min) and M(max) as measured in f_{nx} clock cycles—must obey the relationship:

$$M(\text{max}) - M(\text{min}) < 2^P \tag{7.1}$$

if the RTS values are to provide a valid measure of source clock variation. The RTS size bounds the magnitude of the range of source clock variation that the SRTS method can tolerate and still provide a valid measure of source clock variation. The maximum magnitude of the f_s clock variation M(max) − M(min), which can be accommodated by SRTS, is bounded by the RTS sampling interval N, the ratio of f_{nx}/f_s, and the clock tolerance ε:

$$M(\text{max}) - M(\text{min}) \leq N * \frac{f_{nx}}{f_s} * \varepsilon \tag{7.2}$$

The value of N is fixed to coincide with the number of f_s clock cycles associated with the CBR AAL user information in 8-cell payloads. For the case of DS1 and DS3 service, 47 octets of a cell payload is AAL user data. The RTS sampling interval then corresponds to

$$N = 8 * 8 * 47 = 3008 \text{ source clock cycles}$$

Selecting ε to have a maximum value of 200 ppm and fixing the maximum value of the ratio f_{nx}/f_s to 2, and RTS of 4 bits, satisfies the relationship in Equation (7.1) for the magnitude of variation bound given by Equation (7.2).

DS1 and DS3 clock tolerances are 130 ppm and 20 ppm, respectively; hence, RST can accommodate both of these services. The use of a common SRTS reference clock frequency at both the transmitter's SRTS entity and the receiver's SRTS entity is necessary for interoperability. The reference clock frequencies used with SONET-based Physical Layer transport of ATM are

$$f_{nx} = \frac{(155.52 \text{ MHz})}{2^k} = \frac{[(8 * 9 * 270) \times f_8]}{2^k}$$

where $k = 0, 1, \ldots, 11$ and $f_8 = 8$ kHz, for supporting f_s clock rates from 64 kbps to 132.8 Mbps (132.8 Mbps is the available ATM cell payload bandwidth on a STS-3c with a 1-octet AAL). For the case of DS3, the highest reference clock frequency needed is 38.88 MHz. The f_{nx}/f_s ratio constraint

$$1 \leq \frac{f_{nx}}{f_s} < 2 \tag{7.3}$$

determines the appropriate reference clock to use. For example, the reference clock used for the recovery of a DS1's 1.544-MHz clock is 2.43 MHz.

CBR AAL Mechanism

The CBR AAL provides its service over preestablished AAL connections. The establishment and initialization of an AAL connection is performed through *AAL management* (AALM). The transfer capacity of each connection and other connection characteristics are negotiated prior to or at connection establishment. (The CBR AAL is not directly involved in the negotiation process, which may be performed by management or signaling.) The AAL receives from

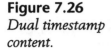

Figure 7.26
Dual timestamp content.

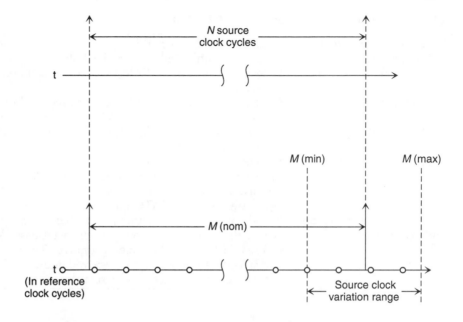

its service user a constant-rate bit stream with a clock. The AAL provides to its service user this constant-rate bit stream with the same clock. The CBR service clock can be either synchronous or asynchronous relative to the network clock: the CBR service is called *synchronous* if its service clock is frequency-locked to the network clock. Otherwise, the CBR service is called *asynchronous*.

The service provided by the AAL consists of its own capability plus the capability of the ATM Layer and the Physical Layer. This service is provided to the AAL user (e.g., an entity in an upper layer or in the Management Plane). The service definition is based on a set of service primitives that describe in an abstract manner the logical exchange of information and control. Functions are performed by the CBR AAL entities are shown in Table 7.8.

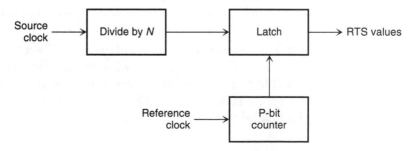

Figure 7.27
Generation of RTS values.

Table 7.8   Functions Performed by CBR AAL

Detection and reporting of lost SAR_PDUs	Detects discontinuity in the sequence count values of the SAR_PDUs and senses buffer underflow and overflow conditions
Detection and correction of SAR_PDU header error	Detects bit errors in the SAR_PDU header and possibly corrects a 1-bit error
Bit count integrity	Generates dummy information units to replace lost AAL_SDUs to be passed to the AAL user in an AAL-DATA.indication
Residual timestamp (RTS) generation	Encodes source service clock timing information for transport to the receiving AAL entity
Source clock recovery	Recovers the CBR service source clock
Blocking	Maps AAL_SDUs into the payload of a CS_PDU
Deblocking	Reconstructs the AAL_SDU from the received SAR_PDUs and generates the AAL-DATA.indication primitive
Structure pointer generation and extraction	Encodes in a 1-octet structure pointer field at the sending AAL entity the information about periodic octet-based block structures present in AAL-DATA request primitives. The receiving AAL entity extracts the structure pointer received in the CS_PDU header field to verify locally generated block structure.

The logical exchange of information between the AAL and the AAL user is represented by two primitives, as shown in Table 7.9 (also see Figure 7.28).

Description of Parameters

AAL_SDU: This parameter contains 1 bit of AAL user data to be transferred by the AAL between two communication AAL user peer entities.

Structure: As discussed, this parameter is used to indicate the beginning or continuation of a block of AAL_SDUs when providing for the transfer of a structured bit stream between communicating AAL user peer entities (structured data transfer service). The length of the blocks is constant for each instance of the AAL service and a multiple of 8 bits. This parameter takes one of the following two values: Start and Continuation. It is set to Start whenever the AAL_SDU being passed in the same primitive is the first bit of a block of a structured bit stream. Otherwise, it is set to Continuation. This parameter is used only when SD service is supported.

Status: This parameter indicates that the AAL_SDU being passed in the same indication primitive is judged to be nonerrored or errored. It takes one of the following two values, Valid or Invalid. The Invalid value may also indicate that the AAL_SDU being

Table 7.9　Primitives for CBR AAL

AAL-DATA.request(AAL_SDU, Structure)	This primitive is issued by an AAL user entity to request the transfer of an AAL_SDU to its peer entity over an existing AAL connection. The time interval between two consecutive AAL-DATA.request primitives is constant and a function of the specific AAL service provided to the AAL user.
AAL-DATA.indication(AAL_SDU, Structure, Status)	This primitive is issued to an AAL user entity to notify the arrival of an AAL_SDU over an existing AAL connection. In the absence of error, the AAL_SDU is the same as the AAL_SDU sent by the peer AAL user entity in the corresponding AAL-DATA.request. The time interval between two consecutive AAL-DATA.indication primitives is constant and a function of the specific AAL service provided to the AAL user.

passed is a dummy value. The use of this parameter and the choice of the dummy value depends on the specific service provided.

Service Expected from the ATM Layer

The AAL expects the ATM Layer to provide for the transparent and sequential transfer of AAL data units, each 48 octets in length, between communicating AAL entities, over an ATM Layer connection, at a negotiated bandwidth and QoS. The ATM Layer transfers the information in the order in which it was delivered to the ATM Layer and provides no retransmission of lost or corrupted information.

Interactions between the SAR and the Convergence Sublayer

The logical exchange of information between the SAR and the Convergence Sublayer is represented by the primitives of Table 7.10.

Description of the Parameters

CSDATA: This parameter represents the interface data unit exchanged between the SAR entity and the CS entity. It contains the 47-octet CS_PDU.

SCVAL: This 3-bit parameter contains the value of the sequence count associated with the CS_PDU contained in the CSDATA parameter.

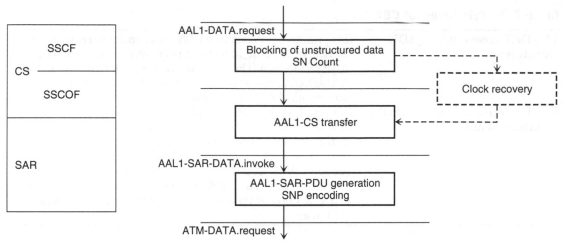

Figure 7.28
AAL 1 functions.

CSIVAL: This 1-bit parameter contains the value of the CSI bit.

SNCK: This parameter is generated by the receiving SAR entity. It represents the results of the sequence number protection error check over the SAR_PDU header. It can assume the value of SN-Valid or SN-Invalid.

Interacting with the Management Plane

The AALM entities in the Management Plane perform the management functions specific to the AAL. Also, the AALM entities, in conjunction with the Management Plane, provide coordination of the local interactions between the User Plane and the Control Plane across the layers.

Table 7.10   SAR Primitives

SAR-DATA.invoke (CSDATA, SCVAL, CSIVAL)	This primitive is issued by the sending CS entity to the sending SAR entity for requesting the transfer of a CSDATA to its peer entity.
SAR-DATA.signal (CSDATA, SNCK, SCVAL, CSIVAL)	This primitive is issued by the receiving SAR entity to the receiving CS entity for notifying of the arrival of a CSDATA from its peer CS entity.

The AAL entities provide the AALM entities with the information required for error processing or abnormal condition handling as an indication of lost or misdelivered SAR_PDUs, and an indication of errored SAR_PDU headers.

AAL1 aspects are revisited in Chapter 8. These constructs are key to early implementations of voice over ATM.

AAL 2

To overcome the problem of allocating bandwidth in CES-based voice, whether structured or unstructured, and to provide flexibility to allow the minimization of delay for voice applications, the industry is pursuing a new AAL: AAL 2. According to proponents, AAL 1 simply cannot be extended to meet these new ATM networking requirements [8].

AAL 2 is an ATM Adaption Layer, specified in ITU-T Recommendation I.363.2 (1997) with the specific mandate to provide efficient voice over ATM services. AAL 2 supports the following features in addition to the AAL 1 adaptation protocol:

- Efficient bandwidth usage through variable bit rate ATM traffic class
- ATM bandwidth reduction support for voice compression, silence detection/suppression, and idle voice channel selection
- Multiple voice channels with varying bandwidth on a single ATM connection

AAL 2 provides bandwidth-efficient transmission of low-rate, short, and variable packets for delay-sensitive applications. AAL 2 is designed to make use of the more statistically multiplexible VBR ATM traffic classes. Therefore, AAL 2 is not limited to ATM connections using the CBR traffic class and can enable voice applications using higher-layer requirements such as voice compression, silence detection/suppression, and idle channel removal [2]. The structure of AAL 2 allows network administrators to take traffic variations into account in the design of an ATM network and to optimize the network to match traffic conditions. See Figure 7.29. This topic is revisited in Chapter 12.

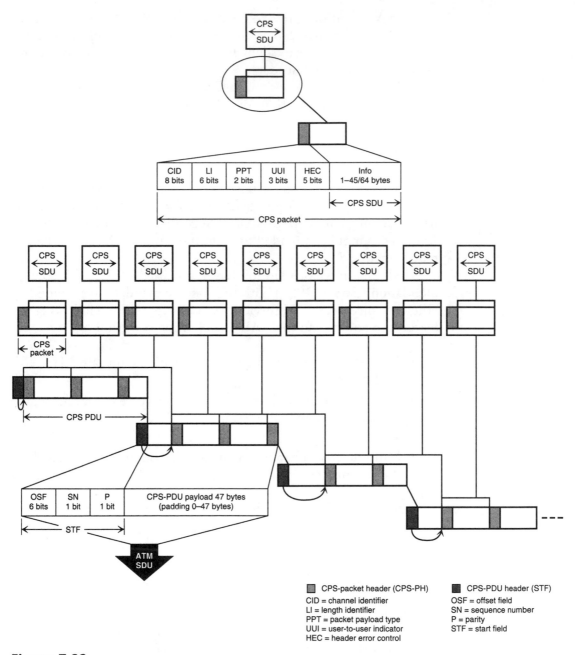

Figure 7.29
AAL 2.

7.6 An Introductory View of PSTN Interworking

The issue of voice support in ATM is thoroughly addressed in Reference [1], and many of the concepts advanced have been standardized in the various VTAO specifications. In preparation for a discussion of the exact Implementation Agreements contained in the 078, 085, 089, and 083 VTOA ATMF documents (Chapters 8, 9, 10, and 11, respectively), this section taken from Reference [1] highlights the issues under discussion. This section provides some of the various background considerations, ideas, philosophies, and alternatives. The VTOA specifications are an exact set of agreements on how interworking and voice support is to be done, so that inexpensive and interoperable equipment can be developed by the vendor community. Figure 7.30 depicts the entire VTOA machinery of Chapters 8 through 11.

PSTN Architecture Issues

This subsection examines how an ATM switch, specifically a carrier network broadband switching system (CN-BSS, or BSS for short) can support voice communication. An overview of the various architectures for the interworking of ATM-based voice with existing voice networks, as well as the rationale for selecting a specific architecture, are presented. Functionality required in the user's equipment is discussed. Voice requirements strictly within an ATM network (i.e., ATM end-to-end without interworking) are also examined.

Some multimedia applications utilizing ATM services may have a telephonic voice component that needs to be satisfied at one end outside the B-ISDN environment. Such ATM-based applications require a mechanism to interwork with existing voice services, narrowband ISDN (N-ISDN) in particular. The phrase "voice over ATM" refers for the rest of the chapter to the interworking between (1) a user accessing the network over an ATM UNI and supplying an information stream over a specified virtual connection, consisting (solely) of digitized 3.1-kHz or 7-kHz speech,[5] and (2) an ISDN-based voice network. The initial goal of this interworking is to achieve *backward compatibility* for limited voice over ATM capabilities; supplementary (e.g., Q.932-based) voice services over ATM are not considered here.

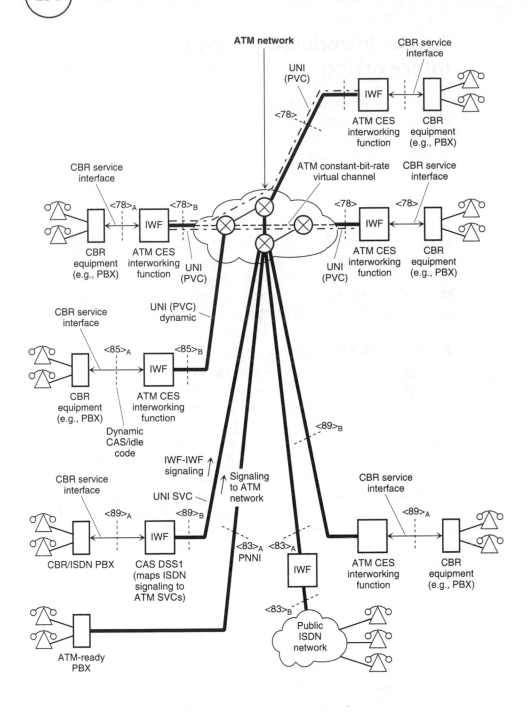

Figure 7.30

VTOA machinery. ⟨78⟩$_A$: af-vtoa-0078.000 structured/unstructured AAL 1 service to PBX (appearance of T1, with signaling support, performance goals, and network mapping to multiple destinations; ⟨78⟩$_B$: af-vtoa-0078.000 ATM UNI traffic descriptors, etc.; ⟨85⟩$_A$: af-vtoa-0085.00 dynamic bandwidth utilization taking CAS-based or idle code pattern– based unused slots out of active status; ⟨85⟩$_B$: af-vtoa-0085.000 ATM UNI traffic descrip- tors, etc.; ⟨89⟩$_A$: af-vtoa-0089.000 trunking (network interworking of ISDN) over ATM. CAS/DSS1 signaling to PBX supported. ISDN messages mapped to ATM SVC signaling. Signaling takes place in three places: IWF to PBX (CAS or ISDN), IWF to ATM network, and IWF to IWF; ⟨89⟩$_B$: af-vtoa-0089.000 ATM SVC signaling; ⟨83⟩$_A$: af-vtoa-0083.000 support of native ATM voice device (e.g., ATM-ready PBX) for communication with ISDN station ATM connection, typically P-NNI and AAL 1/AAL 5 in user plane; ATM SAAL SVC with narrowband bearer capability in Control Plane; ⟨83⟩$_B$: af-vtoa-0083.000 with PNNI- or DSS2-to-DSS1 mapping of B-ISDN messages to ISDN messages.

The dynamics of user applications, CPE capabilities, CPE costs, and ATM transport costs will ultimately determine when it is eco- nomical to provide these capabilities to customers and when cus- tomers might elect to employ them. As a practical matter, voice over ATM must be cost effective to the end user compared to sepa- rate Plain Old Telephone Service (POTS) lines terminating on the user's CPE. (These costs are in the neighborhood of $25 per month plus $6 per hour.)

Figure 7.31 depicts interworking at the conceptual level. An assumption made here (embodied in Figure 7.31) is that the BSS does not directly terminate N-ISDN customers' basic rate or primary rate UNIs. This assumption implies that the BSS is not envisioned to have the functionality equivalent to a Class 5 CO switch. The model is that voice is received over an ATM UNI. Another assumption is that any interworking with a POTS switch is done via an N-ISDN switch (see Figure 7.32). *Note:* This assumption is not mandatory but it simplifies BSS and CPE requirements.

This discussion addresses only a single active voice connection over a VC in the UNI (in order not to have to worry about $n \times 64$- structured signals that require a more complex AAL mechanism— that is, P protocol data units and non-P protocol data units in AAL 1, discussed earlier. (If multiple voice connections are required, multiple VCs can be used, instead of a single VC carrying an $n \times 64$ signal.)

Figure 7.31
Internetworking of BSS with a narrowband switch, conceptual view.

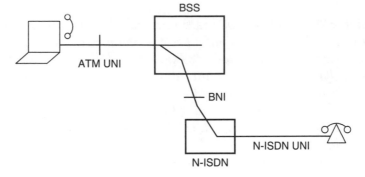

BNI: broadband-to-narrowband interface

Architecturally, the question is: What are the characteristics of the broadband-to-narrowband (BNI) interface? Such characteristics have to be specified for the User Plane of the BNI as well as for the Control Plane. Different (interworking) functionality is required in the BSS and/or N-ISDN switch, depending on the choices made. The BNI can consist of B-ISDN UNI, B-ISDN NNI, N-ISDN UNI-like, N-ISDN NNI, or some other, including "Proprietary."

In the first instance (see Figure 7.33), the interworking function is assumed to take place in the N-ISDN switch; ATM UNI protocols are used between the BSS and the N-ISDN switch. Note the relaying functions both in the User Plane and in the Control Plane. The user signals the BSS; the BSS in turn signals the N-ISDN switch using ATM protocols. Also note that the N-ISDN switch runs a stack toward the ultimate user (assuming that this is ISDN-based).

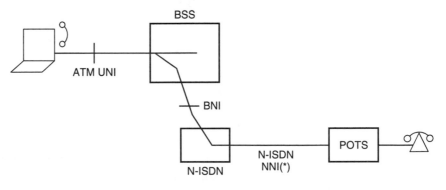

Figure 7.32
Internetworking of broadband switching systems with a POTS switch is accomplished via an N-ISDN switch.

(*) Existing interface/specification
BNI: broadband-to-narrowband interface

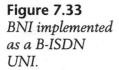

Figure 7.33
BNI implemented as a B-ISDN UNI.

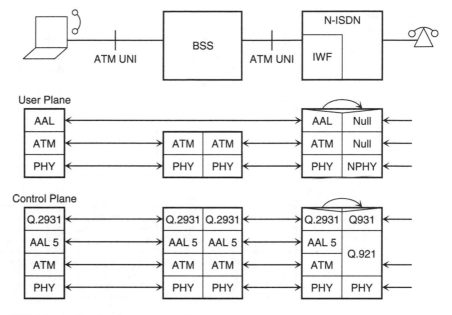

IWF: interworking function
NPHY: N-ISDN PHY

In the second instance (see Figure 7.34), the interworking function is assumed to take place in the N-ISDN switch; a broadband interswitching system interface (B-ISSI) or private network node interface (P-NNI) protocol is implemented between the BSS and the N-ISDN switch. Figure 7.34 depicts Q.2931/ATMF UNI 4.0[6] as the protocol used; however, it can also be the Broadband ISDN User Part (B-ISUP) over AAL 5. Another option, not shown, is to signal outside the B-ISSI and instead use the SS7 network with B-ISUP over MTP 3 (Chapter 5 discussed CCSS7 User Parts). The user signals the BSS; the BSS in turn signals the N-ISDN switch using ATM protocols. Also note that the N-ISDN switch runs a stack toward the ultimate user (assuming that this is ISDN-based).

In the third instance (see Figure 7.35), the interworking function is assumed to take place in the BSS. The interface is called *N-ISDN UNI-like* because the BSS is not expected to terminate local loops, but it can use N-ISDN UNI protocols (the primary rate interface, in particular) over the trunk. In this scenario, the BSS is acting as a PBX as seen by the ISDN network (Q.931, PRI, subservient numbering, etc.). The user signals the BSS; the BSS in turn signals

Figure 7.34
BNI implemented as a B-ISDN B-ISSI.

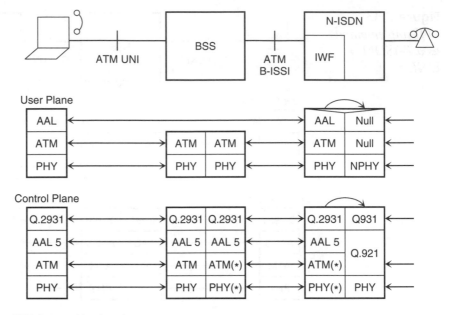

IWF: interworking function
NPHY: N-ISDN PHY

(∗) B-ISSI protocol suite
  −Q.2931 (modified) or
  −B-ISUP over SAAL

the N-ISDN switch using N-ISDN protocols. Also note that the N-ISDN switch runs a stack toward the ultimate user (assuming that this is ISDN-based).

This case has a variant, shown in Figure 7.36. In this variant, the interface is seen as an ISDN primary rate interface/basic rate interface "nailed up" from the BSS to the ISDN switch. The user signals the BSS using ATM protocols; upon such a request, the BSS allocates a pre-nailed-up channel from the pool (an equivalent derived D-channel) to the user, so that the user can signal the N-ISDN switch using encapsulated N-ISDN protocols. Also note that the N-ISDN switch runs a stack toward the ultimate user (assuming that this is ISDN-based).

There is a variant of this scenario (not shown) where the derived signaling channel is nailed up all the way from the user to the N-ISDN switch (this scenario is similar to that shown in Figure 7.36, except that the ATM Control Plane stack does not exist). In

Figure 7.35
BNI implemented as an N-ISDN UNI-like.

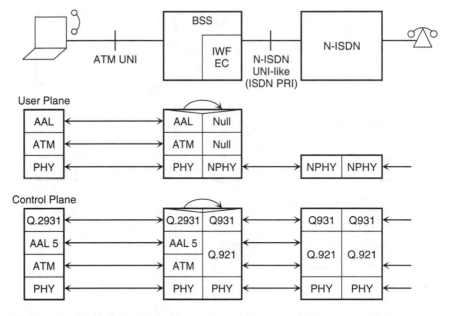

IWF: interworking function
NPHY: N-ISDN PHY
EC: echo control

the previous case, the user signals the BSS on demand to make available a pooled facility (i.e., a nailed-up channel from the BSS to the N-ISDN switch); in this case the PVC nailed-up signaling channel is always there.

In the fourth instance, the interworking function is assumed to take place in the BSS, using N-ISDN NNI protocols (see Figure 7.37). This is similar to the second scenario, except that the interworking burden is placed in BSS. The user signals the BSS using ATM protocols; upon such a request, the BSS signals the N-ISDN switch over SS7 links to establish the voice call. Also note that the N-ISDN switch runs a stack toward the ultimate user (assuming that this is ISDN-based).

Last, vendor-proprietary methods could be used as depicted in Figure 7.38. The user signals the BSS using ATM protocols; upon such a request, the BSS signals the N-ISDN switch using a proprietary protocol stack. Also note that the N-ISDN switch runs a stack toward the ultimate user (assuming that this is ISDN-based). Notice that this approach requires the embedded N-ISDN

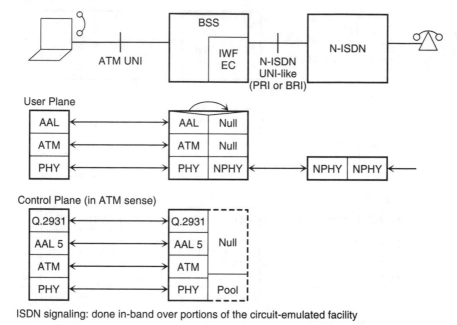

ISDN signaling: done in-band over portions of the circuit-emulated facility

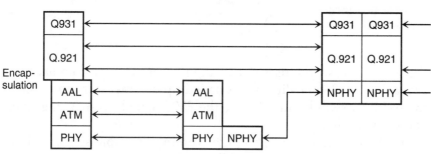

IWF: interworking function
NPHY: N-ISDN PHY
EC: echo control

Figure 7.36
BNI implemented as an N-ISDN UNI-like with in-band ISDN signaling over the ATM access virtual channel.

switch to support this (new) protocol, necessitating some sort of upgrade.

There is a variant of this scenario (not shown) where the vendor-specific protocol runs end to end, that is, directly between the user and the N-ISDN switch (in this case, the BSS is not involved in voice-related signaling).

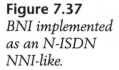

Figure 7.37
BNI implemented as an N-ISDN NNI-like.

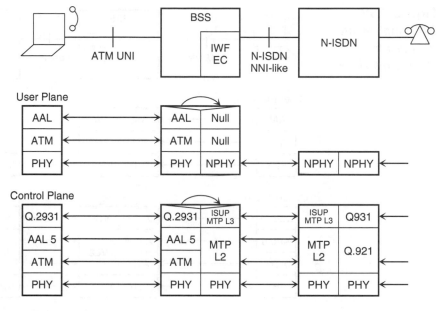

IWF: interworking function
NPHY: N-ISDN PHY
EC: echo control

Discussion of Scenarios

Each of the scenarios described above has advantages and disadvantages, which can fit into a technical category, a business category, or both.

The scenario of Figures 7.33 and 7.34 put the interworking burden on currently deployed switches. It is unlikely that these switch vendors can be persuaded to make the necessary investment in hardware and software to ensure this compatibility.

The scenario of Figure 7.35 places the interworking requirement on the BSS. This is consistent with the way other types of interworking functions currently being contemplated (e.g., frame relay) will be implemented. This scenario is the recommended approach. In the User Plane, access is accomplished by circuit emulation of individual speech-oriented bearer channels using AAL capabilities in the CPE and at the BSS. The user needs to employ Q.2931/ATMF UNI 4.0 signaling in the ATM Control Plane. Interworking of the signaling channel (Q.2931/ATMF UNI 4.0 to Q.931) occurs at the BSS. The *narrowband bearer capability* (N-BC) *information element* (IE) must be included in the broadband SETUP

Figure 7.38
BNI implemented as a vendor-specific interface.

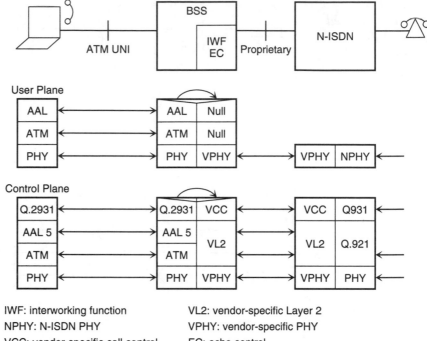

IWF: interworking function
NPHY: N-ISDN PHY
VCC: vendor-specific call control

VL2: vendor-specific Layer 2
VPHY: vendor-specific PHY
EC: echo control

message; this IE will be used by the BSS to launch an N-ISDN SETUP message. The BNI is an ISDN circuit-switched primary-rate bearer channel. One of the disadvantages of this scenario is that the BSS must play a role in the call setup process by intercepting, converting, and interpreting the narrowband signaling messages, as implied by the Control Plane stack shown in Figure 7.35.

The scenario of Figure 7.36 is similar to the scenario of Figure 7.35, except that a circuit-emulated connection is supported transparently through the BSS, between the user equipment and the N-ISDN switch. This user-to-N-ISDN transparent channel is set up between the user and the BSS over a signaling path that *terminates in the BSS* (that is, B-ISDN-to-N-ISDN signaling interworking is not supported in the BSS). Note that the user station still needs to support Q.2931/ATMF UNI 4.0. It is assumed that a pool of (pre-) nailed-up DS0 channels exists between the BSS and the N-ISDN switch. A trunk is selected by the BSS to establish the transparent path from the user to the N-ISDN switch. After the path is set up, the user initiates an in-band N-ISDN signaling exchange with the

N-ISDN switch. The disadvantage of this approach is that the user equipment now needs to support *both signaling stacks* (one for B-ISDN and one for N-ISDN). Another possibility emerges from this discussion, not shown in Figure 7.36, but already alluded to: Have a few DS0 VCs predefined (i.e., PVC-like) from the user, through the BSS, to the N-ISDN to be used to establish voice calls. This requires the user to have a Q.931 stack but not a Q.2931/ATMF UNI 4.0 stack active in the voice station (presumably the user would have a Q.2931/ATMF UNI 4.0 stack somewhere, given that the user is a B-ISDN user by assumption).

The scenario of Figure 7.37 is a more sophisticated version of the scenario of Figure 7.36, as the N-ISDN switch treats the BSS as a switch, via an NNI, rather than a simple PBX-like concentrator. However, the protocol machinery is more complex. The scenario of Figure 7.38 has the disadvantage of being vendor-specific, thereby degrading global interoperability.

Pragmatically Best Architecture

Based on this discussion, the scenario of Figure 7.35 is the approach to support voice over ATM. See Table 7.11.

AAL Issues

Figure 7.35 shows that AAL capabilities are needed in both the CPE and in the BSS. Standards groups have not settled on a choice

Table 7.11   BNI for Voice over ATM at the Physical Architecture Level

Interworking capability:
    Located at the BSS
    Broadband-to-narrowband interface defined to be an ISDN PRI
    BSS looks to N-ISDN as a PBX

User plane access:
    Circuit emulation using AAL 1 capabilities in the CPE and at the BSS
    (AAL-supported CBR path between CPE and BSS)
    ISDN circuit-switched primary-rate channel between BSS and the N-ISDN
    switch

Signaling: User employs Q.2931/ATMF UNI 4.0 signaling in ATM Control Plane
    Bearer capability IE included in the broadband SETUP message
    Bearer capability IE used by the BSS to launch an N-ISDN SETUP message

of AAL type for voice service. AAL Type 1 provides cell sequencing for lost/misinserted cell detection and, optionally, timing recovery (using the SRTS technique) for applications that have stringent jitter requirements.

As discussed in earlier sections, AAL Type 1 provides more-than-sufficient error protection and timing recovery functions to support voice. With the very low cell loss/misinsertion ratios expected in ATM networks, error detection is not considered necessary for single-channel voice support. Also, at 64 kbps, synchronous clock recovery may not be necessary for voice. Instead, receiver-specific methods of recovering timing from buffer fill observation may suffice (e.g., adaptive clocking). Thus, from a technical point of view, AAL 1 functions may not be strictly necessary for voice. However, even if these capabilities are not strictly needed for voice, it may make sense to use AAL 1 coding so that all DS0 signals have the same payload/cell rates. Specifically, 64-kbps unrestricted digital information (data) will presumably take advantage of AAL 1 error detection. Thus, in order not to have different cell rates for 64-kbps voice versus 64-kbps data, it may make sense to use AAL 1 coding for voice for commonality. The costs of using SRTS versus receiver-specific timing recovery methods for voice are not yet well understood. The VTOA specifications do now call for AAL 1 support for voice.

As noted, the AAL 1 functionality supports a *structured* capability in order to establish the boundaries of a group of octets—for example, in the $n\times64$-kbps case. This is a more complicated framing protocol that utilizes alternating non-P and P protocol data units. The P protocol data units provide a pointer that indicates the beginning of the structure of octets. Given the assumption of carrying a *single* voice channel over a VC, the structured mechanism is not required (it will be required when more than one DS0 will be carried over the ATM UNI).

In conclusion, AAL 1 without structure support can be used. Explicit source clock frequency recovery mechanisms do not have to be used for single-channel, 64-kbps voice signals. Instead, a receive buffer is used to smooth out cell delay variations; the buffer may impose some fixed maximum delay (on the order of 2 to 4 ms) for this smoothing function, without introducing adverse delay problems, particularly when the partial-fill method described below is utilized. (*Note:* When cells are filled with 16 octets of speech, cells arrive at a rate of one cell every 2 ms or two cells every 4 ms—this allows the buffer mechanism at the receiving station a certain amount of slack in reading out cells at a constant rate.)

ATM Cell Fill Issues

Figure 7.35 shows that ATM capabilities are needed in both the CPE and in the BSS. This section examines issues associated with the ATM (the same treatment could have been included in the next section under CPE, but the choice was made to cover it here).

As briefly discussed earlier in the chapter, two candidate solutions are feasible [9]:

- *Partial cell fill*   The broadband voice interworking unit (IWU) at the CPE or at the interface to a narrowband network would partially fill cells with less than the 47 (or 48) cell payload octets available. A value of 16-octet cell payload filling introduces a 4-ms round-trip delay due to cell construction. This delay would be considered acceptable.
- *Full cell fill*   The broadband voice interworking unit at the CPE (and at the interface to a narrowband network) would fill cells with 47 octets (voice samples). This would introduce a round-trip delay of approximately 12 ms, and will require echo cancellation at the IWU between the broadband and narrowband networks.

Echo cancelers compute an echo estimate for each direction of a voice channel. This estimate is then subtracted (i.e., removed) from the send-path signal; this cancels the echo and leaves only the near-end speech to be transmitted to the distant end. Typically the canceler constructs a mathematical echo estimate on the near-end path, usually after 200 ms of speech. The following ITU-T recommendations are applicable:

- ITU-T G.131-1996, Control of Talker Echo
- ITU-T G.164-1988, Echo Suppressors
- ITU-T G.165-1993, Echo Cancellers

There are advantages and disadvantages with both approaches identified above. The discussion that follows focuses on these considerations, followed by the suggested approach. Partial fill with only 16 cells could be justified as follows.

ATM is characterized by a degree of overhead, not only at the AAL level, but also at the ATM, at the transmission convergence (mapping) level, and at the physical-medium-dependent (SONET) levels. STS-3c has 27 octets of overhead 8000 times a second—that is, about 2 Mbps. Additional overhead may be encountered in the cell mapping procedure. Another 14 Mbps (approximately) of overhead is generated at the ATM Layer. Another 3 Mbps (approximate) of overhead is generated by the AAL 1 protocol, for an approximate total of 19 Mbps on an STS-3c UNI. While a sense of efficiency and elegance would ostensibly suggest filling the voice cells, at the practical level, this efficiency may be of limited consequence, compared to the 19 Mbps of already existing overhead. Carrying a single voice channel over the UNI would have an additional overhead of 128 kbps (instead of $8000/47 = 170$ fully filled cells per second, we now need to send $8000/16 = 500$ partially filled cells, for a penalty of $[500 * 47 - 170 * 47] * 8 = 128$ kbps). Comparing 128 kbps to 20 Mbps is a trivial incremental percentage of overhead—$(20.12 - 20)/20$ or 0.6 percent more. Carrying 10 voice channels over the UNI would have an additional overhead of 1.3 Mbps. Comparing 1.3 Mbps to 20 Mbps gives an incremental percentage of $(21.3 - 20)/20$ or 6.5 percent more. Carrying 20 voice channels over the UNI would have an additional overhead of 2.6 Mbps. Comparing 2.6 Mbps to 20 Mbps gives an incremental percentage of $(22.6 - 20)/20$, or 13 percent more. Additionally, the overhead affects the access line, which, in practice, already allocates the bandwidth, regardless of whether it is utilized.

Given these observations, one simple approach to voice interworking would be to carry cells with 16-octet fill. This approach eliminates much of the cellularization delay at the source. The BSS can pipeline the voice octets to the N-ISDN switch, eliminating the need for BSS-based echo cancellation functions due to the delays incurred by the cellularization process (more on this below). *This approach eliminates the need to deploy echo cancelers in conjunction with the voice interworking function at the BSS.* This approach would make sense when the volume of internetworked voice over ATM is small, as indications are (multimedia use of ATM will eventually generate more voice, but this will likely be carried end to end over ATM).

The approach of using 47-octet cell fill (full fill) entails the additional complexity and cost of echo cancellation. The considerations for choosing between partial fill and full cell fill (with echo cancelers) are as follows.

Time to market: Partial fill is easier to implement than full cell fill (from a network equipment perspective). Thus, it is reasonable to assume that systems implementing partial fill could be commercially available before systems employing echo cancelers to achieve full cell fill.

Initial equipment costs: The impact of either option on CPE that supports single-channel voice (e.g., a multimedia workstation on an ATM LAN, or a Multipoint Control Unit (MCU) associated with an ATM UNI) should be minimal. It is not unreasonable for CPE to be able to support either full or partial fill. It is expected that multimedia terminals on ATM LANs will likely use higher than telephony-quality audio (for intra-LAN networking), either multiplexed together with other media (as in H.261) or in fully filled cells.

The impact on network equipment is clear: Full cell fill requires the implementation of an echo cancellation function at the point of interworking between the broadband and narrowband networks, while partial fill does not. Standalone echo cancelers of 1980s-vintage operate on an entire T1 transmission system and cost approximately $1500 to $2000 (that is, approximately $60 to $80 per circuit). However, most of this cost has little to do with the actual echo cancellation (DSP) function; these standalone devices must (1) have their own power supplies, cases, and so on; (2) terminate and regenerate a DS1 signal; and (3) support external (maintenance) interfaces. At least one switch manufacturer has integrated echo canceler functions directly into (toll switch) trunk interface circuits, at a far lower per-line cost. An estimate of the (integrated) cost increment associated with echo cancellation is $10 to $40 per circuit (inversely related to the number of circuits sharing a single DSP echo canceler). In the architecture advocated in this book, these narrowband circuits are used as part of a BSS-to-ISDN CO interface and are thus shared (like trunk circuits) by all potential voice over ATM users. Assuming a typical 5:1 line-to-trunk ratio, this implies that the incremental equipment costs of full cell fill amount to $2 to $8 per equivalent voice line.

The echo control function must be integrated into the ATM-to-narrowband interworking equipment (that is, one should not have to rely on utilizing standalone echo cancelers in conjunction with the ATM-to-narrowband interworking equipment. It is not strictly required that echo cancellation functions be performed at this interworking point; however, looking into the ATM-to-narrowband interface from a suitable (i.e., impairment-free) ATM reference point, the equivalent echo return loss on any connection should exceed 30 dB. In practice, this may necessitate the use of echo cancelers integrated into the interworking function. If echo cancelers are included at the interworking point, they should conform to ITU-T Recommendation G.165; the cancellation function should be performed in one direction of transmission only—that is, the echo to be canceled is the far-end echo, if present; the echo cancelers should be capable of handling echoes with a tail delay of at least 32 ms; and the BSS must be able to either disable the echo canceler associated with any narrowband circuit or route around the canceler-equipped circuits based on the bearer capability specified in the bearer capability IE (this is important not for voice transport but for ATM-to-narrowband data interworking).

Usage costs: From both a carrier and end-user perspective, full fill and partial fill are roughly equivalent in terms of usage. Partial fill "wastes" approximately 128 kbps per voice channel, but this is a relatively trivial amount if the true application for initial voice over ATM is backward compatibility with N-ISDN for low volumes of traffic. If the volume of traffic were high, it would be in the end user's best interest to have full cell fill, since the 128-kbps waste is incurred (in this architecture) solely on the user's access line.

To summarize this discussion, partial fill has the advantages of potentially earlier commercial availability and slightly lower per-line network equipment costs, while full cell fill has the advantage of using less bandwidth over the UNI. CPE should be capable of implementing either, or even both.

User Equipment Needed

This section provides some general requirements for CPE handling ATM-based voice.

AAL and ATM Fill

These issues are identical to those described above for the BSS.

Voice Digitization

To properly support voice in an ATM environment, the user's terminal equipment must meet several functional requirements. First, to ensure compatibility with existing networks, the terminal equipment must support standard 64-kbps μ-law PCM encoding (ITU Recommendation G.711). CPE may optionally support 7-kHz audio (ITU Recommendation G.722). *Note:* Other voice coding schemes (e.g., vocoding) may be considered in the future.

Echo Control in CPE

In a traditional telephone network, echo arises in the form of energy reflected back to the user when there is a mismatch of impedance of an analog loop termination (e.g., at the 2- to 4-wire hybrid). If the path is sufficiently short so that the propagation delay is small, then the echo will reach the user quickly enough not to cause a problem (the propagation delay is $\frac{1}{186}$ ms per mile). Delay can also be introduced by signal processing equipment (A/D conversion, buffering, switching, etc.). If the path includes several pieces of equipment that raise the delay to several milliseconds, then echo can begin to become a problem. Finally, there may be far-end injection of signal—for example, when the sender's voice is delivered over a full-duplex speakerphone so that some of the output signal is picked up by the speakerphone's microphone and returned to the sender tens of milliseconds later.

Since the architecture discussed in this chapter is completely digital, the issues of impedance mismatch do not represent critical contributing factors. However, the buffering of the voice before it is sent onto the UNI could become a problem if

1. The digitized buffered signal is applied to the earpiece of the handset at the same time it is transmitted on the UNI. This should not occur, since it does not make sense to convert the voice to a digital signal, then buffer it to cellularize it, then reconvert it in order to apply it to the earpiece—the earpiece signal should come directly from the handset without further processing. Even if the signal was applied at transmission time, it should not constitute a problem if the buffering time is only 4 ms or thereabouts.

2. The signal is reinserted at the remote end and carried all the way back to the sender. Two mitigating factors come into play: (a) Even if the signal were reinjected it should not constitute a problem if the buffering time is only 4 ms or thereabouts, so that the round-trip delay would be small; (b) specifications for echo control are utilized in the design of the CPE.

To ensure that the far-end user experiences acceptable performance, the terminal equipment (TE) should be designed to meet the specification for echo control set forth in EIA/TIA-579, which requires the weighted acoustic *echo path loss* (a measure of the attenuation of echoed signals) of the digital telephone set to be at least 45 dB. The transmit/receive loudness rating must also be consistent with EIA/TIA-579.

Summary of Requirements to Support Interworking User Equipment

The user's terminal equipment must be able to construct protocol data units for the following User Plane protocol stack:

AAL	AAL 1 with/without structure. Explicit source clock frequency recovery mechanisms not used; instead, a receive buffer (imposing some fixed maximum delay) is used to smooth out cell delay variations.
ATM	Full fill of 47 speech octets per cell; 1 voice channel per VC.
PHY	Same PHY employed in the user's UNI.

The user's voice equipment (or the adjunct station of which the voice unit is part) must be able to construct protocol data units for the following Control Plane protocol stack:

Q.2931/ATMF UNI 4.0	Call control capabilities with support for N-ISDN bearer capability
AAL 5	SSCF, SSCOP, AAL 5 common part
ATM	Normal operation
PHY	Same PHY employed in the user's UNI

The CPE must be designed to follow the following specification:

Echo control	Meet the specification set forth in EIA/TIA-579

Network and Network Interface Requirements

In summary, the network must support an SVC ATM UNI with a voice CPE meeting the requirements described above. Interworking is to be supported at the BSS. AAL 1 must be supported. Full cell fill is utilized. Buffers are provided to support smoothing in order to meet cell delay variation tolerance requirements. Lost cells are replaced with dummy cells at the interworking unit.

Note: Full cell fill with AAL Type 1 format will require echo cancelers. These can be located at the interworking site, as described above.

The equivalent echo return loss on any connection should exceed 30 dB. If echo cancelers are included at the interworking point, they should have the following properties: (1) They must conform to ITU Recommendation G.165; (2) the cancellation function is to be performed in one direction of transmission only; (3) the echo cancelers should be capable of handling echoes with a tail delay of at least 32 ms; and (4) the BSS must be able to disable the echo canceler associated with any narrowband circuit or route around the canceler-equipped circuits.

Echo cancelers

- Equivalent echo return loss on any connection should exceed 30 dB.
- Must conform to ITU Recommendation G.165.
- Cancellation function in the direction of transmission only.
- Should be capable of handling echoes with a tail delay of at least 32 ms.
- The BSS must be able to either disable the echo canceler associated with any narrowband circuit or route around the canceler-equipped circuits based on the bearer capability specified in the bearer capability IE.

More specifically, there are the following requirements.

UNI User Plane Capabilities at BSS   In the origination-to-destination path, the IWU must be able to disassemble protocol data units built on the following User Plane protocol stack, for usage by the interworking relaying function:

AAL	AAL 1 with/without structure. Explicit source clock frequency recovery mechanisms not used; instead, a receive buffer (imposing some fixed maximum delay) is used to smooth out cell delay variations.
ATM	Full fill of 47 speech octets per cell; 1 voice channel per VC.
PHY	Same PHY employed in the user's UNI.

In the destination-to-origination path, the IWU must be able to assemble protocol data units built on the User Plane protocol stack just shown (for usage by the interworking relaying function).

UNI Control Plane Capabilities at BSS   In the origination-to-destination path, the IWU must be able to disassemble protocol data units built on the following Control Plane protocol stack, for usage by the interworking relaying function:

Q.2931/ATMF UNI 4.0	Call control capabilities with support for N-ISDN bearer capability
AAL 5	SSCF, SSCOP, AAL 5 common part
ATM	Normal operation
PHY	Same PHY employed in the user's UNI

In the destination-to-origination path, the IWU must be able to assemble protocol data units built on the User Plane protocol stack just shown (for usage by the interworking relaying function).

BNI User Plane Capabilities at BSS   In the origination-to-destination path, the IWU must be able to disassemble protocol data units built on the following User Plane protocol stack toward the N-ISDN switch, for usage by the interworking relaying function:

PHY	ISDN circuit-switched primary rate bearer channel—ISDN User Plane

In the destination-to-origination path, the IWU must be able to assemble protocol data units built on the User Plane protocol stack just shown (for usage by the interworking relaying function).

BNI Control Plane Capabilities at BSS   In the origination-to-destination path, the IWU must be able to disassemble protocol data units built on the following Control Plane protocol stack, for usage by the interworking relaying function:

Q.931	UNI requests are mapped to N-ISDN call control protocols using the bearer capability obtained over the ATM UNI.
Q.921	Normal operation.
PHY	ISDN circuit-switched primary rate bearer channel—ISDN control plane.

In the destination-to-origination path, the IWU must be able to assemble protocol data units built on the Control Plane protocol stack just shown (for usage by the interworking relaying function).

Voice Entirely within an ATM Network

There are cases in which it is preferable to support entirely within an ATM network (i.e., ATM end to end without interworking). The current implicit assumption is that multimedia over ATM will be supported by CPE multiplexing of the video, voice, image, and data components. This predicament arises from the fact that no synchronization of distinct VCs is currently supported by network elements. Even VCs within a given virtual path (VP) are not necessarily guaranteed to be temporally synchronized. It appears likely that for real-time multimedia applications AAL 1 will be used. For store-and-forward multimedia applications (e.g., for messaging), AAL 5 or some other adaptation protocol could be used.

A voice call that is not part of a multimedia session can be supported over an ATM UNI to another ATM UNI, generally using the same techniques discussed earlier. Figure 7.39 depicts the architectural view.

The key aspects of voice support are as follows:

- The originator uses Q.2931/ATMF UNI 4.0 signaling in the Control Plane to establish the end-to-end bidirectional symmetric SVC connection.
- Voice samples are produced according to G.711; echo control according to EIA/TIA-579 [10].
- Both originator and receiver utilize AAL 1 over ATM in the User Plane; receive-end buffering is used for timing.
- There is full fill of 47 speech octets per cell and one voice channel per VC.

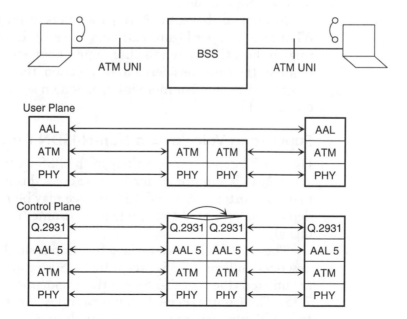

Figure 7.39
Voice support within an ATM network.

- The network does not provide any echo cancellation (full-duplex speakerphones must provide adequate echo management to avoid reinjection of signal).

In the interworking case discussed earlier, the BSS recognized the request over the UNI as a voice request by the presence of the narrowband bearer capability IE. This IE is utilized by the N-ISDN switch to complete the call. This IE is not strictly necessary for a voice connection that is entirely provided over ATM. If the narrowband bearer capability IE is not utilized, another mechanism may be required to identify the VC as a voice-carrying VC; although the BSS does not necessarily need to know the nature of the VC content, the receiving equipment that supports multiple VCs over the interface needs to know that AAL 1 logic must be provided on top of the local ATM Layer for this particular VC (other AALs may be active for other VCs over the UNI). One mechanism is to make the AAL parameters IE mandatory for voice-carrying channels; the subtype field can be coded for voiceband-based on 64 kbps. However, many of the other fields in this IE are not needed (they are needed for more general $n\times64$ channels using clock recovery). This implies some inefficiency. Another way to identify VCs as voice-carrying channels would be to reserve a small number of VCs per interface for voice applications.

As implied above, the AAL parameters IE for the voice over ATM case (i.e., per Figure 7.35) may be sent for the purpose of setting up the VC between the user equipment and the interworking point. In the case considered in this section, the AAL parameters IE is sent end to end. For more information on signaling, refer to Reference [11].

Supporting Voice over a Non-N-ISDN Far-End Platform

Figure 7.32 depicts interworking of the BSS with a POTS switch via an N-ISDN intermediary. In some cases this N-ISDN capability may not exist; a BSS-to-POTS interface may be needed. Figure 7.40 depicts the proposed arrangement (it assumes that the switch is digital).

The User Plane interworking function is similar to that described in Figure 7.35, except that DS0s rather than B-channels are utilized (the user-to-BSS interface is identical to that of Figure 7.35). The Control Plane BSS interworking functions over the BSS-to-POTS interface must support a traditional signaling apparatus;

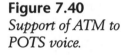

Figure 7.40
Support of ATM to POTS voice.

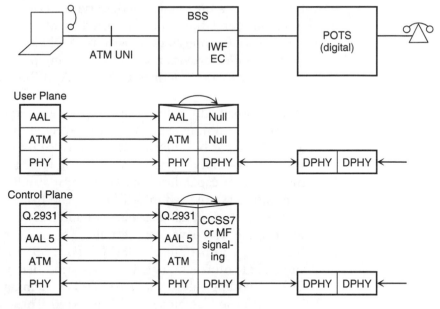

IWF: interworking function
EC: echo control
DPHY: DSO-based physical layer

the signaling can be in-band (associated) MF or it can be via CCSS7. The Control Plane user-to-BSS interface is similar to that described earlier; the AAL parameters IE is utilized to set up the VC between the user and the interworking point in the BSS. Echo control is needed in the BSS.

ITU-T View for Provision of 64-kbps Circuit-Mode ISDN Services

The material that follows is a transcription of Section 6 and Annex E of ITU-T Q.2931, February 1993.

(1) Provision of 64-kbps-Based Circuit-Mode ISDN Services in B-ISDN and Signaling Interworking between N-ISDN and B-ISDN

This clause describes the particular features required to provide 64-kbps-based circuit-mode ISDN services in B-ISDN and signaling interworking between B-ISDN and N-ISDN. For the 64-kbps-based circuit-mode services, the term *N-ISDN services* is also used. This term includes the circuit-mode services described in the I.200 series of recommendations and supported by the Q.931 protocol. For these services, interworking with N-ISDN is possible. This description of service provision and interworking presupposes the communication scenario B defined in Annex A of Recommendation I.580.

Introduction   In order to ease signaling interworking between B-ISDN and N-ISDN, separate services-related information elements are defined for N-ISDN services and B-ISDN services. For the provision of N-ISDN services, basically the Q.931 information elements bearer capability, high-layer compatibility, and low-layer compatibility are used in B-ISDN. In the B-ISDN, these information elements are designated as narrowband bearer capability (N-BC), narrowband low-layer compatibility (N-LLC), and narrowband high-layer compatibility (N-HLC). For their application in B-ISDN, the Q.931 information elements are modified according to the Q.2931 coding rules—that is, octet 3 containing the IE instruction field with the Flag bit set to 0 is inserted. These information elements are defined in Q.2931 subclause 4.6. For the provision of B-ISDN services, new information elements are used, as defined in clause 4.5 of Q.2931. Table 7.12 shows the information elements required for the provision of N-ISDN services in B-ISDN.

Table 7.12   Information Elements in B-ISDN to Provide N-ISDN Services

	IEs used to describe network-relevant bearer attributes	*IEs used to describe low-layer attributes (transparent for B-ISDN)*	*IEs used to describe high-layer attributes (transparent for B-ISDN)*
N-ISDN-related information elements (Section 4.6 of Q.2931)	N-BC	N-LLC	N-HLC
B-ISDN-related information elements (Section 4.5 of Q.2931)	Broadband bearer capability (B-BC) supplemented by: ATM user cell rate QoS parameter End-to-end transit delay	ATM Adaptation Layer (AAL) parameters	—

One major advantage of taking the Q.931 information elements nearly unchanged in B-ISDN is a significant simplification of interworking between B-ISDN and N-ISDN. Another important benefit is that by dividing the service-related attributes into N-ISDN- and B-ISDN-related parts, a decoupling of the B-ISDN-specific information elements from the evolution of the Q.931-based information elements is achieved.

The reason for taking the Q.931 information elements even for the provision of N-ISDN services in a pure B-ISDN environment is that a B-ISDN user cannot know in advance whether the destination of a call will be a B-ISDN (Q.2931) or an N-ISDN (Q.931) terminal. Therefore, no difference is made between the provision of N-ISDN services in a pure B-ISDN environment and the provision of these services in the case of interworking with N-ISDN.

Information Elements for N-ISDN Services in B-ISDN　When N-ISDN services are provided in a B-ISDN environment, in principle the information elements of Q.2931 (e.g., Called Party Number; see Section 4.5 of Q.2931) are used in the same way as for B-ISDN-specific services. However, for the service-related attributes listed in Table 7.12, Q.931 information elements (see top line of Table 7.12) are reused for the N-ISDN services as described below. The following subsections only describe the use of the services-related information elements in the SETUP message. However, in case of service negotiation, they may also be included in the first response message returned to the call-initiating entity.

Bearer Service–Related Information　The B-BC information element is always included in the SETUP message. This information element is mandatory for all services. It is interpreted by the B-ISDN. For N-ISDN services, the N-BC information element is also mandatory in the SETUP message. Unlike the B-BC information element, however, the N-BC information element is transported transparently through the B-ISDN.

The N-BC information element is included in the SETUP message even if no interworking takes place, since the user is not able to know in advance whether the receiver of the SETUP message will be B-ISDN (Q.2931) or N-ISDN (Q.931) equipment.

For N-ISDN services, a value for the ATM cell rate is selected, such that the bit rate of the N-ISDN service (64 kbps or $n \times 64$

kbps) can be transported as the cell payload (i.e., excluding the overhead of the ATM cell and the AAL header) of the ATM cells.

Low-Layer Information   If required for the description of the N-ISDN services, the N-LLC information element is included in the SETUP message. *Note:* The B-ISDN low-layer information (B-LLI) element is used for B-ISDN-specific services.

The N-LLC information element is transported transparently through the B-ISDN. For the provision of N-ISDN services, the inclusion of the AAL parameter information element in the SETUP message is required, specifying AAL Type 1.

High-Layer Information   If required for the description of the N-ISDN services, the N-HLC information element is included in the SETUP message. The N-HLC information element is transported transparently through the B-ISDN.

Interworking N-ISDN to B-ISDN   This section describes the functions performed by a terminal adapter (TA) or network adapter (NA), according to scenario B/I.580.

The objective is that Q.931 information elements simply be relayed through the B-ISDN by the TA or the NA, by the addition of a new octet 3 (IE instruction field).

Bearer Service–Related Information   The Q.931 BC information element is mapped to the N-BC information element by the TA or the NA, by simply inserting the third octet containing the IE instruction field. The Flag bit in this octet is set to 0; that is, the normal error handling procedures as defined in Q.2931 subclause 5.7 apply. In addition to this, the B-BC information element is created by the TA or NA, indicating Bearer Class A and the value Yes for the susceptibility to clipping field. The ATM user cell rate and the QoS parameter information elements are also generated by the TA or NA, evaluating the information of the Q.931 BC information element.

Low-Layer Compatibility Information   The Q.931 LLC information element (if included) is mapped to the N-LLC information element by the TA or NA without change of content. Simply, the new octet 3 is inserted in the same way as described above. The AAL parameter is generated by the TA or NA, indicating AAL Type 1.

High-Layer Compatibility Information The Q.931 HLC information element (if included) is mapped to the N-HLC information element by the TA or NA without change of content. Simply, the new octet 3 is inserted in the same way as described above.

The N-HLC information element is transported transparently through the B-ISDN, except for the cases described in Section 4.6.3 of Q.2931.

Interworking B-ISDN to N-ISDN If a broadband TE (B-TE) initiates a call to a narrowband TE (N-TE), only N-ISDN services will be processed and forwarded by the NA. If a B-ISDN-specific service is selected by the B-TE toward the N-ISDN, then the call should be rejected by the NA with cause code "Service interworking not possible."

Bearer Service–Related Information The B-BC, the ATM user cell rate, and the QoS parameter information element are discarded by the NA.

The N-BC information element is mapped to the Q.931 BC information element by the NA, by simply removing its third octet, without causing other changes to the content.

If no N-BC information element is included, then a B-ISDN service should be assumed and the call should be rejected with cause code "Service interworking not possible."

Low-Layer Compatibility Information The N-LLC information element (if included) is mapped to the Q.931 LLC information element by the NA by simply removing its third octet, without change of the contents.

The AAL parameter information element is discarded by the NA.

If a B-LLI information element is detected by the NA, then the call should be rejected with cause code "Service interworking not possible."

High-Layer Compatibility Information The N-HLC information element (if included) is mapped to the Q.931 HLC information element by the NA by simply removing its third octet, without change of the contents.

If a B-HLC information element is detected by the NA, then the call should be rejected with cause code "Service interworking not possible."

Overlap Sending and Receiving   B-ISDN terminal equipment shall use en-block sending in B-ISDN. This implies, from the B-TE perspective, the mandatory inclusion of the Sending Complete information element in the SETUP message. Since overlap receiving is an allowed procedure in N-ISDN, this procedure is also supported in B-ISDN for incoming calls from the N-ISDN. In order to allow terminal equipment designed for the N-ISDN to be connected to the B-ISDN via a terminal adapter or via a customer's network, the Q.2931 protocol also supports overlap sending. The procedures of Q.2931 for overlap sending and receiving are specified below.

If overlap sending is used, the SETUP message contains either no called number information, or incomplete called number information, or called number information that the network cannot determine to be complete.

On receipt of such a SETUP message, the network starts timer T302, sends a SETUP ACKNOWLEDGE message to the user and enters the Overlap Sending state. When the SETUP ACKNOWLEDGE message is received, the user enters the Overlap Sending state and optionally starts timer T304. After receiving the SETUP ACKNOWLEDGE message, the user sends the remainder of the call information (if any) in one or more INFORMATION messages. The called party number information should be provided by the user in the Called Party Number information element.

If, for symmetry purposes, the user employs timer T304, the user restarts T304 when each INFORMATION message is sent.

The call information in the message that completes the information sending may contain a "sending complete" indication (i.e., the Sending Complete information element). The network restarts timer T302 on receipt of every INFORMATION message not containing a "sending complete" indication.

When a user determines that a received message contains either no called number information, or incomplete called number information, or called number information that the user cannot determine to be complete, and when the user is compatible with the other call characteristic and implements overlap receiving, the user should start timer T302, send a SETUP ACKNOWLEDGE message to the network, and enter the Overlap Receiving state. When the SETUP ACKNOWLEDGE message is received, the network should stop timer T303, start timer T304, enter the Overlap Receiving state, and send the remainder of the call information (if any) in one or more INFORMATION messages, starting timer T304 when each INFORMATION message is sent. The called party number information is provided in the Called Party Number information element. The call address information may contain a "sending complete" indication (i.e., the Sending Complete information element).

Note: If the network can determine that sufficient call setup information will be received by the called user by sending the next INFORMATION message, it is recommended that this INFORMATION message contains the Sending Complete information element.

The user shall start timer T302 on receipt of every INFORMATION message not containing a "sending complete" indication.

Following the receipt of a "sending complete" indication, or the determination that sufficient call information has been received, the user should stop timer T302 (if implemented) and send a CALL PROCEEDING message to the network. Alternatively, depending on internal events, the user may send an ALERTING or CONNECT message to the network.

Note: The CALL PROCEEDING message in this case will cause the originating exchange to send a CALL PROCEEDING message to the originating user, if not already sent.

At the expiration of timer T302, the user should either send a CALL PROCEEDING, ALERTING, or CONNECT message if sufficient information has been received, or initiate clearing in accordance with Section 5.4 of Q.2931 with cause no. 28, "invalid number format" (incomplete number), if it determines that the call information is definitely incomplete.

At the expiration of timer T304 the network initiates call clearing in accordance with Section 5.4 of Q.2931 with cause no. 28, "invalid number format" (incomplete number), sent to the calling user, and cause no. 102, "recovery on timer expiry," sent to the called user. If, following the receipt of a SETUP message or during overlap receiving, the user determines that the received call information is invalid (e.g., invalid called party number), the user should initiate call clearing in accordance with Section 5.4 of Q.2931 with a cause such as one of the following:

#1   unassigned (unallocated) number
#3   no route to destination
#22   number changed
#28   invalid number format (incomplete number)

Upon receipt of the completed call information, the user may further perform compatibility checking functions.

Notification of Interworking Interworking of B-ISDN with N-ISDN requires the support of the progress indicator values specified in Recommendation Q.931 by the B-ISDN. The following principles shall apply:

1. In the case of interworking with N-ISDN, all progress indicator values applying for N-ISDN interworking should be relayed to B-ISDN and then transported transparently through the B-ISDN.

2. In the case of a call leaving or entering B-ISDN at the NA, the NA should not generate a Q.931- and Q.2931-Progress indicator information element. The Q.931-Progress indicator information element should be mapped to the Q.2931-Progress indicator information element by adding or removing octet 3, depending on the direction of the call.

(2) Annex: Mapping Functions to Support 64-kbps-Based Circuit-Mode ISDN Services in B-ISDN and Interworking between N-ISDN and B-ISDN (Q.931/Q.2931)

Use of the N-LCC and the B-LLI Information Elements in B-ISDN The N-LCC and B-LLI information elements should be used in Q.2931 as described by the following items:

1. The N-LLC information element is used to determine end-to-end attributes on N-ISDN circuit-mode services supported in a B-ISDN. This information element should not be used for B-ISDN-specific services. In particular, this information element is used by a B-ISDN terminal emulating a N-ISDN service and between a TA (connecting an N-ISDN-TE to B-ISDN) and a B-ISDN network.

2. For B-ISDN-specific services, the B-LLI information element is used consistent with Q.2931.

3. Either the N-LLC or the B-LLI information element will be used in a call, not both.

4. If B-ISDN-specific terminals are connected to B-ISDN that do not support emulation of N-ISDN services, only the B-LLI information element is used, not the N-LLC information element.

The use of the N-LLC and B-LLI information elements is illustrated in Figure 7.41.

Mapping Functions between B-ISDN-Related Information Elements and N-ISDN-Related Information Elements This section specifies the processing and the detailed mapping of the service-related information elements performed by a network adapter installed between B-ISDN and N-ISDN. The communications scenario is described in Recommendation I.580, Annex A, scenario B. It should be noted that the functions and the mapping described in this section also apply to a terminal adapter (TA) at the UNI connecting an N-ISDN terminal to a B-ISDN network.

Interworking functions between N-ISDN and B-ISDN are provided only for circuit-mode 64-kbps-based N-ISDN services. Interworking functions to support packet-mode and frame-mode bearer services are for further study.

For the interworking functions between N-ISDN and B-ISDN, the following principles apply:

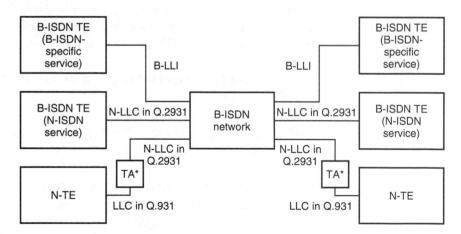

Figure 7.41
Illustration of the N-LLC and BLLI IEs in Q.2931.

* The LLC information is transferred transparently across the TA except for changes required by the different coding rules.

1. If B-ISDN-specific service is requested at the Q.2931 side of the NA, the call should be rejected.

2. If the NA receives a request for an N-ISDN service at its Q.931 side, it will select an ATM user cell rate for the B-ISDN side that is able to carry the 64-kbps (or $n \times 64$-kbps) bit rate of the N-ISDN service.

3. If the NA receives a request for an N-ISDN service at its Q.931 side, it will select Bearer Class A (CBR, CO, end-to-end timing required) and AAL Type 1 as default values for the B-ISDN side. The value for the susceptibility to clipping field in the B-BC is set to Yes.

4. In the direction from Q.2931 to Q.931, the NA places the information elements to be transferred to the N-ISDN side into the ascending order required by Recommendation Q.931.

Detailed Mapping Functions for the Direction Q.2931 to Q.931
The detailed mapping functions performed by the NA for the direction from Q.2931 to Q.931 are illustrated by the examples that follow.

The NA will relay the N-BC, N-LLC, and N-HLC information elements transparently to the N-ISDN. No further processing is required, except for changes needed to accommodate the different coding rules. B-BC, ATM user cell rate, QoS parameter, and AAL parameter information elements are only B-ISDN-related and are therefore not needed by the NA to generate the N-ISDN-related information elements. These information elements are discarded.

B-ISDN User Requests N-ISDN Bearer Service "3.1-kHz Audio"
See Table 7.13.

B-ISDN User Requests N-ISDN Telephony Teleservice   See Table 7.14.

Detailed Mapping Functions for the Direction Q.931 to Q.2931
The detailed mapping functions performed by the NA for the direction from Q.931 to Q.2931 are illustrated by the examples that follow.

The NA will relay the BC, LLC, and HLC information elements transparently to the B-ISDN. No further processing is required,

Table 7.13 Mapping Performed by NA for 3.1-kHz Audio Bearer Service (Direction Q.2931 to Q.931)

Q.2931	Q.931
Emulation of the N-ISDN bearer service 3.1-kHz audio	3.1-kHz audio bearer service
N-BC	BC
3.1-kHz audio	3.1-kHz audio
Circuit mode	Circuit mode
64 kbps	64 kbps
G.711 μ-law	G.711 μ-law
N-HLC	HLC
Optional	Present, if provided
N-LLC	LLC
Optional	Present, if provided
B-BC	
Bearer Class A	—
Susceptibility to clipping	—
ATM user cell rate	
Equal to 64 kbps	—
Quality of service	
ffs	—
AAL parameters	
AAL Type 1	—
SSCS attributes: ffs	—

except for changes needed to accommodate the different coding rules. B-BC, ATM user cell rate, QoS parameter, and AAL parameter information elements are generated by the NA using default values and the information provided by the Q.931 information elements. The susceptibility to clipping field of the B-BC information element in Q.2931 is always set to Yes.

N-ISDN User Requests the 3.1-kHz Audio Bearer Service See Table 7.15.

N-ISDN User Requests the Telephony Teleservice See Table 7.16.

Table 7.14   Mapping Performed by NA for N-ISDN Telephony Teleservice (Direction Q.2931 to Q.931)

Q.2931	Q.931
Emulation of N-ISDN telephony teleservice	Telephony teleservice
N-BC	BC
Speech	Speech
Circuit mode	Circuit mode
64 kbps	64 kbps
G.711 μ-law	G.711 μ-law
N-HLC	HLC
First high-layer characteristics identified to be used in the call	First high-layer characteristics identified to be used in the call
High-layer protocol profile: telephony	High-layer protocol profile: telephony
N-LLC	LLC
Optional	Present, if provided
B-BC	
Bearer Class A	
Susceptibility to clipping	—
ATM user cell rate	
Equal to 64 kbps	—
Quality of service	
ffs	—
AAL parameters	
AAL Type 1	
SSCS attributes: ffs	—

References

1. D. Minoli and M. Vitella. *Cell Relay Service and ATM for Corporate Environments*. New York: McGraw-Hill, 1994.

2. D. Minoli and E. Minoli. *Delivering Voice over IP Networks*. New York: Wiley, 1998.

3. T. Ferrugia, Fore Systems. Personal communication (August 1997).

4. D. Minoli and J. Amoss. *Broadband and ATM Switching Technology*. New York: McGraw-Hill, 1998.

5. B. Kittams. "Proposal for a Liaison to T1X1." *Contribution to T1 Committee T1S1.5/94-027*, Dallas, TX. January 10–14, 1994.

Table 7.15   Mapping Performed by NA for Audio Bearer Service (Direction Q.931 to Q.2931)

Q.931	Q.2931
3.1-kHz audio bearer service	Emulation of the audio bearer service
BC	N-BC
3.1-kHz audio	3.1-kHz audio
Circuit mode	Circuit mode
64 kbps	64 kbps
G.711 μ-law	G.711 μ-law
HLC	N-HLC
Optional	Present, if provided
LLC	N-LLC
Optional	Present, if provided
—	B-BC
	Bearer Class A
	Susceptibility to clipping
—	ATM user cell rate
	Equal to 64 kbps
—	Quality of service
	ffs
—	AAL parameters
	AAL Type 1
	SSCS attributes: ffs

6. R. C. Lau. "Synchronous Frequency Encoding Technique for Circuit Emulation." *SPIE Conference on Visual Processes and Image Communication*, September 1989.

7. D. Minoli. *Video Dialtone Technology: Digital Video over ADSL, HFC, FTTC, and ATM.* New York: McGraw-Hill, 1995.

8. M. McLoughlin. "A Management Briefing on Adapting Voice for ATM Network, A Comparison of AAL 1 versus AAL 2." *General DataCom White Paper* (1997).

9. W. O. Covington, Jr., and M. E. Vitella. "Voice Transport on an ATM Broadband Network." *GLOBECOM '89*: 1921–1925.

10. *Acoustic-to-Digital and Digital-to-Acoustic Transmission Requirements for ISDN Terminals,* Electronics Industry Association, EIA/TIA-579 (March 1991).

11. D. Minoli and G. Dobrowski. *Signaling Principles for Frame Relay and Cell Relay Services.* Norwood, MA: Artech House, 1994.

Table 7.16   Mapping Performed by NA for Telephony Teleservice (Direction Q.931 to Q.2931)

Q.931 Telephony teleservice	Q.2931 Emulation of telephony teleservice

BC
  Speech
  Circuit mode
  64 kbps
  G.711 μ-law
	N-BC
	  Speech
	  Circuit mode
	  64 kbps
	  G.711 μ-law

HLC
  First high-layer characteristics
    identified to be used in the call
  High-layer protocol profile:
    telephony
	N-HLC
	  First high-layer characteristics
	    identified to be used in the call
	  High-layer protocol profile:
	    telephony

LLC
  Optional
	N-LLC
	  Present, if provided

—	B-BC
	  Bearer Class A
	  Susceptibility to clipping

—	ATM user cell rate Equal to 64 kbps
—	Quality of service ffs

—	AAL parameters
	  AAL Type 1
	  SSCS attributes: ffs

Notes

[1]Specifically over af-uni-0010.002, UNI 3.1—ATM Forum User Network Interface Specification version 3.1 (September 1994).

[2]Also note that, although the CES ATMF specification has a DS3 version, there would seem to be little commercial interest for this at this time.

[3]Some of this material is based on Reference 1.

[4]Bellcore asserts that its U.S. Patent No. 5,260,978 for Synchronous Residual Timestamp (SRTS) Timing Recovery in a Broadband Network may apply to the ATM Adaptation Layer Type 1 (AAL 1) ANSI Standard (T1.630-1993) referenced in the VTOA Circuit Emulation Service.

[5]Other VCs on the same UNI may contain other traffic.

[6]ITU-T Q.2931-1995, Broadband Integrated Services Digital Network (B-ISDN); Digital Subscriber Signaling System No. 2 (DSS2); User-Network Interface (UNI) Layer 3 Specification for Basic Call/Connection Control, is the international signaling standard. A related specification is ITU-T Q.2951-1995, Stage 3 Description for Number Identification Supplementary Services Using B-ISDN Digital Subscriber Signaling System No. 2 (DSS2)—Basic Call.

CHAPTER 8

VTOA Voice over ATM: Circuit Emulation Service

This chapter presents an encapsulated and much abridged description of the ATM Forum's VTOA Circuit Emulation Service Interoperability Specification Version 2.0 (af-vtoa-0078.000), January 1997. This chapter is based on the ATM Forum specification cited. This material is for pedagogical purposes only. Developers, engineers, and readers requiring more information should acquire the specification directly from the ATM Forum. The document is 92 pages long and contains very detailed requirements; in standards parlance the information contained in this chapter is informative only. Figure 8.1 puts the spec in context.

8.1 Introduction to af-vtoa-0078.000

The af-vtoa-0078.000 document, referred to as the Circuit Emulation Service Interoperability Specification (CES-IS), specifies the ATM Forum's interoperability agreements for supporting CBR traffic over ATM networks (e.g., PCM-based voice) that comply with the Forum's other interoperability agreements. Note that all of the specific types of CBR service and/or specific interfaces identified within the specification need not be supported by a vendor in order to be compliant.

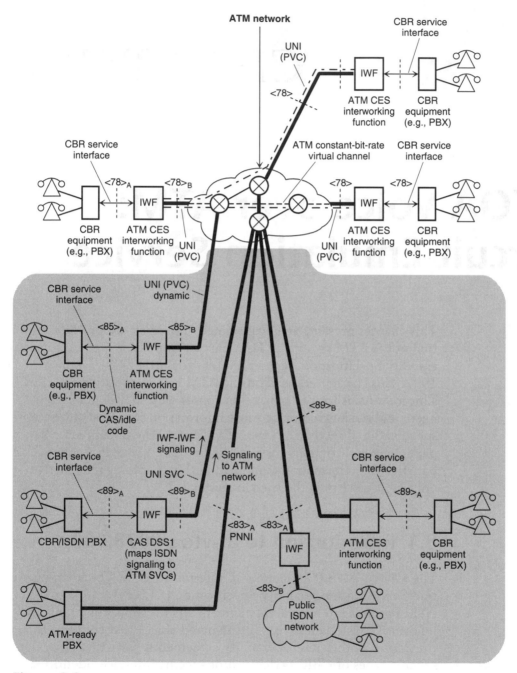

Figure 8.1
VTOA 0078.000.

The CES-IS specifically covers the following types of CBR service:

1. Structured DS1/E1 $n \times 64$-kbps (fractional DS1/E1) service
2. Unstructured DS1/E1 (1.544-Mbps, 2.048-Mbps) service
3. Unstructured DS3/E3 (44.736-Mbps, 34.368-Mbps) service
4. Structured J2 $n \times 64$-kbps (fractional J2) service
5. Unstructured J2 (6.312-Mbps) service

The E-hierarchy is used in Europe and the J-hierarchy is used in Japan. In the synopsis that follows, only the North American aspects are covered in some detail. Interested readers and developers should refer directly to af-vtoa-0078.000 for the E/J details.

The scope of the CES-IS is limited to the essential agreements needed to reliably transport these bit rates across ATM networks that comply with the ATM Forum's interoperability agreements. Specifying all the agreements needed to support a full-service offering (for example, ATM-based video telephony) is explicitly beyond the scope of the af-vtoa-0078.000 document.

Figure 8.2 provides a reference model for circuit emulation services. It shows two ATM circuit emulation service (CES) interworking functions (IWFs) connected to an ATM network via physical interfaces defined in the ATM Forum UNI Specification. The CES IWFs are also connected to standard constant-bit-rate (CBR) circuits (e.g., DS1/DS3, J2, or E1/E3), which may originate, for example, on a user's PBX. The job of the two IWFs is to extend the constant-bit-rate circuit to which they are connected across the ATM network. They are to do this in a manner that is transparent to the terminating equipment* of the CBR circuit. This means that the ATM portion of the connection should retain its bit integrity—that is, analog signal loss cannot be inserted and voice echo control cannot be performed. Thus, for facilities intended to carry voice or multimedia services, any required echo control must be performed either by the terminal equipment or before the ATM CES IWF is encountered. The assumption in the CES-IS is that using AAL 1 over ATM constant-bit-rate virtual channels is a simple, general, and effective method of addressing this type of application.

---

*The service interface may use a connector such as the RJ48C or RJ48M, as specified in T1.403.

Figure 8.2
Reference model.

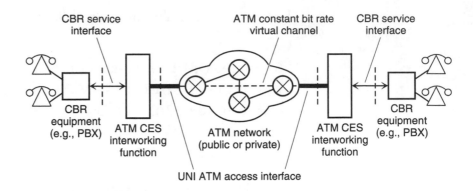

An ATM UNI physical interface has two characteristics that are relevant when supporting CES:

1. *Bandwidth*   The ATM interface must provide adequate bandwidth to carry $n\times64$ or unstructured traffic after segmentation.
2. *Timing*   The ATM interface can be used to convey timing traceable to a primary reference source from the ATM network to the CES interworking function, where external connection to network timing is not supported.

8.2 Structured DS1/$n\times64$-kbps Service

A number of applications currently use $n\times64$-kbps services. For example, there are a number of DTE interfaces and video codecs that are capable of operating at $n\times64$-kbps rates for $n > 1$. The following variations are supported:

- $n\times64$ service represents all modes of the structured DS1/E1 and J2 $n\times64$-kbps service.
- DS1 $n\times64$ service represents all modes of structured DS1 $n\times64$-kbps service in which the two IWFs involved are emulating DS1-based $n\times64$-kbps service supplied via a DSX-1 interface, T1.102-1993 Revised.
- DS1 $n\times64$ basic service represents DS1 $n\times64$ service with no support for carrying channel-associated signaling (CAS).

- DS1 *n*×64 service with CAS represents DS1 *n*×64 service with support for carrying CAS.
- Logical *n*×64 service represents all modes of structured DS1 *n*×64-kbps service in which the non-ATM-related functions of the two IWFs involved are left unspecified.
- Logical *n*×64 basic service represents logical *n*×64 service with no support for carrying CAS.
- Logical *n*×64 service with CAS represents all logical *n*×64 service with support for carrying CAS (also, there are E/J hierarchy services).

Figure 8.3 shows the relationships among the members of the *n*×64 services family. Note that the above does not include any indication of specific support for Common Channel Signaling (CCS) services. The current version of the af-vtoa-0078.000 specification makes no particular provisions for its use in CCS systems, but this specification does not preclude its use in CCS systems. Specific provisions for its use in CCS systems are currently undergoing further study.

Service Description

n×64 service is intended to emulate a point-to-point fractional DS1, E1, or J2 circuit. The service is typically accessed via either 1.544-Mbps DSX-1 (T1.102—1993 Revised) interfaces, 2.048-Mbps (G.703) interfaces, or 6.312-Mbps (JT-G.703a) interfaces. For DS1, *n* of the 24 timeslots available at the DSX-1 interface, where

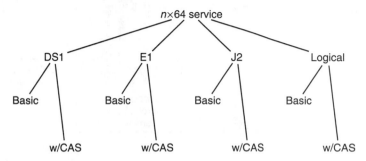

Figure 8.3
VTOA-supported CESs.

Basic = without explicit signaling support
w/CAS = with CAS support

$1 \leq n \leq 24$, are carried across the ATM network and reproduced at the output edge. For E1, $1 \leq n \leq 31$. For J2, $1 \leq n \leq 96$.

Because the $n\times64$ service can be configured to use only a fraction of the timeslots available on the service interface, it is possible to allow several independent emulated circuits to share one service interface, as shown in Figure 8.4. The capability of allowing several AAL 1 entities to share one service interface, where each AAL 1 entity is associated with a different virtual channel connection (VCC), allows for functional emulation of a DS1/DS0, E1/DS0, or J2/DS0 digital cross-connect switch.

In this configuration, the ATM Layer is responsible for multiplexing and demultiplexing several VCCs, one to each AAL 1 entity. Each AAL 1 entity is responsible for performing segmentation and reassembly on one VCC. The timeslot mapping function is responsible for assigning the stream input and output from the SAR process to specific time slots in the service.

Figure 8.5 shows an example cross-connect configuration in which two PBXs are connected across an ATM backbone to a central office switch. One virtual channel might carry ten timeslots

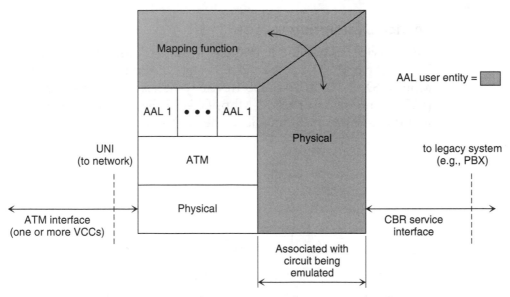

Figure 8.4
DS1/E1/J2 structured service interworking function—layering perspective.

between one PBX and the central office switch; another virtual channel might carry ten timeslots between the other PBX and the central office switch. At the pair of IWFs near the central office switch, the two virtual channels are reassembled, and a total of 20 timeslots are carried across the last DS1/E1/J2 link connecting the central office switch and its CES IWF. Although the *n*×64 service should be useful in providing a cross-connect service, it is outside the scope of the current CES-IS to specify cross-connect service.

Multiple CES IWFs providing *n*×64 service may be used to provide multiple AAL 1 entities, allowing several *n*×64 connections to be multiplexed onto a single service interface, with each connection utilizing different 64-kbps channels of the service interface.

Framing and Timeslot Assignment

DS1 *n*×64 service is capable of interfacing with circuits using extended superframe format (ESF). DS1 *n*×64 service may also support superframe format (SF) framing at a DS1 service interface. The *n*×64 service will carry any group of *n*×64-kbps timeslots, where *n* can be 1 to 24, 1 to 31, or 1 to 96 for DS1/E1 and J2, respectively. The timeslots assigned to a virtual channel are not required to be

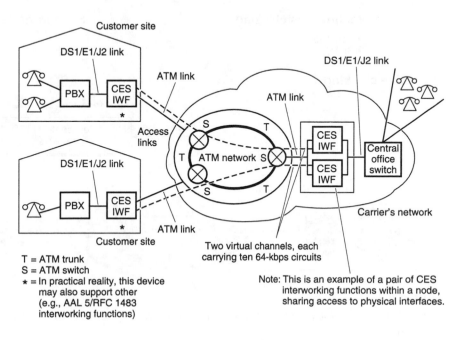

Figure 8.5
Cross-connect example.

T = ATM trunk
S = ATM switch
★ = In practical reality, this device
    may also support other
    (e.g., AAL 5/RFC 1483
    interworking functions)

Note: This is an example of a pair of CES
    interworking functions within a node,
    sharing access to physical interfaces.

contiguous. The CES IWFs must deliver octets at the output in the same order as they were received at the input. The $n{\times}64$ service also must maintain 125-μs frame integrity across a virtual channel.

Clocking

The DS1/E1/J2 $n{\times}64$-kbps service requires the use of synchronous circuit timing, as recommended by ITU I.363.1 (see Figure 8.6 and 8.7). In order to support this synchronous clock recovery by the attached end-user equipment, the following requirements are stated in the specification:

- Any $n{\times}64$ service IWF will provide a means by which a time source traceable to a primary reference source (PRS) may be supplied.

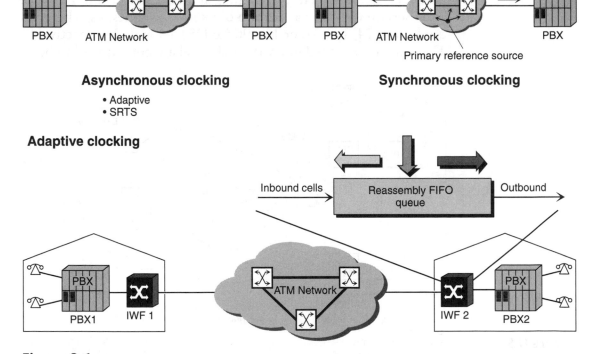

Figure 8.6
Circuit timing—clock recovery: generating the correct clock at the exit point of the ATM network.

- For DS1 service, an IWF service interface will provide 1.544-MHz timing to external DS1 equipment.

These requirements assume that the IWF provides the required synchronous circuit timing to the external equipment via the CES service interface itself (this does not preclude the provision of the synchronous circuit timing to the external equipment via a separate physical interface).

Jitter and Wander

The following performance requirements are supported (for North America):

- Jitter measured at the output of the IWF service interface and tolerated at the input of the IWF service interface must meet ANSI T1.403 and G.824 for DS1 circuits.
- Wander must meet ANSI T1.403 and G.824 for DS1 circuits.
- ANSI T1.403-1995 specifies that wander will not exceed 28 UI (18 μs) peak to peak in any 24-hour period. Recommendations G.823 and G.824 require that network wander be maintained at less than 10 μs over any 10,000-s interval (approximately 3 hours).

Facility Data Link

This section applies only to DS1 ESF $n\times64$ service and J2 $n\times64$ service.

The DS1 ESF facility data link associated with the service interface is terminated at the ESF/G.704 sublayer in the interworking function. The DS1 ESF facility data link is used to carry once-per-second performance report messages as described in T1.403. These messages carry information on numbers of CRCs, framing errors, line code violations, and other impairments detected over the last second.

For DS1, the CES IWF will terminate the facility data link as specified in ANSI T1.403-1995. DS1 performance–related information from T1.403-compliant FDL messages will be stored in the IWF's Management Information Base (MIB) (Section 8 of af-vtoa-0078.000).

Figure 8.7
More clocking considerations for CES.

SDT Timing

A CES IWF in SDT mode needs to merge multiple received data streams into a DS1/E1 frame which requires every source clock be synchronized to the destination service clock (1.544 MHz for DS1 and 2.048 MHz for E1) in order to prevent buffer overflow or underflow. This implies that all the source clocks and the service clock must be in synchronization. The ideal clocking that satisfies the requirement is the synchronous timing mode. In the case that a traceable clock is not available, as in most private networks, plesiochronous timing mode is the only other means which incurs data slipping whose performance depends on the accuracy of the plesiochronous clock. The ATM network interface of IWF may offer a traceable clock but needs to offer at least a high accuracy clock that the IWF can utilize for synchronous timing and falling back to plesiochronous timing mode should the network clock lose the traceable source. In a less likely scenario that if the clocks of the CBR service user equipment involved in a crossconnect are traceable, then loop timing is used.

Free running	Line transmit and receive clocks are not related to any clock sources, 1.544 Mbps ± 50 ppm for DS1 and 2.048 Mbps ± 50 ppm for E1.
Asynchronous	Asynchronous:Timing is supplied by the CBR service equipment. The recovered CBR service equipment line receive clock at the transmitting CES IWF is carried through the ATM network to the receiving CES IWF where it is recovered using either adaptive or SRTS clock recovery method. This clock constitutes the CBR service equipment line transmit clock at the receiving CES IWF.
Plesiochronous	Timings are supplied by CES IWFs to CBR service equipment at both ends, but not carried through the ATM network. They are sourced from high precision independent clocks with controlled frame slips, typically derived from the network timing module with ±4.6 ppm precision. (User equipment is recommended to loop its recovered receive clock to its transmit clock.)
Synchronous	Synchronous:Timing is supplied by CES IWFs to CBR service equipment at both ends, but not carried through the ATM network. The clock is traceable to a common source.
Loop Timing	The line received clock is looped to the line transmit clock with the assumption that user equipment are traceable to a Primary Reference Source (PRS).

Figure 8.7
(Continued)

UDT Timing

A CES IWF in UDT mode maps a single received data stream into a DS1/E1 frame. Though synchronous and plesiochronous timing modes are applicable to UDT clocking, asynchronous timing mode, where the clock is recovered from the data stream, is more robust and commonly used. There are two methods of recovering the transmitter service clock in asynchronous timing mode, namely, Synchronous Residual Time Stamp (SRTS) and adaptive clock (also known as FIFO centering).

Adaptive Clock

In the adaptive clock method, the source CES IWF just sends the data to the destination CES IWF over the network and the destination CES IWF writes the received data into a buffer and then reads it with a local DS1/E1 service clock. The fill level of the buffer controls the local clock frequency by continuously measuring the fill level around the a median position and feeding this measurement to drive a phase-locked loop which in turn drives the local clock. The selection of the buffer size will be to prevent buffer overflow and underflow and at the same time not to introduce excessive delay.

Synchronous Residual Time Stamp

The SRTS method uses the residual time stamp to measure and convey information about the frequency difference between a common reference clock derived from the ATM network and a DS1/E1 service clock. The same derived network reference clock is assumed to be available at both the source and destination CES IWFs. If the common network reference clock is unavailable or the CES IWFs traverse two or more networks that are not synchronized, then the SRTS will be operating in the plesiochronous network mode. In general, SRTS provides better jitter and wander performance than the adaptive clock method.

Bit-Oriented Messages and Alarms

This section applies only to DS1 $n \times 64$ service. For DS1 using ESF, the IWF must terminate bit-oriented messages for yellow alarms and loopback as described in T1.403. Loopbacks are handled as described in TR-NWT-000170. Several kinds of alarms can be detected at the point where the service interface is received by the IWF. Definition of alarm states is given in T1.403 for DS1, G.704 for E1, and JT-G.704 for J2. Refer to af-VTOA-0078.000 for the required support by the IWF.

Signaling Bits

The *n*×64 service can support signaling in one of two modes of operation: *with channel-associated signaling* or *without CAS*. *n*×64 service with CAS requires direct recognition and manipulation of the signaling bits by the CES IWF. This mode is necessary to support *n*×64 applications requiring DS1 robbed-bit signaling or E1 CAS support. Conversely, non-CAS mode, or basic service, requires no direct CAS support by the CES IWF. Basic service can be used to support *n*×64 applications not requiring signaling or those that provide signaling using common channel signaling (e.g., as used in N-ISDN) or provided by other means.

All *n*×64 service IWFs will provide basic service. This mode is compatible with N-ISDN applications, as well as many video codecs. *n*×64 service IWFs may also provide *n*×64 service with CAS. This mode is required for much existing PBX and voice telephony equipment.

Service QoS

This section describes the minimal service performance characteristics required by *n*×64 service.

End-to-End Delay   End-to-end delay requirements are application-specific and are beyond the scope of this specification. ITU-T Recommendation G.114 provides considerable guidance on the subject of delay.

Error Ratios   *Bit error ratio* (BER) is the ratio of the number of bit errors to the total number of bits transmitted in a given time interval. There are no specific bit error ratio requirements for *n*×64 service other than those implied by the errored second and severely errored second requirements in ANSI T1.510-1994, Network Performance Parameters for Dedicated Digital Services—Specifications.

Service performance is also measured in terms of *errored seconds* (ES) and *severely errored seconds* (SES). Performance objectives for errored seconds and severely errored seconds are given in ANSI T1.510-1994 for DS1 and in G.826 for E1.

AAL 1 Requirements

The *n*×64 service will use the structured data transfer (SDT) mode as defined in I.363.1. ANSI document T1.630, and Bellcore GR-

1113-CORE also contain descriptions of AAL 1 structured data transfer mode.

A significant source of delay in the $n\times64$ service is the *cell payload assembly delay*, or the amount of time it takes to collect enough data to fill a cell. This period of time can be reduced by sending cells that are only partially full, rather than waiting for a full 46- or 47-byte payload before sending each cell. This reduces delay at the expense of a higher cell rate. Partial cell fill is an optional feature of a CES IWF; if available, the number of bytes to be sent in each cell can be set when the virtual channel is established, either through configuration for PVCs or by ATM UNI 3.1 signaling for SVCs.

The $n\times64$ service interworking function is capable of sending cells without dummy octets. However, the $n\times64$ service may reduce cell payload assembly delay by introducing dummy octets to complete the cell payload, as outlined in ITU I.363.1, 1996. It should be noted that the cell padding technique described in I.363.1 requires a fixed number of payload (i.e., service interface) octets per cell, resulting in a variable number of pad bytes per cell, depending on the presence of the AAL 1 structure pointer. When padding is used with structured data transfer, it should be noted that I.363.1 requires that the structure pointer span both payload and pad bytes. For example, a structure pointer with the value 46 always indicates the first octet of the second cell in a pair, no matter how much padding might be present in each cell.

AAL User Entity Requirements

This section provides requirements for the AAL supporting CES.

Cell Coding

AAL 1 as specified in ITU-T document I.363.1 has the capability to delineate repetitive, fixed-size blocks of data, each block being an integral number of octets in size. This capability is used in the $n\times64$ service to carry n DS0 timeslots, organized into blocks.

For a block size of one octet, corresponding to a single DS0 stream (i.e., $n = 1$) with basic service, AAL 1 provides block delineation merely by aligning each AAL user octet with an ATM cell payload octet.

For a block size greater than one octet, AAL 1 uses a pointer mechanism to indicate the start of a structure block. This AAL Type 1 Convergence Sublayer (CS) specification requires the pointer to be inserted at the first opportunity in a cell with an even sequence count value (i.e., 0, 2, 4, 6) as indicated by the Convergence Sublayer Indication (CSI) bit of the AAL 1 header being set to 1. The SDT pointer must be inserted in a cell payload with an even sequence count once and only once in each set of eight cell payloads corresponding to an AAL 1 sequence count cycle (i.e., 0, 1, 2, 3, 4, 5, 6, 7). If no structure block begins with an eight-cell sequence, then a pointer value of 127 will be inserted in cell number 6 of the cycle. For more on SDT pointer generation and processing, refer to ITU Recommendation I.363.1.

The layout of the $n{\times}64$ service data within the structure blocks—or cell coding—varies with the type of $n{\times}64$ service being supported, as described below. Logical $n{\times}64$ service may use any of the coding approaches described below. (*Note:* The need for a common method to transport CAS signaling transitions for DS1, E1, J2, and voice compression requires further study.)

Cell Coding for DS1/n×64 Basic Service   To encode $n{\times}64$ into AAL 1 SDTs without carrying signaling bits, a block is created by collecting n octets—one from each of the n timeslots to be carried—and grouping them in sequence. See Figure 8.8 for an example showing the block structure for $n{\times}64$ where $n = 3$. The block size for $n{\times}64$ basic mode is always n octets. DS1, E1, and J2 $n{\times}64$ basic service will encode $n{\times}64$ service data in an AAL 1 structure of size n.

Cell Coding for DS1/n×64 with CAS   Circuits that carry the ABCD signaling bits end to end may also be emulated with the CES IWF, if the CAS mode option is provided. A special AAL 1 structure format is used to carry emulated circuits with CAS. In this format, the AAL 1 block is divided into two sections, the first of which carries the $n{\times}64$ payload, the second of which carries signaling bits that are associated with the payload.

In CAS mode, the payload part of the structure is one multiframe in length. For $n{\times}64$ DS1 with ESF framing, this portion of

Figure 8.8
Example single-frame structure format for 3×64 kbps.

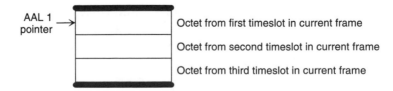

AAL 1 pointer →

Octet from first timeslot in current frame

Octet from second timeslot in current frame

Octet from third timeslot in current frame

the AAL 1 structure is *n* times 24 in length. For *n*×64 E1 using G.704 framing, the payload portion of the AAL 1 structure, called the *payload substructure*, is *n* times 16 octets in length. For *n*×64 J2 using JT-G.704 framing and signaling, the payload portion of the AAL 1 structure is *n* times 8 octets in length. In each case, the first octet in the AAL 1 structure is from the first of the *n* timeslots in the first frame of a multiframe.

The second portion of the AAL 1 structure, called the *signaling substructure*, contains the signaling bits that are associated with the multiframe. For DS1 and E1, the ABCD signaling bits associated with each timeslot are packed two sets to an octet and placed at the end of the AAL 1 structure. If *n* is odd, the last octet will contain only four signaling bits and four zero pad bits. For J2, which utilizes a single signaling bit per channel, the signaling bits associated with each timeslot are packed eight sets to an octet and placed at the end of the AAL 1 structure. If *n* is not a multiple of 8, the last octet will contain only the remaining number of signaling bits and the rest of the octet will be padded with zero bits.

The AAL 1 structure pointer is used to indicate the first octet of the payload substructure.

An example of the AAL 1 structure for DS1/E1 *n*×64 circuits with CAS is shown in Figure 8.9. In this example, *n* is set to 3, so each AAL 1 block contains payload from three timeslots, plus the three sets of signaling bits present in one multiframe.

Packing of the signaling bits for DS1 and E1 is done by using bits 8..5 of the first octet for the first set of signaling bits, bits 4..1 of the first octet for the second set of signaling bits, and so on. Bits 4..1 of the last octet of the signaling substructure will be unused and will be set to zero if the VCC is configured to carry an odd number of timeslots. Figure 8.10 shows the assignment of bits to the signaling substructure.

DS1 with superframe format can also be carried with a CES IWF. For SF format, the AAL 1 structure is made the same size as the equivalent extended superframe format structure by sending two SF multiframes together in one AAL 1 block, instead of one multiframe as is done in ESF framing. For SF format, the signaling octets at the end of the AAL 1 structure contain AB signaling bits from the two SF multiframes in the structure. Figure 8.11 shows the signaling substructure detail for an example circuit of *n* = 3. In this example, signaling bits AB are from the first SF multiframe in the AAL 1 structure, while bits A'B' are from the second SF multiframe.

Figure 8.9
Example multi-frame structure for 3×64-kbps DS1/E1 with CAS.

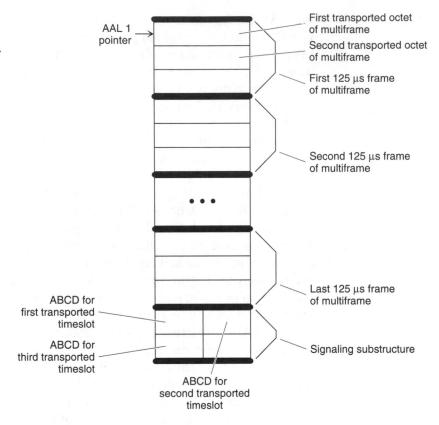

Table 8.1 gives the size of the AAL 1 structure in octets for a few different values of *n*. The parameter *n* gives the number of 64-kbps timeslots derived from a single access line to be transmitted over one VCC. A value of $n = 1$ corresponds to a single 64-kbps circuit; $n = 6$ corresponds to 384 kbps; $n = 30$ corresponds to the full E1 payload of 1.920 Mbps.

Figure 8.10
Example DS1/ESF and E1 signaling substructure.

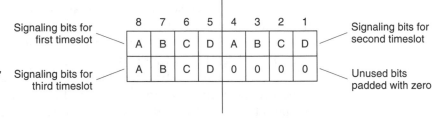

Figure 8.11
Example DS1/SF signaling substructure.

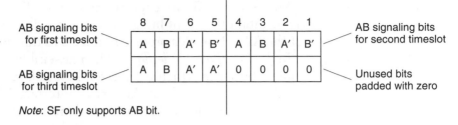

Note: SF only supports AB bit.

It should be noted that, in the case of DS1 with CAS, the ABCD bits may be present in the payload substructure in addition to being in the signaling substructure. In circumstances of both normal operation and alarm conditions such as trunk conditioning, valid signaling must be sent in the signaling substructure.

If CAS mode operation is enabled for DS1, the downstream IWF may only obtain ABCD signaling bits from the signaling substructure.

Loss/Error Response

The IWF will contain a function that reassembles a sequence of AAL 1 cells into streams of octets for transmission by the DS1/E1/J2 service interface. This reassembly function must cope with a variety of errors and impairments, including lost cells, late cells, and misinserted cells.

Lost and Misinserted Cells   The reassembly unit may detect lost and misinserted cells by processing sequence numbers in the AAL 1 headers. If cell loss is detected, dummy cells consisting of 46 or 47 octets will be inserted when bit count integrity can be maintained. The content of the inserted octets is implementation-dependent.

Depending on implementation, there will be a point at which too many cells will have been lost to maintain bit count integrity; at this point, the AAL 1 receiver may have to locate the next AAL 1 structure pointer to reacquire framing.

Table 8.1   Sample AAL 1 Structure Sizes for $n \times 64$ Service with CAS

	Structure Size in Octets				
Framing	n = 1	n = 6	n = 24	n = 30	n = 96
DS1/ESF	25	147	588	n/a	n/a
DS1/SF	25	147	588	n/a	n/a

Misinserted cells are expected to be rare. The reassembly unit may maintain bit count integrity where possible by dropping cells that the AAL 1 header processor detects as misinserted.

Buffer Overflow/Underflow   The reassembly function will require a buffer in which the reassembled cell stream is stored before it is transmitted out the service interface. The size of this buffer will be implementation-dependent, but it must be large enough to accommodate expected cell delay variation (CDV), while small enough not to introduce excessive delay in the emulated circuit. This buffer will be subject to overflow or underflow if slight clocking differences exist between the node at which segmentation takes place and the node at which reassembly takes place. Buffer underflow may also result from unexpectedly large CDV. The $n\times64$ service IWF will be required to perform controlled frame slips if the reassembly buffer encounters an overflow or underflow (i.e., *starvation*) condition. The data inserted in case of underflow is implementation-dependent.

8.3 DS1/E1/J2 Unstructured Service

A large number of applications utilize DS1, E1, and J2 interfaces today, making use of the entire bandwidth. The following services are supported.

- Unstructured service represents all modes of the unstructured DS1/E1 and J2 unstructured service.

- DS1 unstructured service represents unstructured service at a nominal bit rate of 1.544 Mbps in which the two IWFs involved are emulating a DS1 circuit supplied via a DSX-1 interface.

- DS1 logical unstructured service represents unstructured service at a nominal bit rate of 1.544 Mbps in which the non-ATM-related functions of the two IWFs involved are left unspecified.

Service Description

DS1/E1/J2 unstructured CBR service is intended to emulate a point-to-point DS1, E1, or J2 circuit. The service is accessed via either a 1.544-Mbps DSX-1 interface, a 2.048-Mbps G.703 interface, or a 6.312-Mbps JT-G.703a interface. The service is defined as a *clear channel pipe*, transparently carrying any arbitrary 1.544-Mbps (2.048-Mbps for E1 and 6.312 Mbps for J2) data stream. The end-user timing source for these interface signals is not necessarily traceable to a PRS.

Note that framing formats other than standard SF, ESF, G.704, or JT-G.704 formats cannot be supported by all SONET/SDH installed equipment. If CES service for such nonstandard framing formats is offered by an exchange carrier, the carrier may have difficulty in maintaining the service interface due to the lack of facility support for operations and maintenance functions such as performance monitoring, facility loopbacks, and so forth.

The DS1/E1/J2 unstructured service also provides an optional feature that allows nonintrusive performance monitoring of the link if SF, ESF, G.704, or JT-G.704 framing is used.

Figure 8.12 shows the DS1/E1/J2 unstructured service from a layering perspective. For this service, the CES interworking function has two Physical Layers, one for the CBR circuit to be emulated and one for ATM. Linking the CBR Physical Layer with the AAL 1 Layer is a *mapping function*. In unstructured service, the mapping function simply maps every bit between the AAL 1 Layer and the 1.544-, 2.048-, or 6.312-Mbps service interface. From an ATM perspective, everything shaded in Figure 8.12 represents an AAL user entity, and that is how we refer to the shaded portions in the CES-IS. For the *logical* versions of the circuit emulation services, the CES-IS leaves the non-ATM portions identified in the figure (i.e., the CBR Physical Layer and CBR service interface) unspecified.

In reference to framing, the DS1/E1/J2 unstructured service carries any arbitrary 1.544-Mbps (2.048-Mbps for E1 and 6.312 Mbps for J2) data stream.

In reference to clocking, the DS1/E1/J2 unstructured service has two modes for timing user equipment attached to the service interface (previously described):

1. *Synchronous mode*, in which timing is supplied to attached DS1/E1/J2 equipment via the IWF service interface and may be traceable to a primary reference source
2. *Asynchronous mode*, in which timing is supplied by an independent clock in the attached equipment and carried transparently through the ATM network

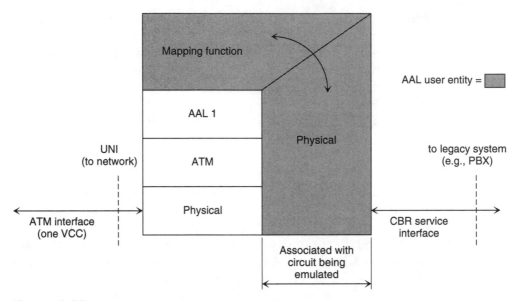

Figure 8.12
DS1/E1/J2 unstructured service interworking function—layering perspective.

When asynchronous timing is supplied by the attached equipment, the end-user timing source for this asynchronous timing may or may not be traceable to a PRS. Whether an interface signal is traceable to a PRS impacts the choice of clock recovery method. If asynchronous CES service is being provided to a CBR interface that does not use timing traceable to a PRS, then SRTS may not be supportable. In order to support SRTS application when the CES IWF does not use timing traceable to a PRS, the CES IWF must have available for its use a reference clock that is common to the reference clock being used by the CES IWF at the other end of the connection.

A CES IWF must implement at least one of the two clocking modes for DS1/E1/J2 unstructured service and may offer both modes. Two interworking functions must be configured for the same clocking mode in order to interoperate.

If asynchronous mode is used, timing will be properly accepted from user equipment as long as that timing is within ±130 ppm for DS1 (as specified in T1.403-1995), ±50 ppm for E1 (as specified in G.703), and ±30 ppm for J2 (as specified in JT-G.703a). Note that the 130-ppm tolerance for DS1 is intended to support older DS1 equipment. Newer equipment will be within ±32 ppm.

Jitter and wander may be present at the output of the emulated circuit, introduced, for example, by imperfections in clock recovery at the output of the CES IWF. For circuits using the asynchronous timing mode, there are two techniques for recovering clock: SRTS and adaptive. While the two techniques can produce equal jitter performance, they may differ in the amount of wander present at the output of the IWF.

Wander requirements apply to network-synchronous signals (i.e., those traceable to a PRS), but the same requirements may be applied to an asynchronous signal if the wander is defined as relative to the clock source rather than to an absolute reference. ANSI technical subcommittee T1E1, the group responsible for T1.403 and T1.404, is studying this area with input from T1X1.3.

Jitter measured at the output of the IWF service interface and tolerated at the input of the IWF service interface will meet ANSI T1.102 and G.824 for DS1 circuits with any clocking mode.

Jitter measured at the output of the IWF service interface and tolerated at the input of the IWF service interface will meet G.823 for E1 circuits with any clocking mode. If synchronous clocking or asynchronous clocking with SRTS clock recovery is used, wander must meet ANSI T1.403 and G.824 for DS1 circuits. ANSI T1.403-1995 5.7.5 specifies that wander will not exceed 28 UI (18 μs) peak to peak in any 24-hour period. Recommendations G.823 and G.824 suggest that network wander be maintained at less than 10 μs over any 10,000-s interval (approximately 3 hours). If the asynchronous clocking mode is used with adaptive clock recovery, the resulting wander will depend on the CDV characteristics of the ATM network used to interconnect interworking functions and might not meet recommendations specified in T1.403, G.823, or G.824.

Note: For circuit emulation service, ITU-T Recommendation I.363.1 and ANSI T1.630 specify the SRTS method of timing recovery to guarantee/meet performance requirements (jitter and wander) of G.823 and G.824. If either IWF connects to DS1, E1, or J2 equipment in the public network, the public network operator may require that SRTS be used.

AAL 1 Requirements

Data transfer service type: The unstructured service will use the unstructured data transfer (UDT) mode as defined in T1.630 and I.363.1.

Cell utilization: In accordance with ANSI T1.630, the IWF will fill the entire 47-octet cell payload with DS1/E1/J2 data.

AAL User Entity Requirements

Unstructured data transfer does not rely on any particular data format. Bits received from the service interface are packed into cells without regard to framing. Note that no particular alignment between octets in DS1, E1, and J2 frames and octets in an ATM cell can be assumed with unstructured data transfer. However, correct bit ordering must be used. Considering the 376 contiguous bits that will be packed into the SDU, the first bit received on the DS1/E1/J2 line is placed in the most significant bit of the first octet of the SDU, and placement proceeds in order until the last bit is placed in the least significant bit of the 47th octet of the SDU.

Clock Recovery

The unstructured service may carry network-synchronous (i.e., traceable to a PRS) or asynchronous DS1, E1, or J2 circuits. In an asynchronous situation, the input service clock frequency must be recovered at the output IWF. There are two techniques for recovering this clock (previously described), *synchronous residual timestamp* (SRTS) and *adaptive.* Either technique may be used, although SRTS may give better control over wander introduced into the emulated circuit, depending on the wander generation mechanisms.

For circuit emulation of both network-synchronous and asynchronous signals, the SRTS clock recovery technique requires a network reference clock (i.e., traceable to a PRS); information on the distribution of network timing may be found in ANSI document T1.101 and in ISO/IEC 11573.

SRTS

The SRTS technique measures the service clock input frequency against a networkwide synchronization signal that must be present in the IWF and sends difference signals, called *residual timestamps,* in the AAL 1 header to the reassembly IWF. At the output IWF, the differences can be combined with the networkwide synchronization signal, to re-create the input service clock. Note that this networkwide synchronization signal must be traceable to a PRS.

If SRTS is provided, it will be used as specified in T1.630 and I.363.1.

The *network-derived clock frequency* used in the SRTS algorithm will be 2.43 MHz for both DS1 and E1 circuit emulation.

Adaptive

The adaptive technique does not require a networkwide synchronization signal to regenerate the input service clock at the output IWF. A variety of techniques could be used to implement adaptive clock recovery. For example, the depth of the reassembly buffer in the output IWF could be monitored as follows:

1. When the buffer depth is too great or tends to increase with time, the frequency of the service clock could be increased to cause the buffer to drain more quickly.

2. When the buffer contains fewer than the configured number of bits, the service clock could be slowed to cause the buffer to drain less quickly.

Wander may be introduced by the adaptive clock recovery technique if there is a low-frequency component to the cell delay variation inserted by the ATM network carrying cells from the input to output IWF.

8.4 Unstructured DS3/E3 Service

Applications may utilize DS3/E3 interfaces today, either utilizing the entire bandwidth or through the use of multiplexing performed in end systems. The following services are supported:

- Unstructured DS3/E3 service, all modes of the unstructured DS3/E3 service
- Unstructured DS3 service, unstructured DS3/E3 service at a nominal bit rate of 44.736 Mbps in which the two IWFs involved are emulating a DS3 circuit supplied via a DSX-3 interface
- Logical unstructured DS3 service, unstructured DS3/E3 service at a nominal bit rate of 44.736 Mbs in which the non-

ATM-related functions of the two IWFs involved are left unspecified

Unstructured DS3/E3 service is intended to emulate a point-to-point DS3 or E3 circuit. The service is accessed via either a 44.736-Mbps DSX-3 interface or a 34.368-Mbps G.703 interface. The service is defined as a *clear channel pipe*, transparently carrying any arbitrary 44.736/34.368-Mbps data stream. The end-user timing source for these interface signals is not necessarily traceable to a PRS.

Note that framing formats other than standard DS3 or E3 formats cannot be supported by all SONET/SDH installed equipment. If CES service for such nonstandard framing formats is offered by an exchange carrier, the carrier may have difficulty in maintaining the service interface due to the lack of facility support for operations and maintenance functions such as performance monitoring and facility loopbacks.

Refer to af-vtoa-0078.000 for details.

8.5 ATM Virtual Channel Requirements

The subsections that follow specify traffic parameters and tolerances as defined in A.6 of the UNI 3.1 Specification. The requirements described in this section must be met by the ATM network that provides an end-to-end ATM connection, i.e., from the input ATM interface to the output ATM interface in Figure 8.2.

Quality of Service Class 1 for circuit emulation from the ATM Forum UNI Specification Version 3.1 Appendix A will be used.

Traffic Parameters and Tolerances

Traffic policing may be performed on cells generated by the CES interworking function and transported by the ATM network.

The CDV tolerance parameter of the usage parameter control (UPC) should take into account any cell delay variation caused by the introduction of OAM (Operations/Administration/Maintenance) cells. The CDV tolerance should also account for any CDV that occurs in the intervening multiplexing and switching devices between the interworking function and the UPC device.

In the context of this specification, CDV tolerance is considered a network option and is currently not subject to standardization.

The following sections give the peak cell rate (PCR) for various versions of the CES interworking function. For unstructured DS1, the PCR on CLP = 0 + 1 required for AAL 1 transport of 1544-kbps user data is 4107 cells per second.

In the structured $n \times 64$ basic service, if partial cell fill is not used and n is greater than 1, the PCR on CLP = 0 + 1 required for AAL 1 transport of $n \times 64$ basic service is $\|(8000 \times n)/46.875\|$ cells per second (where $\|x\|$ means "smallest integer greater than or equal to x"). If partial cell fill is used, the PCR is $\|(8000 \times n)/K\|$, where K is the number of AAL user octets filled per cell. If partial cell fill is not used for 64-kbps basic service (i.e., when n is equal to 1), the PCR on CLP = 0 + 1 required for AAL 1 transport is $\|8000/47\|$ cells per second. If partial cell fill is used, the PCR is $\|8000/K\|$, where K is the number of AAL user octets filled per cell.

For structured $n \times 64$ service with CAS the PCR on CLP = 0 + 1 required for AAL 1 transport of DS1 $n \times 64$ service with CAS is:

1. No partial cell fill, n even:
   $\|8000 \times [n \times 49/48]/46.875\|$
2. No partial cell fill, n odd:
   $\|8000 \times [(1 + n \times 49)/48]/46.875\|$
3. Partial cell fill, n even, K the number of AAL 1 user octets filled:
   $\|8000 \times [n \times 49/48]/K\|$
4. Partial cell fill, n odd, K the number of AAL 1 user octets filled:
   $\|8000 \times [(1 + n \times 49)/48]/K\|$

These rates are derived by dividing the effective user octet rate (including block overhead) by the number of user octets carried per cell.

Because all of the signaling bits are grouped together at the end of the AAL 1 structure, virtual channels supporting DS1, E1, and J2 $n \times 64$ service with CAS will suffer some jitter in cell emission time. For example, an IWF carrying an $n \times 64$ E1 circuit with $n = 30$ and CAS enabled will, on average, emit about 10.5 cells spaced by 191.8 µs, followed by a cell carrying CAS bits after a gap of only

130 µs. This jitter in cell emission time must be accommodated by peak rate traffic policers.

Cell Transfer Delay

Overall delay is often critical for circuit emulation applications, particularly those involving voice. Delay introduced by the ATM network interconnecting CES IWFs is composed of two components: *Maximum delay* gives the largest expected cell delay between entrance and exit of the ATM network; *cell delay variation* (CDV) gives the uncertainty in the delay that might be experienced by any particular cell.

Circuit emulation equipment must have reassembly buffers large enough to accommodate the largest CDV present on a virtual channel to prevent underflow or overflow, with resulting reframe or slip events. At the same time, it should be noted that reassembly buffers larger than required to accommodate CDV will result in excessive overall delay.

The number of intervening switches, and their queue management, and line speeds have a significant impact on the distribution of CDV that must be handled by the reassembly buffer in the destination IWF. There are currently no standards that define a bound on CDV; however, some information on CDV and reassembly buffer sizes can be found in GR-1110-CORE and TA-TSV-001409. The BICI 1.1 specification gives an approximation of how CDV accumulates across multiple nodes. Implementors are advised to design the reassembly buffer in excess of these values, possibly making the size of the reassembly buffer configurable to optimize the jitter versus absolute delay trade-off in various configurations.

The amount of CDV that the reassembly process can accommodate is configured with the MIB entry atmfCESCdvRxT. This entry allows the network provider to configure the maximum cell arrival jitter that the reassembly process will tolerate in the cell stream without producing errors on the CBR service interface. This parameter may be set to a small value if the connection will produce minimal CDV and a large value if the connection will produce large CDV.

An informative example of the implementation of a receiver that uses the atmfCESCdvRxT parameter is as follows: The receiver will place the contents of the first cell to arrive after an underrun into the receive buffer in a position such that it will be played out at least one CDVT (atmfCESCdvRxT) later.

8.6 Signaling for CES SVCs

This section specifies ATM UNI 3.1 signaling between the IWFs that support CES. There is no mapping specified between signaling that pertains to traditional DS1, E1, J2, and $n\times64$ services and ATM UNI 3.1 signaling. The call/connection control procedures of UNI 3.1 apply. The following section details the content of the setup message. CES signaling places no explicit constraints on other signaling messages. Note that UNI 3.1 SVC support is optional for the CES IWF. The following sections are applicable only when such SVC support is provided (the reader should refer to af-vtoa-0078.000 for full details).

Addresses and Identifiers

All CES SVCs are point to point. As with all SVCs, the endpoints must be identified during call setup with an ATM address; these may be of any of the three formats identified in Section 5.1.3 of the UNI 3.1 Specification. Additional identifiers in the broadband low-layer information (B-LLI) information element (IE) distinguish the particular type of CES SVC being set up.

SETUP Message Contents

Section 5.3.1.7 of the UNI 3.1 Specification lists the mandatory and optional information elements in the SETUP message. This CES specification places constraints on the values of certain fields in the following mandatory information elements:

1. ATM traffic descriptor
2. Broadband bearer capability
3. QoS parameter

The following sections describe those constraints.

Table 8.2   Broadband Bearer Capability IE Field Values
for CES SVCs

Field	Value
Bearer class	'1000 0' BCOB-X
Traffic type	'001' constant bit rate
Timing requirements	'01' end-to-end timing required
Susceptibility to clipping	'00' not susceptible to clipping
User Plane connection configuration	'00' point to point

The following information elements (which in general are optional) are required for CES signaling:

1. The AAL parameters information element
2. The broadband low-layer information element

The required contents of these information elements are discussed in the following sections.

The other information elements identified in UNI 3.1 Section 5.3.1.7 as optional remain optional for CES SVCs; this CES specification places no constraints on the values of the fields in these optional information elements.

ATM Traffic Descriptor

For CES SVCs, the following two fields in this information element must be specified:

1. Forward peak cell rate CLP = 0 + 1
2. Backward peak cell rate CLP = 0 + 1

The values for these fields should be calculated as specified in Section 5.1.

Table 8.3   QoS Parameter IE Field Values
for CES SVCs

Field	Value
QoS Class Forward	'0000 0001' QoS Class 1
QoS Class Backward	'0000 0001' QoS Class 1

Table 8.4   AAL Parameters IE Field Values for *n*×64 Service SVCs

Field	Value
AAL type	"0000 0001" AAL Type 1
Subtype	"0000 0010" circuit transport
CBR rate	"0000 0001" 64 kbps
	"0100 0000" *n*×64 kbps, *n* > 1
Multiplier	The value *n* for *n*×64 kbps. Omit field for 64-kbps case.
Structured data transfer block size	Size in octets, as defined in Section 2.3.1
Partially filled cells method	*K*, the number of AAL user octets filled per cell; see Section 2.2.2. Omit field if partial cell fill is not used.

The best effort indicator and the traffic management options identifier must be omitted. We recommend that the other fields be omitted as well.

Broadband Bearer Capability

Table 8.2 specifies the values for the fields in this information element.

Quality of Service Parameter

Table 8.3 specifies the values for the fields in this information element.

Table 8.5   AAL Parameters IE Field Values for DS1 Unstructured Service and DS1 Logical Unstructured Service SVCs

Field	Value
AAL type	"0000 0001" AAL Type 1
Subtype	"0000 0010" circuit transport
CBR rate	"0000 0100" 1544 kbps (DS1)
Source clock frequency recovery method	"0000 0000" Null (synchronous circuit transport)
	"0000 0001" SRTS method (asynchronous circuit transport)
	"0000 0010" adaptive method (asynchronous circuit transport)

Table 8.6   AAL Parameters IE Field Values for DS3 Unstructured Service and DS3 Logical Unstructured Service SVCs

Field	Value
AAL type	"0000 0001" AAL Type 1
Subtype	"0000 0010" circuit transport
CBR rate	"0000 0111" 44736 kbps (DS3)
Source clock frequency recovery method	"0000 0000" null (synchronous circuit transport)
	"0000 0001" SRTS method (asynchronous circuit transport)
	"0000 0010" adaptive method (asynchronous circuit transport)

The coding standard field in this information element will be coded as "11" when operating over ATM Forum–compliant networks. However, when interfacing to an ITU-conformant network that is not ATM Forum–compliant, the coding standard will be coded "00" and the QoS Class Forward and QoS Class Backward are each coded "0000 0000," meaning QoS Class 0—Unspecified QoS Class.

Table 8.7   Broadband Low-Layer Information IE Field Values for CES SVCs

Field	Value
User information Layer 3 protocol (octet 7)	"01011" ISO/IEC TR 9577
ISO/IEC TR 9577 initial protocol identifier (IPI; octet 7a, 7b)	IPI is coded "1000 0000" to indicate IEEE 802.1 SNAP identifier. Hence, octets 7a and 7b are coded as "0100 0000" and "0000 0000," respectively.
Organizational unit identifier (OUI) (octets 8.1–8.3)	x'00 A0 3E' ATM Forum OUI
Protocol identifier (PID) (octets 8.4–8.5)	x'00 00' ignored for unstructured service
	x'00 06' DS1/E1/J2 $n\times64$ basic service
	x'00 07' E1 $n\times64$ service with CAS
	x'00 08' DS1 SF $n\times64$ service with CAS
	x'00 09' DS1 ESF $n\times64$ service with CAS
	x'00 0B' J2 $n\times64$ service with CAS

ATM Adaptation Layer Parameters

The values in this information element vary with the particular choice of CES. Tables 8.4 through 8.6 specify the field values for $n \times 64$ service, DS1 (+ logical) unstructured service, and DS3 (+ logical) unstructured service, respectively. If the called party does not accept these parameters, it should release the call with cause no. 93 ("AAL Parameters Not Supported").

Broadband Low-Layer Information

This information element identifies that the signaling entities are ATM Forum CES AAL user entities as specified in this CES-IS. It also identifies the specific service and coding approach for $n \times 64$ service. (See Table 8.7.)

CHAPTER 9

VTOA Dynamic Bandwidth Utilization

This chapter presents an encapsulated and much abridged description of the ATM Forum's VTOA Specifications of (DBCES) Dynamic Bandwidth Utilization (af-vtoa-0085.000), July 1997. This chapter is based on the ATM Forum specification cited. This material is for pedagogical purposes only. Developers, engineers, and readers requiring more information should acquire the specification directly from the ATM Forum. Figure 9.1 puts the spec in context.

9.1 Introduction to Dynamic Bandwidth Utilization: 64-kbps Timeslot Trunking over ATM Using CES

The objective of af-vtoa-0085.000 is to specify a method for enabling dynamic bandwidth utilization in an ATM network based on detecting which timeslots of a legacy TDM trunk from a PBX or multiplexer are active and which are inactive. When an inactive state is detected in a specific timeslot, the timeslot is dropped from the next ATM structure and the bandwidth it was using may be reutilized for other services (e.g., CBR/VBR/UBR/ABR applications at the same UNI/channel). This method may be applied utilizing

365

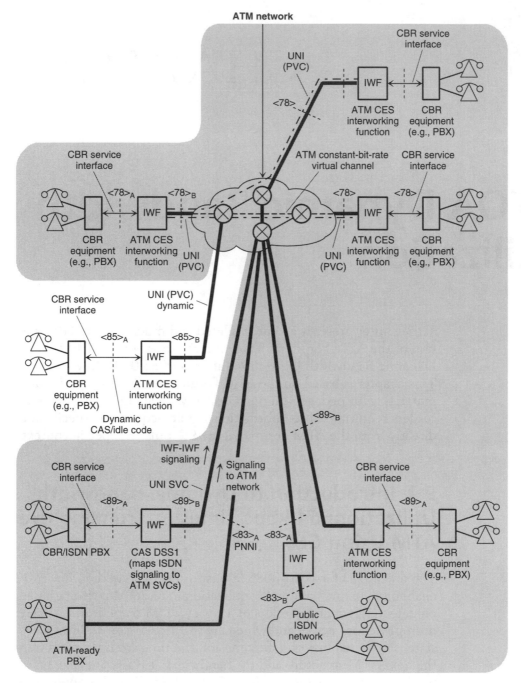

Figure 9.1
af-vtoa-0085.000.

any practical technique of timeslot activity detection, such as CAS or CCS. Following are some possible approaches to idle state detection. The af-vtoa-0085.000 specifications are applicable in both PVC and SVC ATM network configurations without the need to create any special signaling messages or elements. The transport of the active timeslots using this specification utilizes the standardized CES structured DS1/E1 $n \times 64$-kbp/s service defined in ATM Forum Document af-vtoa-0078.000.

To meet the requirements of af-vtoa-0085.000 it is necessary to be able to detect the idle status of each of the timeslots. One of the following methods may be used.

- *Idle detection utilizing idle code pattern* The idle status of a timeslot can be detected (at the transmitting IWF) by detecting the continuous occurrence of an idle code pattern in that timeslot's data for some specified interval. This section addresses the requirements for detecting this idle status.

- *Idle detection using AB signaling bits in CAS* With channel-associated signaling, the value of the AB bits used to determine the idle status of the timeslots on a given connection should be user configurable (this allows the IWF's user to configure the values on the basis of the supported terminal equipment and match the values on the two sides of the virtual connection). In most instances, only the A and B signaling bits need be considered (the C and D signaling bits are often used for echo canceler control, billing metering pulses, etc.). Table 9.1 defines the patterns used in the majority of applications of relevance to circuit emulation service (also refer to Chapter 5 for additional discussion of signaling).

Table 9.1 Idle Detection States

Signaling Type	*Transmit*		*Receive*	
Idle State Patterns	*A*	*B*	*A*	*B*
E&M/PLAR	0	d	0	d
FXO—ground start	1	d*	0	1
FXO—loop start	d	1	0	d
FXS—ground start	0	1	1	d*
FXS—loop start	0	d	d	1

"d" indicates a "don't care" bit—either 0 or 1.

*Optionally check for 1 here.

Figure 9.2 depicts a reference configuration for DBCES. The ATM device shown may be a physical or a functional entity that provides several interfaces to users as well as to other network elements. Included in this device is the circuit emulation interworking function (CES IWF), which is the subject of this document's specifications. This interworking function performs the following functions:

- Circuit emulation services (CES) structured DS1/E1 $n\times64$-kbp/s service per ATM Forum af-vtoa-0078.000
- Timeslot activity detection
- Dynamic structure sizing (DSS) of the AAL 1 structure that correlates with the active timeslots in the TDM to ATM direction
- Recovering the active timeslots from the AAL 1 structure, in the ATM to TDM direction, and placing them in the proper slots in the TDM stream
- Placing the proper signals (e.g., ABC&D) in each of the timeslots of the recovered TDM stream

The function shown as "ATM queue with DBU" in Figure 9.2 represents the ATM queue in the device (ATM CPE) that is respon-

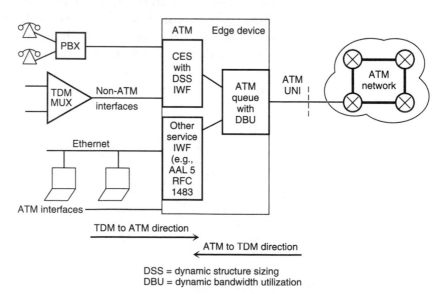

Figure 9.2
Reference configuration for trunking with dynamic bandwidth utilization.

sible for queuing and transmitting the cells from the different interfaces into any given common ATM interface. The dynamic bandwidth utilization (DBU) entity assigns a fixed bandwidth (cell rate) to each of the CES interworking functions, which corresponds to the maximum structure size expected to be handled. When all the provisioned timeslots in a given CES IWF are active, this entire bandwidth is needed for serving that CES IWF. When some of the CES IWF's timeslots are not active, the IWF dynamically reduces the size of the structure, thus transmitting a lower cell rate to the ATM queue. The DBU capability in the queue can then temporarily assign the bandwidth not used by its "owner" IWF to another service. This capability would provide bandwidth for UBR-type services without having to reserve MCR/PCR, thus increasing the effective bandwidth utilization on the ATM interfaces. The DBU capability itself is beyond the scope of this specification. However, to take advantage of this capability, CES IWFs that meet this specification are required. The interworking function requirements summarized above are expanded in the sections that follow.

The following definitions highlight key concepts of the af-vtoa-0085.000 specification.

Dynamic structure sizing (DSS) is the ability of a CES interworking function to dynamically adjust the size of the AAL 1 structure up or down based on the number of active timeslots contained in the DS1/E1 trunk undergoing circuit emulation. The structure has a maximum size, defined below, which is set at the time of configuring the IWF.

Configured structure is the maximum-size AAL 1 structure when all provisioned (assigned) timeslots of a given trunk are active. This is predetermined by the maximum number n of the 64-kbps timeslots provisioned on the trunk at the time of configuring the IWF. n may represent a full or a fractional DS1 or E1 frame. As an example, a full DS1 has a configured structure that accommodates the contents of 24 timeslots ($n = 24$), which corresponds to a (maximum) payload of 576 octets of user information and 12 octets signaling in the case of CAS (see Figure 9.3). Another example is a fractional DS1/E1 trunk utilizing only 4×64-kbps timeslots. In this case the configured structure accommodates the contents of only 4 timeslots ($n = 4$), which corresponds to a (maximum) payload of 96 octets of user information and 2 octets signaling in the case of CAS. The order and position of the assigned timeslots in the

DS1/E1 frame is configured at the user's discretion and is accommodated via a bit mask as explained below.

Active structure is the AAL 1 structure containing the information from actually active timeslots at any given instance. Inactive timeslots are not mapped into the AAL 1 structure altogether. There are two types of active structures:

- *Active structure type 1:* This is an active structure that contains a bit mask.
- *Active structure type 2:* This is an active structure that does not contain a bit mask.

The bit mask is usually transmitted only in structures containing a pointer (the only exception is when transitioning from all inactive slots to at least one active slot, in which case there may be one structure with a bit mask that does not have a pointer). This approach minimizes the bandwidth consumption (less frequent bit mask transmission) and provides deterministic location of the bit mask after the pointer.

Inactive structure is a structure one to four octets long transmitted when all timeslots are inactive. It contains only a bit mask full of zeros, with a parity bit of value 1, and no payload or signaling substructure.

The *bit mask* is a bit pattern that indicates the activity status of the provisioned (assigned) *n* timeslots. This bit pattern is always created by the ATM transmitter and enclosed in the AAL 1 struc-

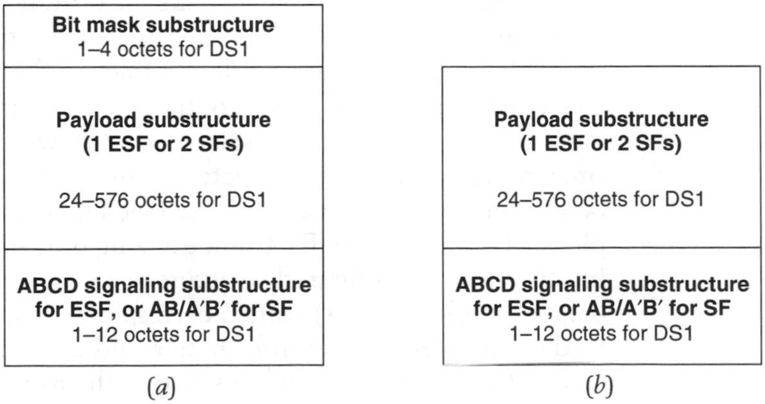

Figure 9.3
CES with CAS:
(a) active structure
type 1 (with bit
mask) for DS1
(see spec for E1);
(b) active structure
type 2 (without bit
mask) for DS1
(see spec for E1).

Bit mask substructure 1–4 octets for DS1
Payload substructure (1 ESF or 2 SFs) 24–576 octets for DS1
ABCD signaling substructure for ESF, or AB/A'B' for SF 1–12 octets for DS1

(a)

Payload substructure (1 ESF or 2 SFs) 24–576 octets for DS1
ABCD signaling substructure for ESF, or AB/A'B' for SF 1–12 octets for DS1

(b)

ture, as explained in the specifications, to enable the ATM receiver to correctly place the retrieved timeslots in the DS1/E1 frame that it reconstructs.

9.2 Interworking Function (IWF) Requirements

Following are the requirements of the IWF to support DBCES:

- The IWF is expected to be capable of performing the CES functions per Circuit Emulation Services Structured DS1/E1 *n*×64 kbps Service specification af-vtoa-0078.000.
- The IWF is expected to be capable of performing activity detection based on CAS, CCS, or another method.
- The IWF is expected to be capable of performing all the required functions described in af-vtoa-0085.000.
- The use of ATM signaling (UNI 3.1 or equivalent) for supporting SVCs in the IWFs is desirable but not mandatory.

At the time of configuring the IWF, the number and order of the configured structure timeslots is determined by the user and must be matched between the two IWFs at the ends of the virtual connection. Note that the bit mask indicates only the numerical order of the assigned timeslots in the configured structure and not the absolute timeslot position in the 24 slots of the DS1 (or E1) frame.

9.3 Specification of the Active and Inactive Structures

As stated above, the active structure has two types: active structure type 1 (with bit mask) and active structure type 2 (without bit mask).

Figure 9.3 shows the two types of active structure for the case of DS1/E1 frames utilizing CAS. Figure 9.4 shows the same for the case of DS1/E1 using CCS. It should be noted that there is no limitation on the use of superframe or extended superframe structures per the CES specification document as illustrated in Figure 9.3. However, as noted in Chapter 5, most modern CPE (e.g., PBXs) support ESF since, in North America, the trend for the transmission facilities is heavily tilted toward ESF.

Active Structure Type 1 (with Bit Mask)

Active structure type 1, with bit mask, will be formatted as shown in Figure 9.3a. In order to assure that the location of the bit mask within the structure is deterministic, consistent, and simple to find, the following approach is used: Whenever an active structure type 1, which will start with a bit mask, is used, a structure pointer will always be used to indicate the boundary of the structure except in the following condition. The first active structure following an inactive structure (transition from all inactive timeslots to at least one active timeslot) may not have a pointer. This requirement is illustrated in Figure 9.5. As shown, the pointer points to the beginning of the bit mask that is the first field in the new structure.

Note that AAL 1 structure pointers will be utilized for all DBCES connections, even when the number of configured channels is equal to 1. (The CES specification defines that the $n = 1$ case in basic service mode would not use pointers.) This is required by the DBCES IWF in order to allow the indication of an active structure with bit mask once every eight cells, even when n is equal to 1.

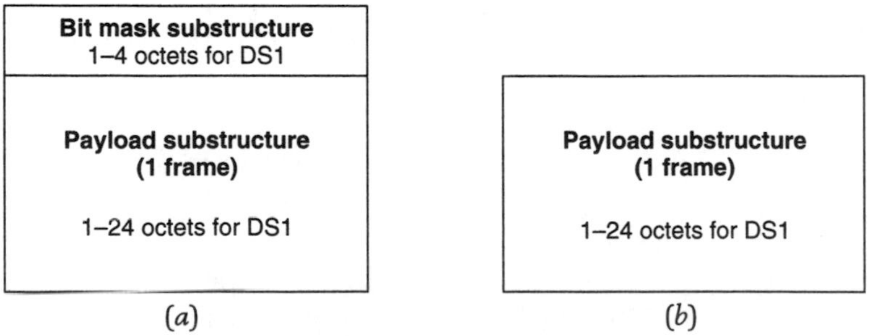

Figure 9.4
CES with CCS:
(a) active structure
type 1 (with bit
mask) for DS1
(see spec for E1);
(b) active structure
type 2 (without bit
mask) for DS1
(see spec for E1);
af-vtoa-0085.000.

(a)

Bit mask substructure
1–4 octets for DS1

Payload substructure
(1 frame)

1–24 octets for DS1

(b)

Payload substructure
(1 frame)

1–24 octets for DS1

Figure 9.5
Illustration of the beginning of a type 1 active structure (af-vtoa-0085.000).

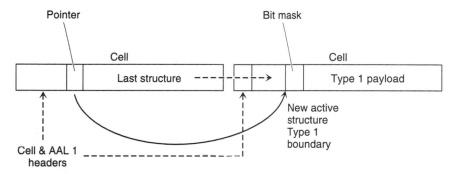

Bit Mask Format

The af-vtoa-0085.000 specification calls for the following, with respect to the bit mask.

The bit mask will be one to four octet(s) long depending on the number of assigned timeslots corresponding to the configured structure. Note that a single parity bit must always be included in the bit mask following the bit representing the highest-order time-slot (see Figure 9.6). For 1 to 7 assigned timeslots, the bit mask will be one octet. For 8 to 15 assigned timeslots, the bit mask will be two octets. For 16 to 23 assigned timeslots, the bit mask will be three octets. The bit mask will be four octets for 24 (full DS1 frame) to 31 (full E1 frame) assigned timeslots.

The number of bits used in a bit mask will be equal to the number of assigned timeslots (n) in the configured structure with one bit correlating to each assigned timeslot, plus one bit for the parity error check, following the format specified below. All unused bits in the bit mask are set to zero.

The bit mask bit assignment will be as illustrated in Figure 9.6. The first bit (LSB) indicates the activity status of the first assigned timeslot in the configured structure. This is the timeslot that has the lowest numerical order among all assigned timeslots in the configured structure. The second bit (next to the LSB) in the bit mask indicates the activity status of the second assigned timeslot (that has the next numerical order higher than the first slot's), and so on. The most significant bit in the bit mask (the highest numerical order bit in the highest numerical order octet) correlates to the highest numerical order assigned timeslot.

The bit mask represents the relative position (numerical order) of the assigned timeslots in the configured structure. This require-

Figure 9.6
Bit mask format.

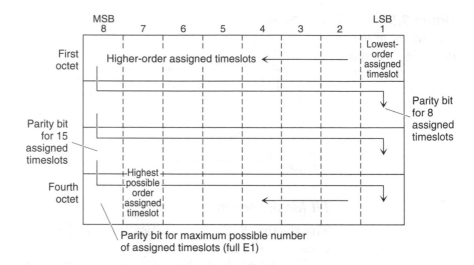

ment is based on the fact that the assignment of timeslots is not required to be the same on the transmitting and receiving ends of a virtual connection.

A bit value of (logical) 1 indicates that the corresponding timeslot is active; a zero value indicates an inactive timeslot.

An odd parity bit is used for error protection of the bit mask. The parity bit is located at the end of the bit mask in bit $n + 1$, where bit n corresponds to the highest-order timeslot in the configured structure (see Figure 9.6 for bit order).

When the error protection field of the bit mask indicates an error, the receiver uses the previously received correct bit mask instead of the current one.

When an error is detected in the bit mask, CAS signaling will not be updated in the corresponding timeslots until the receiver has received a valid bit mask.

Payload and Signaling Substructures

The payload and signaling substructures are formatted as defined in the current ATM Forum CES Structured DS1/E1 n×64 kbps Service specifications in af-vtoa-0078.000. The primary difference between af-vtoa-0078.000 and af-vtoa-0085.000 is that the payload and signaling in the BDCES specification are made up only of active timeslots, while in the other specifications they may be all active, a mix of active/inactive, or all inactive. Nevertheless, the formats are all the same. In vtoa-0085-based edge devices, if no time-slots are active, the payload and signaling substructures are empty.

Active Structure Type 2 (without Bit Mask)

This type of structure is formatted as shown in Figure 9.3b. The difference between this structure and a type 1 (active structure with bit mask) is the absence of the bit mask and the AAL 1 structure pointer. This type of structure will be used only when an AAL 1 structure pointer is not used. The payload and signaling substructures are identical to the substructures described above.

Inactive Structure

This structure will be one to four octets, as described in the bit mask requirements above. All bits except the $n + 1$ bit are set to zero. The $n + 1$ bit is the parity bit and will be of value 1 for correct structure. n is the number of assigned timeslots in the subject VC, that is, the maximum number of timeslots that can be active on this VC. See Figure 9.6 for format. This type of structure is used only when all assigned timeslots are inactive.

9.4 Procedures

In the following discussion, *transmitter* refers to the IWF transmitting into the ATM network and *receiver* refers to the IWF receiving from the ATM network.

Configuration

Each IWF is configured by assigning specific timeslots corresponding to each virtual connection in each direction of transmission. This is the $n \times 64$-kbps bandwidth defined in the af-vtoa-0078.000 specification. This may be the full DS1/E1 line or a fraction thereof. In addition, the following parameters (which are beyond the scope of the ATMF specification) must be configured for each timeslot for proper operations:

- Definition of the signaling bit combinations, in both directions, that constitute idle, not idle, and blocking states

- Insertion of the idle code on the receive side (when the slot has not been transmitted due to being inactive on the transmit side)

In full-duplex connections, both directions contain the same number of assigned timeslots ($n \times 64$), but generally different timeslot positions in the DS1/E1 frame. The following procedures address one direction of transmission. The procedures for the other direction are identical.

Transmitter

The transmitting IWF determines each timeslot's activity status from the information received from both the local and remote DS1/E1 equipment in the signaling bits related to this timeslot. The transmitting IWF will then format the TDM active timeslots into one of the two AAL 1 structure types discussed above. At the beginning of transmission from a quiescent state, or whenever the number of active timeslots changes, an active structure with bit mask (type 1) will be transmitted at the next available opportunity. From a quiescent (inactive) state, this is the first transmitted cell. Periodic use of type 1 active structure, which contains a pointer, is required to assure proper structure alignment in the receiver. To comply with ITU-T Recommendation I.363-1, which requires transmission of one structure with a pointer every eight cells, the following apply.

- A structure pointer will be transmitted every eight cells. An active structure type 1 with bit mask will be transmitted for every structure pointer that is not a dummy pointer. (This requirement will be met whenever there is any number of active timeslots of 1 to n, with n as the maximum number of configured timeslots.)
- An active structure type 2 (without bit mask) will be transmitted all other times. (This requirement will be met whenever there is any number of active timeslots of 1 to n, with n as the maximum number of configured timeslots.)

It should be noted that a pointer accompanying active structure type 1 has the same interpretation as the pointer in the existing

ITU-T and ANSI standards, that is, it indicates the number of octets between it and the beginning of the next structure.

Receiver

The receiving CES IWF will calculate the length of the payload/signaling substructure from the value of the bit mask that is located at the beginning of the payload of active structure type 1.* The calculated length will be used as the length of all subsequent type 2 structures (structures without bit mask) until the next bit mask (type 1 structure) is received. The new bit mask either verifies or changes the calculated length.

Following the four-timeslot-configured structure example, and assuming all are active, the bit mask value indicates four active slots. The payload length for CAS is, therefore, 4×24 (assuming DS1). The signaling substructure length is 2 (following the CAS specification in the CES). Total payload/signaling substructure length equals 98. The same example for CCS yields a payload/signaling size of four octets. The receiver will identify the beginning of the payload/signaling substructure at M octets after the beginning of the type 1 active structure, which is identified by the pointer. M is equal to the number of octets in the bit mask.

Notice this rule results from the fact that the pointer (in type 1 structures) points to the beginning of the total structure, which always starts with the bit mask. In the four-timeslot example, $M = 1$. Therefore, the payload/signaling substructure starts one octet after the beginning of the type 1 structure.

In the type 2 active structures, the beginning of the payload/signaling substructure is at the beginning of the entire structure because there is no bit mask.

All Timeslots Inactive

When all assigned timeslots transition from at least one active to all inactive, the following requirements apply. Upon the detection of

---

*For the case of CAS, this calculation is performed by multiplying the number of active indication bits in the bit mask by 24 for DS1 (16 for E1), and adding $N/2$ octets for signaling substructure. For the case of CCS or basic service, the structure payload size is always the number of active timeslots (the CCS timeslot is included in the count if present in the subject structure).

all timeslots being inactive, the transmitter will send an inactive structure following the first pointer after detecting the all-inactive state. The last cell containing active structure will be completely transmitted at the active structure rate before reducing the rate to the inactive structure rate. The transmitter will continue to transmit cells containing the inactive structure at a cell rate greater than one cell every 0.5 second. This is to ensure that a loss-of-signal state is not declared. The IWF receiver, receiving cells meeting the previous requirement, will cause the IWF to transmit idle code in the time-slots of the receiving DS1/E1 line associated to the subject VC. The specific code will be user-programmable. Otherwise, the receiver may indicate loss of signal and the IWF sends AIS on the receiving DS1/E1 line.

Upon detection of one or more timeslots becoming active, the transmitter will send a type 1 active structure following the last inactive structure. The time lapse between detecting a timeslot becoming active and transmission of the first cell containing this slot's information will not exceed 50 ms. The receiver will detect the transition to active status by detecting a valid nonzero bit mask following the all-zero bit masks (inactive structures) it has been receiving during the idle period. Upon detecting this state, the receiver interprets the associated structure as a type 1 active structure and begins reassembling the active slots' data and sending them on the correlating timeslots in the receiving DS1/E1 line.

9.5 Additional Requirements

The reader should consult af-vtoa-0085.000 for information on the following related/required issues:

- ATM virtual channel requirements
- Traffic parameters and tolerances
- DBCES cell rate
- ATM virtual channel payload type and CLP
- Signaling (the UNI 3.1 SVC support is optional for the DBCES IWF)
- SETUP message/call initiation procedures
- Management

CHAPTER 10

VTOA Interworking with Narrowband/ISDN Services

This chapter presents an encapsulated and much abridged description of the ATM Forum's VTOA specifications for ATM Trunking Using AAL 1 for Narrowband Services (af-vtoa-0089.000), Version 1, July 1997. This chapter is based on the ATM Forum specification cited. This material is for pedagogical purposes only. Developers, engineers, and readers requiring more information should acquire the specification directly from the ATM Forum. Figure 10.1 puts the spec in context.

10.1 Introduction to ATM Trunking Using AAL 1 for Narrowband Services

This section provides a description of issues surrounding the ATM trunking application.

Goals and Approach

As noted in Chapter 8, the ATM Forum's Circuit Emulation Service Interoperability Specification Version 2.0 (af-vtoa-0078.000) is lim-

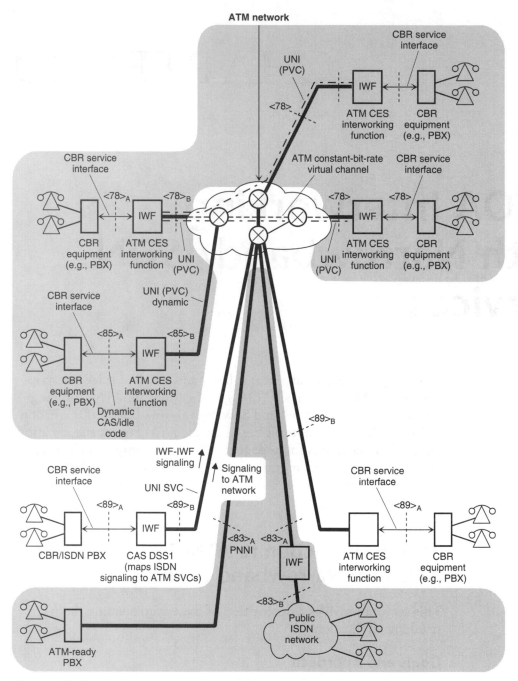

Figure 10.1
af-vtoa.0089.000.

ited to structured DS1, E1, $n\times64$-kbps, and J2 service, and to unstructured DS1, E1, DS3, and E3 service. It is based on the establishment of a facility with a fixed number of circuits (channels) between two endpoints. There are needs, especially in the enterprise networking environment, to extend these capabilities to provide additional features as related to the use of ATM backbone and narrowband access resources. The af-vtoa-0089.000 specification provides those extensions by defining capabilities to allow:

1. Allocation of resources on an as-needed basis, which may be based on expected or actual traffic loading
2. Traffic from/to multiple endpoints (e.g., PBXs, key systems) to share those allocated facilities
3. Calls to be routed to the desired destination facilities, which eliminates the need to dedicate specific narrowband channels to every destination

ITU-T Recommendation I.580-1995, General Arrangement for Interworking between B-ISDN and 64-kbps ISDN, identifies the following interworking scenarios for ATM networks and narrowband (ISDN) networks, as depicted in Figure 10.2:

1. Interconnection of an ATM terminal/network and a narrowband terminal/network (service interworking)
2. Interconnection of two narrowband networks via an ATM network (ISDN network interworking over ATM)
3. Interconnection of two ATM networks via a narrowband network (ATM network interworking over ISDN)

The af-vtoa-0089.000 specification addresses only scenario #2, in which the user interfaces and services are the same as those that are currently provided by the narrowband network.[1] This capability is also called *ATM trunking* or *ATM tunneling.* The specification utilizes and builds upon existing standards and does not include any new speech coding methods; it specifies how the existing coded speech is mapped into the ATM cells.[2]

The specification defines the capabilities of the interworking function (IWF) to provide a means for the interconnection of two narrowband networks through an ATM network via ATM trunks.

Figure 10.2
Communication scenarios in interworking between ATM networks and narrowband networks.

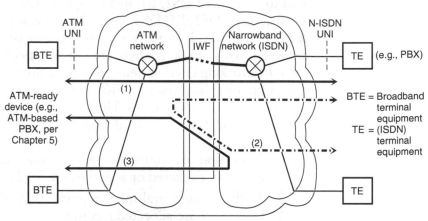

(1) Service interworking
(2) Network interworking of narrowband ISDN over ATM
(3) Networking interworking of ATM over narrowband ISDN

The IWFs provide the necessary adaptation functions to interconnect narrowband equipment to the ATM network. This specification defines the IWF as a logical function that communicates with a peer IWF on the other side of the ATM network. *The two narrowband networks can be thought of as two user ISDN/T1-ready PBXs.* The more general scenario of two telephone company (carrier) ISDN networks that need to be interconnected over an ATM "cloud" is not addressed at this time by the specification.

An ATM trunk is defined as one or more ATM virtual connections that carry a number of 64-kbps narrowband channels and associated signaling between a pair of IWFs. The only constraint placed on the number of narrowband channels per virtual connection, the number of virtual connections per ATM trunk, and the number of ATM trunks per IWF is the addressing mechanisms inherent in the ATM signaling upon which this capability is built.

The IWF may be a standalone device with physical interfaces to the ATM network and the narrowband network or it may be integrated into either the ATM network equipment or the narrowband network equipment, for example, a PBX or ISDN switch.

This specification is limited to *network interworking functions* (service interworking is outside the scope of the specification). The IWF terminates the narrowband signaling protocol in order to perform routing on a per-call basis for the 64-kbps channels to the appropriate destination IWF. The IWF transfers the service information, including the identity of the called user, transparently through the ATM connection. UNI 3.1[3] is used in the specification.

Service Requirements

The following service requirements are important and are addressed in af-vtoa-0089.000.

Call-by-call routing is necessary to route calls on a per-call basis to make more effective use of the transmission and switching capabilities of the ATM network. This allows integration into one physical narrowband interface of multiple access circuits carrying calls destined for different far ends. This reduces the need for tandem circuit switches. To provide this function, the IWF should be able to understand the signaling messages for call setup and call clearing and be able to establish ATM trunks to more than one remote IWF.

Bandwidth on demand is necessary to allocate the bandwidth only when needed. The IWF provides this capability by allowing the establishment of facilities (VCCs) either based on predetermined traffic patterns or when a new call setup requires it.

Bandwidth sharing is necessary to share the bandwidth with other types of service (e.g., data or other PBX). The IWF provides the flexibility for efficient use of bandwidth by freeing up unneeded bandwidth for use by other services.

Support of DS1/E1 with signaling—DSS1, and E&M (CAS) with DTMF signaling—is also a requirement.

Network Interconnection Configurations

Figure 10.3 shows the six potential network interconnection configurations of ATM trunking using AAL 1 for narrowband services (the VTOA specification addresses only configurations I, II, and V), which are as follows:

I. Connection of private narrowband networks via private ATM networks

II. Connection of private narrowband networks via public ATM networks

III. Connection of public narrowband networks via public ATM networks

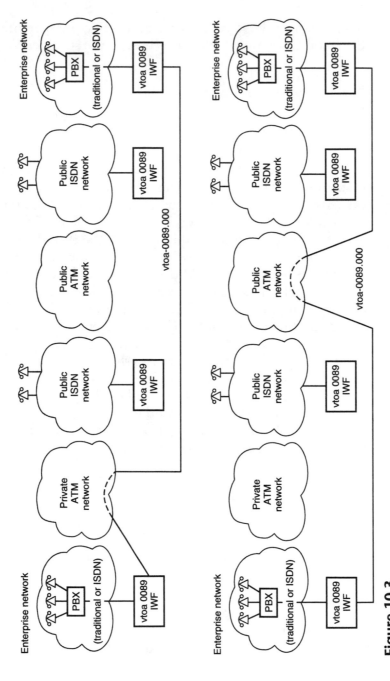

Figure 10.3
Network interworking options.

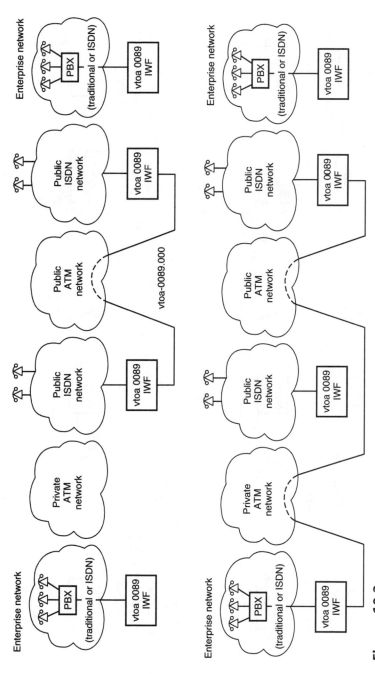

Figure 10.3
(Continued)

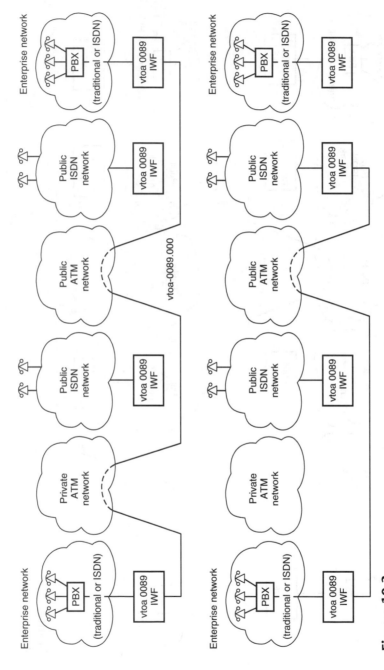

Figure 10.3
(Continued)

IV. Connection of private narrowband network and public narrowband network via both private ATM networks and public ATM networks

V. Connection of private narrowband networks via both private ATM networks and public ATM networks

VI. Connection of public narrowband network and private narrowband network via public ATM networks

The *ATM trunking narrowband network–to–ATM network* interworking scenario can be supported only in *private ISDN network–to–private ATM network* interworking (configuration I). It can also be supported in a private narrowband network to a public ATM network that supports the DSS2 message flows between IWFs described below (configurations II & V).[4] The traffic carried by the trunking described in the specification includes speech and voiceband telephony services such as fax and voiceband modem services and the narrowband signaling associated with these services. Figure 10.4 depicts the most straightforward application of the specification.

The af-vtoa-0089.000 service provides support for both 64-kbps bearer channels and $n\times64$-kbps channels; however, no specific procedures for maintaining timeslot integrity of the channels between the narrowband network are described for the support of $n\times64$-kbps by the IWF. Furthermore, the narrowband signaling protocols at the two narrowband interfaces must be the same, namely, DSS1 or E&M (CAS) signaling. The IWF does not support any signaling protocol conversion between narrowband devices.

10.2 Switched Trunking Service for 64-kbps Channels

This section discusses the mechanisms identified for the transport of 64-kbps narrowband channels across an ATM network with network interworking functions. Figures 10.5 and 10.6 depict the two ATM trunking mechanisms that are addressed. In the *one-to-one mapping*, each 64-kbps channel is mapped into one ATM VCC. In the *many-to-one mapping*, multiple 64-kbps channels are mapped into one ATM VCC.

Figure 10.4
Basic application of vtoa-0083.000.

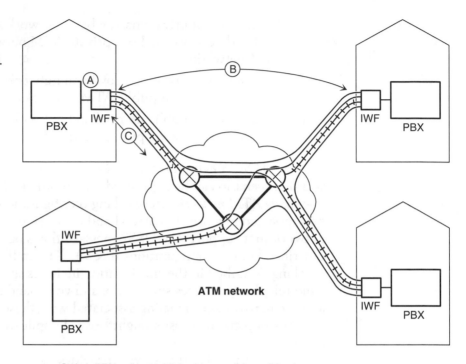

— Switch PBX cells established on a call-by-call basis
▬ ATM trunks
+ Access line

A — Signaling for narrowband interface

B — IWF-to-IWF signaling

C — ATM signaling

There are functions that are common to both mechanisms, and there are functions that are specific to each mechanism. Both mechanisms use one IWF-to-IWF signaling connection to transport narrowband DSS1 signaling messages between two IWFs within an SSCF-UNI/SSCOP/AAL 5 cell stream. For CAS applications, the IWF-to-IWF signaling is performed in-band using DTMF and ABCD bit mapping onto AAL 1 (as specified in af-vtoa-0078.000) and is carried in the same VCC as the 64-kbps channels.

Functions Applicable to Both One-to-One and Many-to-One Cases

Figure 10.7 shows the reference configuration for ATM trunking for narrowband services. Private or public narrowband networks are

Figure 10.5
ATM trunking one-to-one mapping.

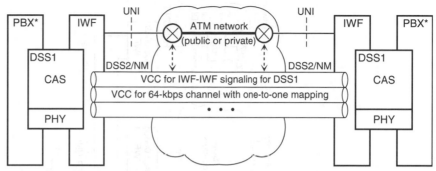

*More generally, an ISDN switch/network

shown connected to interworking functions, which in turn are connected to either public or private ATM networks through physical interfaces. The narrowband networks connect to the IWFs over DS1/E1 facilities.[5] The job of the IWFs is to adapt the incoming signals from the narrowband networks into a suitable format for carriage over the ATM networks and vice versa. ATM connections are set up over the ATM networks between appropriate IWFs to support the desired number of adapted 64-kbps narrowband channels.

The IWF for ATM trunking using AAL 1 provides a call-by-call switched service to the narrowband network. For the support of N-ISDN out-of-band D-channel signaling, the IWF terminates the narrowband signaling and transports all narrowband messages in a signaling connection setup with the remote IWF. For the support of channel-associated signaling (e.g., traditional T1-based PBXs), the IWF terminates the narrowband signaling and signaling information is transported in the same ATM virtual connection that carries the

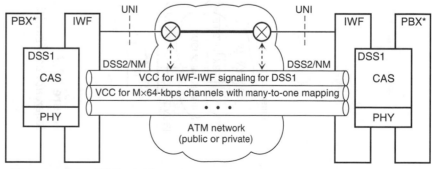

Figure 10.6
ATM trunking many-to-one mapping.

*More generally, an ISDN switch/network

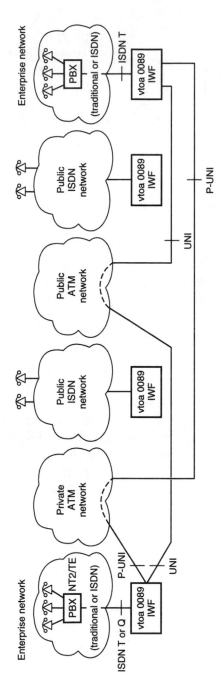

Figure 10.7
Reference configuration.

390

voice information. For effective support of voice devices, such as PBXs and/or key systems, it is important that certain performance metrics be met in the network. Table 10.1 depicts recommended goals in af-vtoa-0089.000 for a number of pertinent factors.

General Functionality of the IWF

The functionality of the IWF is listed in Table 10.2.

IWF Functionality with N-ISDN Signaling The functionality of the IWF located at the interface between a narrowband ISDN and a broadband network, is described next, as listed in af-vtoa-0089.000.

Trunks on E1 or DS1 facilities, with their associated out-of-band signaling channels, terminate on a narrowband switch function, which routes the 64-kbps channels from the incoming trunks so that channels that need to use the same path across the ATM network may be grouped. Multiple outputs are multiplexed together and presented to a mapping function, where the octets belonging to individual 64-kbps channels are mapped into the payload of AAL 1 ATM cells belonging to a given VCC. These ATM cells are carried by the VCCs connecting IWFs across the ATM network.

The out-of-band signaling channels are also presented to the call handling function so that the call handling function can control the narrowband switch function. The call handling function uses the services of *signaling AAL* (SAAL) and AAL 5 to transfer the narrowband signaling messages across the ATM network to a peer IWF in a separate VCC.

Table 10.1   Performance Goals/Approaches

Delay	ATM trunking for narrowband services introduces some additional delay to that encountered for the transport over the ATM network, because of buffering to accommodate cell delay variation introduced by the ATM network, and cell assembly/disassembly delay. Echo control measures are recommended on all speech connections where end-end delay exceeds that specified in G.131.
Error performance	The error performance of trunked narrowband channels is impacted by cell errors, cell loss, and cell misinsertion in the ATM network. Appropriate cell loss compensation is required in the IWF.
End-to-end delay	End-to-end delay requirements are application-dependent and are beyond the scope of af-vtoa-0089.000. ITU-T Recommendation G.114 provides considerable guidance on the subject of delay.
Error ratios	Service performance is also measured in terms of errored seconds (ES) and severely errored seconds (SES). Performance objectives for ES and SES are given in T1.510 for DS1 and in G.826 for E1.

Table 10.2   IWF Functionality

Signaling termination	Extracts signaling from and inserts signaling into the narrowband interface.
Call handling	Interprets the call setup and release signals from the connected narrowband equipment, including selection of the destination for each call.
Switching	Enables any combination of channels from the narrowband side to be connected, on a call-by-call basis, to any combination of ATM trunks. This consists of copying the data octets from individual timeslots from the DS1/E1 side into the desired channel positions on the ATM side, and vice versa.
Multiplexing	Combines channels from multiple sources from the narrowband side toward ATM trunks to the ATM network.
Mapping and adaption	Inserts the 64-kbps channels into the allocated channel positions in the VCC according to af-vtoa-0078.000.
VCC management	Allocates/deallocates VCCs to distant PBXs as needed to support the traffic.

If the VCCs to carry narrowband signaling messages and 64-kbps channels are controlled by the IWF, then the call handling function also generates messages as defined in UNI 3.1 for setting up these VCCs. Otherwise, the VCCs are established by network management procedures.

The call handling of the IWF is limited to setup and release of point-to-point connections and does not include other services such as supplementary services.

IWF Functionality with Channel-Associated Signaling   The functionality of the IWF located at the interface between a narrowband network and a broadband network and utilizing CAS, is described next, as listed in af-vtoa-0089.000.

Trunks with CAS for supervisory signaling and DTMF for address signaling on E1 or DS1 facilities terminate on a narrowband switch function, which routes the 64-kbps channels from the incoming trunks so that channels that need to use the same path across the ATM network may be grouped. Multiple outputs are multiplexed together and presented to a mapping function, where the octets belonging to individual 64-kbps channels are mapped into the payload of AAL 1 ATM cells belonging to a given VCC. These ATM cells are carried by the VCCs connecting IWFs across the ATM network.

The narrowband switch function also presents the narrowband signaling (supervisory and address signaling) to a call handling function. This call handling function controls the narrowband switch function in order to route the individual 64-kbps channels to the correct VCC. The narrowband signaling information is transported in the same ATM VCC as the associated speech information.

If the VCCs to carry 64-kbps channels are controlled by the IWF, then the call handling function also generates messages as defined in UNI 3.1 for setting up these VCCs. Otherwise, the VCCs are established by network management procedures.

Signaling

The signaling required includes signaling on the narrowband interface, IWF-to-IWF signaling, and IWF-to-ATM network signaling.

Signaling for Narrowband Interface The signaling between the IWF and the narrowband network may be via either DS1 or E1 at the Physical Layer with either narrowband ISDN (ITU-T Q.931) or CAS signaling (ITU-T G.704 and ANSI/TIA/EIA-464-B).[6]

IWF-to-IWF Signaling The signaling protocols between the IWFs of interest in North America can be one of the following and is the same as that used between the connected narrowband equipment and the IWF: DSS1 ISDN (ITU-T Q.931) or CAS (E&M with wink start and DTMF according to ANSI/TIA/EIA-464-B). The two subsections that follow provide more information on the signaling function support.

ATM Signaling This is required to set up SVC tunnels/trunks through the ATM network.

Signaling for N-ISDN Figure 10.8 shows the protocol reference model for DSS1, highlighting the signaling requirements in the interworking function to interface narrowband and ATM networks. Signaling associated with 64-kbps channels carried between two IWFs is transported across the ATM network in the signaling AAL (SAAL) cell stream within a separate VCC. It allows the signaling for narrowband ISDN 64-kbps calls to remain in the narrowband domain from end to end. This separate VCC may be established as a PVC or as an SVC as shown in Figure 10.9. Refer to af-vtoa-0089.000 for additional details about the entire signaling process.

Signaling for Channel-Associated Signaling Figure 10.10 shows the protocol reference model for the support of channel-associated signaling. The IWF terminates narrowband CAS supervisory signaling and DTMF address signaling. When a narrowband

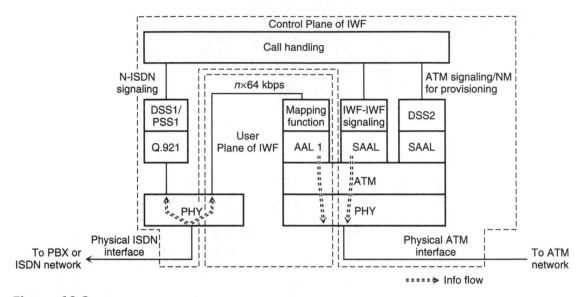

Figure 10.8
IWF reference model for DSS1 applications.

channel becomes active, the IWF, based on the called party number, finds the ATM address of the destination IWF. If there is no ATM VCC to the destination IWF available to carry the call, the IWF sets up an ATM VCC to carry the call. This is shown in Figure 10.11. If there is an ATM VCC to carry the call to the destination IWF, the 64-kbps channel is mapped into the VCC.

Refer to af-vtoa-0089.000 for a discussion of glare management. (Glare was discussed in Chapter 5, and as applied to this environment is the condition that occurs when two IWFs seize the same allocated channel position or "slot" of the same ATM VCC at about the same time such that the IWF-IWF signaling setup indications cross; for N-ISDN, this occurs when both sides generate an N-SETUP message at about the same time; for CAS, glare is detected when the return off hook in the wink lasts beyond 350 ms.)

ATM Signaling   ATM signaling is used between the IWF and the ATM network to set up SVCs for IWF-IWF signaling (for the case of N-ISDN signaling only) and SVCs for the 64-kbps channels across the ATM network. The call/connection control procedures of UNI 3.1 are used. Refer to af-vtoa-0089.000 for a discussion of

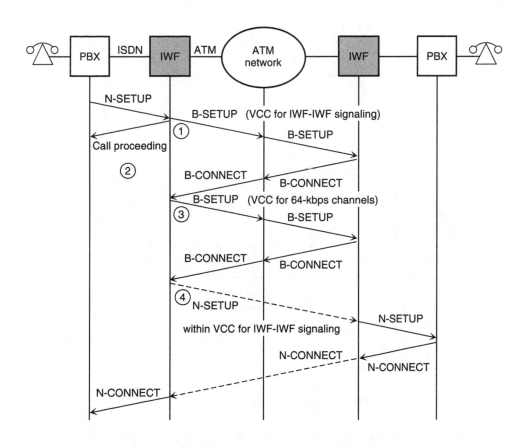

Note 1: Based on the called party number in the N-ISDN SETUP message, the IWF finds the ATM address of the destination IWF. If the VCC for the IWF-IWF signaling does not already exist, the IWF sets up a VCC for the IWF-IWF signaling.

Note 2: Depending on the time to set up the VCCs, it may be necessary to send a call proceeding message in order to avoid failures due to expiring timer.

Note 3: The IFW sets up a VCC for the 64-kbps channel(s) using the broadband SETUP message with the B-LLI IE to identify the VCC.

Note 4: After the VCC to carry the narrowband call is established, the IWF sends a narrowband SETUP message to the destination IWF over the IWF-IWF signaling connection. This N-SETUP contains the VCCI value from the B-LLI IE of the B-SETUP. For many-to-one mapping, it also contains the number of the selected channel in the identified VCC.

Figure 10.9
Information flows when VCCs do not exist (af-vtoa-0089.000).

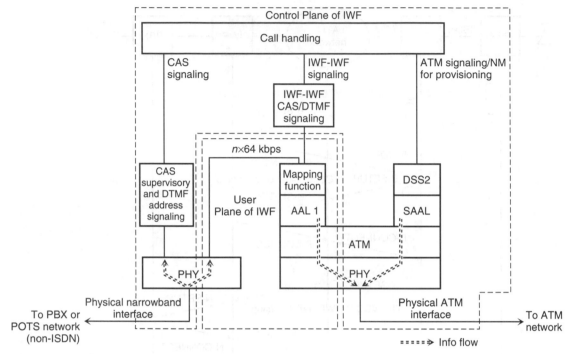

Figure 10.10
IWF reference model to support channel-associated signaling.

such related signaling topics as addresses and identifiers for switched virtual channels (SVCs), SETUP message contents, and handling of error conditions.

ATM Adaptation Layer

For the transport of IWF-IWF signaling to support N-ISDN (out-of-band) signaling, AAL type 5 is used. For the User Plane, AAL 1 is used. As noted in Chapter 7, AAL 1 as specified in ITU-T recommendation I.363.1 has the capability to delineate repetitive, fixed-size blocks of data, each block being an integral number of octets in size. This capability is used to carry multiple DS0 timeslots organized into blocks. For a block size of one octet, corresponding to a single DS0 stream (i.e., $n = 1$), AAL 1 provides block delineation by aligning each AAL user octet with an ATM cell payload octet. For a block size greater than one octet, AAL 1 uses a pointer mechanism

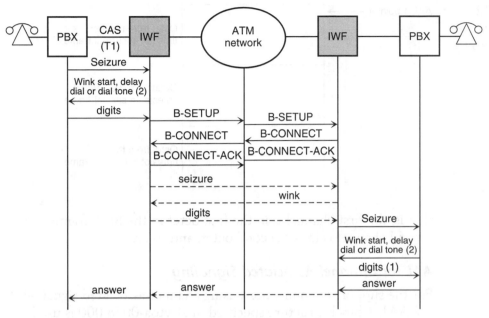

Figure 10.11
Information flows when no VCC exists for 64-kbps channel (af-vtoa-0089.000).

to indicate the start of a structure block. The pointer operation should be as described in ITU-T Recommendation I.363.1, which requires the pointer to be inserted at the first opportunity in a cycle of eight cells, as delimited by the AAL 1 header sequence number 0 through 7.

AAL for N-ISDN (out-of-band) Signaling

For the support of connections using N-ISDN (out-of-band) signaling, to encode multiple 64-kbps channels into the AAL 1 SDT, a block is created by collecting *n* octets—one from each *n* number of 64-kbps channels—and grouping them in sequence. See Figure 10.12 for an example that shows the block structure for three 64-kbps channels. The block size for *n*×64 channels is always *n* octets.

For the many-to-one mapping, the channel number in the channel ID IE corresponds to the position number in the SDT frame;

Figure 10.12
Example structure format for 3×64 kbps.

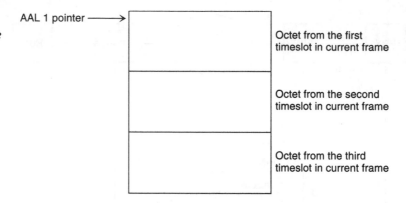

AAL 1 pointer ———→

Octet from the first timeslot in current frame

Octet from the second timeslot in current frame

Octet from the third timeslot in current frame

that is, the first channel is in the first octet in the SDT frame, the second channel is in the second octet, and so on.

AAL for Channel-Associated Signaling

For the support of connections using channel-associated signaling, the AAL 1 block structure specified in af-vtoa-0078.000 is used; however, the limit of 24 or 31 channels for DS1- and E1-based systems, respectively, will not apply. The number of channels per VCC is limited to 128. Speech information and DTMF tones are carried by the payload portion of the AAL 1 block. The channel-associated signaling bits are carried by the signaling portion of the AAL 1 block.

Functions Applicable to One-to-One Mapping

For the support of N-ISDN (out-of-band) signaling, an ATM VCC is required between a pair of IWFs for the transport of IWF-IWF signaling. For the support of CAS, the narrowband signaling information is transported with the same ATM VCC that carries voice information. In either case, for the User Plane, an ATM VCC is required for each 64-kbps channel. This VCC can either be set up and released individually for each voice call or it can be reused for a number of consecutive voice calls. The number of such VCCs between a pair of IWFs is limited by the connection identifier used in the B-LLI information element, which can identify up to 8192 different connections for each direction. Since the individual 64-kbps calls are mapped onto separate ATM VCCs, the IWF does not require a switching functionality. Refer again to Figure 10.5.

Functions Applicable to Many-to-One Mapping

For the support of N-ISDN (out-of-band) signaling, an ATM VCC is required between a pair of IWFs for the transport of IWF-IWF signaling. For the support of channel-associated signaling, the narrowband signaling information is transported on the same ATM VCC that carries voice information. For either case, for the User Plane, an ATM VCC is required to carry multiple 64-kbps channels. The IWF establishes an appropriate number of many-to-one mapping connections between two IWFs. The establishment can be done through ATM signaling or through management. Refer again to Figure 10.6.

10.3 Specific Support Mechanisms

The reader should refer to the VTOA specification for Information Element Contents—for example, ATM Adaptation Layer parameters, ATM traffic descriptors, broadband bearer capability, broadband low-layer information element, and quality of service parameters. The reader should also refer to the specification for signaling mechanisms to establish VCC for 64-kbps channels, including ATM Adaptation Layer parameters, ATM traffic descriptor, broadband bearer capability information element, broadband low-layer information, and quality of service parameter. Similarly, the specification should be consulted for IWF-IWF signaling. The specification also contains informative material on clocking issues. Clocking is always an important consideration that must be given detailed attention.

Notes

[1]By contrast, af-vtoa-0083.000 specifies the functions to be performed by a native ATM terminal and an IWF to provide service between B-ISDN-attached terminals and/or N-ISDN-attached terminals.

[2]Transport of compressed voice with optional activity detection is not addressed and may be the subject of future revisions.

[3]UNI 4.0 may optionally be employed.

[4]The VTOA Technical Committee indicates that further study is needed to determine how public narrowband networks interworking with either public or private ATM networks would support ATM trunking (configurations III, IV, and VI).

[5]Specifically, for the support of N-ISDN, the interface between the N-ISDN network and the IWF is defined in I.431 (ISDN primary rate interface). For the support of channel-associated signaling, the interface between the narrowband network and the IWF may be DS1 as defined in ANSI/TIA/EIA-464-B (or E1 as defined in G.703). The interfaces between the IWF and the ATM network can be any one or more ATM Forum/ITU-T UNI specifications.

[6]Dial pulse address signaling is not supported.

CHAPTER 11

VTOA Voice Telephony over ATM to the Desktop

This chapter presents an encapsulated and much abridged description of the ATM Forum's VTOA specifications for Voice and Telephony over ATM to the Desktop (af-vtoa-0083.000), Version 1, May 1997. This chapter is based on the ATM Forum specification cited. This material is for pedagogical purposes only. Developers, engineers, and readers requiring more information should acquire the specification directly from the ATM Forum. Figure 11.1 puts the spec in context.

11.1 Introduction to Voice and Telephony over ATM to the Desktop Specification

The af-vtoa-0083.000 specification is the ATM Forum's interoperability agreement for supporting voice and telephony over ATM to the desktop via a *native ATM terminal*. This is a device that can place a G.711 bit stream onto an AAL, onto an ATM layer, and onto an ATM network. Such a terminal could conceivably be an ATM-attached PC, an ATM-ready PBX, an ATM-ready voice-mail system, or the like. The af-vtoa-0083.000 specification identifies the features required to provide voice and telephony service in B-ISDN. It

401

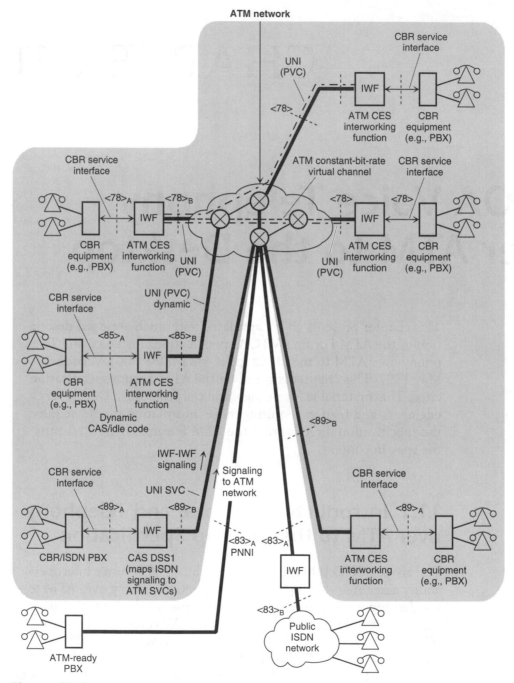

Figure 11.1
af-vtoa-0083.000.

describes the functions to be performed by the native ATM terminal and an interworking function (IWF) to provide service between B-ISDN-attached terminals and/or N-ISDN-attached terminals, be they public or private. The document specifies the particular features required to support signaling interworking between B-ISDN and N-ISDN. The requirements for support of UNI 4.0 supplementary services are also described (but are not covered in this synopsis).

The af-vtoa-0083.000 specification applies to the transport of a single 64-kbps *A*-law or μ-law (ITU-T Recommendation G.711) voiceband signal. Alternative coding for voice transport (e.g., high-quality voice, compressed voice) and silence removal are currently outside the scope of the specification. Only the signaling interworking with an N-ISDN interface is covered. This document is based on PNNI 1.0, UNI 4.0, ITU-T Recommendation I.580 on N-ISDN interworking, and ITU-T Recommendations Q.2931, Q.2951, and Q.2957 on DSS2 signaling. It covers the interworking scenario where a user on a B-ISDN is accessing N-ISDN services offered by an N-ISDN, through an IWF. Three types of attachment are considered in the specification:

- Broadband terminal equipment (B-TE) to private or public B-ISDN
- Private B-ISDN to public N-ISDN
- Private B-ISDN to private N-ISDN

Figure 11.2 depicts the reference configuration for af-vtoa-0083.000. Note, however, that the interworking between a public B-ISDN and a public N-ISDN, including the B-ISUP and the N-ISUP protocols, is outside the scope of the specification. Also note that the signaling between a public B-ISDN and a private B-ISDN is specified in UNI 4.0. The service requirements for N-ISDN service are described in ITU-T Recommendation I.231 for the circuit-mode bearer service and in I.251 and I.257 for the supplementary services supported in this specification.

11.2 Native ATM Terminal Equipment

The specification makes the following assumption about the functional requirements of the native ATM terminal: The native ATM

Figure 11.2
Reference configu-
ration (af-vtoa-
0083.000).

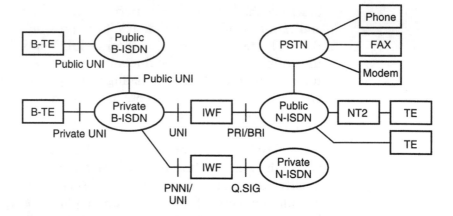

terminal equipment (B-TE) is able to establish a voice communication through a B-ISDN on a per-call basis. The traffic is 64-kbps
PCM-encoded voice. Each voice call uses one VCC. The B-TE may
invoke supplementary services on a per-call basis. A B-TE has either
a public UNI to a public B-ISDN or a private UNI to a private
B-ISDN. The protocol support of the terminal at the S_B reference
point is as described below.

User Plane

Physical Layer: The Physical Layer is any of the Physical Layers
defined by the ATM Forum.

   ATM Layer: The specification of the ATM Layer is as defined
in section ITU-T Recommendations I.150 and I.361, including
OA&M cells for F4 and F5 management information flows.

   AAL: A B-TE attached to a private B-ISDN has the option of
using either the AAL 1 specification for voiceband signal transport
as described in ITU-T Recommendation I.363.1, or the AAL 5 as
specified in ITU-T Recommendation I.363.5. However, a B-TE
attached directly to a public B-ISDN may have to support the AAL
1 specification for voiceband signal transport to conform to the
public B-ISDN offerings. It is most important that two B-TEs be
able to connect directly to one another and not require that an
interworking function be inserted into the VCC to transcode
between different User Plane formats (AAL 1 for voice and AAL
5). Therefore, it is required that all B-TEs implement a common
User Plane format—in the sense that they can *accept* incoming calls

whose signaling indicates the use of that format (it is not required, though, that all B-TEs establish their outgoing calls using only the common format; a B-TE may choose to use the alternate format instead). Since all B-TEs must implement AAL 5 to support Control Plane signaling, the common User Plane format is specified to be AAL 5.*

Application Level—Voice Bit Stream: The voice stream is encoded as 64-kbps PCM μ-law or *A*-law, as described in ITU-T Recommendation G.711. The B-TE may transmit either μ-law or *A*-law signals, according to the guidelines of G.711, and it must be capable of receiving both μ-law or *A*-law signals.

Control Plane

Lower Layers: The Physical Layer and the ATM Layer are as above. The signaling AAL (SAAL) layer is as specified in Section 4.1 of UNI SIG 4.0 (af-sig-0061.000).

Upper Layers: Basic call/connection control signaling. The procedures of section 6/Q.2931, "Procedures for the Support of 64-kbps-Based Circuit-Mode ISDN Services in B-ISDN and Access Signaling Interworking between N-ISDN and B-ISDN" and Appendix II.2.2/Q.2931 apply, as modified per UNI 4.0, "Basic Point-to-Point Call." Broadly, the requirements are as follows (af-vtoa-0083.000/Q.2931).

A B-TE will code the N-BC information elements as in Table 11.1, the broadband bearer capability information element as in Table 11.2, the ATM traffic descriptor information element for AAL 1 for voice as in Table 11.3, the ATM traffic descriptor infor-

---

*Per af-vtoa-0083.000, the following AAL 5 requirements are imposed: Voiceband information will use the message mode service. The SSCS is null, thus the AAL-SDU is mapped to one CPCS-SDU (no SSCF and no SSCOP). The CPCS-PDU payload may be up to 40 octets, in increments of 8 octets, with 40 octets as the preferred value. Therefore, the SAR sublayer is trivial: the AAU bit in the payload type of the ATM header is always set to 1 to indicate the end of a SAR-SDU. The CPCS user-to-user indication (CPCS-UU), in the CPCS trailer, should be set to 00000000. The use of this octet for other purposes is reserved for further study. The length field in the CPCS trailer may be coded as 8 to 40. The cell rate for AAL 5 should be 8000 divided by payload_length cells/s (64 kbps × 1 octet/8 bits × 1 cell divided by payload_length octets). For a full fill cell, the cell rate is 200 cells/s. This implies a cell construction delay of 125 μs × payload_length. For a full fill cell, the cell construction delay will be 5 ms.

Table 11.1 N-BC Information Element

Octet	Information element field	Field value
3	Information transfer capability	Speech (not to be used for fax or modem) or 3.1-kHz audio
4	Transfer mode	Circuit mode
	Information transfer rate	64 kbps
4.1	Absent	
5	User information Layer 1 protocol	Recommendation G.711 μ-law or Recommendation G.711 A-law
5a–7	Absent	

mation element for AAL 5 for voice as in Table 11.4, the quality of service parameters information element as in Table 11.5, the AAL parameters information element for AAL 1 for voice as in Table 11.6, and the AAL parameters information element for AAL 5 for voice as in Table 11.7.

Some interworking functions listed in Q.2931 are not supported in af-vtoa-0083.000 (refer to the specification for details). Some supplementary services—for example, calling line identification presentation (CLIP), calling line identification restriction (CLIR), connected line identification presentation (COLP), connected line identification restriction (COLR), subaddressing (SUB), and user-to-user signaling (UUS) Service 1—are supported. Refer to the ATM Forum specification for details.

11.3 Interworking Function

This section is summarized from af-vtoa-0083.000; more details can be found in the original documentation.

Table 11.2 Broadband Bearer Capability Information Element

Octet	Information element field	Field value
5	Bearer class	BCOB-A
5a	Absent	
6	Susceptibility to clipping	Susceptible to clipping
	User Plane connection configuration	Point-to-point

Table 11.3 ATM Traffic Descriptor Information Element for AAL 1 Voice

Octet	Information element field	Field value if no OA&M cells are used*	Field value if 1 OA&M cell/s is used†	Field value with maximal OA&M support‡
5	Absent			
6	Absent			
	Forward peak	0000 0000	0000 0000	0000 0000
7.1	cell rate	0000 0000	0000 0000	0000 0000
7.2	(CLP = 0 + 1)	1010 1011	1010 1100	1010 1111
7.3		(171 cells/s)	(172 cells/s)	(175 cells/s)
	Backward peak	0000 0000	0000 0000	0000 0000
8.1	cell rate	0000 0000	0000 0000	0000 0000
8.2	(CLP = 0 + 1)	1010 1011	1010 1100	1010 1111
8.3		(171 cells/s)	(172 cells/s)	(175 cells/s)

*These values are based on an AAL for voice (i.e., AAL type 1 with a payload of 47 octets per cell) for user information and no cell rate allocation for OA&M cells.

†These values are based on an AAL for voice (i.e., AAL type 1 with a payload of 47 octets per cell) for user information and on 1 cell/s allocation for OA&M cells.

‡These values are based on an AAL for voice (i.e., AAL type 1 with a payload of 47 octets per cell) for user information and the following cell rate allocation for OA&M: 2% of the user cell rate and an additional 1 cell/s.

Functional Requirements

The IWF converts the voice traffic on the B-ISDN (ATM network) to voice traffic on the N-ISDN (narrowband telephony network). On both sides, the traffic is 64-kbps PCM-encoded voice. One ATM VCC is mapped to one N-ISDN channel dynamically on a per-call basis. For that purpose, the IWF also maps the B-ISDN signaling information (on VC = 5) to N-ISDN signaling information (on the D-channel). To preserve service integrity, the IWF attempts to keep intact as much as possible the information of the signaling channel. In the opposite direction from the N-ISDN to the B-ISDN, an inverse set of operations to the above is performed.

Interfaces and Protocols

This section specifies mapping requirements to interwork between N-ISDN and B-ISDN at the IWF. It also proposes interworking configurations and a protocol reference model. The interworking configurations shown in Figure 11.3 are derived from scenario B, case 1 of Annex A/I.580. Also, it allows for the use of AAL 5 for the transport of voiceband information. When the N-ISDN is a public net-

Table 11.4 **ATM Traffic Descriptor Information Element for AAL 5**

Octet	Information element field	Field value if no OA&M cells are used*	Field value if 1 OA&M cell/s is used†	Field value with maximal OA&M support‡
5	Absent			
6	Absent			
	Forward peak cell rate	0000 0000	0000 0000	0000 0000
7.1		0000 0000	0000 0000	0000 0000
7.2	(CLP = 0 + 1)	1100 1000	1100 1001	1100 1101
7.3		(200 cells/s)	(201 cells/s)	(205 cells/s)
	Backward peak cell rate	0000 0000	0000 0000	0000 0000
7.1		0000 0000	0000 0000	0000 0000
8.2	(CLP = 0 + 1)	1100 1000	1100 1001	1100 1101
8.3		(200 cells/s)	(201 cells/s)	(205 cells/s)

*These values are based on an AAL type 5 payload of 40 octets per cell for user information and no cell rate allocation for OA&M cells. For a payload of less than 40 octets, the filled value should be 8000 divided by payload_length, encoded in binary format.

†These values are based on an AAL type 5 payload of 40 octets per cell for user information and on 1 cell/s allocation for OA&M cells. For a payload of less than 40 octets, the filled value should be 8000 divided by payload_length + 1, encoded in binary format.

‡These values are based on an AAL type 5 payload of 40 octets per cell for user information and the following cell rate allocation for OAM: 2% of the user cell rate and an additional 1 cell/s. For a payload of less than 40 octets, the filled value should be 8000 divided by payload_length × 1.02 + 1, encoded in binary format.

work, the signaling protocol between the B-ISDN and the IWF is DSS2, and the signaling between the IWF and the N-ISDN is DSS1. When the N-ISDN is a private network, the signaling protocol between the B-ISDN and the IWF is PNNI signaling or DSS2, and the signaling protocol between the IWF and the private N-ISDN is PSS1 (Q.SIG).

Two B-ISDN private networks can be connected through an N-ISDN network (public or private), or a B-ISDN network can be connected to narrowband devices (N-ISDN or analog) through an N-ISDN. The S and T reference points are described in ITU-T Recommendation I.411. The S_B and T_B reference points are described in ITU-T Recommendation I.413. The Q reference point is described in ISO/IEC 11579-1.

Table 11.5 **Quality of Service Parameters Information Element**

Octet	Information element field	Field value
5	QoS-class forward	Unspecified QoS class
6	QoS-class backward	Unspecified QoS class

Table 11.6 AAL Parameters Information Element for AAL 1 for Voice

Octet	Information element field	Field value	
5	AAL type	0000 0000	AAL for voice

In Figure 11.3, at the *T* reference point, the user side of the interface is at the left and the network side of the interface is at the right. At the *T₍B₎* reference point, the user side of the interface is at the left and the network of the interface is at the right if the IWF maps messages one to one; if the IWF fully terminates the call control protocol, the user side and the network side can be reversed.

A private B-ISDN may consist of a multitude of devices, including a private ATM switch or a network of private ATM switches. A private N-ISDN may consist of a multitude of devices, including a PBX or a network of PBXs.

Public N-ISDN In this interworking scenario, the N-ISDN sees the IWF as a B-TE or as a PBX. Depending on which side is the user side, the private B-ISDN sees the IWF either as a B-TE or as a public B-ISDN.

Private N-ISDN In this interworking scenario, the private N-ISDN sees the IWF as another N-ISDN node in the private N-ISDN network. Similarly, the private B-ISDN sees the IWF as another B-ISDN node in the private B-ISDN network.

In some scenarios, the IWF may be integrated, as shown in Figure 11.4, either with the private B-ISDN, in which case there would be no physical PNNI or UNI between the private B-ISDN and the IWF, or with the private N-ISDN, in which case there would be no real Q reference point between the IWF and the private N-ISDN. When the IWF is integrated, some of the require-

Table 11.7 AAL Parameters Information Element for AAL 5

Octet	Information element field	Field value	
5	AAL type	0000 0101	AAL type 5
6.1	Forward maximum	Any multiple of 8 between 8 and	
6.2	CPCS-SDU size	40, encoded in binary format	
7.1	Backward maximum	Any multiple of 8 between 8 and	
7.2	CPCS-SDU size	40, encoded in binary format	
8	SSCS-type	Absent (preferred), or 0000 0000 null	

Figure 11.3
Interworking configurations.

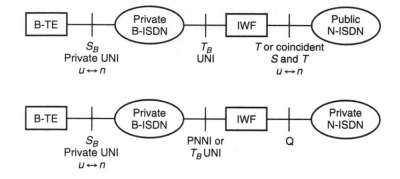

ments may not apply; for example, if the IWF is integrated with the private B-ISDN, there will be no PNNI at the IWF.

User Plane

Figure 11.5 illustrates the user information (User Plane) interworking applicable to the same reference configuration. In the User Plane, the role of the IWF is to convert between TDM-encoded voiceband information and ATM cell-based voiceband information.

Control Plane

This section describes the protocol machinery for the control plane.

Protocol Reference Model

Figure 11.6 illustrates the signaling interworking (Control Plane).

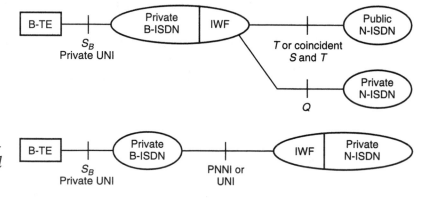

Figure 11.4
Additional interworking configurations for integrated IWF.

Figure 11.5
User information (User Plane).

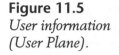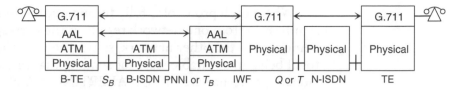

Public N-ISDN In the Control Plane, the role of the IWF is to act as a protocol converter between DSS2 and DSS1. The SAAL Layer should be as specified in Section 4.1 of UNI SIG 4.0 (af-sig-0061.000).

Private N-ISDN In the Control Plane, the role of the IWF is to be a protocol converter between PSS1 and DSS2 or PNNI signaling. The SAAL Layer should be as specified in Section 4.1/UNI SIG 4.0 (af-sig-0061.000) for DSS2 signaling or in section 6.1.2.2/PNNI.0 (af-pnni-0055.000) for PNNI signaling.

Basic Call/Connection Control Signaling

Interworking between the N-ISDN basic call signaling protocol and the B-ISDN basic call/connection control signaling protocol is achieved either by fully terminating each protocol within the IWF or by a one-to-one mapping of messages.

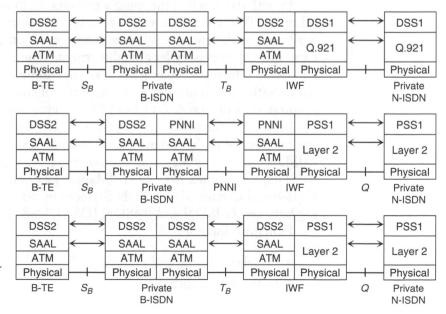

Figure 11.6
The signaling interworking (Control Plane).

Where each protocol is fully terminated, a message of global significance from one network results in the corresponding message being sent to the other network, subject to the other network's protocol being in a suitable state for sending that message. Messages of global significance are SETUP, ALERTING, CONNECT, PROGRESS, and the first call clearing message (DISCONNECT, RELEASE, or RELEASE COMPLETE). When mapping the first call clearing message from one network onto the first call clearing message to be sent to the other network, the choice of message to be sent will depend on the requirements of the other network's protocol (e.g., a RELEASE COMPLETE message as a first call clearing message from the B-ISDN can result in a DISCONNECT message being sent to the N-ISDN, unless it is the first response to a SETUP message from the N-ISDN). Messages of local significance (all other messages) are terminated in the IWF if received and should be generated in the IWF in accordance with the requirements of the protocol. Protocol timers run in accordance with the requirements of the two protocols.

Where messages are mapped one to one, each message from one network will be mapped onto the corresponding message of the other network, consistent with and with the exceptions detailed in af-vtoa-0083.000.

In both cases, when mapping a message from one protocol to the other, the IWF will pass on each received information element that is allowed in the corresponding message of the other protocol and carry out any necessary length adjustment. When sending a message, additional information elements may have to be generated in accordance with the requirements of the protocol concerned and the requirements of Annex E/Q.2931 (see af-vtoa-0083.000 for details).

In general, the procedures of Section 6/Q.2931, "Procedures for the Support of 64-kbps-Based Circuit-Mode ISDN Services in B-ISDN and Access Signaling Interworking between N-ISDN and B-ISDN," and Annex E/Q.2931, "Mapping Functions to Support 64 kbps-Based Circuit-Mode ISDN Services in B-ISDN and Interworking between N-ISDN and B-ISDN (DSS1/DSS2)," apply.

Functions include:

- Overlap sending and receiving
- Instruction indicators

- Call clearing
- Connection acknowledgment
- Restart procedure

11.4 Timing Issues

The voice and telephony services of the N-ISDN are synchronous services. To minimize service defects, public networks are synchronized to primary reference standards. ANSI T1.101 and ITU-T Recommendation G.811 describe for accuracy requirements for synchronization in public networks. A timing relationship is therefore required when a B-TE is connected to the N-ISDN via an IWF. The PCM codec in the B-TE may have to be synchronized to the network clock of the N-ISDN. There are three distribution mechanisms available (timing derived from a network-based clock—that is, the Physical Layer—when available, is the preferred timing distribution mechanism):

- Network-based (Physical Layer)
- Adaptive (ATM and/or AAL Layer)
- Independent (free running clock)

Refer to Chapter 7 for a brief review of timing and to af-vtoa .0083.000 for a more complete description.

11.5 Delay and Echo Issues

Appropriate echo control measures are recommended on all speech connections where the end-to-end delay exceeds that specified in section 3.1/G.131. Additional guidance is provided in G.176. Also refer to af-vtoa-0083.000 for a more complete description.

11.6 Addressing Issues

The requirements of section 3/UNI Signaling 4.0 and the guidelines of Annex 1/UNI Signaling 4.0 concerning E.164 apply. In addition to the numbering plans supported by UNI 4.0 (E.164 or other), there is a need to support telephony numbers in a N-ISDN private numbering plan (PNP). PNP specifies private N-ISDN numbers (i.e., telephone numbers used within a private numbering plan and not conforming to E.164). Refer to af-vtoa-0083.000 for a more complete description.

CHAPTER 12

Adapting Voice for ATM Networks:

A Comparison of AAL 1 versus AAL 2, and a Case Study of APEX Voice Service Module by General DataComm*

12.1 Introduction

This chapter discusses the concepts related to voice over ATM services and, in particular, details the use of ATM Adaptation Layer 1 (AAL 1) versus ATM Adaptation Layer 2 (AAL 2) to adapt voice for ATM networks. It also provides a case study of GDC's APEX voice technology.

AAL 1 has been standardized in both the ITU-T and ANSI since 1993, is incorporated in the ATM Forum specifications for circuit emulation services (CES), and is offered by several ATM equipment manufacturers. However, although AAL 1 is offered by many vendors—including General DataComm (GDC)—AAL 1 should not be considered an optimum solution for voice over ATM.

*This chapter was contributed by Mike McLoughlin, Keith Mumford, and Joe Birch, General DataComm (GDC).

415

In the development of ATM (or broadband) standards, AAL 1 found its niche as a way to allow ATM to replace time division multiplexing (TDM) circuits at fixed rates such as 1.536 Mbps (T1) or 2.048 Mbps (E1). The use of AAL 1 was subsequently extended to allow replacement of 64K circuits (or traditional digital voice circuits), providing a means to convey voice on ATM backbones instead of TDM infrastructures. AAL 1 was not initially developed to optimize voice over ATM applications, but is considered a de facto standard in the absence of a real specification.

This chapter will show that voice over ATM is best served by utilizing AAL 2's variable-bit-rate (VBR) service rather than the less efficient AAL 1 constant bit rate (CBR), which suffers from permanently allocated bandwidth that is poorly utilized and inefficient.

Although AAL 2 improves ATM network efficiency for voice over ATM, there are cases where the use of AAL 1 is quite appropriate. These cases will be explored briefly in this chapter.

Recognizing that AAL 1 was not an optimal solution for voice over ATM, some equipment manufacturers have developed proprietary solutions that increase network efficiency. Obviously, proprietary solutions for voice over ATM can reap benefits, but they may also negate interoperability.

Rather than pursue proprietary voice over ATM solutions, progressive vendors opted to participate in the development of AAL 2, which not only provides support for an optimum VBR voice over ATM solution, but ensures network and product interoperability. For details of GDC's AAL 2 solution, see section 12.6 "APEX Voice Service Module" at the end of the chapter.

Prior to AAL 2, users desiring to implement voice over ATM had to either live with the limitations of AAL 1 or select proprietary voice over ATM solutions. Now that AAL 2 has reached technical completion, all ATM network planners must consider using AAL 2 for VBR voice over ATM applications.

This discussion starts out with a description of AAL 2.

12.2 Introduction to AAL 2

This section details the protocol of the newly developed ATM Adaptation Layer 2 (AAL 2) and provides examples of the use of AAL 2 for voice over ATM.

A brief overview of the ATM AAL 1 protocol is also included to allow differentiation between AAL 1 and AAL 2. By now readers will be familiar with AAL 1, which has been standardized in both the ITU-T and ANSI since 1993, is incorporated in the ATM Forum specifications for circuit emulation services, and is offered by several ATM equipment manufacturers. However, few know the details of the AAL 2 protocol. Starting with an overview of the AAL 1 protocol should simplify the process of understanding AAL 2.

AAL 2 had its beginnings in a contribution to Committee T1S1.5 entitled "Short Multiplexed AAL (SMAAL)" in September 1995, which was authored by John Baldwin of Lucent. SMAAL was first introduced to the ITU-T at the May 1996 meeting of Study Group 13 in Geneva. At this meeting, AAL 2 was initiated under the temporary name of AAL-CU (for *composite user*). The work on AAL-CU was given high priority within the subgroup of Study Group 13 associated with AAL development. This resulted in arguably the most rapid and stable development of any recommendation within the ITU-T.

From inception in May 1996 to technical agreement on February 28, 1997, AAL 2 was completed in the record time of nine months. This was primarily due to a concerted effort by the ITU-T membership that had a singular goal in mind: to develop an AAL geared to the support of packetized voice and data over ATM, with full backing of the ATM Forum.

While the ITU-T was developing the protocol for AAL 2, input from the ATM Forum VTOA (Voice Telephony over ATM) working group substantiated the critical need in the market for an AAL that fully satisfied the requirements for voice over ATM.

The cooperation between the ATM Forum, which identified market needs, and the protocol experts at the ITU-T resulted in a new AAL that is ideally suited for voice over ATM applications: AAL 2.

AAL 2 is defined in the ITU-T Recommendation I.363.2 that was determined at the Study Group 13 meeting in Seoul, Korea, in February 1997 and was to be approved at the September 1997 Study Group 13 meeting in Toronto.

12.3 The ATM Adaptation Layer

As noted in previous chapters, the ATM Adaptation Layer (AAL) performs functions required by the User, Control, and Management planes and supports the mapping between the ATM Layer and the next-higher layer. The functions performed in the AAL depend upon the higher-layer requirements. In short, the AAL supports all of the functions required to map information between the ATM network and the non-ATM application that may be using it.

Different Adaptation Layers exist to carry traffic as diverse as packet-based or isochronous (T1 or E1) over the ATM backbone. AALs are standardized in the ITU-T I.363.x series of recommendations. The two most commonly implemented are AAL 1 (per I.363.1), which supports isochronous transmission—circuit emulation, for example—and AAL 5 (per I.363.5), which supports carrying packet data, such as frame relay, over ATM.

ATM Adaptation Layer 1 (AAL 1)

As defined in ITU-T Recommendation I.363.1, AAL 1 provides the following services to the AAL user (see also Chapter 7):

- Transfer of service data units with a constant source bit rate and the delivery of them with the same bit rate
- Transfer of timing information between source and destination
- Transfer of structure information between source and destination
- Indication of lost or errored information not recovered by AAL 1, if needed.

The primary application for AAL 1 is circuit emulation, that is, to provide a constant-bit-rate service, enabling simplistic isochronous transports of leased lines across the ATM backbone. To achieve this, AAL 1 typically uses the ATM CBR service category definition, which specifies the peak cell rate (PCR), cell loss ratio (CLR), and cell delay variation (CDV) necessary in the ATM network to support the application. This cell flow is independent of information contained within the service rate—that is, cells continue to flow on the ATM virtual circuit even when there is no traffic.

The ATM Forum's Circuit Emulation Interoperability Specifications, Versions 1 and 2, define the overall architecture and specification for this kind of application.

In addition to the constant cell flow using AAL 1, the information payload contained within each cell is set by the basic structure of AAL 1 (Figure 12.1). The information payload for AAL 1 is always 47 octets, the basic structure used for circuit emulation. Optional structures for AAL 1 add additional overhead, reduce the information payload, and are used for structured circuit emulation. When assessing the use of AAL 1 for voice over ATM, it is significant to note that the AAL 1 protocol has the following limitations:

- Only a single user of the AAL can be supported.
- Reducing delay requires significant additional bandwidth.
- Bandwidth is used even when there is no traffic.
- Voice is always 64K or bundles of 64K ($n\times64$).
- No standard mechanism in the AAL 1 structure for compression, silence detection/suppression, idle channel removal, or common channel signaling (CCS).

ATM Adaptation Layer 2 (AAL 2)

The basic functions of the AAL 2 protocol are consistent with AAL 1, in that both enhance the service provided by the ATM Layer to support functions required by the next-higher layer. However, AAL 2 goes beyond AAL 1 by defining a structure that includes functions supporting higher-layer requirements neither considered nor possible within the structure of AAL 1.

AAL 2 provides for the bandwidth-efficient transmission of low-rate, short, and variable packets in delay-sensitive applications. It enables support for both variable-bit-rate and constant-bit-rate applications within an ATM network. VBR services enable statistical multiplexing for the higher-layer requirements demanded by voice applications, such as compression, silence detection/suppression, and idle channel removal. AAL 2's VBR and CBR capabilities

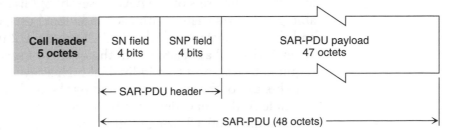

Figure 12.1
AAL 1 SAR-PDU.

mean that network administrators can take traffic variations into account when designing an ATM network and to optimize the network to match traffic conditions.

In addition, AAL 2 enables multiple user channels on a single ATM virtual circuit and varying traffic conditions for each individual user or channel.

The structure of AAL 2 also provides for the packing of short-length packets into one (or more) ATM cells, and the mechanisms to recover from transmission errors. In contrast to AAL 1, which has a fixed payload, AAL 2 offers a variable payload within cells and across cells. This functionality provides a dramatic improvement in bandwidth efficiency over either structured or unstructured circuit emulation using AAL 1.

In summary, AAL 2 provides the following advantages when compared with AAL 1:

- Bandwidth efficiency
- Support for compression and silence suppression
- Support for idle voice channels
- Multiple user channels with varying bandwidth on a single ATM connection
- VBR ATM traffic class

The structure of AAL 2, as defined in ITU-T Recommendation I.363.2, is shown in Figure 12.2.

AAL 2 is divided into two sublayers: the Common Part Sublayer (CPS) and the Service-Specific Convergence Sublayer (SSCS).

AAL 2 Common Part Sublayer

Fully defined in I.363.2, the CPS provides the basic structure for identifying the users of the AAL, assembling/disassembling the variable payload associated with each individual user, error correction, and the relationship with the SSCS. Each AAL 2 user can select a given AAL-SAP associated with the quality of service (QoS) required to transport that individual higher-layer application. AAL 2 makes use of the service provided by the underlying ATM Layer. Multiple AAL connections can be associated with a single ATM Layer connection, allowing multiplexing at the AAL Layer. The

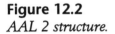
Figure 12.2
AAL 2 structure.

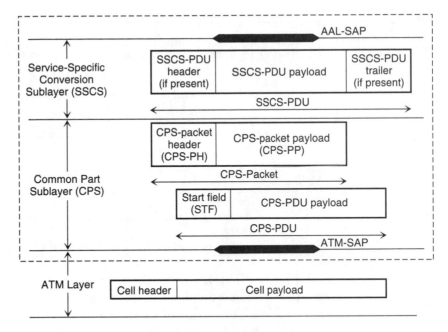

AAL 2 user selects the QoS provided by AAL 2 through the choice of the AAL-SAP used for data transfer.

AAL 2's CPS possesses the following characteristics:

- It is defined on an end-to-end basis as a concatenation of AAL 2 channels.
- Each AAL 2 channel is a bidirectional virtual channel, with the same channel identifier value used for both directions.
- AAL 2 channels are established over an ATM layer permanent virtual circuit (PVC), soft permanent virtual circuit (SPVC), or switched virtual circuit (SVC).

The multiplexing function in the CPS merges several streams of CPS packets onto a single ATM connection. The format of the CPS packet is shown in Figure 12.3.

Key fields of the CPS packet are the channel identifier (CID), the length indicator (LI), and the user-to-user indication (UUI) fields. These are defined below.

CID field   This uniquely identifies the individual user channels within the AAL 2 and allows up to 248 individual users within each AAL 2 structure. Coding of the CID field is shown below.

Figure 12.3

Format of the AAL 2 CPS packet.

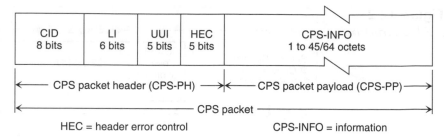

| CID 8 bits | LI 6 bits | UUI 5 bits | HEC 5 bits | CPS-INFO 1 to 45/64 octets |

←——— CPS packet header (CPS-PH) ———→|←——— CPS packet payload (CPS-PP) ———→

←————————————————— CPS packet —————————————————→

HEC = header error control   CPS-INFO = information

Value	Use
0	Not used
1	Reserved for layer Management peer to peer Procedures
2–7	Reserved
8–255	Identification of AAL 2 user (248 total channels)

LI field   This identifies the length of the packet payload associated with each individual user and assures conveyance of the variable payload. The value of the LI is one less than the packet payload and has a default value of 45 octets, or it may be set to 64 octets.

UUI field   This provides a link between the CPS and an appropriate SSCS that satisfies the higher-layer application. Different SSCS protocols may be defined to support specific AAL 2 user services or groups of services. The SSCS may also be null. Coding of the UUI field is as shown below:

Value	Use
0–27	Identification of SSCS entries
28, 29	Reserved for future standardization
30, 31	Reserved for layer management (OAM)

After assembly, the individual CPS packets are combined into a CPS-PDU payload, as shown in Figure 12.4. The offset field identifies the location of the start of the next CPS packet within the CPS-PDU. For robustness, the start field is protected from errors by the parity bit and data integrity is protected by the sequence number.

AAL 2 Service-Specific Convergence Sublayer

In ITU-T Recommendation I.363.2, the SSCS is defined as the link between the AAL 2 CPS and the higher-layer applications of the

Figure 12.4
*Format of the AAL
2 CPS-PDU.*

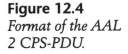
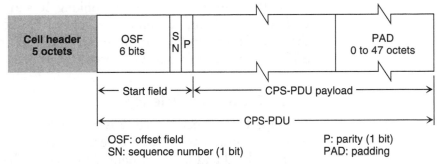

OSF: offset field
SN: sequence number (1 bit)

P: parity (1 bit)
PAD: padding

individual AAL 2 users. Several SSCS definitions that take advantage of the AAL 2 structure for various higher-layer applications are planned.

A null SSCS, already understood and used in conjunction with the AAL 2 CPS, satisfies most mobile voice applications. This is clearly evidenced by the consolidation of the ATM Forum VTOA Mobile and VTOA Landline Trunking Subgroups into a single VTOA Trunking Group.

To satisfy higher-layer requirements associated with data and AAL 2 configuration messages—called *AAL 2 negotiation procedures,* or ANP—an SSCS for segmentation/reassembly (temporarily called I.SEG) is in development within the ITU-T Study Group 13.

For peer-to-peer application interoperability, a standard SSCS to satisfy voice trunking over ATM has yet to be defined, but standards work is progressing rapidly in this area. Work on an SSCS for trunking was added to new work items in Study Group 13 at the February 1997 meeting. Parallel activities are ongoing in the ATM Forum VTOA Trunking Group under the program that is now titled "ATM Trunking Using AAL 2 for Narrowband Services" (previously called "VTOA Landline Trunking Phase 2").

It is expected that the ATM Forum will identify a critical market need for a SSCS for trunking and that the ITU-T will respond quickly with an appropriate protocol standard.

Recognizing the need for a new Adaptation Layer to satisfy voice applications, and understanding the relationship between the ITU-T and the ATM Forum, a number of vendors are working on the completion of the AAL 2 standard and in parallel develop ATM products that are compliant with AAL 2.

With regard to an SSCS for trunking, it is important to continue to drive toward completion of this standard in both the ITU-T and the ATM Forum and is committed to incorporation of a standard SSCS for trunking in our ATM products.

AAL 2 Protocol Efficiency

An important aspect of AAL 2 is packet fill delay, which allows the network operator to set a time period during which AAL 2 PDUs are assembled and then segmented into cells. The setting of packet fill delay allows the operator to alter the delay characteristic of voice into the ATM adaptation phase of AAL 2. Different voice circuits may have different minimum delay requirements, and it is important to be able to trade off delay and efficiency within the voice over ATM environment.

Table 12.1 shows the relationship between the packet fill delay and the AAL 2 PDU payload required to support a single voice channel. For example, for a single 32K ADPCM voice channel with a packet fill delay setting of 2 ms, each AAL 2 PDU goes out with an 8-byte payload supporting the voice channel. If the value of packet fill delay is doubled to 4 ms, then each 32K ADPCM voice channel will fill 16 bytes in every AAL 2 frame before being sent into the ATM network.

Table 12.2 lists both PCM and 32K ADPCM channels with various packet fill delay parameters to provide a basic understanding of the protocol efficiency for AAL 2. However, while evaluating the protocol payload and overhead may have meaning for a statistician, it is totally removed from the real benefit of AAL 2, which is significant reduction in bandwidth requirements for a given application. To allow multiplexing within an AAL, additional overhead is required, but the net result is vastly improved bandwidth efficiency.

Table 12.1   Packet Fill Delay versus AAL 2 PDU Payload

Packet Fill Delay (ms)	*CPS Header (bytes)*	*32K ADPCM*	*64K PCM*
2	3	8-byte payload	16-byte payload
4	3	16-byte payload	32-byte payload
6	3	24-byte payload	48-byte payload
8	3	32-byte payload	64-byte payload

Table 12.2 **AAL 2 Protocol Efficiency**

Channel Header (bytes)		*Payload*	*Efficiency (%)*
32K ADPCM (4 ms)	3	16-byte payload	84
32K ADPCM (8 ms)	3	32-byte payload	91
PCM (4 ms)	3	32-byte payload	91
Default LI	3	45-byte payload	94
Maximum LI	3	64-byte payload	96

AAL 2 Bandwidth Efficiency

Due to the complexity of dealing with both fixed and statistical compression in a voice channel (for example, ADPCM and silence suppression) and the further complication of packing these voice channels into ATM cells, it is difficult to provide a simple formula to calculate the theoretical ATM bandwidth needed to support a voice service inside the ATM network. However, the following examples help to illustrate the bandwidth efficiency that may be expected from an AAL 2 VBR voice service.

Figure 12.5 shows how an AAL 2 PDU supporting six 32K ADPCM channels with a packet fill delay value of 4 ms would be structured.

Further examples of the structure of an AAL 2 PDU with varying values for packet fill delay are shown in Figures 12.6 through 12.8.

Table 12.3 shows the use of AAL 2 for six channels, given the parameters of basic compression factor (none or 32K ADPCM), the encoding delay value, packet fill delay, and support for silence suppression on or off (assuming 50 percent silence). The absolute

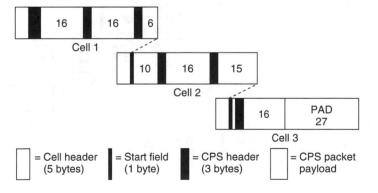

Figure 12.5
Six channels of 32K ADPCM with 4-ms packet fill delay.

Figure 12.6
Six channels of 32K ADPCM with 6-ms packet fill delay.

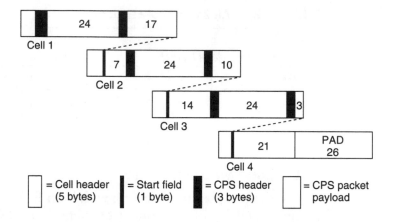

bandwidth required to support the service within an ATM trunk is shown in the last column.

AAL 2 Voice over ATM Trunking Efficiency

Another possible way to view the efficiency of an AAL 2 connection is to identify how many voice channels may be carried over a fixed-bandwidth ATM trunk between ATM network elements.

Figure 12.9 shows the number of voice channels that can be carried over a T1 ATM trunk using AAL 2. The *x*-axis represents the value of packet fill delay, and the *y*-axis shows the number of

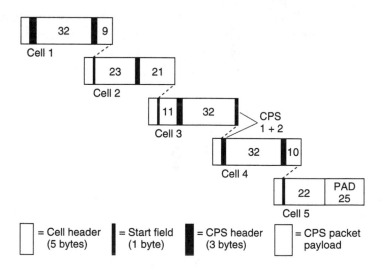

Figure 12.7
Six channels of 32K ADPCM with 8-ms packet fill delay.

Figure 12.8
One channel of 64K PCM and five of 32K ADPCM with 4 ms. packet fill delay.

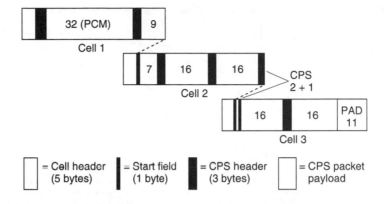

voice channels carried. Plots are shown for both 64K PCM and 32K ADPCM cases in the AAL 2 frame.

Note that, using 64K PCM inside an AAL 2 frame, a maximum of 18 channels can be supported with a delay of up to 8 ms. But for the 32K ADPCM encoded channels, a maximum of 35 channels may be supported.

If silence suppression is included, significant gains can be seen. Assuming that a voice circuit contains 50 percent silence and that 20 percent of all channels are idle at any one time, we see that the number of 64K PCM channels supported by AAL 2 more than doubles from 18 to 45 with 8 ms of packet fill delay by adding silence detection/suppression and idle channel removal. (See Figure 12.10.) When 32K ADPCM compression is added, the T1 trunk can accommodate up to 87 high-quality, multiplexed voice channels.

Table 12.3   Bandwidth Required Using AAL 2 for Six Voice Channels

No. of Channels	Channel Rate	AAL	Packet Fill Delay (ms)	Silence Suppression	Bandwidth (kbps)
6	64K	2	6	No	495
6	32K	2	4	No	318
6	32K	2	6	No	283
6	32K	2	8	No	265
6	64K	2	6	Yes	198
6	32K	2	4	Yes	128
6	32K	2	6	Yes	113
6	32K	2	8	Yes	106

Figure 12.9
*Number of AAL
2 voice channels
in a DS1 trunk
with variable
packet fill delay
(ms) without
silence suppres-
sion.*

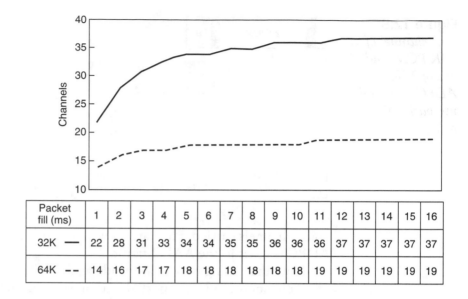

Packet fill (ms)	1	2	3	4	5	6	7	8	9	10	11	12	13	14	15	16
32K —	22	28	31	33	34	34	35	35	36	36	36	37	37	37	37	37
64K ––	14	16	17	17	18	18	18	18	18	18	19	19	19	19	19	19

Finally, considering the fact that when these voice channels are not busy (e.g., overnight) the bandwidth being used for voice is available for other applications (remote server archiving or software download, for example), then ATM networks begin to emerge as the only viable underlying technology for efficient wide area multi-service networking.

The next section provides a detailed comparison of the benefits and improvements in efficiency afforded by using AAL 2 for voice over ATM in lieu of using AAL 1.

12.4 Options for Transporting Voice in ATM Networks

As mentioned elsewhere in this book, today there are three standards-based methods that can be used for the transport of voice traffic over ATM networks:

1. AAL 1: circuit emulation
2. AAL 1: structured circuit emulation
3. AAL 2: variable-bit-rate voice over ATM

Figure 12.10
Number of AAL 2 silence-suppressed voice channels in a DS1 trunk with variable packet fill delay (ms).

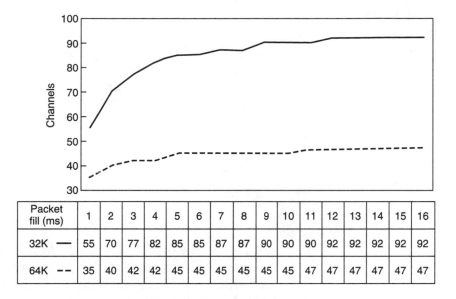

Packet fill (ms)	1	2	3	4	5	6	7	8	9	10	11	12	13	14	15	16
32K ―	55	70	77	82	85	85	87	87	90	90	90	92	92	92	92	92
64K --	35	40	42	42	45	45	45	45	45	45	47	47	47	47	47	47

Circuit emulation allows the user to establish an AAL 1 ATM connection to support a circuit, such as a full T1 or E1, over the ATM backbone. Structured circuit emulation establishes an AAL 1 $n \times 64$-kbps circuit, such as a fractional T1 or E1, over the ATM backbone. VBR voice over ATM uses an AAL 2 connection to provide highly efficient voice over ATM support.

This section discusses the first two alternatives, describing their relative advantages and disadvantages, and introduces a third option, that of variable-bit-rate voice over ATM.

Circuit Emulation

Unstructured circuit emulation is the ATM Forum–specified approach based on using an AAL 1 CBR ATM connection to carry a full T1 or E1 circuit—or full T3 and E3 circuits—between two points in the network (Figure 12.11). This connection may typically be used to carry end-to-end transparent circuits between time division multiplexers or digital PBXs.

Carrying voice over ATM in this manner is by far the simplest method to implement and deploy, but it is inefficient for two main reasons:

1. The support of an emulated circuit inside an ATM network actually requires significantly more bandwidth than neces-

Figure 12.11
*Typical basic cir-
cuit emulation
application.*

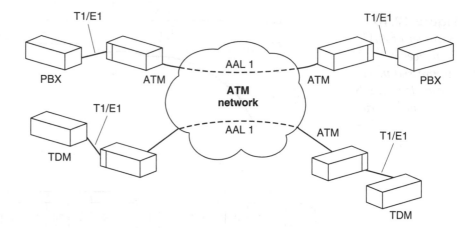

sary. Due to the overhead in the ATM cell and in the AAL 1
Layer, the ATM connection always requires 12 percent more
bandwidth than the circuit it is carrying. For example, a
1.536-Mbps DS1 circuit carried across an ATM backbone
requires 1.73 Mbps of ATM bandwidth.

2. The emulated T1/E1 circuit is typically configured as a
point-to-point ATM permanent virtual circuit and, as such, is
always active, even if the service is not transmitting data or
voice. For example, when the emulated T1/E1 carries a circuit between digital PBXs, the bandwidth is permanently
allocated, even if there are no voice calls active. The bandwidth cannot simply change to meet new network or application topology requirements.

This simple but inflexible and inefficient approach to transport-
ing a full T1 or E1 over ATM does not take advantage of the fact
that, for data services, the bandwidth profile may be bursty, as in
most LAN applications. Furthermore, for voice applications, all voice
channels are transmitted even when there are no voice calls active
on the link. Therefore, not only is the bandwidth requirement excessive, but there is no opportunity to take advantage of statistical gain,
which is a key factor for migrating to an ATM network.

Structured Circuit Emulation

Using structured circuit emulation for voice over ATM offers some
improvement over basic circuit emulation, as it allows AAL 1 ATM

connections to be established for $n\times64$-kbps circuits as opposed to a full T1 or E1.

Figure 12.12 shows three digital PBXs connected in a mesh over the ATM backbone using structured circuit emulation. Individual groups, or bundles, of timeslots are mapped to ATM circuits that are sized for a portion of, rather than all, the timeslots within the E1 or T1 PBX trunks. Unlike circuit emulation, which is transparent to traffic, structured circuit emulation must recognize each timeslot to allow routing of individual channels between PBX trunks. Recognition of each timeslot allows the network to convey in-band channel-associated signaling (CAS) on a per-channel basis. However, structured circuit emulation cannot accommodate out-of-band signaling protocols such as ISDN Q.931 or Q.SIG.

Although the ability to establish more granular $n\times64$-kbps circuits between endpoints in the network seems to be an improvement over the full E1 or T1, the additional bandwidth requirements needed to establish an $n\times64$-kbps circuit over ATM are often overlooked. This can be disadvantageous due to the trade-offs involved in efficiency versus delay characteristics for voice services. Minimal delay is very important for voice networks, as delay in the network can lead to excessive echo on voice circuits—and to the need for echo cancellation.

In basic circuit emulation, adaptation delay is minimal as the T1 or E1 bit stream is processed and segmented without regard to the framing structure within the signal. In structured circuit emulation, care must be taken to operate only on those timeslots that are to be transported across the ATM network. If an ATM cell is completely filled with information before being transmitted (this is the most efficient case), then each cell must wait for 47 sample times (47 octets of voice or data) until it is filled with data.

In the most efficient case with a fill rate of 47 samples, an AAL 1 circuit that transports six channels requires an ATM connection at a rate of 443 kbps. Using structured circuit emulation with partial cell fill (i.e., cells are partially filled with data and the remainder becomes overhead) would result in a lower delay, but requires higher bandwidth for the ATM connection. If partial fill is used with a fill rate of 24 samples, or octets, the result is an ATM bandwidth requirement of 866 kbps for the very same six channels.

A traditional T1 or E1 network requires 384 kbps for six channels versus 443 kbps (best case) or 866 kbps (with 24-sample par-

Figure 12.12
Typical structured circuit emulation application.

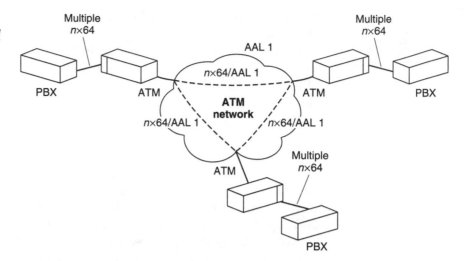

tial fill) using structured circuit emulation. As such, the best case requires 15 percent more bandwidth, and the reduced delay/partial fill case requires more than double the bandwidth of traditional TDM.

Overall, structured circuit emulation allows improved granularity for establishing fractional T1 or E1 circuits over ATM networks. However, the high penalty in bandwidth requirements and engineering challenges created by excessive delay may be overlooked. The cost of the additional bandwidth to support the service with low delays may outweigh the gains to be made by using structured circuit emulation.

Variable-Bit-Rate Voice over ATM

To overcome the excessive bandwidth needed for structured circuit emulation and provide the flexibility to allow the network operator to control delay on voice services, a new Adaptation Layer is required. AAL 1 simply cannot be extended to meet these new ATM networking requirements.

AAL 2 is a new ATM Adaptation Layer, specified in ITU-T Recommendation I.363.2 (1997) with the specific mandate to provide efficient voice over ATM services. A number of vendors including General DataComm actively participated in the development of this new standard by providing technical expertise and contributions necessary for successful determination of the specification in February 1997.

AAL 2 provides bandwidth-efficient transmission of low-rate, short, and variable packets for delay-sensitive applications and is designed to make use of the more statistically multiplexable variable-bit-rate ATM traffic classes. Therefore, AAL 2 is not limited to ATM connections using the CBR traffic class and can enable voice applications using higher-layer requirements such as voice compression, silence detection/suppression, and idle channel removal. The structure of AAL 2 allows network administrators to take traffic variations into account in the design of an ATM network and to optimize the network to match traffic conditions.

12.5 When to Use AAL 1

As shown in the previous section, AAL 2 offers significant benefits over AAL 1 in bandwidth efficiency. Thus AAL 2 should be used when all network elements (ATM nodes) within an ATM network support an AAL 2 adaptation capability. However, if a network element cannot support AAL 2, configuring AAL 1 connections for voice to this node allows transport of voice through the non–AAL 2 portion of the network.

In addition to using AAL 1 for interoperability with nodes that do not support AAL 2, some applications are adequately supported with AAL 1. In fact, they cannot utilize the benefits of AAL 2. A typical application of this type is interconnection to an Internet service provider, as shown in Figure 12.13.

In this application, the user access lines are traditional voice lines connecting with a voice end office. However, these user access lines serve a dual purpose: access to a public voice network and Internet access. The ATM network, as deployed, is not part of the voice network, but rather provides interconnection from the Class 5 voice switch to the two ISPs. In this application, the ATM network traffic is entirely modem data, which is adequately served with AAL 1 and cannot take advantage of the statistical gain associated with AAL 2 voice traffic.

The use of AAL 1 is also well suited to applications where the ATM network provides the functional equivalent to a digital cross-connect system in TDM networks. An example of this is shown in Figure 12.14. Physical connections are made between the PBX, TDMs, channel banks, and other traditional voice/data equipment and the ATM backbone. Through structured circuit emulation, the ATM network provides routing for DS0s or $n \times$ DS0s, allowing for

Figure 12.13
Internet access via an ATM backbone.

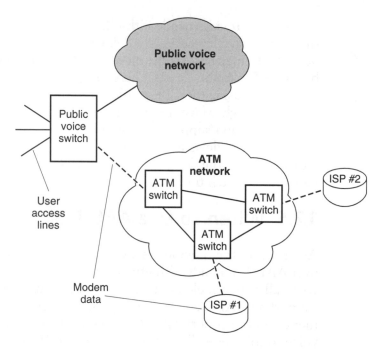

interconnection of the voice/data equipment. Figure 12.15 depicts how configuration of virtual circuits within the ATM network creates this cross-connect function for the interconnection of external customer equipment. This type of configuration demonstrates the flexibility of the ATM network, providing for unlimited mesh connectivity.

12.6 The APEX Voice Service Module

The General DataComm APEX switch has supported basic voice over ATM services since early 1993 via one of the first commercially available circuit emulation interfaces. Recent enhancements to the product family enabled more comprehensive circuit emulation services, such as structured circuit emulation for T1 and E1 connections.

With many GDC contributions to the standards bodies involved in setting the direction for this vital feature, the GDC APEX product family now enables service providers and enterprise ATM users for the first time to efficiently multiplex voice, video, and data over a common ATM backbone using industry standards.

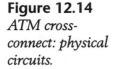

Figure 12.14
ATM cross-connect: physical circuits.

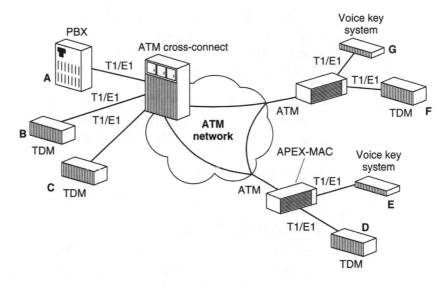

While many ATM vendors are now beginning to roll out basic structured circuit emulation interfaces, GDC is providing an interface that not only allows backward compatibility with these devices, but offers future-proof, standards-based, VBR voice internetworking across an ATM network.

The APEX Voice Service Module (VSM) is a voice over ATM interface for the APEX family of ATM WAN switches and multiservice access concentrators, accepting up to four full ports of T1 or E1 voice (96 or 120 channels) and providing adaptation to ATM cell flows.

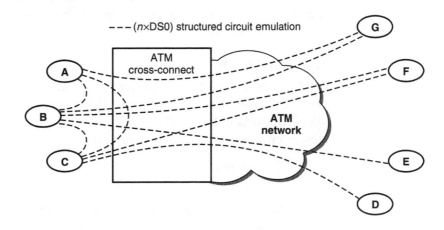

Figure 12.15
ATM cross-connect: virtual circuits.

The VSM provides per-voice-circuit ADPCM compression, silence detection/suppression, and idle channel removal, and can interpret both channel-associated and standards-based common channel signaling schemes, such as ITU-T Q.931 and ETSI/ANSI Q.SIG.

Significantly, the VSM supports both AAL 1 encoding for backward compatibility with structured circuit emulation interfaces and AAL 2 encoding for standards-based VBR voice over ATM services.

VSM Key Benefits

Following are the key benefits of the VSM.

Bandwidth Reduction

AAL 2 technologies reduce the bandwidth required for voice traffic. The efficiencies gained via AAL 2 lead to extensive reductions in the amount of information transmitted across the backbone, as well as savings in infrastructure costs.

Integration of Voice, Video, and Data

For the first time, an ATM product supports standards-based VBR voice, data, and video in a single multiservice concentrator with a common ATM backbone.

Lower Start-up Cost

GDC's modular approach to voice over ATM within the VSM allows network designers to start with an entry-level CBR AAL 1 and VBR AAL 2 solution. Value-added voice features such as voice compression and silence suppression can be added as a simple upgrade when required.

Standards Based

GDC is committed to supporting the latest voice over ATM specifications through a highly programmable firmware environment. The VSM supports both the ITU-T I.363.1 and I.363.2 specifications, as well as emerging VTOA standards for:

1. Circuit emulation services V 2.0
2. ATM trunking using AAL 1 for narrowband services
3. ATM trunking using AAL 2 for narrowband services

Therefore, you can be sure that your GDC VSM will adapt to meet new requirements emerging from the standards committees.

Compatibility with Other Vendors' Equipment

GDC's VBR voice over ATM technology offers support far in advance of that which most other vendors deliver. However, the capability to support basic structured circuit emulation guarantees interoperability with other vendors' equipment.

High Density

The APEX VSM offers four times the port density per slot than competing, proprietary VBR voice over ATM solutions. This means lower costs per port for provisioning voice services over the ATM backbone.

Future-Proof Solution

The VSM is designed to be as future-proof as possible, with completely software-upgradeable ATM Adaptation Layers, voice processing, and signaling capabilities.

VSM Key Features

VSM has the following *physical specifications:*

- Quad port E1 or T1 digital connections
- Modular capacity for up to 120 voice over ATM channels
- Up to 120 bundles per module

Its *bandwidth efficiency* provides for

- Simultaneous AAL 1 and AAL 2 support
- Voice compression
- Silence detection and suppression
- Idle channel removal
- User-configurable packing time

Other key features include

- Flexibility (ATM circuit options and simultaneous voice and data support)
- Echo cancellation
- Automatic fax/modem bypass
- T1/E1 signaling options: channel-associated signaling (AB signaling) and common channel signaling (LAP-D signaling)
- Trunk conditioning
- Network management

Physical Specifications

Quad Port E1/T1 Digital Connections   Each VSM supports up to four T1 or E1 interfaces, providing connectivity for up to 96 (T1) or 120 (E1) voice and data channels into the ATM network. An APEX-NPX easily supports a configuration of two E3 ATM interfaces and sixty E1 interfaces, yielding 1800 voice channels in a single, cost-effective, voice over ATM system.

Modular Capacity up to 120 Voice Channels per Controller There may be network planners with smaller, but just as important, voice and data networking requirements. The VSM has been specially designed to provide maximum architectural flexibility to meet the varying demands of ATM and voice networks throughout the world.

Table 12.4 shows that, for very simple AAL 1–only requirements, the basic VSM provides a straightforward platform for up to four ports of structured circuit emulation over an ATM network, with the added capability to perform both common channel and channel-associated signaling interpretation. The basic VSM also supports AAL 2 capability, including idle channel removal, which provides significant advantages over AAL 1 in some cases.

However, should the need arise for VBR voice over ATM support, the addition of a single daughter card will provide either 48 (T1) or 60 (E1) channels of VBR voice capability. These voice channels may be selected arbitrarily from any of the 96 or 120 channels available on the VSM. Even with the daughter card installed, it is still possible to configure all channels as structured circuit emulation and bypass the additional voice-processing capabilities, such as compression.

Table 12.4 Comparison of Five Voice Service Module Versions

	T1 Hierarchy	*E1 Hierarchy*
VSM	Basic VSM supporting two or four E1/T1 interfaces, 96 (T1) or 120 (E1) voice channels, AAL 1 structured circuit emulation, AAL 2, idle channel removal, and CAS/CCS signaling support	
VSM/48	Basic module plus 48 channels of voice compression/echo cancellation and silence suppression	
VSM/60		Basic module plus 60 channels of voice compression/echo cancellation and silence suppression
VSM/96	Basic module plus 96 channels of voice compression/echo cancellation and silence suppression	
VSM/120		Basic module plus 120 channels of voice compression/echo cancellation and silence suppression

The further addition of a second daughter card provides an extra 48 or 60 channels of VBR voice capability, bringing the total number of VBR voice-processing channels to 96 or 120 per card.

In this way, network planners can start off with a low-cost, entry-level system and be assured of a simple migration path to full-featured VBR voice over ATM for each of the four T1 or E1 interfaces.

Up to 120 Bundles per Module Voice or data channels with the same destination can be grouped together in *bundles*. A bundle is a single ATM virtual channel connection (VCC) that serves multiple narrowband trunk circuits. These narrowband channels are carried within ATM cells over the virtual connection, and the corresponding narrowband signaling messages may be carried within the same (or a different) bundle.

Bundles provide:

- A reduction in the number of permanent virtual circuits (PVCs) in the ATM network by aggregating multiple voice channels within a single ATM connection
- Bandwidth efficiency, by better utilization of the ATM cell payload
- Reduced delay, by increasing the packing density of the ATM cell with multiple channels and therefore reducing the fill time

Each VSM supports up to 120 bundles, with a minimum bundle size of 1 channel, and a maximum of 120 channels. Both contiguous and noncontiguous channels within the T1 or E1 frame may be aggregated into a single bundle (Figure 12.16).

Each bundle can be configured to carry the number of voice channels appropriate for the particular route being served. With AAL 2 support, the actual bandwidth used by a bundle at any point in time is dependent upon voice activity. For example, voice channels may be dynamically added to or removed from the AAL 2 bundle, depending upon whether a phone is on-hook or off-hook. This flexibility to alter the size of the bundle, instead of dimensioning by peak rate requirements, enables the released broadband capacity to be used for other (nonnarrowband) services.

In fact, the APEX VSM can take timeslots from any of its four physical interfaces and map them into a single ATM VCC, or bundle, up to 120 (E1), or 96 (T1) channels (Figure 12.17).

The ability to place large numbers of compressed, silence-removed voice channels into a single ATM VCC, to pipe these statistically across an ATM backbone, and to reassemble into high-quality voice channels at the receiving end is an extremely efficient method of hauling voice traffic over a long distance using a switched ATM network.

Bandwidth Efficiency

Simultaneous AAL 1 and AAL 2 Support   A key feature of the VSM is its ability to "talk" both ATM AAL 1 and AAL 2 protocols in the ATM network. This ensures that both data and voice services may be adequately supported within the VSM and that additional voice features such as compression, silence suppression, and idle bandwidth detection can be efficiently treated in the adaptation process.

In fact, not only does the VSM support AAL 1 and AAL 2 protocols, AAL 5 is also an inherent part of the VSM structure. AAL 5

Figure 12.16
Contiguous and noncontiguous timeslots in a single bundle.

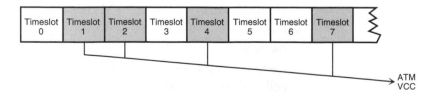

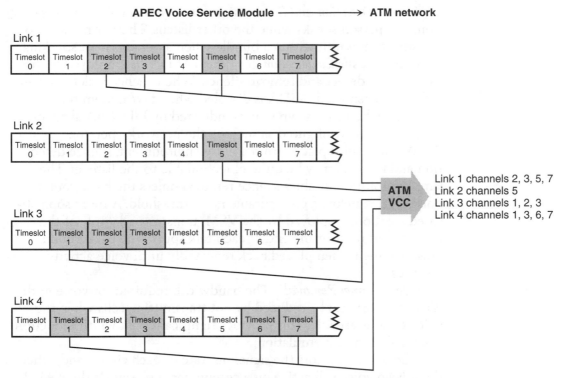

Figure 12.17
Multiple channels from each physical interface may form a single ATM VCC.

carries signaling messages efficiently between voice networking elements and will support N-ISDN to B-ISDN interworking in the future. Overall, the VSM is a future-safe solution to the networking needs of today that will also address emerging technologies and functions.

Voice Compression   Initially, the VSM will support G.726 32K ADPCM voice compression simultaneously on all 96 or 120 voice channels. ADPCM 32K compression provides a 2-to-1 bandwidth savings over the standard 64K PCM encoding used by most PBXs, while still providing very high voice quality at the receiver. Each incoming voice channel can be individually configured for compression or no compression.

The future-proofed VSM architecture allows for additional voice compression algorithms to be added or substituted via software upgrade.

Silence Detection and Suppression   In a typical voice conversation, one person speaks while the other listens. There is no need to transmit bandwidth within a bundle when a person is not speaking. An *advanced silence detection algorithm* (ASDA) is employed within the VSM to detect and remove silence. When silence is detected, no cells are transmitted. ASDA is disabled when fax/modem tones are detected, when a data-type call is indicated by ISDN signaling, or when statically configured as such by the network operator.

When a call is placed from a noisy environment, silence detection and removal may be quite objectionable to the listener. The simplest solution disables silence removal unless the background noise level is below a configurable noise threshold. A more sophisticated solution, employed by the VSM, transmits a sample of the background noise at the end of each talk spurt. The background noise sample is then played back repeatedly until voice activity resumes.

Idle Channel Removal   The bandwidth required for voice in the ATM network can be reduced by not transmitting cells when the voice circuits are idle. This provides significant bandwidth reduction over AAL 1 circuit emulation.

The VSM monitors the signaling state of each circuit and, when there is no voice call active on a certain channel, signals the AAL 2 Layer to stop transmitting cells for that channel in the AAL 2 PDU.

When this bandwidth is freed it can be used by other applications. A typical example is the enterprise network in which, during the day, voice traffic is very heavy, while at night it may drop to near zero. A remote archiving program begins to run across the network at night. The bandwidth that was being used for voice during the day is now used for data overnight.

Configurable Packet Fill Delay   APEX VSM includes a configurable packet fill delay parameter, with selectable values from 2 ms to 8 ms, which is used to control the delay-versus-efficiency aspects of each AAL 2 connection.

For example, setting packet fill delay to 4 ms for a particular AAL 2 connection means that the tolerable packing delay allowed on that connection is 4 ms. The AAL 2 interface will ensure that the efficiency of that connection matches that required to maintain a 4-ms packing time.

Higher values of packet fill delay generally mean more efficient AAL 2 circuits (less bandwidth required), but with a larger delay.

Flexibility

ATM Circuit Options   The VSM supports the use of ATM PVCs, soft PVCs (SPVCs), and switched virtual circuits (SVCs) within the ATM network. Basic voice services may use PVC/SPVCs, while more efficient voice networking may make use of the common channel signaling protocol to dynamically construct end-to-end switched voice calls on demand using ATM SVCs.

Simultaneous Voice and Data Transport   The VSM supports an $n{\times}64$-kbps circuit type for the transmission of data via bundles. On circuits of this type, voice compression, silence detection, idle detection, and fax/modem tone detection are all disabled. $n{\times}64$-kbps data streams can be transmitted using AAL 1 adaptation and are end-to-end compatible with ATM devices employing structured circuit emulation for data connectivity.

Echo Cancellation

In an ATM network, factors contributing to the delays experienced by voice services can be caused by:

Compression time: The time taken to compress a voice channel down from 64-kbps PCM

Cell assembly time: The time taken to pack the voice or compressed voice into an ATM cell

Network delay: The time taken to transmit the cell from one end of the ATM network to the other

Decompression time: The time taken to decompress the voice channel back to 64-kbps PCM

In voice networks, excessive delay introduced by the transmission network may be critical due to the echolike effect that results from the reflected signal at the receiving end. While a little delay is tolerable in a normal voice call, delays above a certain level tend to cause an echo that is confusing to the listener and can reduce a conversation to a series of mistimed, half-spoken sentences.

In particular, if channel bundles are not employed, the cell assembly delay can be significant even at 64 kbps. This delay gets much worse when reduced-bandwidth (compressed) voice is assembled into cells.

To counteract this phenomenon, voice networks often use echo cancelers external to the network to negate the echo. However, these external units are typically bulky, expensive, or both. An integrated echo cancellation system in the VSM provides the capability to cancel inherent echoes for up to 120 channels of voice simultaneously. The VSM echo cancellation system complies with the ITU-T G.165 specification and can be manually configured to *on* or *off* per channel. The VSM echo cancellation function is adaptive, is dynamically calculated for each individual channel within the module, and supports a tail length of up to 16 ms.

Automatic Fax/Modem Bypass

Fax and high-speed modem signals cannot tolerate the signal degradation associated with voice compression. The VSM can be configured (on a per-channel basis) to automatically detect a fax or modem call and to switch the circuit to an uncompressed 64-kbps path (with echo cancellation and silence detection/removal disabled).

Fax and modem channels are detected using tone detectors to monitor active voice circuits for fax and modem handshake sequences. When such tones are detected, voice compression is disabled and the circuit is switched to 64 kbps. The circuit bandwidth remains at 64 kbps until the call is completed. The next call on this circuit returns to the configured compression rate.

T1/E1 Signaling Options

Channel-Associated Signaling (A/B Signaling)   Channel-associated signaling (on-hook/off-hook detection) may be interpreted by the VSM and employed to add, or drop, individual channels dynamically from a bundle. The E1 VSM uses timeslot 16 for identifying and processing the signaling bits. The T1 VSM employs robbed-bit signaling for identifying and processing the ABCD signaling bits.

If the bundle is transported over the ATM network using either a PVC or an SPVC, CAS may be used for reducing or increasing the bandwidth of an AAL 2 connection by adding or removing an active or idle voice channel from the ATM trunk. When SVCs are used in the ATM network, the VSM can dynamically create ATM connections on a call-by-call basis. Signaling can be configured within the VSM on a per-channel basis and allows support for a wide range of channel types, as shown in Table 12.5.

Table 12.5   Supported Channel Types

E1	SSR2 Line Signaling Digital Version Q.421 Q.424
T1	TR 43801 Section C
	Sleeve Ground Dial Pulse (SGPO)
	Dial Pulse (DPO/DPT)
	E&M
	Foreign Exchange (FXO/FXS)
	Off-Premise Extension (OPX)
	Multifrequency Signaling
	Revertive Pulse (RPO/RPT)
	Sleeve Dial Pulse (SDPO)
	Duplex (DX)
	Private Line Auto Ring Down (PLAR)
	Pulse Link Repeater (PLR)
	Ring Down (RD)

Common Channel Signaling (N-ISDN Signaling)   Two narrowband ISDN common channel signaling protocols are supported within the VSM:

Q.931: A signaling protocol associated with public ISDN networking

Q.SIG: A newer protocol designed for private PBX interconnection

Each T1/E1 interface can be configured for either Q.931 or Q.SIG. As with channel-associated signaling, bandwidth reduction benefits are derived from processing common channel signaling messages. However, the maximum benefit is derived when these narrowband signaling protocols interwork with ATM SVCs.

Consider a private PBX application where the VSM processes Q.SIG commands and routes individual voice calls over SVCs. Network complexity is much simpler than in a more traditional Q.SIG deployment using fixed-bandwidth leased lines. The VSM's ability to place on-demand, switched calls between PBX systems eliminates tandem voice switching, and greatly reduces the number of voice trunks in the network.

Support for these narrowband ISDN protocols allows for extended features that are not supported in CAS, such as calling line identification (CLI, or caller ID), clear channel 64K, and switched $n\times64$-kbps multirate ISDN circuits. The VSM allows these supplementary services to be passed transparently through the ATM network between PBXs.

Through the Q.931 interface, the APEX VSM offers a standards-based primary-rate ISDN connection and can connect and accept messages from ISDN-compatible devices other than PBXs. For example, a dial-up ISDN router can place switched ISDN calls across the APEX network as if it were connected to the public ISDN.

ATM Signaling Support

While CAS and CCS support offer a narrowband signaling interface, it is also important to understand the broadband ATM signaling capabilities of the ATM device. The key to determining if any given ATM product satisfies both current network implementations and future ATM network extensions is not merely checking that narrowband signaling protocols are supported. Network planners must determine that the ATM product offers expansion for both narrowband and ATM (or broadband) signaling and ensures proper interworking.

Networks using narrowband signaling, whether it be CAS or CCS, are widely deployed. Both product features and standards for these networks are mature and well understood. However, product features and standards for broadband signaling are, by comparison, still rather immature and continuously evolving.

There are four solutions for the ATM broadband interswitch signaling. These are proprietary SVCs, the Interim Interswitch Signaling Protocol (IISP) and Private Network Node Interface (PNNI) from the ATM Forum, and the Broadband ISDN User Part, or B-ISUP (B-ICI in ATM Forum specifications). The GDC APEX product line currently offers support for the IISP and in the future will also offer both PNNI- and B-ISUP-based interfaces.

Trunk Conditioning

The VSM fully supports all aggregate T1/E1 failures, such as local and remote alarms in T1. These failure conditions associated with the full T1/E1 trunks are reported on both ends of the connection, and appropriate actions are taken on all channels associated with the failure.

Virtual circuit (VC) failures are monitored on the ATM interface. Appropriate actions are taken on each individual voice channel in the VC.

Table 12.6   **Voice Service Module Feature Matrix**

Features	*VSM*	*VSM/48*	*VSM/96*	*VSM/60*	*VSM/120*
AAL 1 support	Yes	Yes	Yes	Yes	Yes
AAL 2 support	Yes	Yes	Yes	Yes	Yes
Maximum voice and data channels					
2 Ports T1	48	48	48	48	48
4 Ports T1	96	96	96	96	96
2 Ports E1	60	60	60	60	60
4 Ports E1	120	120	120	120	120
Maximum channels with voice processing (e.g., compression)					
2 Ports T1	0	48	—	—	—
4 Ports T1	0	48	96	—	—
2 Ports E1	0	—	—	60	—
4 Ports E1	0	—	—	60	120
$n\times64$-kbps voice (AAL 1/AAL 2)	Yes	Yes	Yes	Yes	Yes
$n\times64$-kbps data (AAL 1/AAL 2)	Yes	Yes	Yes	Yes	Yes
Idle channel removal	Yes	Yes	Yes	Yes	Yes
ADPCM 32K voice compression	No	Yes	Yes	Yes	Yes
Echo cancellation	No	Yes	Yes	Yes	Yes
Silence detection/suppression	No	Yes	Yes	Yes	Yes
Configurable packing time	Yes	Yes	Yes	Yes	Yes
Channel-associated signaling (CAS) support	Yes	Yes	Yes	Yes	Yes
Common channel signaling (Q.SIG) support	Yes	Yes	Yes	Yes	Yes
Common channel signaling (Q.931) support	Yes	Yes	Yes	Yes	Yes
Fax/modem bypass	N/A	Yes	Yes	Yes	Yes
Compatible with ATM Forum T1/E1 Circuit emulation service	Yes	Yes	Yes	Yes	Yes
Downloadable signaling, compression, and adaptation processing	Yes	Yes	Yes	Yes	Yes
SNMP managed	Yes	Yes	Yes	Yes	Yes

Network Management

The APEX VSM is fully managed via an SNMP MIB agent within the APEX system. Additionally, a craft port allows the user to view and instruct the MIB from a local or remote RS232 interface.

VSM Feature Matrix

Table 12.6 identifies the capabilities of each of the five APEX VSM products.

Index